KU-788-722

# BRIEF CONTENTS

# CONTENTS

# INTERNET
**2ND EDITION**
# COMMERCE
## DIGITAL MODELS FOR BUSINESS

*Elaine* **LAWRENCE**

*Brian* **CORBITT**

*Jo-anne* **FISHER**

*John* **LAWRENCE**

*Alan* **TIDWELL**

John Wiley & Sons Australia, Ltd

BRISBANE • NEW YORK • CHICHESTER • WEINHEIM • SINGAPORE • TORONTO

Second edition published 2000 by
John Wiley & Sons Australia, Ltd
33 Park Road, Milton, Qld 4064

Offices also in Sydney and Melbourne

Typeset in 10/12 pt New Baskerville

First edition 1998

© E. Lawrence, B. Corbitt,
J. Fisher, J. Lawrence and A. Tidwell 1998, 2000

National Library of Australia
Cataloguing-in-publication data

---

Internet commerce: digital models for business.

2nd ed.
Includes index.
ISBN 0 471 34167 3.

1. Electronic commerce.   2. Business enterprises —
Computer networks. I. Lawrence, Elaine.

658.054678

---

Cover and internal design by Liz Wiffen
Cover image and images used in internal design:
© Digital Vision 1999

Printed in Singapore
10 9 8 7 6 5 4 3 2 1

CHAPTER 5    **Electronic payment systems**    *(Brian Corbitt)*    102

# PREFACE

We were very thrilled with the success of the first edition of this textbook and thank our readers for their kind words of encouragement. The book won the Australian Publishers Award for Excellence in the Tertiary Technology Section in 1999. In the two years that have passed since the first edition of this textbook, there has been an explosion of Internet activity. According to Martin Butler of the Butler Group in Europe:

> *By 2010 . . . most of commerce will be executed in a realtime environment by intelligent software agents. They will be able to make millions of decisions a second — there will be no time for management meetings to decide on pricing structures. One thing is certain: we are consistently underestimating the pace and magnitude of the changes taking place.*

> (Butler, M. 2000, Butler Group, www.butlerforums.com)

This burgeoning use of the Internet demands that employees and managers understand and be skilled in Internet commerce practices in order for their businesses to gain a competitive advantage. The second edition of *Internet Commerce: Digital Models for Business* has updated the material for the rapidly emerging field of Internet/electronic commerce. This new edition places the study of Internet commerce within an international and national framework. It includes many new case studies and Business and Legal insites to illustrate the emerging trends and features. The multidisciplinary team of authors has covered the business, management, technical and legal aspects of this exciting area of commerce on the Internet.

## Objectives of the book

After completing the book, students will:

- have received a thorough grounding in electronic commerce on the Internet
- know the stakeholders in electronic commerce and their capabilities and limitations in the strategic convergence of technology and business
- understand the rapid changes taking place in electronic commerce
- be aware of the new technologies of importance to electronic commerce
- have been exposed to important research and development trends in the area.

As an additional resource, Elaine Lawrence, in collaboration with John Wiley and Sons Australia, will maintain a web site (see www.johnwiley.com.au/tertiary/internet-commerce) to keep readers abreast of recent changes with timely updates. This text also includes a variety of other special features, including:

- clearly identified learning outcomes
- Business and Legal insites with thought-provoking content allowing for ample class discussion. Questions are generally worded to allow for change and innovation over the next few years.
- discussion and research exercises at the end of each chapter
- case studies with discussion and research questions and exercises
- further reference material giving readers additional material and resources
- key terms, making the text ideal for quick reference and study
- appendixes of web sites listed in the chapter, allowing for quick and easy access
- a glossary.

The authors hope that lecturers and students will find this new edition, web site and supplements useful and valuable adjuncts to their study of Internet commerce.

# ABOUT THE AUTHORS

### Elaine Lawrence

Elaine Lawrence, BA, GradDip Commercial Computing, MACS, MBIT, is a senior lecturer in the School of Computing Sciences, University of Technology, Sydney. Her research interests are in Internet commerce and networking. She is a founding member of the Internet/intranet consulting business, Cyber.Consult. As well, Elaine has written 'Setting up a shopfront' (1998) and 'Virtual tax reform (1999) in the series *Hands-on Solutions: E-commerce* for CCH Australia, Ltd.

### Brian Corbitt

Brian Corbitt, BA, DipEd, BSc, GradDip Careers, MEd Studs, PhD, MACEA, MQIEA, is Professor of Electronic Commerce at Victoria University of Wellington and teaches in the School of Communications and Information Management. Previously he worked in electronic commerce at both the University of Melbourne and Monash University. Professor Corbitt specialises in electronic commerce policy development, analysis and implementation, and in business modelling and electronic commerce trade relationships. His published research includes reports to public and private agencies on smart cards, implementation of electronic commerce in SMEs (small- and medium-sized enterprises) in Australia, intranets, electronic commerce implementation in South-East Asia, and electronic commerce policy implementation.

### Jo-anne Fisher

Jo-anne Fisher is a director and member of the board of ETC Electronic Trading Concepts Pty Ltd, a leading Asia–Pacific e-business strategy and solutions firm. Prior to joining ETC, Jo-anne established the first Australian Centre for Electronic Commerce in 1995, and initiated the first university-based e-commerce courses in Australia. Jo-anne has been working in the field of e-commerce for over 12 years. She has extensive consulting experience in eStrategy development, eProcurement, SME eBusiness initiatives, eCommunity development and management, online education (eLearning) and more recently eHealth. Jo-anne is an Honorary Fellow of Deakin University with the Electronic Commerce Group in the School of Management Information Systems.

### John Lawrence

John Lawrence, LLB, BSc (Hons) Civil Engineering, MBA, is a barrister practising in the areas of electronic commerce, environmental and planning laws, construction and building disputes, and contract law. He is a Registered Legal Practitioner, New South Wales, and a member of the New South Wales Bar Association; the Institution of Engineers, Australia; and the Institute of Arbitrators and Mediators, Australia.

### Alan Tidwell

Alan Tidwell, BA, MS, PhD, is a senior lecturer in the e-commerce program in the Macquarie Graduate School of Management, Macquarie University. His speciality is human communication and relationships. He is a founding member of the Internet/intranet consulting business Cyber.Consult.

# ACKNOWLEDGEMENTS

The authors would like to thank the team at John Wiley and Sons Australia, who have helped in the production of this book.

We are also grateful for the insightful reviews and advice from the reviewers Dr Celia Romm, Central Queensland University; Paul O'Brien, University of Sunshine Coast; Noel Brown, University of Southern Queensland; Peter Chomley, RMIT University; and Graham Wrightson, University of Newcastle.

**Images**

© The Australian Broadcasting Corporation. Reproduced with permission (p. 85); Reproduced with permission of Ansett Australia (p. 176); Reproduced by permission of ANZWERS (p. 27); The ASX screen shot is reproduced by the publisher with the permission of the Australian Stock Exchange Limited (p. 58); Commonwealth of Australia — Copyright. Reproduced with permission (p. 224); © Autobytel. Reproduced with permission (p. 55); ©Addison-Wesley Longman, Inc. Reprinted by permission of Addison-Wesley Longman (p. 292); Reproduced with permission of the Department of Employment, Workplace Relations and Small Business Entry Point Management Branch (p. 294); Screen shot reproduced by permission of Britannica.com.au (p. 8); © University of Technology, Sydney. Reproduced by permission (p. 34); Reproduced with permission by Dell Computer. Copyright © 2000 (p. 80); Reprinted by permission of DoubleClick, Inc. (NASDAQ: DCLK) (p. 172); Reproduced courtesy of dpunkt.verlag (p. 123 top); Courtesy of employment.com.au (p. 199); © FishNet Security. Reproduced with permission (p. 281); © Ford. Reproduced with permission (p. 198 bottom); © 2000 Gateway, Inc. Reproduced by permission (pp. 38 and 66); Reprinted with permission. © Harris Technology (p. 82); Hertz Australia Pty Ltd (p. 122 top); Reproduced by permission of Hilton-Adelaide (p. 40); Reprinted by permission of Sancella Pty Ltd (p. 87); Courtesy of Lucent Technologies, Inc. © 2000. Lucent Technologies, Inc. All rights reserved. Lucent and the Innovation Ring logo are registered trademarks of Lucent Technologies, Inc. (p. 192); Reproduced with permission of Medical Benefits Fund of Australia Ltd (p. 123 bottom left); Screen shot reprinted by permission from Microsoft Corporation (p. 63 bottom); Reprinted with the permission of National Australia Bank (p. 123 bottom right); Reproduced with the permission of National Australia Bank and MasterCard International (p. 123 centre right); Netscape Netcenter website © 2000 Netscape Communications Corporation. Screen shots used with permission (pp. 62 and 63 top); © 2000 ninemsn. Reproduced with permission (p. 64); Financial Services Technology Consortium (FSTC) © 1998 FSTC (p. 118); © Chris Payne (p. 12); Courtesy of Queensland Transport (p. 123 centre left); Reproduced by permission of Greg Norman Interactive (p. 88); Reproduced by permission of Sofcom © 2000 (p. 35); Courtesy Sydney Water (p. 16); © Telstra Corp. Ltd. Reproduced by permission (p. 122 bottom right); Reproduced with permission (p. 33); © John Wiley & Sons Australia (p. 194); © John Wiley & Sons, New York. Reprinted by permission of John Wiley & Sons, New York (pp. 37, 41 and 159); © Wine Planet (p. 39); Reproduced with permission of Woolworths (p. 198 top)

**Text**

Reprinted by permission of Addison-Wesley Longman (tables 1.2 and 3.1); Commonwealth of Australia — Copyright. Reproduced by permission (p. table 1.1); Reprinted with permission of IDG Communications Australia (pp. 130 and 139–40); From *CyberTimes*. The *New York Times* on the Web. © 1999 The *New York Times* Company. Reprinted by permission (pp. 255–7); Reprinted with permission of the *E-Commerce Times* © 1999–2000 Triad Commerce Group, LLC. All rights reserved (pp. 295–7); Reproduced with permission of *E-Commerce Today* (pp. 210 and 219); Reprinted from the September 1999 issue of *Fast Company* Magazine. All rights reserved (p. 289); Reproduced by permission by Oxford University Press (p. 84); © *Time*, Inc. Reprinted by permission (pp. 273–4); © Knapp Communications (pp. 149–50); © 1999 by CMP Media Inc., 600 Community Drive, Manhasset, NY 11030, USA. Reprinted from *Information Week* with permission (p. 126); © 1999 by CMP Media Inc., 600 Community Drive, Manhasset, NY 11030, USA. Reprinted from *InternetWeek* with permission (p. 286); Reproduced with permission of Strategic Publishing — a division of Fairfax Business Publications (pp. 71–5); Netcraft Ltd. Reproduced with permission (tables 4.4 and 4.5); Copyright Penton Media, Inc. 1100 Superior Ave, Cleveland, Ohio, 44114 (pp. 160–3); © *Red Herring* Magazine, reprinted with permission (p.302); © Schlumberger Industries International SA. Reproduced with permission (pp. 132–4); Reproduced with permission of Robin Cover, Managing Editor of the 'XML Cover Pages' web site (www.oasis-open.org/cover/) (p. 57); Courtesy Sydney Water (pp. 15–16); Dan Tebbutt is an IT and Internet journalist who has worked in Sydney, San Francisco and Melbourne (pp. 242–4); © 1999 by CMP Media Inc., 600 Community Drive, Manhasset, NY 11030, USA. Reprinted from *TechWeb* with permission (pp. 282–3); Reprinted with permission of VerticalNet (pp. 277–8); Copyright © 1994–2000 Wired Digital, Inc. All rights reserved (pp. 287–8).

CHAPTER

1

# Introduction  to Internet commerce

## LEARNING Outcomes

You will have mastered the material in this chapter when you can:

- understand and define electronic commerce and Internet commerce
- understand the difference between the Internet and the World Wide Web
- know the main Internet commerce players and their capabilities and limitations in the strategic convergence of technology and business
- understand the impact of the World Wide Web on the Internet and on businesses
- give practical examples to illustrate the theory of creative destruction
- understand the rapid changes taking place in electronic commerce and Internet commerce.

'... *it would be a gross error for firms and organisations — or governments for that matter — to think they can safely shelve consideration of the Internet as a core business and trade tool for a year or two. This is not an option if we want to reap the benefits of increasing output, exports and jobs that can, and should, flow from skilful use of Internet commerce. We need to move now.*'

Tim Fischer, former Deputy Prime Minister and Minister for Trade, in Department of Foreign Affairs and Trade 1999, *Driving Forces on the New Silk Road: The Use of Electronic Commerce by Australian Businesses*, Commonwealth of Australia, Canberra, p. iii

# INTRODUCTION

*(form of technology)*

The **Internet**, a network of computer networks that has no central control or organisation, is changing the way people think about and do business. From its military, research and academic background, it has evolved into a serious business tool. In Australia, organisations are using the Internet to satisfy communication, network and research needs and, increasingly, to sell goods and services online to consumers able to pay using secure credit cards and digital cash. The exponential growth in the use of the Internet underpins the fact that it is growing faster than any other technology in history. The number of people with Internet access grew from 2.3 million in 1995 to well over 300 million in 1998.[1] The number of Internet hosts (computers linked to the Internet) grew from one million in 1993 (when it began to be used as a commercial tool) to around 20 million by mid-1997 and 30 million by early 1998.[2] Australia, which traditionally has been very quick in its uptake of new technology and ideas, has not been as entrepreneurial with electronic commerce on the Internet and has been rated as a 'straggler' by a Forrester Research study of countries that are adopting electronic commerce. New Zealand, by contrast, is classified as a 'sprinter'.[3] Researchers have identified four waves of Internet development and in table 1.1 it is noted that Australia has been included in wave 2.

| TABLE 1.1 | FOUR WAVES OF INTERNET DEVELOPMENT | |
|---|---|---|
| **WAVE** | **COUNTRIES** | **CHARACTERISTICS** |
| wave 1 | United States, Canada and the Nordics | Characterised by early adoption in universities and government in the 1980s. These countries are among the heaviest commercial users of the technology. |
| wave 2 | the rest of the European Union, Australia, New Zealand, Japan, Republic of Korea, Taiwan, Singapore, Hong Kong and Israel | Characterised by high level of private and public sector interest in developing broad information societies. Extensive commercial use although focus on consumer applications varies widely. |
| wave 3 | developing countries across South-East Asia, China, Brazil, Argentina, South Africa, Egypt, and smaller island states such as Tonga, Fiji, Barbados and French Polynesia | Characterised by high levels of interest in initiating and developing business applications of online commerce. |
| wave 4 | least developed countries or other countries that deliberately shun Internet use | Characterised to date by unattractive investment environment. In some countries there have been attempts to ban the Internet for political and social reasons. |

**SOURCE:** Department of Foreign Affairs and Trade 1999, *Creating a Clearway on the New Silk Road: International Business and Policy Trends in Internet Commerce*, Commonwealth of Australia, Canberra, p. 8

The *Global Internet Banking Report: An Asia-Pacific-Japan Perspective* showed that Australia and Canada have the most advanced online banking capability.[4] This book will look at the many examples of Australian and international Internet business success stories and show how such success has been achieved.

# DEFINITIONS OF ELECTRONIC COMMERCE AND INTERNET COMMERCE

There has been an explosion of names to identify doing business electronically, such as electronic commerce, e-commerce, iCommerce, Internet commerce and digital commerce. In this book, we will use the terms 'electronic commerce' and 'Internet commerce' interchangeably. Electronic commerce can be defined as the buying and selling of information, products and services via computer networks today and in the future, using any one of the myriad of networks that make up the Internet.[5] However, Kalakota and Whinston point out that electronic commerce has many definitions depending on the perspective from which you view it. These ideas have been summarised in the following table.

| TABLE 1.2 | ELECTRONIC COMMERCE FROM FOUR PERSPECTIVES |
|---|---|
| **PERSPECTIVE** | **DESCRIPTION** |
| communications | to deliver information, products/services and payments over the telephone, communication networks or other means |
| business | to automate business transactions and work flows |
| service | to cut service costs while improving the quality of goods and increasing the speed of service delivery |
| online | to provide the capability of buying and selling products and information over the Internet and other online services |

*SOURCE:* R. Kalakota and A. Whinston 1997, *Electronic Commerce: A Manager's Guide*, Addison-Wesley, United States, p. 3

While the Internet was established in the 1960s in the United States, it was not until the 1990s that its commercial potential started to be realised. Prior to that, the Internet was an academic and research tool for government, educational and non-profit organisations that was subsidised by the government and kept strictly out of reach of the business community. In the mid-1980s the National Science Foundation (NSF) created a high-speed, long-distance telecommunications network into which other networks could be linked. (Other organisations now support this link.) By 1991 NSF dropped its restrictive usage policy and allowed in many commercial sites.[6] This development, along with the arrival of the **World Wide Web**, caused the business community to take notice of the Internet. The Web is a graphical **hypertext** environment that operates within the Internet. It supports multimedia presentations, which include audio, video, text and graphics. The protocol (a set of rules, procedures and standards) that underpins the Web is hypertext transfer protocol (HTTP) and the protocol for doing business on the Web is secure hypertext transfer protocol, which provides a basis for secure communications, authentication, digital signatures and encryption.

# WEB BROWSERS, INTERNET COMMERCE AND SECURITY

A web **browser** is a piece of software that allows the user to access information in the form of sound, text, graphics and video clips on the Internet. Browsers such as **Netscape** Navigator and Microsoft's Internet Explorer (combined with supporting software) provide an interface to the Web via **hypertext transfer protocol (HTTP)** or other types of Internet tool such as **file transfer protocol (FTP)** or Gopher.

The secure hypertext transfer protocol enables:
• browsers to encrypt information being sent to a server, digitally sign requests and authenticate the identity of a server
• servers to encrypt replies, to digitally sign replies and authenticate the identity of browsers.

Prior to the establishment of the Web, the Internet was text-based, command-driven and user-unfriendly. Once multimedia became part of the scenario, businesses started to see the potential in using it. Two features are encouraging businesses to use the Internet: codification and distribution. Codification refers to the organised storage of information in a computer system (e.g. ASCII text and standards for storing photographs, videos and audio). Distribution refers to the ability to use **hypertext markup language (HTML)**, a programming language used to create a web page that allows codified information to be shared globally (as well as **email**), no matter whether the information is text, photographs or embedded web pages.[7] Entrepreneurs quickly saw the real business possibilities that the Web offered. A new standard called **extensible markup language (XML)** allows developers to develop custom tags such as <item-number>, <item-name> and <item-price>. Such a language will enable browsers and web **servers** to implement transaction processing tasks. In fact just as HTML allows for open text publishing, XML will bring open database publishing.[8]

## Uniform resource locators and business significance

**Uniform resource locators (URLs)**, also known as universal resource locators, are addresses for web pages on the Internet. Users are able to enter these addresses into their browser software and make direct connections with the relevant web pages. Table 1.3 shows some example URLs and table 1.4 explains the meanings and uses of these protocols.

Internet Commerce: Digital Models for Business

| TABLE 1.3 | UNIFORM RESOURCE LOCATOR (URL) EXAMPLES | |
|---|---|---|
| **PROTOCOL** | **WEB SERVER OR COMPUTER NAME** | **DIRECTORY NAME AND/OR FILENAME** |
| file:// | /CI/Digital Commerce/ | INTRO/index.htm |
| telnet:// | 138.25.78.8 | (login library) |
| gopher:// | info.anu.edu.au:70 | /11/OtherSites/othergophers |
| news: | news.newusers.questions | |
| http:// | www.ssw.com.au | /index.htm |
| https:// | www.davidjones.com.au | |
| ftp:// | ftp.deakin.edu.au | /pub/pc-net/ |

| TABLE 1.4 | PROTOCOL MEANINGS AND USES | |
|---|---|---|
| **PROTOCOL** | **ACTION** | **PURPOSE** |
| file:// | retrieve local HTML and multimedia files | useful for editing purposes |
| telnet:// | log onto and work on a remote computer | useful for checking out external libraries' resources |
| gopher:// | access text-based menu system | useful for searching and receiving documents |
| news: | read messages from discussion groups | communicating with wide range of people on topics of mutual interest |
| http:// | retrieve text and multimedia to a local computer | linking a user's browser client to a web server |
| https:// | to secure transactions | encrypting credit card transactions |
| ftp:// | download files from remote computer | e.g. downloading software |

# THE GROWTH OF COMMERCIAL DOMAIN NAMES

The Internet commercial domain (indicated on a URL by '.com') was the fastest growing segment over the last two years. In Australia there are now so many commercial domains registered that some companies are going offshore to Norfolk Island to register their **domain names** (see case study 1 at the end of this chapter). Many Australian companies are also registering their business names in the United States where it is cheaper and where a country code (e.g. Australia's country code is '.au') is not added. Some Australian cyber businesses believe that having a '.au' on their domain name could deter overseas shoppers from dealing with them. Discussions are ongoing about setting up new domains, such as '.firm' and '.store'. Obviously for businesses it is important to have a URL that reflects the business name. For example, an Internet/intranet consulting and training business called Cyber.Consult has a registered domain name and virtual server at www.cyberconsult.com.au. Thus, it is easy for people to quickly work out what a business address is, whether it is for BHP, David Jones or Cyber.Consult. It is vitally important for companies to register their Internet addresses as there have been cases of people registering well-known brand or company names and then asking the legitimate company for money to buy the 'Net' name. Registration of commercial domain names in Australia and elsewhere has been characterised by some problems (see the case studies at the end of this chapter).

## HISTORY OF ELECTRONIC COMMERCE

Electronic data interchange (EDI) and email have been used for years in work flow and re-engineering applications. By October 1999 America Online had over 20 million subscribers. Many large businesses and government departments in Australia have insisted that their suppliers use EDI if they wanted to continue supplying them. As a result, some companies who could not afford such expensive hardware and software lost contracts. However, the Internet combined with EDI offers businesses the opportunity to become part of the digital commerce phenomenon in the twenty-first century. Harris Technology in Sydney has a successful web site and also uses EDI to communicate with its supplier.

Automation in the financial services industry began with back office functions (e.g. cheque processing in the 1960s), followed by new systems for credit card processing and wire transfers. Next, teller stations in local branches were automated to allow direct entry of particular transactions and direct access to customer account information. In the 1980s automation went from behind the counter to the customers via automatic teller machines (ATMs). In Australia the customer acceptance of ATMs was not particularly fast, but ATM-style banking is now very popular. The concept of digitally transferring funds (electronic funds transfer or EFT) between banking institutions has expanded to personal banking with ATMs, ATM cards and point-of-sale machines. In the 1990s the personal computer moved from the office to the home, and financial institutions are extending their technology to bring services to customers' personal computers (or telephones) at home and at work. The institutions have found such facilities lower the cost of servicing customer transactions, while increasing revenue sources. These facilities also make the institutions more competitive in customer service, which leads to increased customer loyalty.[9]

'A paradigm shift is driving new business practices within the financial services industry. Financial institutions desire to build new computer systems across an open platform to handle the shift to secure digital transactions. Four critical issues are impacting the speed of the evolution:
- the need for improved technology to ensure the security of the transaction
- the availability of a variety of payment protocols
- system reliability for twenty-four hours a day times seven days a week operations
- the flexibility of the platform to absorb new capabilities as they become available.'[10]

# BUSINESS REVOLUTION AND INTERNET COMMERCE

Just as the banks have seen how computer networks improve their viability, businesses have started to recognise that the Internet allows:
- company and consumer transactions over public networks for home shopping and banking
- transactions with trading partners using EDI
- information-gathering, such as market research
- information distribution transactions.[11]

# THE THEORY OF CREATIVE DESTRUCTION

Ways of doing business have been dramatically changed by the use of information technology — old ways of dealing with customers, suppliers and employees have been destroyed and replaced by radical new ways. Harvard economist Peter Schumpeter calls this creative destruction. He believes that what has been destroyed is more important than what has been retained and that only by destroying old ways of doing business can new ways be created.[12] Let us consider an example that is very common in Australia. With the restructuring of businesses in Australia, many middle managers found themselves without jobs. These were often people in their late forties who had identified closely with the firms for which they had worked over the past 20 years. Many of these people had to destroy their way of marketing themselves as potential loyal employees and become sole practitioners. They could no longer find positions that would enable them to have secretaries, assistants and various support mechanisms to get them through the working day. For such people to survive, they had to reinvent themselves and become proficient in the use of information technology themselves. If they obtained a private consulting job, they had to do all the parts of the job themselves, such as typing the report, preparing the invoices, doing their own research and running the modelling software.

Old business practices had to be thrown out and new information technology practices brought in. For example, Encyclopædia Britannica, now Britannica.com.au, had to reinvent the way it presented and sold its encyclopedic database. At first the company resisted the move to digital media; however, continued growth of technology forced it to re-evaluate its business strategy. In 1994 it decided to market its encyclopedia as a CD-ROM and as a subscription-based Internet service. The CD-ROM entered the market at a retail price of more than A$1200. This high price did not attract the expected business and the company was forced to reduce the price to A$199, which has proved to be a much more attractive proposition for buyers. The CD-ROM includes the entire text version of the *Encyclopædia Britannica*, plus articles from the *Britannica Book of the Year*, links to relevant web sites and helpful tools to assist students with homework. The encyclopedia is also available on DVD (digital video disc). To further add value to its product, Britannica.com.au offers *Britannica Online* (www.eb.com, see **home page** below), a subscription-based Internet service featuring the entire *Encyclopædia Britannica* and other special features and tools, including an encyclopedia for younger students. Britannica.com.au continues to reposition itself from a traditional publishing company into a twenty-first century media company. In October 1999 Britannica.com.au launched a free online information service at www.britannica.com.au. The service contains the entire encyclopedic database as well as current information such as news, weather, markets and sport, content from leading category magazines, books and links to 130 000 web sites classified and rated by Britannica's editorial team. *Encyclopædia Britannica* is still available in print form, but is now also packaged with the CD-ROM version.

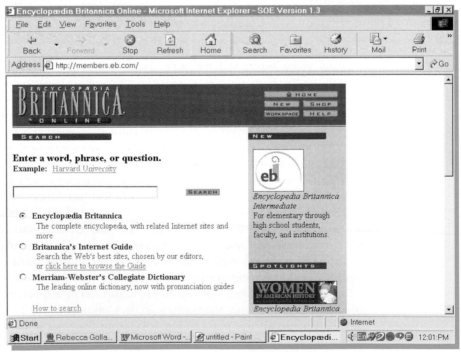

**FIGURE 1.1:** Home page for Britannica Online

# WHAT THE INTERNET MEANS FOR BUSINESSES IN AUSTRALIA

It is important for businesses to have an idea of what Internet commerce can offer before they try the Internet. Below are some of the key points of what Internet commerce can mean for businesses.[13]

## Strategic competitive advantages

The Internet and **intranets** give businesses the opportunity to improve their internal business processes and customer interfaces to create a sustainable, competitive advantage. If businesses take up the challenge quickly, they have the opportunity to leapfrog over the competition. Many Australian employment agencies have been quick to see the potential of listing job vacancies online. Morgan and Banks encourage online résumé applications. This has in turn led to a radical rethink on how to write résumés and has led to specialists setting up businesses to advise on résumé construction for the Web. Such résumés should contain key words that will be picked up by web search engines. This will be further explored in chapter 8.

## Managers need to be aware of the potential

Managers must be educated so they can see the possibilities of the Internet. In Australia managers are often technically illiterate and proud of it. If this is the case, it is difficult for them to see the advantages that are offered by the Internet. It is important that executive education on the Internet be put in place to ensure that opportunities are not lost.

In an Andersen survey of 150 Australian Chief Executive Officers in 1998, most agreed that e-commerce would revolutionise business in five years, but four out of five surveyed then said they did not consider e-commerce to be one of their top priorities. They felt information technology was a cost rather than an opportunity.

As the new digital economy grows, more and more people are connected and share data between desktops while collaborating on projects. An interesting management tool that allows employees to flourish in an innovative and creative environment is the Business-of-One program. In such a model employees see themselves not as workers but as a business of one where they can contribute business opportunities. Employees thus run their work in an entrepreneurial way and are encouraged to own their duties. It is apparent that as downsizing occurs, the idea of the business of one (as an Internet business) becomes attractive.[14]

Different companies in Australia have undertaken different tactics to ensure that their staff become aware of the potential of the Internet. Sydney Water and Australian Water Technologies embarked on an Internet Awareness Program in early 1995. Cyber.Consult was engaged to run seminars for all staff, from top management down to support staff, to alert them to the potential of the Internet. After a series of seminars, a Vocational Education Training Accreditation Board (VETAB) accredited introductory course on the Internet and the Web was offered to all members of the corporations. This course forms part of the corporations' strategy of upgrading their staff's information technology skills. A course in electronic commerce on the Internet has been developed by Cyber.Consult as the corporations are interested in exploring the possibility of using the Internet commercially. Sydney Water customers are able to pay their water rates via the St George Bank web page.

Sydney company Internet Training and Support designed its course 'Untangle the Web' specifically for businesspeople who are apprehensive about using the Web and need to gain confidence and competence quickly. They use games, music and advanced learning techniques to convert fear into fun in their Internet courses.

In Australia, some organisations have merely set up a web site to demonstrate that they are technically 'with it'. This was a reasonable strategy in 1995, but in the twenty-first century it is vital to be more than a mere presence. Organisations should be transforming themselves into new digital commerce centres and be prepared to open digital markets. This digital marketing opportunity provides sellers with the opportunity to personalise their goods and services to one consumer at a time — the antithesis of mass marketing. Browser **cookies** (files that a web server stores on a user's computer) allow companies to create a more personalised web interaction for consumers, but this is fraught with danger if companies don't ask users for permission first.

Some Australian companies have shied away from the Internet because they had security fears but at least they have seen the value of the intranet within the organisation. Use of intranets to enable employees to carry out tasks such as ordering hardware or software or requesting leave demonstrates the value of such a user-friendly interface. It can also pave the way for the organisation to communicate with the outside world on the Internet and communicate with suppliers and customers via intranets and **extranets**.

The term 'extranet' refers to a specialised and customised online information service provided by a company to its valued clients (either individuals or organisations). These can be suppliers (upstream) and other business partners (e.g. legal advisers, side-stream), rather than just the customers (downstream). It uses Internet connectivity and web technology as its platform. The differences (between the Internet and an extranet) are that an extranet has a specific audience and therefore is designed to satisfy the information needs of that audience.[15] (See Business insite on Fairfax.)

Email is another facility that can make doing business easier. Once companies see the value of email they generally realise that it is a truly valuable business tool for the organisation. Now that HTML-enhanced email is available, businesses can save lots of money by using email rather than normal post (known as 'snail mail') or faxes. Collaboration with others is the great advantage of doing business on the Internet. Team-building is made easier by the nature of the collaborative development aspect of the Internet. Netscape has launched its 1997 product under the name of 'Netscape Communicator' to underscore the value of the Internet in terms of communication. Lotus' product Domino builds on the background of **groupware**, which is an application that is networked to allow users to share data and maximise human interaction. Microsoft is now offering voice email.

One great advantage of the Internet is its potential for real-time training and **conferences**. Businesses are able to utilise **Internet protocol television (IP/TV)** and videoconferencing to deliver training right to the employee's desktop. Groups of people and individuals in different locations can hold interactive meetings. Using inexpensive software such as Microsoft's Net-Meeting, employees can see one another on screen and even collaborate using electronic whiteboard software, which can be used interactively.

# Fairfax AdOnline

A exciting project by Fairfax called AdOnline has made various impacts on some of the key areas of traditional newspaper operations and illustrates some emerging trends relevant to new ways of doing business due to the presence of the Internet. It is an example of a business-to-business e-commerce extranet.

AdOnline is a suite of software modules that allow selected and favoured clients, who are regular advertisers in either the *Sydney Morning Herald* or the *Age*, to place advertisements into these publications directly from their own back-end systems via the Internet. These advertisements are entered into the two Fairfax proprietary, back-end **legacy systems** without having to liaise with the call centres (known as the 'phone room' in the industry). AdOnline leverages the Internet substantially as the medium of transfer of information between the advertiser and the company's two main publishing systems.

AdOnline was conceived almost two years ago so that Fairfax could be seen as a 'leading edge' force in the electronic media and e-commerce as well as maintaining the reputation as a dominant player in the print media.

This project has seen the potential of the World Wide Web being realised by Fairfax to the extent that every advertisement that appears in the printed products now also appears on the Fairfax web sites. These ads are also categorised automatically as they are being placed on the web site so that they can be searched based on various user criteria. The big benefit here is that multiple databases can be searched simultaneously.

For instance, if **web surfers** were searching for an exotic vintage car they could enter the search criteria (e.g. red, less than $20k, good condition, MGB, pre-1965 etc.) and the search would look through the *Sydney Morning Herald*, the *Age*, the *Illawarra Mercury*, *Newcastle Herald* etc. How long would that take if they were to actually look through the printed products themselves? Interesting statistics became apparent such as MGBs are cheaper in Melbourne than in Sydney! This type of statistic was not necessarily available to the public prior to such databases being available.

Figure 1.2 provides an overview of the major components in the AdOnline project and also indicates some of the networking protocols that are used to allow this project to operate.

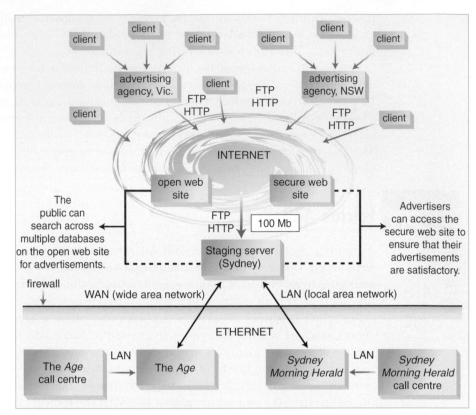

**FIGURE 1.2:** Overview diagram of Fairfax's AdOnline architecture.
**SOURCE:** C. Payne 1999, 'Extranets — a quiet business revolution page', Thesis for Master of Science, University of Technology, Sydney, p. 67

One of the major selling features of the AdOnline project is the option advertisers now have to supply additional multimedia information about the item they are selling. At the moment, this feature is limited to only real estate vendors and is primarily designed to allow video clips of properties for sale.

So, as well as a conventional textual description of the property for sale, along with the usual photographic image of the property, the advertiser can, for no extra cost, supply a video clip of the property including an audio commentary if required. All pieces of such advertisements can be delivered to either or both of the major publishers through the common medium of the Internet.

**SOURCE:** Chris Payne, Advertising Development Manager, John Fairfax Holdings Ltd

### EXERCISES

1. Do some research to find out what is meant by the following terms:
   (a) proprietary, back-end legacy systems
   (b) firewall
   (c) **wide area network (WAN)**
   (d) **local area network (LAN)**
   (e) **ethernet**.
2. Prepare a table that outlines the advantages of the AdOnline system to Fairfax, advertisers and the public.
3. Discuss any disadvantages you see in such a system.

# POSSIBLE RISKS IN INTERNET COMMERCE

## Security issues

Businesses are cautious because they fear that hackers will break into their networks and steal valuable information. It must be remembered that security issues have always been associated with computer networks. There are many techniques that have been developed over the years to combat security problems and these will be addressed in chapter 6. Netscape produces the Secure Server and Secure Sockets Layer protocol to combat security problems, while Microsoft has produced the Microsoft Commerce Server and IBM has SecureWay. Microsoft has launched an e-commerce framework called BizTalk, which acts as a translation engine between systems operating on Internet protocols, legacy systems and enterprise resource planning systems, such as SAP and EDI platforms.

## Shopping experience issues

Many people believe that shopping via computers will not take off because people view shopping as an entertainment or social event. This may have been so when women were not so widely represented in the work force. A working woman often finds shopping, especially grocery shopping, a chore. In 1997 retail sales in large shopping centres slumped and research in the United States points to the fact that women are not keen on going to large shopping centres once a week to do their shopping. The St George Bank used an effective advertisement aimed at working women for its Internet banking facilities. It pointed out that while the woman in the advertisement did not have time to get through her various chores during her lunch break, at least she could do all her banking from the comfort of her own home. Advertisements for Internet shopping concentrate on the 'Wouldn't you rather be at home!' theme.

## Micropayments or microtransactions issues

Critics have stated that until micropayments (small payments using, for example, digital cash) and microtransactions (small fee transactions down to 10 cents) are available, on-line shopping will fail. Electronic payment systems that allow for such transactions will be covered in chapter 5.

## Lack of standards issues

Internet commerce shows how technological advances leapfrog legal and government regulations and standards. Some attempts to set up standards included Secure Electronic Transactions (SET), a secure communication standard that could be used for handling credit cards over the Internet. In June 1998, SET (www.setco.org) awarded the right to use the SET trademark to the first four vendors of SET compliant software, namely Globeset Inc, Spyrus/ Terisa Systems, Trintech and Verifone Inc. Other standards include Open Buying on the Internet (OBI), which can be found at www.openbuy.org. These and others will be addressed in more detail in chapters 5 and 6.

## Lack of bandwidth

It takes a lot of transmission capacity, or bandwidth, on the Internet to transmit graphics, audio and video. The bandwidth of the communication channels that hook up computers to the Internet are measured in bits per second. Businesses claim that lack of bandwidth will kill opportunities on the Internet. Telstra's Big Pond Cable web site allows download speeds of nearly 3 Mbps but this service is mainly restricted to residential districts in metropolitan areas. However, in May 1999 Telstra's Carrier Services group introduced a new low cost, asymmetric satellite service for all of the 40 Big Pond direct points of presence (POPs) in Australia and will utilise high-quality international satellite transmission on multiple 45 Mbps links from the United States. As well, Telstra is introducing a proxy cache service for capturing and storing frequently visited web sites locally in order to reduce the costs and time involved in downloading web sites from overseas and interstate. Web information will be stored in local cache farms in each capital city of Australia. Cable & Wireless Optus' Spinnaker services approximately 30 per cent of the major ISPs in Australia. Optus Spinnaker's presence in this market has also generated an extra 200 megabits of international capacity in 1999, approximately double the Australian total of the same time last year. Spinnaker offers access to New Zealand and some Asian countries such as Hong Kong and China at domestic traffic rates. Satnet has 4 Mbps bandwidth on PanAmSat 2. Users are guaranteed a minimum of 128 Kbps but this may go up to 400 Kbps. Ozemail is also involved in an Internet trial with the Austar satellite TV service.[6]

## STAKEHOLDERS IN INTERNET COMMERCE

One of the exciting possibilities with Internet commerce is the fact that a single person can start doing business on the Internet. Below are listed some of the companies and areas that have profited as a result of the rise of the Internet and its commercialisation.

- software developers, such as Sausage Software and Superior Software
- hardware companies, such as Banksia modem manufacturers. (By November 1999, 1.7 million households [25 per cent of all households] were connected to the Internet. The increase in the number of households with home Internet access was more than double the increase in the number of households with home computers over the 12 months to November 1999.[17])
- access providers, such as Ozemail and BigPond
- telephone companies, such as Telstra, AAPT and Cable & Wireless Optus
- system integrators, such as JavaSoft

- consultants and trainers, such as Cyber.Consult (www.cyberconsult.com.au), Apt Strategies (www.aptstrategies.com.au) and Internet Training and Support
- buyer and seller services, such as search engines and portals (e.g. Yahoo!, Dogpile, MetaCrawler, WebCrawler, anzwers.com.au, Wombat search engine, http://ozsearch.com.au)
- information publishing engines, such as Adobe
- shopping malls, such as Sofcom, ShopSafe
- home users, who use the Internet for banking and bill payment
- students. (It is New South Wales government policy that every school has an Internet connection.)
- employees, who may use intranets such as that at Sydney University
- business-to-business opportunities (see Cisco Systems at www.cisco.com, and the Business insite on the Fairfax site)

## Using intranets to boost efficiency

### The Intranet: a new way for Sydney Water

Sydney Water has actually had two intranets.

The first one was called the WaterWeb. It was designed in-house by the Software Development Unit with only limited input from other businesses. The intent was to demonstrate a pilot version, deploy it and then build upon it.

The eyes of the management were opened to (some of) the potential of this new tool. An Intranet Project Team was formed in December 1997 that comprised representatives from each of the other businesses as well as a technical resource from Software Development. The charter of this team was to 'support the Corporation's drive to be a communications-enabled company by ensuring the professional development of the intranet and determining design content and content development guidelines'.

The team went to open tender to obtain some external advice and expertise in the design and development of our intranet. The successful tenderer was the Nethead Nemas Group (NNG).

The site was developed, the content compiled and loaded, and publishing guidelines were approved and broadcast. Content coordinators were nominated and trained. Five months after the project was initiated, Sydney Water's new intranet (the ConnectNet) was implemented in April 1998.

The key benefits from the development of a more integrated intranet facility for the organisation have been:
- information is more accessible and driven by business processes
- a corporate-wide ability to convey relevant information has been established
- management and reporting information is quickly and easily disseminated
- the adherence to 'best practice' in relation to information management
- the sharing of information between the various businesses throughout the organisation.

The WaterWeb is now a far more dynamic facility that enables staff to access a diverse range of information on any number of topics from personnel to complex scientific data concerning water quality. Sydney Water has approximately 4500 staff spread over more than 50 sites from Wollongong to the Blue Mountains.

Along with icons allowing access to the usual functions (e.g. Help, Search, Links, Feedback, My Page), there is also a corporate message board and a PeopleFinder facility, which stores all of the organisation's people and their contact details.

The contents of the ConnectNet are accessed through four gateways:

- 'Internal', which stores all corporate documents like policies and procedures and pages for several business units
- 'Customers', which houses the Customer Complaint System (newly developed) and details of upcoming marketing or public relations events
- 'Environment', which contains information about environmental issues, educational programs, legislative amendments. It also has the eGuide which canvasses issues such as:
  - ecologically sustainable development and due diligence
  - education and awareness
  - resources
  - environmental heritage
  - environmental impact assessment.
- 'Business', which has information on a host of issues such as the liaison with the newly formed Sydney Catchment Authority, Year 2000 issues and concerns as well as copies of the Operating Licence and group business plans.

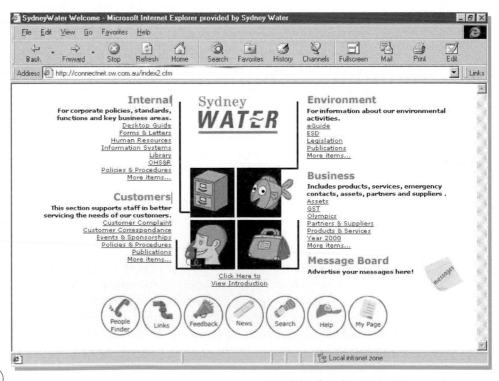

**FIGURE 1.3:** Sydney Water's intranet home page

The Intranet project is considered to be critical to the ongoing development of the organisation and various businesses are developing their own intranet pages to store more business-specific content. Several significant projects are underway including the measurement and reporting of intranet usage, and content archiving. Sydney Water now has an internal web master and will increasingly use the site as a business application front-end, as well as a communications and publishing tool

**SOURCE:** Paul Saunders, Business Analyst, Sydney Water Corporation

### EXERCISES

1. Discuss the business advantages and disadvantages of introducing an intranet into a corporation as a first step to moving out to the Internet and later to Internet commerce.
2. Select a company that you know has an intranet and investigate its development, outlining any problems that were encountered.

## SUMMARY

This chapter has covered the history of electronic commerce. It has shown how electronic commerce started in the financial area and is now spreading to cover all aspects of commercial transactions over the World Wide Web. Businesses will have to reinvent themselves, change some business processes and even destroy some of their usual ways of doing business. Strategies for new business planning and implementation have been introduced and will be covered in more depth in chapter 2. The growth of the Internet and intranets has provided new job opportunities and new ways of applying for jobs have developed. Businesses that want to stay competitive and viable must embrace the opportunities of setting up digital markets if they wish to survive in the next millenium.

**key terms**

| | | |
|---|---|---|
| browser | groupware | intranet |
| conference | home page | legacy system |
| cookies | hypertext | local area network (LAN) |
| domain name | hypertext markup | Netscape |
| email | language (HTML) | server |
| ethernet | hypertext transfer protocol | uniform resource locator |
| extensible markup | (HTTP) | (URL) |
| language (XML) | Internet | web surfers |
| extranet | Internet protocol television | wide area network (WAN) |
| file transfer protocol (FTP) | (IP/TV) | World Wide Web |

# Case Study ① — THE ESTABLISHMENT OF ICANN — INTERNET CORPORATION FOR ASSIGNED NAMES AND NUMBERS

## GOVERNMENTS ENDORSE PRIVATE SECTOR INTERNET

**Singapore, 2 March 1999.** A powerful group of governments today endorsed the establishment of the private-sector model for the technical administration of the Internet. In a critical milestone for the establishment of the new market-led technical management structure, nearly 20 national governments from around the world reinforced the need for market-led solutions to the fast-moving evolution of the Internet. Their actions confirmed the principles first put in motion by the United States government in July 1998.

Until late 1998, the Internet's technical administration was performed by or on behalf of the United States government.

The Governmental Advisory Committee of the Internet Corporation for Assigned Names and Numbers (ICANN) concluded its inaugural meeting today by endorsing the principles behind the creation of ICANN and committing themselves to play a constructive role in support of its processes.

The national governments were joined by representatives of key multi-lateral governmental organisations and treaty organisations, including the European Commission, the International Telecommunications Union, the Organisation for Economic Cooperation and Development, and the World Intellectual Property Organisation.

'Today represented a significant milestone in the establishment of ICANN,' said Australia's Dr Paul Twomey, the Chairman of the Governmental Advisory Committee. 'We saw a broad cross-section of the community of nations express strong support for the idea that the Internet is best managed by the Internet community itself.'

The meeting was attended by representatives of 17 nations, including Argentina, Australia, Bhutan, Brazil, Canada, China, France, Japan, Korea, Mexico, Peru, Singapore, Spain, Sri Lanka, Tuvalu and the United States. Germany's representative also attended today's meeting on behalf of the President of the European Union.

Dr Twomey stated, 'The governments and organisations attending today's meeting represent the vast majority of Internet users. They also reflected some of the most innovative policy approaches to the use of the Internet.'

For example, Tuvalu has recently made Internet history by entering a lucrative commercial arrangement for the marketing of its .tv country code top level domain (ccTLD).

The discussions in Singapore covered a broad range of issues, including matters of structure and organisation, as well as significant policy issues such as the administration of ccTLDs.

The Governmental Advisory Committee is not a decision-making inter-governmental organisation, but a forum for providing advice to ICANN. Under ICANN's bylaws, the ICANN Board may refer matters to the Governmental Advisory Committee, or the Governmental Advisory Committee may raise issues and make recommendations on its own initiative.

A web site for the Governmental Advisory Committee has been established, which can be accessed through the ICANN home page (http://www.icann.org).

**About ICANN**

The Internet Corporation for Assigned Names and Numbers (ICANN) is a new, non-profit, international corporation formed to oversee a select number of the Internet's core technical management functions. Between now and September 2000, ICANN is slated to gradually take over responsibility for coordinating domain name system management, IP address space allocation, protocol parameter assignment coordination, and root server system management.

In the past, many of these functions have been handled by the US Government or its contractors and volunteers. This informal structure represented the spirit and culture of the research community in which the Internet developed. However, the growing size and international importance of the Internet has necessitated the creation of a technical management body that is both more formalised in structure, and more fully reflective of the geographic diversity of the Internet community.

ICANN is a non-profit corporation with an international board of directors. Its initial board is led by interim chairman Esther Dyson, and has members drawn from several nations. This initial board is finalising ICANN's by-laws and procedures and working to pave the way for a smooth and stable transition from the present administrative system.

The initial board members will be replaced by board members selected by four different constituency groups, collectively representing a broad range of the Internet's technical and user communities around the globe.

Under the MoU [memorandum of understanding], ICANN has already accredited an initial group of five new competitive registrars (America Online, CORE, France Telecom, Melbourne IT and register.com), as part of a test of the Shared Registration System, which will permit competition among multiple registrars in this very public component of the Internet's underlying technology. Following completion of the test and the negotiation of an acceptable registry agreement with Network Solutions, at least 52 other companies from around the world will also be eligible to offer registration services alongside Network Solutions, heralding a new era of full and open competition.

**SOURCE:** Press release © 1999, Internet Corporation for Assigned Names and Numbers

## RESEARCH QUESTIONS

1. Do some research to find out what is meant by the following: 'Tuvalu has recently made Internet history by entering a lucrative commercial arrangement for the marketing of its .tv country code top level domain (ccTLD)'.
2. What is the situation now in registering a commercial domain site in Australia? Please note that Australian commercial sites may register in other countries such as the United States, Norfolk Island, Anguilla etc.
3. Outline what ICANN has achieved since its inaugural meeting.
4. What have been some of the most significant achievements of the National Office of the Information Economy (see www.noie.gov.au)?
5. In Australia, the registration of commercial domain names has had a turbulent history. Do some research and write a report outlining the history of commercial domain names in Australia from 1994 onwards.

# Case Study 2 — GETTING A DIGITAL BUSINESS ONLINE

In this case study there are some important web sites you should investigate.

### Registering a web site

The Internet has one system for the allocation of IP addresses (numbers) and another system for the allocation of domain names. The numbers have been under the control of the Internet Assigned Names Association (IANA), which is to become the Internet Corporation for Assigned Names and Numbers (ICANN) www.icann.org).

The transitional IANA web site (www.iana.org) has information on IP addressing and its role in the domain name system (DNS).

People in Australia who need an IP address or block of addresses go firstly to their Internet service provider who in turn goes to its upstream registry, AUNIC (www.aunic.net). There are appropriate regional registries at APNIC (www.apnic.net).

There are two types of top-level domains, generic and country codes:

- generic — .com, .org, .net, .edu, .gov, .mil, .int
- country — .au, .ca, .jp, .nz, .sg.

Robert Elz from the University of Melbourne was delegated the responsibility by IANA of administering the '.au' domain; 'edu.au' and 'gov.au' went to Geoff Huston of Telstra Internet; 'net.au' to Chris Chaundy of Connect.com.au; 'com.au' to Peter Gerrard of Melbourne IT; and 'asn.au' to Michael Malone of iNet Technologies.

The new body to oversee domain names here is au Domain Administration (auDA) (www.auda.org.au), which has taken over from the Australian Domain Name Administration (ADNA), which had no real power. The new body will be self-funded from membership fees and other administrative fees. Some of the more contentious issues of membership qualifications, e.g. citizenship, have been passed to the National Office of the Information Economy (www.noie.gov.au) to resolve.

The administration of the 'com.au' domain is undertaken by the Internet Names Australia (INA) (www.ina.com.au) — a division of Melbourne Information Technologies Australia Pty Ltd.

### TABLE 1.5 — MAJOR DOMAIN NAME ENTITIES

| NAME OF BODY | WEB ADDRESS |
| --- | --- |
| Internet Assigned Numbers Authority (IANA) | www.iana.org |
| Internet Network Information Centre (interNic) | www.internic.net |
| Internet Corporation for Assigned Names and Numbers | www.icann.org |
| American Registry for Internet Numbers | http://arin.net |
| Asia-Pacific Network Information Centre | http://apnic.net |
| Internet Names Australia | www.ina.com.au |
| Australian Domain Name Administration | www.auDA.org.au |
| NetRegistry | www.netregistry.au.com |

**SOURCE:** A. Macpherson, 'Business-to-business transactions', *Hands-on Solutions: E-commerce*, CCH Australia, 1999, pp. 22–7

## RESEARCH QUESTIONS

1. There has been discussion of the fact that we need more generic domains if Internet commerce continues to grow. Some of the ideas put forward include the provision of such domains as .firm, .shop, .biz, etc. What is the situation with these ideas now?

2. Can a business register a business name that is a common dictionary word; for example, if the company was named Hills Hoist, could it register as http://www.hills.com.au?

3. The Norfolk Island computer guru, Robert Ryan, managed to get a .nf country code for the island despite the fact that it is not a separate country from Australia. This has meant that companies are able to register as http://www.mycompanyname.com.nf without having to follow the dictionary rule or other rules. Do a search of the Internet and see how many .com.nf entities you can find. Write a report on any that appear to be breaking the common dictionary rule.

4. What is your opinion of the 'no commonly used dictionary words in the domain names' rule? Justify your answer.

5. Do some research on the site NetRegistry (www.netregistry.com.au). How does its philosophy, method of registrations, cost and speed of registration differ from Internet Names Australia (www.ina.com.au)?

## QUESTIONS

1. In this chapter you have been given two examples of the theory of creative destruction. See if you can find examples of how this theory might apply in any one of the following industries: travel, automobile, banking and leisure.

2. After carrying out some research, write a short paper on the history of the Internet in Australia or your choice of country.

3. Debate the following statement: 'Internet shopping will fail as it does not allow for a social shopping experience'.

4. Debate the following statement: 'Australian managers are technically illiterate and keyboard phobic'.

5. Do some research on how companies are using email and inexpensive software such as Microsoft's NetMeeting to enhance both inter- and intra-organisational communication.

## SUGGESTED READING

Gates, B. 1999, *Business @ The Speed of Thought: Using a Digital Nervous System*, Microsoft Press, United States.

Kalakota, R. and Whinston, A. 1996, *Frontiers of Electronic Commerce*, Addison-Wesley, United States.

McKeown, P. and Watson, R. 1996, *Metamorphosis — A Guide to the World Wide Web and Electronic Commerce*, John Wiley and Sons, Inc., United States.

Mougayer, W. 1997, *Opening Digital Markets*, CyberManagement, Canada.

Phillips, M. 1998, *Successful E-commerce*, Bookman, Australia.

**END NOTES**

1. Department of Foreign Affairs and Trade 1999, *Creating a Clearway on the New Silk Road: International Business and Policy Trends in Internet Commerce*, Commonwealth of Australia, Canberra, p. 3.
2. Headcount (www.headcount.com), quoted in Department of Foreign Affairs and Trade, op. cit., p. 3.
3. Forrester Research Incorporated, *Forrester Ranks World Economies for eCommerce*, 30 April 1997, press@forrester.com, www.forrester.com.
4. Hickman, B. 1997, 'Internet banking services to soar', *Australian*, 8 April 1997, p. 3.
5. Kalakota, R. and Winston, A. 1996, *Frontiers of Electronic Commerce*, Addison-Wesley, United States, p. 5.
6. McKeown, P. and Watson, R. 1996, *Metamorphosis: A Guide to the World Wide Web and Electronic Commerce*, John Wiley and Sons, New York, p. 6.
7. ibid., p. 14.
8. Panko, R. 1999, *Business Data Communications and Networking*, 2nd edn, p. 413, www.prenhall.com/panko.
9. Flanagan, P. 1997, 'Internet funds transfer', *University of Technology, Sydney, Masters Project*, June 1997, p. 27.
10. Coleman, A. 1997, *Java Commerce: A Business Perspective*, JavaSoft, www.javasoft.com/products/commerce/bizper.html.
11. Kalakota and Winston, op. cit., p. 2.
12. McKeown and Watson, op. cit., p. 2.
13. Mougayer, W. 1997, *Opening Digital Markets*, CyberManagement, Canada, pp. 113–8.
14. Harrison, L. G. 1997, *Harrison on Leadership*, July 1997, www.altika.com/leadership.
15. Tjhai, P. '1997 will be the year of the "extranet"', Computers Section, *Australian*, 18 June 1996, p. 34, and Payne, C. 1999, Extranet — the quiet business communication revolution, MA thesis for Science (Computing), University of Technology, Sydney.
16. Mehlman, J. 1999, 'The right stuff: access technologies', *Australian Personal Computer*, May, p. 94.
17. Australian Bureau of Statistics 1999, Continued Growth in Australian Internet Access, media release, 1 March 2000, 22/2000.

# Business models for Internet commerce

## LEARNING Outcomes

You will have mastered the material in this chapter when you can:

- ◉ understand the various models that can be applied to Internet commerce
- ◉ discuss the pros and cons of each model
- ◉ use strategic planning principles for Internet commerce.

'The basis of competition and wealth creation in the digital economy is not good use of information, quality, process re-engineering, speed, effective decision making, empowerment or other countless management techniques popular today. It is business model innovation.'

Don Tapscott, Chairman of the Alliance for Converging Technologies, in R. Kalakota and M. Robinson 1999, *E-Business: Roadmap for Success*, Addison-Wesley Longman, p. xiii

# INTRODUCTION

When the World Wide Web caught the imagination of marketing and businesspeople, it was only a matter of time before commercialisation of the Web became a reality. Even before the Web made its appearance in the early 1990s, some far-sighted people had seen the potential of doing online business using email. However, because the Internet had its roots in academia and research, commercialisation was usually frowned upon until the early 1990s. Remember that there is no 'cookbook' approach to Internet commerce. If you look at the success stories over the past few years it is interesting to note that those who have been successful have devised their own models. They have often been young, entrepreneurial, risk-taking individuals. In this chapter we will examine some of the successful business models that have been used to establish businesses on the Internet. In the second part of the chapter we will look at using the Internet Commerce Customer Service Life Cycle model and the Integrated Internet Marketing model.[1]

# BUSINESS MODELS

No matter what business model the fledgling electronic business adopts, it is possible to adapt essential disciplines of successful management techniques to participate in online business on the Internet.[2] The key strategies that are put forward as being essential for establishing a successful presence on the Internet are:

- planning
- controlling
- monitoring
- adjusting
- managing quality.

Each of these strategies will be dealt with in the context of providing advice for businesses wishing to maximise their cyber potential. Methods for building a commercial presence on the Internet include the following models:

- Poster/Billboard model
- Online Yellow Pages model
- Cyber Brochure
- Virtual Storefront
- Subscription model
- Advertising model
- 3.5.7 model
- Auction/Reverse Auction model
- Affiliation model
- Portal model.

MANAGING QUALITY

PLANNING

MODELS

Poster/Billboard
Online Yellow Pages
Cyber Brochure
Virtual Storefront
Subscription
Advertising
3.5.7
Auction
Reverse Auction
Affiliation
Portal

MONITORING

CONTROLLING

ADJUSTING

MANAGING QUALITY

**FIGURE 2.1:** Strategies and models for a successful Internet presence

# Poster/Billboard model

The **Poster/Billboard model**,[3] a low-cost strategy for beginners, is concerned with the posting of enticing 'come-on' information for others to read and take action on. For example, a business using email must ensure it places the business address on all communications. Web pages should carry an automatic reply address, so that users need only click on the hypertext link to open the email composition window. Because email is capable of handling HTML-embedded text, it is easy to include your 'clickable' http://address in your signature block at the end of your emails — a cheap and efficient way of advertising your site. Both email and HTTP addresses should also appear on advertisements, letterheads, memos, faxes and business cards. It is essential to avoid mass unsolicited emailing, which only serves to irritate potential customers by clogging up their inboxes. Such email is analogous to junk mail in a person's home or business mailbox.

# Online Yellow Pages model

Businesses using the **Online Yellow Pages model**,[4] which represents a greater investment in money, create a menu, with each item on the menu pointing towards other sources and proving further information. These menus can be created on **Gopher** servers, bulletin boards, the Web and **wide area information**

**server (WAIS).** This model creates a higher profile for businesses. A user or customer is able to access business information by conducting a search either by name or by industry and business type. A site location identified by either a map or photograph may be used. When accessed, the site will contain such information as products or services and prices, any special offers and methods of payment.

## Cyber Brochure model

The **Cyber Brochure model**,[5] which is slightly more sophisticated than the Online Yellow Pages approach, provides for information sheets, brochures and information items. The emphasis here is on the information itself with only a small amount of space given over to promotional material.

## Virtual Storefront model

The **Virtual Storefront model**[6] is a full information service designed to include the marketing of a business's services and products and/or online purchasing and customer support. In cyberspace such transactions are increasingly being conducted entirely online through encrypted two-way data traffic between the consumer and the 'virtual store'. The product or merchandise purchased through either of these methods is then generally delivered to the purchaser at a later date by mail. In the case of information, software or entertainment products, however, the goods may simply be downloaded to the consumer's hard drive through the network connection. This is the most sophisticated model requiring more planning, time, money and effort.[7]

## Subscription model

Use of the **Subscription model**[8] has been borrowed from publishing. Just as a consumer might subscribe to a monthly or weekly magazine, so a consumer is able to subscribe to an online version of a magazine or any product with updated versions offered on an on-going basis. It is becoming increasingly prevalent among businesses whose products can be delivered online, as can be seen by the practice of selling software by subscription in order to facilitate the timely dissemination of version upgrades to customers. This has been used successfully by Netscape to allow users to upgrade to new versions of the browser.

## Advertising model

The **Advertising model**[9] has been used by web sites such as search engine web pages (see figure 2.2). They offer advertising space on their web pages to obtain revenue. They use targeted advertising so that if a consumer goes to a search engine, such as Lycos, to search for cars for sale, advertisements for Holden or Ford might appear as banner advertisements on the search result page. Such one-to-one targetted marketing has excited many business entrepreneurs. Obviously the web site has to be able to attract large numbers of people (of an appropriate demographic) if it is to sell advertising space.

Note the banner advertisment at the top of the screen.

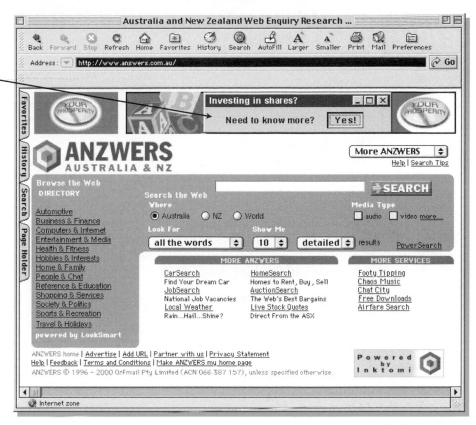

**FIGURE 2.2:** ANZWERS — an online search engine specifically for Australian and New Zealand users (www.anzwers.com.au)

The advertising model is appropriate primarily for service-oriented, online businesses. However, a site could lose business by advertising another company's business products in the online environment. Cross-marketing, the sale of complementary goods in conjunction with another good, is the major exemption. For example, a surfboard manufacturer might accept advertising from a supplier of 'surfie' type clothing or accessories. In Australia, the earthmover and civil contractor company RP Equipment runs an online guide (www.rpdata.net.au/equip/) to new and used heavy equipment on the Internet. It also advertises a huge range of cars, utilities, light commercial vehicles, four-wheel drives and motor bikes online. If the cyber business offers valid opportunities for advertisers to convey their messages to an appropriate demographic, it may have a chance in attracting advertisers to contribute to the success of the new business.[10]

# 3.5.7 model

The **3.5.7 model**[11] lays the foundation for commercial success by using the Internet as a business communication tool. The key points of the 3.5.7 model are outlined in the Business insite on the next page.

# The 3.5.7 model

The 3.5.7 model can be used to plan a new web presence or rework an existing one. The model can essentially be broken down into three areas: three steps to a better focus, five strategies to evaluate the potential of a web presence and seven tactics to be used as a framework for building specific plans.

### Three steps to a better focus

These three points outline why businesses on the Internet have not yet made millions of dollars and why they should still maintain their presence.

1. The Internet is not a sales transaction tool — yet. Its acceptance may parallel consumers' acceptance of ATMs and take a few years.
2. Communication is where the money is. Most companies should realise the real potential for Internet commerce lies in its cheap communication costs.
3. You need new thinking, new strategies and a new approach — lateral, adventurous thinking is required.

### Five-dimensional strategy

These five strategies each point to a key element of doing business online. Businesses should evaluate how each of these strategies could be better served through an online web presence.

1. communicating with existing customers
2. providing service and support
3. communicating with prospects
4. augmenting traditional business communication (what could be done on the Internet that is not being done now because of time or money constraints)
5. internal communications

### Seven-point tactical guide

The following points provide tactics that can be improved using the Internet. Each tactic is a general framework on which to build specific plans.

1. building brand awareness and loyalty
2. direct-response promotions
3. education of the marketplace
4. product demonstration and distribution
5. public relations/press relations
6. research and product development
7. service and support

### EXERCISES

1. Discuss the statement 'Communication is where the money is'. Do you agree or disagree that the real potential for Internet commerce lies in cheap communication costs? Why or why not?
2. Locate web sites that illustrate each point in the seven-point tactical guide and justify your choices.
3. Visit the site www.successful.com to find out more about this business model.
4. Select a potential online business, such as a newsagency or soft-drink maker, and prepare a report illustrating how you could apply the 3.5.7 model to that business.

## Auction and Reverse Auction models

Originally online auctions were used as a way for computer manufacturers to offload surplus material quickly. In the United States it was collectors of items and memorabilia such as 'Beanie Babies' and back issues of the *Saturday Evening Post* that propelled the growth of online auctions using the **Auction model**.

The web site www.priceline.com developed the **Reverse Auction model** where bidders set their price for items such as airline tickets or hotel rooms and a seller decides whether to supply it.[12]

## Affiliation model

The **Affiliation model** encourages web-site owners to sign up under what is known as an associate or affiliate program. For example Amazon invites web-site owners to sign up to sell the bookseller's inventory. Once approved, the affiliate is sent an email with instructions on how to set up links and banner ads. These affiliates do not directly sell but merely direct web surfers to the online store, which takes and fills the order. The merchant then pays the affiliate a small set fee for playing the rainmaker.[13]

## Affiliate programs

Several large Internet companies such as Amazon run what is known as affiliate programs. If you have a web site, you are able to enrol as an affiliate. Once approval has been given, you are given instructions via email on how to set up links and banner advertisements. Once set up, your web site simply directs your visitors to the online stores, which take and fill the orders. These merchants in turn pay you a percentage of each sale or a small set fee for forwarding on the customer.

A book called *Digital Darwinism* by Evan Schwartz outlines the way in which affiliate programs are taking off. It claims that affiliate programs make more sense than banner advertisements, which require payment in advance and do not guarantee traffic or sales.

Web sites, such as Refer-It, that list affiliate programs and network sites, such as LinkShare, beFree and DirectLeads, make it easy for web masters to join up. Refer-It also lists the top 10 programs and gives affiliate programs ratings.

### EXERCISES

1. Do some research to ascertain whether this Affiliate model is proving profitable for:
   (a) the affiliates
   (b) the companies offering the affiliate programs.
2. Schwartz and the web master of Refer-It have commented that this 'model is still green and more innovations are coming'. Do some research to see what is now happening with this model and what innovations, if any, have taken place.

## Portal model

A **Portal model** web site is designed to offer a variety of Internet services from a single convenient location.[14] The goal of the portal is to be designated as your potential customer's browser's start-up page. This model reached a peak in 1998, then seemed to subside in early 1999 only to make a comeback in late 1999. Most portals offer certain free services such as a search engine; local, national and worldwide news; sports and weather; references such as directories and maps; shopping malls; and email and chat rooms. In Australia users of the popular web email service Hotmail are directed automatically to the Channel 9 Television and Microsoft portal www.ninemsn.com.au when they log out of the email screen. Other popular portals include such major search engines as Altavista, Excite, InfoSeek, Lycos and Yahoo!

# STRATEGIES TO SUCCESSFULLY IMPLEMENT THE BUSINESS MODELS

Regardless of what type of business presence you wish to establish on the Internet, it is vital to carry out the five strategies of planning, controlling, monitoring, adjusting and managing quality.[15] Obviously, the size of the business will restrict the number of personnel involved in the operation, but the disciplines can be adapted for any business wishing to establish an electronic commercial presence.

## Planning

The potential Internet business user should devise an effective plan outlined in a business/user requirements document, which covers strategies and schedules. This document should establish the baseline for the establishment of a presence on the Internet. For example, if the business is going to use the Online Yellow Pages, Cyber Brochure, Advertising or Virtual Storefront models, particularly on the Web, it will need to plan a vibrant home page so that potential customers will stay longer at the site and/or continue to return to the site. It might be necessary to hire a professional firm to design the entire commercial site, particularly if you are intending to link up a database to the home page or if you need help designing attractive graphics.

## Controlling

The cyber business should have a documented and well-defined structure that covers all the people involved (including the potential customers), duties, job descriptions and responsibilities. The customers must keep returning regardless of what model the business chooses. For example, added incentives may be attached to the home page to ensure return visits. If the business uses an outside consultant, it might be beneficial to be attached to that consultant's home page, particularly if that consultant can provide lots of return business to the site. Develop a budget and work out costs for every aspect of the business, such as creating web documents, storage costs, **firewalls**, credit card transaction costs, download charges and consulting charges.[16] (See the case study at the end of this chapter.)

# Monitoring

During the setting up of the business presence on the Internet, it is vital to keep close checks on time and money expenditure. If using an outside consultant, it is necessary to get competitive quotes from designers and to budget for software, hardware and design upgrades. Service providers are often upgrading their special deals so the Internet business must monitor these as well. If the business is using an already established web site, ask about the kind of traffic the site receives on a daily, weekly or monthly basis. This will help the business judge the value of the advertising and promotion being conducted by the server service.[17]

# Adjusting

Because the Internet is not a standard medium, the establishing of a presence will be ongoing. If the business chooses the Cyber Brochure, Online Yellow Pages, Advertising or Virtual Storefront model, it must rely on a combination of stunning graphics, audio clips, video clips, **Java applets** and continually refreshed content to enable the business to attract **bookmarking**, that is, subscribers who save and revisit the address of an interesting page.[18] Obviously, it is vital that such visually interesting pages do not take too long to load or the potential consumer will not bother to wait. It is also appropriate for businesses to move through the models as their needs change.

# Managing quality

The cyber business must also have a commitment to quality. To be able to deliver quality it is essential to have a quality management system and it is the responsibility of the person in charge of quality to meet customer requirements. Publicity on the Internet costs a fraction of the price of the print medium so it is vital to ensure that only top quality information goes out to the customers. Quality management should be seen as an integral part of each of the other four strategies. **Listserv** software enables worker groups to communicate and can act as a **total quality management** tool. This can help team members keep in touch and involved even when travelling. Group members can get hold of the most up-to-date versions of collaborative work and provide current versions and comments to all members simultaneously.[19] Australian businesses have used a combination of the business models to set up shop on the Internet with some excellent results. It is vital that users are not presented with error messages such as 'JavaScript Error: www.mycompany.com, line 20. Start glide is not defined'. This shows a lack of quality control.

# USING THE POSTER/BILLBOARD MODEL

This most simple model allows businesses to use email headers and footers, signature blocks or greeting cards to advertise their business. Businesses should put their email address on all electronic and non-electronic communications. A business can set up an automated reply mailbox, which will send out standard material in reply to a request for information. Mailbox information might be set up as follows:

**Internet/Intranet Training**
**for**
**Government & Business**
**Telephones: + 61 2 9968 4803**
**+ 61 2 9869 0628**
**Fax: + 61 2 9968 3015**

**http://www.cyberconsult.com.au**

**E-mail: cyberconsult@acslink.net.au**

*FIGURE 2.3:* Sample signature file

Listservs can also be used to send out information and discussion of business issues. Email order forms can be attached. It is important to realise that many lists prohibit advertising but will allow a short signature file. Some businesses are using this model to mail virtual floral bouquets or greeting cards. Businesses can gather a lot of important information via email listservs.

# USING THE ONLINE YELLOW PAGES MODEL

The advantages of the Online Yellow Pages model can be realised by remembering how effective the paper-based Yellow Pages are in advertising a firm's goods. If you take the concept online, the added attractions involved include being able to:
• search for a business by type or name
• see the location of the business on a map.
Obviously the key point about this model is the fact that you are able to communicate cheaply and effectively with existing and potential clients.

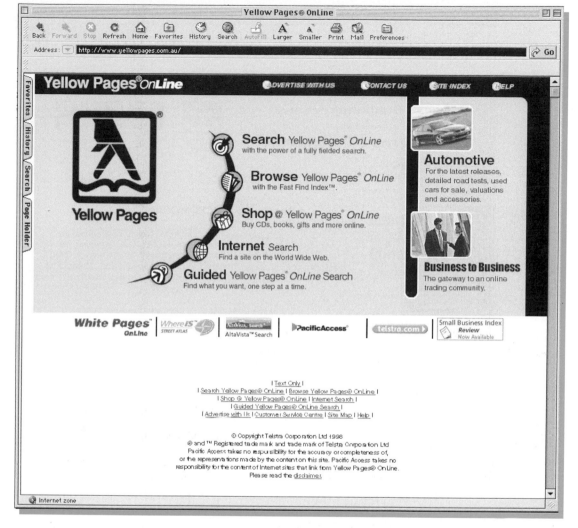

**FIGURE 2.4:** Home page of the online Yellow Pages (www.yellowpages.com.au)

## USING THE CYBER BROCHURE MODEL

There are many advantages of the Cyber Brochure model. Instead of setting up and printing out expensive paper brochures, your company can have colourful, interactive brochures that can be easily updated. For example, the School of Computing Sciences at the University of Technology, Sydney has saved a lot of advertising money through the use of the cyber brochure for its Continuing Professional Education program. The brochure can be easily updated when new course dates are announced, clients can enrol online, and courses can be added and deleted as necessary.

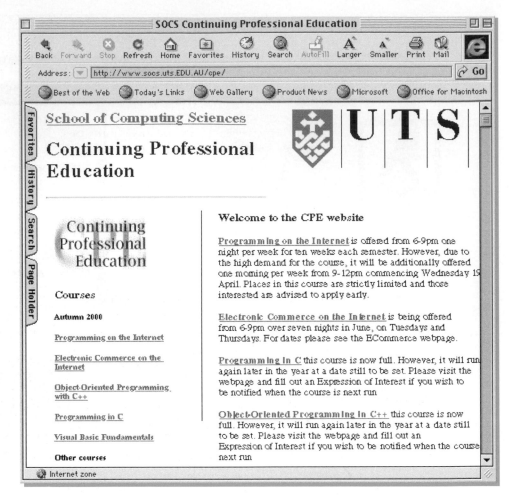

**FIGURE 2.5:** Continuing Professional Education (CPE) web page (www.socs.uts.edu.au/cpe/)

## USING THE VIRTUAL STOREFRONT MODEL

A virtual storefront is a full information service with online purchasing and customer support. This is a popular way of selling on the Internet and nowadays there are providers, such as the Melbourne company Sofcom, who take out a lot of the pain of setting up a virtual storefront. Potential clients are guided through the intricacies of setting up a commercial web site via the use of **wizards**. Clients are then able to design their own site and evaluate its impact before making a decision to allow Sofcom to host their site. There are a number of online shopping malls, especially in the United States, where merchants offer a broad assortment of goods and services from a number of different manufacturers. This represents a form of one-stop shopping similar to the physical retail shopping mall concept.

Another example of this model in Australia is the grocery chain, Woolworths, which provides an online shopping channel at www.woolworths.com.au. Potential purchasers register online before any trading is permitted. Once registered the purchaser is able to use a login name and password to access the site and select goods to place into a 'shopping basket' The total is then added up and submitted. The online shopper is able to nominate a time for delivery and method of payment, for example via portable EFTPOS or credit card at the time of delivery. There is a charge for picking the order and a charge for delivery. As the shopper returns to the site a master list of groceries is presented to the online shopper thus making the shopping easier as the weeks go by. The important advantage from the customers' perspective is that the order-processing time is greatly reduced as the traditional paper trail is significantly shorter and there is less human intervention in processing the order as there is no need to rekey the purchase order information. As the customer is able to make purchase choices from an electronic catalogue there are likely to be fewer ordering errors.

**FIGURE 2.6:** Sofcom's Shopping Mall. Sofcom helps firms set up commercial sites (www.sofcom.com.au).

# YELLOW PAGES LOOKS OFFSHORE

MARK HOLLANDS
☐ **Internet**

YELLOW Pages publisher Pacific Access has expanded its Internet ambitions, striking an alliance with a Hong Kong-based company to help Australian companies import and export goods online.

Pacific Access has signed an exclusive deal with Asian sources to build a Web portal aimed at matching buyers and sellers across a range of industries in a bid to give an overseas dimension to the Yellow Pages web site, which recently began offering to construct dedicated web sites for customers.

A subsidiary of Telstra, it already has a successful line of domestic online titles such as White Pages, Search Australasia, Whereis Online, and the local franchise for AltaVista.

The new web site will be called Australian Sources.

Asian Sources, with a global reputation as the publisher of 350 specialist trade magazines, already attracts more than 50 000 sales inquiries a week for 4000 Asian-based suppliers and manufacturers, which offer an estimated 72 000 products on its portal.

Its key customers in the Asian region include the 100 largest buyers in the world, including American retailer Wal-Mart, Kmart and Toys R Us. Australian companies Dick Smith Electronics, Coles Myer and Woolworths also use the portal.

Pacific Access chief executive Andrea Polmear said the alliance had given her company the opportunity to widen its client base beyond small businesses — the core of the Yellow Pages clientele.

'This deal offers the next stage in the development of the online economy in Australia,' Ms Polmear said.

'We are giving local manufacturers and suppliers the opportunity to expand their reach overseas and trade online. Enabling these companies to trade will put us in the driving seat.'

A pilot site was being constructed for Australian Sources that would look similar to its Asian counterpart, she said.

Her company would approach suitable Yellow Pages clients to participate in the site, and would seek new business, she said.

'Our aim is to provide an affordable web site that has a global brand,' Ms Polmear said.

Pacific Access would offer to build client sites that would feature 20 to 30 products. 'All our development will be done locally,' she said. 'The task of building micro-sites is within our organisation's capability.

'We have already built several thousand for our Yellow Pages customers in the past five months. The popularity of that service has exceeded our expectations by five times.'

The Australian Sources site will work along the lines of the traditional advertising model, with a charge being made for each product a company promoted on the portal.

The transaction engine for the site is a proprietary suite called Asian Sources e-Trade, which is currently used by more than 400 companies around the world, including Fujitsu and Reebok.

Asian Sources senior vice-president Howard Finger said the aim was to 'make it easier for buyers and sellers'.

**SOURCE:** The *Australian*, 21 September 1999, p. 49, www.news.com.au

### EXERCISES

1. How has Yellow Pages moved from being an example of the Yellow Pages model to a Portal model?
2. What are the advantages of the Portal model for buyers and sellers? What are the disadvantages?
3. It has been stated that the Portal model has struggled to maintain popularity. Do some research to ascertain the popularity or otherwise of this Internet business model.

# OTHER POPULAR BUSINESS MODELS

Two other popular business models are the Internet Commerce Customer Service Life Cycle and the Integrated Internet Marketing model ($I^2M$).

## The Internet Commerce Customer Service Life Cycle

The **Internet Commerce Customer Service Life Cycle** establishes four distinct, yet recurring, stages in the relationship between the service and the customer: determining requirements, assisting acquisition, encouraging ownership and helping retirement.[20]

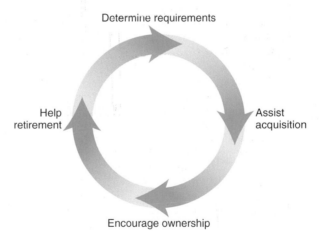

**FIGURE 2.7:** Internet Commerce Customer Service Life Cycle. **SOURCE:** P. McKeown and R. Watson 1996, *Metamorphosis: A Guide to the World Wide Web and Electronic Commerce*, John Wiley and Sons, Inc., United States, p. 133

### Determine requirements

The major advantage of the Web is that it allows businesses to help customers determine their needs. If a person wishes to arrange to stay at a hotel for a holiday, he or she can visit the web site of a hotel chain, examine the types of room available and the amenities and location, and then book his or her stay over the Internet. Some online computer sellers, such as Gateway 2000 Australia, are also allowing customers to determine their own needs. These companies allow potential clients to build the computer of their dreams online and price it. An added advantage here is that the client is actually doing the work rather than a company's salesperson. Interestingly many clients actually prefer being in charge of determining their own needs via computer rather than relying on a salesperson.

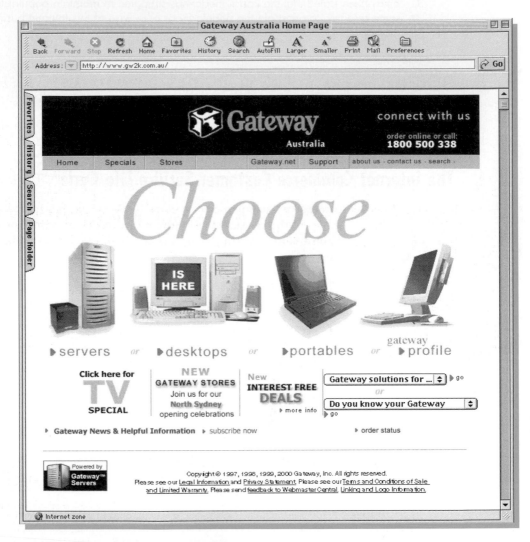

**FIGURE 2.8:** Home page of Gateway 2000 Australia (www.gw2k.com.au)

## Assist acquisition

The Web can help customers acquire products easily. The Co-op Bookshop (www.coop-bookshop.com.au), an online bookshop, serves as a model for what the library interface of the future could look like. If you are interested in buying a book, you are able to search by title, author or book type. The Co-op Bookshop was Australia's first online academic and general bookshop. The online shopper can search one million titles and books can be ordered online.

The Co-op Bookshop has a visitor's room where news is updated regularly and it hosts live online interviews with authors. Wineries and liquor outlets in Australia have also taken to Internet commerce quickly. The web site of a Sydney-based liquor outlet, Wine Planet, which started online ordering throughout Australia in 1998 is shown below. The Wine Planet site's features include wine reviews from leading wine writers and food and wine matching. Web site visitors are encouraged to join the Wine Lovers Club, where they can access 'My Cellar', a personal cellaring database that allows them to keep track of their wine collection.

**FIGURE 2.9:** Home page of Wine Planet, winner of the 1999 AFI/Telstra Web Award for Best E-commerce Site in Australia (www.wineplanet.com.au)

## Encourage ownership

It is always advantageous if customers feel some loyalty to the brand or product that they are buying. Internet commerce allows the business to support the customer on an ongoing basis, such as providing answers to **frequently asked questions (FAQs)** or providing online registration for hotel rooms. The Hilton hotel chain ensures that frequent users feel part of the Hilton family by encouraging them to join its Hilton HHonors club and earn free travel benefits.

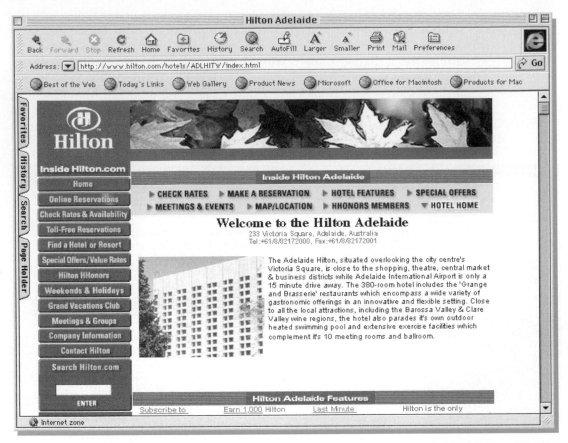

**FIGURE 2.10:** Home page of the Adelaide Hilton Hotel
(www.hilton.com/hotels/ADLHITW/index.html)

### Help retirement

The Web can also help the customer dispose of a service or product by providing, for example, online resale or classified ads. A computer retail company could offer classified advertisements for resale of computers and accessories. Web sites could offer customers tips on how to safely dispose of environmentally unfriendly material such as laser printer cartridges.

## Integrated Internet Marketing model

The **Integrated Internet Marketing model** (**I²M**) promotes using the Internet to market products and services, shape customers' attitudes and maintain corporate image. The central idea is to develop a coherent marketing strategy.[21] There are a number of ways to do this, including those described on the following pages.

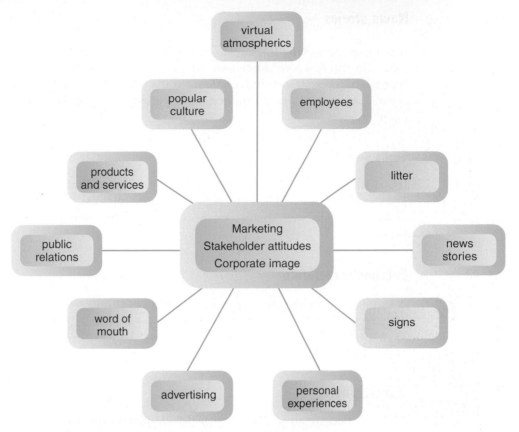

**FIGURE 2.11:** Integrated Internet Marketing model.
**SOURCE:** P. McKeown and R. Watson 1996, *Metamorphosis: A Guide to the World Wide Web and Electronic Commerce,* John Wiley and Sons, Inc., New York, p. 137

## Virtual atmospherics

The web site should allow the customer to experience an organisation's atmosphere without actually being there. For example, the web sites for resorts on the Great Barrier Reef achieve **virtual atmospherics** by the use of stunning visual images of the islands.

## Employees

It is imperative that the communication component of the Internet, such as email, listservs and intranets, are used to empower employees and solve problems. The Internet allows for the cascading of communication, where information can move through all levels of the company quickly, cheaply and effectively.

## Litter

Unfortunately the very immediacy of the Internet can lead to electronic pollution. Web businesses should ensure that their links are up-to-date and that old information is taken off.

## News stories

It is apparent that the Internet is now being used as a way of breaking news. In Australia the first announcement of the death of a cancer victim using the Northern Territory's euthanasia law was made on the Web. Many information technology companies announce their products on the Web before issuing press releases.

## Signs

It is advantageous if businesses can use their logos effectively on web pages. For example, they may use them for navigation aids on their site. Ansett uses a shell to allow web surfers to move through the web pages for Hayman Island.

## Personal experience

A business might decide to give clients an opportunity to try before they buy. This is particularly easy if you are a company with a product that can be demonstrated over the Internet easily, such as a software company. Music companies are able to offer sound bites from a featured CD.

## Advertising

This has been dealt with earlier in the chapter in the sections on the Advertising model (see page 26).

## Word of mouth

Bad news travels fast on the Internet. Companies can monitor newsgroups and lists to ensure that nothing damaging is being spread about the business. Some companies also use the newsgroups to test some of their new ideas.

## Public relations

Increasingly the Web is being used as a public relations tool. Press releases, particularly government releases, are often posted on the Web first.

## Products and services

The Web is a great way to distribute product information. This distribution could be, for example, conducted using the Cyber Brochure model. Companies can also use their customer base to support one another by, for example, establishing a listserv or newsgroup or by setting up a FAQs page. Computer companies have found this a very useful way to keep their customer base up to date with changes.

### Popular culture

If your product is part of popular culture, the business can benefit, for example, by having it as a clearly labelled product in virtual network games. In car races, the cars featured might be Holdens and Fords, both of which are part of the popular culture in Australian motor sports. The Sydney Opera House has become a symbol for Sydney and graphics of it adorn many web pages. The upcoming Olympic Games at Sydney in the year 2000 obviously features as a link in many commercial sites. By associating commercial sites with popular icons, cyberbusinesses can increase product and brand knowledge.

## SUMMARY

In this chapter we have studied the various business models that are appropriate to Internet commerce. As this is a developing field, it is vital to remain alert and be aware as new models make their appearance. The models described in this chapter were the Poster/Billboard model, the Online Yellow Pages model, the Cyber Brochure model, the Virtual Storefront model, the Subscription model, the Advertising model, the 3.5.7 model, Auction/Reverse Auction model, the Affiliation model, the Portal model, the Internet Commerce Customer Service Life Cycle and the Integrated Internet Marketing model.

It is important to realise that as your web site evolves, business models might have to be adapted to suit the changing needs of the business. Whatever model(s) is adopted it is important to plan, control, monitor, adjust and manage quality.

### key terms

*Advertising model*

*Affiliation model*

*Auction model*

*bookmarking*

*Cyber Brochure model*

*firewalls*

*frequently asked questions (FAQs)*

*Gopher*

*Integrated Internet Marketing model ($I^2M$)*

*Internet Commerce Customer Service Life Cycle*

*Java applets*

*listservs*

*Online Yellow Pages model*

*Portal model*

*Poster/Billboard model*

*Reverse Auction model*

*Subscription model*

*3.5.7 model*

*total quality management*

*virtual atmospherics*

*Virtual Storefront model*

*wide area information server (WAIS)*

*wizards*

The online auction business has become the most lucrative commerce strategy on the Web and has been by far the biggest growth sector in the already booming US e-commerce industry. Auction sites covered 15 per cent, or US$1.4 billion, of the US e-commerce market last year, with the market leader eBay growing its customer base from 850 000 in June 1998 to 3.8 million by March 1999.[22] In contrast to this figure, Keegan stated eBay's registered users nearly doubled in the three-month period from April to June 1999 from 1.2 million to 2.1 million.[23] Bryant estimates that there are 5.6 million registered eBay users.[24]

Instant access and distribution have allowed Internet business to do in the past two years what media moguls did over a generation or more ago. Online auctions have become so popular that there is a web site dedicated to news about them along with independent services in www.auctionwatch.com.[25] The following list is of some types and specific examples of an online auction.[26]

- Sold.com.au. This site does not charge buyers, so if users register, they can buy items without having to supply their credit card details or any other financial details over the Internet. Buyers pay when they pick up the item or when it is delivered by the seller. Sellers pay a listing fee and a sales transactions fee.
- Classic auction. In this type of auction the starting bid is the lowest price a seller will accept.
- Reserve auction. In this type of auction the seller enters a low starting price to encourage bids but requires a sale when the reserve price is met.
- Dutch auction. In this type of auction, sellers list several items so that bidders may bid for entire lot or choose any quantity.
- Robobid. This is a proxy agent on Sold.com.au that automatically bids on the users' behalf up to the maximum they have said they are willing to pay.

## RESEARCH QUESTIONS

1. For your research visit two auction sites on the Internet and outline the way in which they work.
2. The auction model has been popular in the United States for years but did not start to take off in Australia until 1999. Do some research to discover why this was so.
3. Investigate the popularity of the Auction model on web sites from two other countries.
4. Visit the Priceline.com site and write a report on the way they have implemented their model.
5. Investigate the use of the Reverse Auction model in Australia or a country of your choice.

**QUESTIONS**

1. What sorts of details could a hotel chain provide to assist potential clients in picking a hotel that matches their travel plans?

2. Select a product that a computer retailer might sell, such as printers, scanners and zip drives. What sort of details about this product could an online computer company provide to their clients?

3. What advantages/disadvantages do Internet customers have over free-call customers when ordering flowers, photographs, books or clothes?

4. What advantages do you see with web ordering for a company?

5. How can companies using the Web ensure that the customer owns the service?

6. Can you think of an effective way to use the Web for the retirement phase of the Internet Commerce Customer Service Life Cycle? Outline your ideas in a short report.

7. Take each phase of the customer service life cycle (requirements, acquisition, ownership and retirement) and find sites that illustrate support for each phase.

8. Take each point of the $I^2M$ model and discuss how you would use it for a commercial site.

9. Do a search for a product on the Web (preferably not a book). Look at the web sites. What kind of business model has been used by the various organisations? Are the sites effective in terms of attracting you as a consumer? Why or why not?

**SUGGESTED READING**

Angell, D. and Heslop, B. 1995, *The Internet Business Companion — Growing Your Business in the Electronic Age*, Addison-Wesley, United States.

Butler, M., Power, T. and Richmond, C. 1999, *The E-Business Advantage*, The Ecademy, www.ecademy.com.

Ellsworth, J. H. and Ellsworth, M. V. 1994, *The Internet Business Book*, John Wiley and Sons, New York.

Kosiur, D. 1997, *Understanding Electronic Commerce: How Online Transactions Can Grow Your Business*, Microsoft Press, United States.

McKeown, P. and Watson, R. 1996, *Metamorphosis: A Guide to the World Wide Web and Electronic Commerce*, John Wiley and Sons, Inc., United States.

Kalakota, R. and Robinson, M. 1999, *E-Business: Roadmap for Success*, Addison-Wesley Longman, United States.

Power, T. and Jerjian, G. 1999, *The Battle of the Portals*, The Ecademy, www.ecademy.com.

**END NOTES**

1.  McKeown, P. and Watson, R. 1996, *Metamorphosis: A Guide to the World Wide Web and Electronic Commerce*, John Wiley and Sons, New York, p. 132.

2.  De Marco, A. 1994, 'The five essential disciplines for successful projects', *The Source*, Australian Computer Society, Queensland, July, pp. 6–8.

3.  Ellsworth, J. H. and Ellsworth, M. V. 1994, *The Internet Book*, John Wiley and Sons, New York, p. 66.

4.  ibid., p. 66.

5.  ibid., p. 66.

6.  ibid., p. 66.

7.  ibid., p. 67.

8.  Fedewa, S. 1996, *Business Models for 'Internetpreneurs'*, Internet Entrepreneurs Support Service, Los Angeles, www.entrepreneurs.net/iess/articles/art4.html.

9.  ibid.

10. ibid.

11. Settles, C. 1996, *The 3.5.7 for Maximising Your Business On-Line*, www.successful.com/357artic.html.

12. Sarno, T. 1999, 'Going, going, gone online', Icon, *Sydney Morning Herald*, 17 July, p. 6.

13. Rowe, C. 1999, 'Top sites pay you for sales! Read how', Biz.Com, *Sydney Morning Herald*, 6 September, p. 41.

14. Shelly, G., Cashman, T., Vermaat, M. and Walker, T. 1999, *Discovering Computers 2000*, Shelly Cashman Series, Course Technology, Cambridge, United States.

15. De Marco, op. cit., pp. 6–8.

16. Angell, D. and Heslop, B. 1995, *The Internet Business Companion — Growing Your Business in the Electronic Age*, Addison-Wesley, United States.

17. ibid., p. 144.

18. Robotham, J. 1995, 'On the Internet: firms say it pays to advertise', *Sydney Morning Herald*, 29 January, p. 9.

19. Ellsworth and Ellsworth, op. cit., p. 32.

20. McKeown and Watson, op. cit., p. 132.

21. McKeown and Watson, op. cit., p. 137.

22. Burton, T. 1999, ' Fairfax ups ante for online sales', *Sydney Morning Herald*, 30 June, p. 28.

23. Keegan, P. 1999, 'Online auctions: from seedy flea markets to big business', *Upside*, vol. 11, no. 7, pp. 70–81.

24. Bryant, G. 1999, 'The garage sales hit the big time', *Business Review Weekly*, vol. 21, no. 35, www.brw.com.au.

25. Pradham, S. 1999, Online auction/reverse auction models: an Australian perspective, paper for subject 'Commerce on the Internet', at the University of Technology, Sydney, November, p. 2.

26. Sarno, T, op. cit., p. 6.

# CHAPTER 3

# Technology basics

## LEARNING *Outcomes*

You will have mastered the material in this chapter when you can:

- distinguish between the Internet, an intranet and an extranet
- describe the communications infrastructure supporting electronic commerce
- explain the various methods of Internet connection
- define and explain the meaning of the protocols used in electronic commerce
- explain client/server computing
- distinguish between fat client and thin client systems
- explain why the Web is popular for personal use, commerce and trade
- describe examples of commercial solutions using the World Wide Web.

*'The creation of the World Wide Web ... has been one of the Internet's most exciting developments that propelled the Internet into the public eye and caused the business world to take Internet technologies seriously ... Aside from the Internet's technical progress ... its sociological progress has been phenomenal ... It seems headed for even greater prominence in the next millenium.'*

M. Chesher and R. Kaura 1998, *Electronic Commerce and Business Communications*, Practitioner Series, Springer, London, pp. 89–90.

# INTRODUCTION

Electronic commerce is concerned with electronic ways of doing business. However, there is a need to also understand how various technologies support electronic commerce. These technologies can be used in the trading or mercantile process/interaction between businesses, between consumers and businesses, and between consumers and consumers.

The technology basics that need to be understood include the communications infrastructure that allows electronic transmission of data and the structure and role of the World Wide Web and other networks.

This chapter will focus on the technology that underpins electronic commerce. It is important to note that those who use this medium do not have to have a detailed understanding of the technologies that enable and support it, but they should have some understanding of what the technologies do.

In this chapter, two key themes will be discussed: the Internet and how it works, and the technologies that make electronic commerce work.

# ALL THE NETS

The Internet, **intranets**, **extranets** and the World Wide Web dominate media reports about telecommunications, business-to-business electronic trading, business-to-consumer commerce and the developing use of electronic commerce throughout the world.

It is the Internet that has made electronic commerce and worldwide trade from one office possible.

## The Internet

The Internet, a linkage of many small computer networks throughout the world, works because there are agreed rules, or **protocols**, about how information is exchanged. These links are created through wires and various forms of communication system.

Specific drivers and **search engines** were developed to facilitate information exchange over the Internet. This exchange has been enhanced with graphics, audio and video transmission, and interactive communication.

The Internet has been adopted as a tool which assists business transactions, promotes products, allows interactive news broadcasts (e.g. CNN), provides news in text and visual form (e.g. Sydney Olympics web sites), supports causes and activities to address social injustice, entertains, enables research and acts as an alternative publishing house (e.g. *MISQ* and *Information Systems Journal* at www.blackwell-science.com/products/journals/isj.htm). The Internet has become a conduit for immediate knowledge, information and communication.

# Intranets

Intranets are computer networks that are privately developed and operated within an organisation. They rely on the standards and protocols of the Internet to operate, and invariably are protected by various forms of security to guard the internal operations of the user organisation. Intranets operate as separate networks within the operations of the Internet (see figure 3.1).

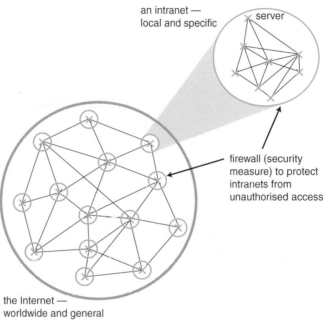

an intranet — local and specific

server

firewall (security measure) to protect intranets from unauthorised access

the Internet — worldwide and general

**FIGURE 3.1:** Intranets and the Internet

# Extranets

An extranet is a collaborative network that uses Internet technology to link businesses with their suppliers, customers or other businesses that share common goals. Extranets are usually linked to business intranets where information is either accessible through a password system or through links which are established collaboratively. They can also be private worldwide networks that operate on protocols that are either the same as the Internet or specifically developed for those networks. Each of these networks is, unlike the Internet, not always in the public domain. SITA (Société Internationale Telecommunications et Aéronautique) is a company that runs a private network that operates throughout the world supporting the booking systems of most international airline systems and companies. This system is totally owned by the users and protected from public use by various security systems.

Other users of extranets include newsgroups, where new ideas or information is shared between companies or groups of companies. Training programs also can be shared and operated through extranets. SITA provides online training to customers and its own employees, using Lotus Notes software. Other companies use software that they have developed, called groupware. Sometimes this extends into shared catalogues that list all component parts or products that are of use to both suppliers and customers. Suppliers of aircraft parts, for example, would value being able to access Boeing's catalogues. However, the possibility of catalogues, booking systems and shared groupware being exposed to public access or to capture by computer hackers, demands that attention be paid to appropriate security measures. Details of various security systems used to protect intranets and extranets are outlined in chapter 6.

These various networks, the Internet, intranet and extranet, perform different functions in electronic commerce (see figure 3.2). These functions are explained below.

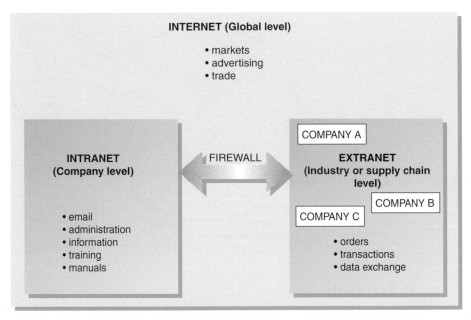

**FIGURE 3.2:** The role of different networks in electronic commerce

# HOW THE INTERNET WORKS

The Internet operates within a structure that has existed to support other technologies, including telecommunications, and uses agreed standards and protocols. The Internet enables businesses to collect information, add value to information, conduct trade and communicate with suppliers and customers.

The Internet operates by taking data (such as an email message, a file, a document or a request for a file), dividing it into separate parts called packets and transmitting those packets along the best available route to the destination computer. Packet switching allows data to be broken up into packets and sent over different routes to their destination. Once there, they are reassembled into meaningful information. The software used for packet switching on the Internet is the communications protocol called **transmission control protocol/Internet protocol (TCP/IP)**.

The Internet works on an infrastructure that covers all of the media necessary for moving information. The infrastructure that works with and complements the Internet includes private corporate networks, cable and satellite television and telecommunication networks (see figure 3.3).

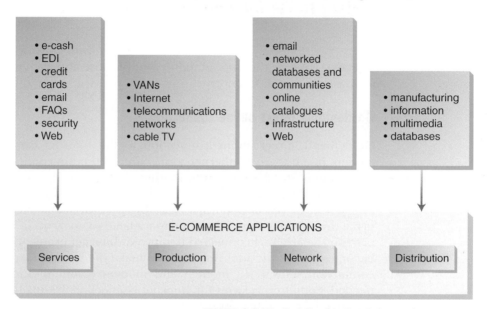

**FIGURE 3.3:** The building blocks of electronic commerce

# Telecommunication infrastructure of the Internet

A number of existing telecommunication technologies support the Internet and facilitate electronic commerce. Technologies for telephone connections form a worldwide network of cables, satellites and microwave dishes, which allows the transmission of signals. The Internet transmits digital signals, which can readily use these existing telecommunication systems. In the last decade new physical networks have been established throughout the world to provide many areas with access to cable television. The transmissions that flow over the Internet can also use these networks.

To use these physical telecommunication systems to gain access to the Internet, consumers, businesses or individuals need to be able to connect to one of the systems, either in the workplace or at home. The physical part of the Internet includes networks and communication lines owned and operated by many different companies and organisations. Large organisations such as universities or global companies often provide permanent, 24-hour, seven-days-a-week access for students and employees. Other people might connect to the Internet via an online service, such as America Online. An Internet service provider (ISP), such as Davnet or Optusnet, is an organisation that has a permanent connection to the Internet and sells temporary connections to others for a fee. Such local ISPs connect to regional host computers operated by national service providers, such as Telstra or Optus. Regional host computers are connected to the major networks that carry most of the Internet communication traffic by high-speed communication lines called backbones, which could be compared to highways that connect major cities across the country.

# Connecting to the Internet

There are four ways that businesses and individuals can connect to the Internet. Each method serves a different purpose and each would be suitable for businesses of different types and sizes.

## On-demand, direct online connection

On-demand, direct online connection to the Internet can be either via a modem or a LAN (e.g. **ethernet** connection). Ethernet connections are a communications standard for transmitting data between computers. Most PC modems transmit data at between 28.8 Kbps and 56 Kbps. Cable modems can transmit at speeds of 500 Kbps to 2 Mbps. As the name suggests, a user can make this type of connection whenever a need to do so occurs. In a direct connection the machine connected has its own **Internet protocol (IP)** address and becomes part of the Internet itself. To make the connection, special Internet connection software, a modem and modem communications software are needed. Software packages for Internet connection are readily available from commercial computer stores and from ISPs.

## On-demand terminal connection

An alternative online method of connecting to the Internet is by connecting to another machine that is connected directly to the Internet, and therefore part of it. In this type of connection there is no need to purchase special software. Only a modem and modem communications software are needed. Such connections are not as flexible as direct connections and do not perform as many tasks.

## Offline connection

An offline connection provides a user with access to the Internet no matter whether they are or are not connected. Information is downloaded and stored on a hard disk either by a user or by a user's agent when connected to the Internet. This downloaded information from the hard disk is then available to the user to access at any time. Special software is loaded on to a computer which when connected to the Internet will allow material to be downloaded. This could be data transferred from one company to another or email messages sent in different time zones. This special software will allow replies written or sent in the offline period to be sent automatically once the machine is reconnected online to the Internet. This process is cheap but quite inflexible.

## Supported connection methods

Supported connection to the Internet involves the use of more complex methods. The most common is connection by ethernet or by serial connections using SLIP and PPP protocols. These are discussed in the next section.

# What is a protocol?

A protocol is a set of traffic rules, procedures and standards designed to allow the transmission of data and information. For successful transmission these rules have to be accepted. Across the Internet there can be only one protocol or set of rules, otherwise computers would not be able to link to each other. In the process of communication on the Internet the protocol established allows two-way communication simultaneously (called the duplex mode for data transmission). This communication process is best illustrated by the Web and by telephone systems in operation in most places throughout the world. In some networks, including private networks where **electronic data interchange (EDI)** has been established, the links can be simpler. EDI transmission can be a simple one-way operation (called the simplex mode of data transmission) or it can be a transmission where data is exchanged both ways (the duplex mode). However, in most instances, this transmission occurs in only one direction at a time. This is called the half-duplex mode of data transmission and illustrates how simply business communication and interaction can occur (see figure 3.4).

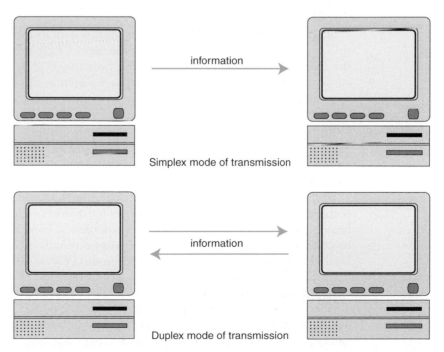

*FIGURE 3.4:* Simplex and duplex modes of data transmission

The most basic protocol of the Internet is the use of TCP/IP processes. This protocol allows users of the Internet to:

- send and receive messages (email)
- find information, interact with other businesses and buy products
- find information about personal details of people who have developed and placed personal material on a specific site (home pages)
- exchange of data (EDI) and business information
- download software that can assist the user to do more operations on the Internet.

Other protocols have also become commonly used on the Internet. These include **point-to-point protocol (PPP)**, **serial line Internet protocol (SLIP)** and **post office protocol (POP)**. It is the development of these types of protocol that has enabled more complex operations to occur using the Web.

In the early days of development of the Internet most research institutions, government agencies and businesses were connected to smaller **local area networks (LANs)** within these organisations. The most common connection was via ethernet. There were few, if any, point-to-point links, which were the most common in telecommunications systems prior to the development of the Internet. One of the reasons for the lack of these simple point-to-point connections was the lack of a standard or protocol. PPP[1] was developed to provide that standard and to manage IP addresses at a host server for the Internet. PPP permits a computer connected to a server via a serial line (such as a modem) to become an actual node on the Internet and enables anyone to connect from home, a business or a hotel room through a telephone connection. This link allows individuals or businesses to receive, send and store email, and browse the Web.

SLIP connects the user (business or individual) to the Internet and allows the user to use the Internet in the same way as PPP, except that SLIP allows the user to send and receive files using only the TCP/IP protocol. (PPP also allows the user to transmit using other forms such as AppleTalk.) However, for most users of the Internet this is not an issue as most individuals and businesses use TCP/IP only. PPP has been developed by many of the Internet service providers running commercial access to the Internet for individuals and small businesses. PPP enables the service provider developers to establish an automatic login that provides the user with a password and automatic dialling of a telephone number to gain access to the Internet.

POP[2] allows users to log into the electronic host, download messages to their computer and upload messages to the host for delivery over the network. In businesses, or through a service provider, there is a computer that receives all incoming email messages. A POP email program (such as Netscape Mail, Pegasus Mail or Eudora) downloads the email from the POP server to a local computer.

## The World Wide Web

The most recent improvement in the attributes of the Internet has been the development of the World Wide Web.[3] The Web allows the user to interchange and interconnect documents using hypertext. This process allows the user to create an interlinked, sometimes interactive, process where one document retrieved from the Internet can be used to establish a link to another document. This link is activated when the user clicks on a **hotlink** or hyperlink (a word, picture or feature highlighted within a document), which triggers the link to another document located on another computer in some other location in the world. The protocol that enables these hotlinks is called hypertext transfer protocol (HTTP). Figure 3.5 shows some examples of hotlinks or hyperlinks embedded in the text of a web page.

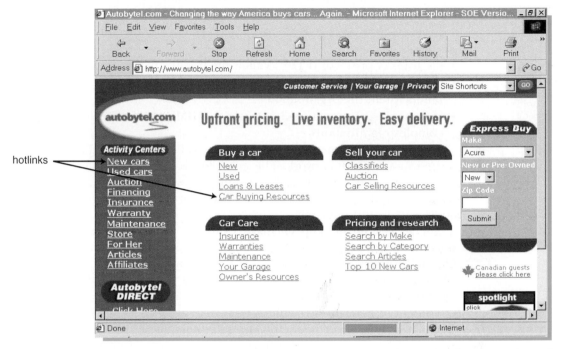

**FIGURE 3.5:** Hotlinks on the Autobytel web page (www.autobytel.com/)

## Global hypertext publishing with HTML and HTTP

In the 1980s the International Standards Organisation released the specifications of a **standard generalised markup language (SGML)**. This protocol defined documents in a plain text using tags that were embedded in the text to specify the definition. Hypertext markup language (HTML) is a form of SGML with a specified document type definition. HTML is a language used to describe how a web browser[4] (e.g. Netscape Navigator or Microsoft's Internet Explorer) will display a text file retrieved from a server.[5] HTML allows the developer of a web page to define hyperlinks between that document and any others that the author might think are important to link together. HTML also allows the developer of a document on the Web to define any multimedia objects that are included in the document. To enable consistent transmission of documents on the Web, HTTP was developed and adopted. This is a multimedia transport protocol. It does not process the packages of data it transmits, but rather is a mechanism that allows users to search for information or data. Further, it allows databases to interact and information to be manipulated.

HTTP defines computer links to the Web when those computers support software that allows them to freely interact with other computers. Those that provide the links are called web servers. HTTP, and the ability of servers to support it, is what defines the Web and differentiates it from other networks. This protocol and the ability to support it also define the Web within the Internet. Web servers have become the places where home pages of all sorts have been developed and stored. The transmission of data within these pages relies on the simplicity and speed of HTTP.

In addition to the TCP/IP and HTTP protocols, the Internet uses other protocols such as:

- file transfer protocol (FTP) to allow the transfer of files between computers
- **simple mail transfer protocol (SMTP)** to enable mail transfer between computers within the organisation
- **multipurpose Internet mail extensions (MIME)** to enable mail transfer in complex organisations.

Web servers are computers which run the HTTP process and which are connected to a TCP/IP network. The web address that identifies other web sites and specific web pages is called a uniform resource locator (URL). It is a means of specifying a resource by incorporating the protocol, machine address, path and filename.

The **extensible markup language (XML)** is a data format for structured document interchange on the Web. A markup language is a mechanism to identify structures in a document. XML is a markup language for documents which contain structured information. Structured information is common in most documents and has two elements:

1. content (e.g. pictures, graphics, text, etc.)
2. the role that the content plays in the document. Where the content is located in the document influences the meaning given to it (e.g. a statement in a footnote is an addendum or an explanation, text in the document is usually structured by headings which indicate what is to come).

XML specification defines a standard way to add markup to documents but it is different to HTML.

In HTML the tag sets and tag semantics are fixed by protocols established by the World Wide Web Consortium (W3C) and are firmly established within existing browsers such as Internet Explorer. XML does not fix the tag sets or the semantics used. It really enables the user to define tags and the structured relationships between them. Like SGML, it supports structured documentation but XML is designed for applications, especially richly structured documents, using the Web.

Active server pages (from Microsoft) allow for the creation of dynamic Internet sites by putting databases on the Internet. Customers can search company databases to retrieve updatedd information.

JavaScript is an interpreted scripting language that allows developers to add scrolling messages and data input forms to web pages. It is easier to learn than Java.

**Adaptations of XML**

## HRM MARKUP LANGUAGE (HRMML)

**June 18, 1999.** Structured Methods has developed Human Resource Management Markup Language (HRMML), an XML-based markup language for job postings, job descriptions and résumés.

A new draft of the HRMML specification is now available for download. HRMML 'currently is described in two draft Document Type Definitions (DTDs), one for résumés and one for job postings. The two DTDs have many common elements, which are contained in shared modules.

HRMML was developed to be broadly applicable to the needs of employers, recruiters, recruit-ing data aggregators and Internet job sites. Whether and how specific elements are used will depend on the requirements of the particular implementation. Many organisations will be able to implement a selective profile for the broader DTD and still be able to exchange a core set of data with organisations using a different profile.'

According to a recent announcement from Chuck Allen, the new release of HRMML 'includes more than 300 pages of documentation, which is included in the HRMML distribution file. You are free to use, modify or redistribute the DTD and documentation.'

## ACORD — XML FOR THE INSURANCE INDUSTRY

**June 16, 1999.** The web site of ACORD (Agency Company Organisation for Research and Development) describes a joint initiative in which XML-based vocabularies for the insurance industry are now being developed in a fast-track effort.

'ACORD and the Independent Insurance Agents of America's Agents Council for Technology (ACT) have entered into a joint initiative to deliver to the industry within 120 days, a standardised vocabulary for XML, based on the ACORD ObjX and AL3 standards', announced Gregory A. Maciag, President and CEO of ACORD.

'This joint initiative will help prevent the potential growth of non-standard DTDs (Documentation Type Definitions) which would lead to multiple, uncoordinated and more costly efforts to standardise SML transactions for the industry', said Maciag.

'The "fast track" approach re-emphasises the industry ACORD's permanent commitment to lead the way in standardising the exchange of insurance-related data by leveraging our ObjX development... [in order to develop a widely accepted standard. The parties] are all committed to working together to produce the minimum specifications required to facilitate the initial deployment of the XML-based insurance application in a consistent, standardised fashion... Developing these XML definitions is a step toward full ObjX implementations and is part of ACORD's mission to build bridges between AL3 and ObjX.'

ACORD currently has defined an XML-based render form Transaction; it has 'a standard object model' which will be given to member companies. [ACORD is also] 'now in the process of working on other transactions including request quote and establish account. These transactions are based on our UML model, and a standard DTD, which we are defining with the help of its members.'

*SOURCE:* R. Cover 1999, 'The SGML/XML Web page', www.oasis-open.org/cover/news1999Q2.html

## QUESTIONS

1. What are the differences between HTML and SGML?
2. How is XML applicable to other database web-based businesses?
3. How has ACORD used XML?

## Uniform resource locators

The HTML document that forms a web site is defined by a URL. This URL is a protocol or standard that gives the address or location of any web site. Each URL defines the Internet protocol being used, the server on which the web site is stored or located, and the path which will transmit the document.

In the web site shown in figure 3.6:

- the protocol is http:// (hypertext transfer protocol)
- the server address is www.asx.com.au. This address specifies the server where the site is stored and then the country where the server is located. In this case, it is in Australia.

The location of the two servers listed below are defined in their URLs. The path of the resource of each of these URLs is not defined.

- .bradford.ac.uk (United Kingdom)
- .mail.bdg.co.th (Thailand)

However, in the following URL the protocol, server and path of each resource are all specified:

http://www-cec.buseco.monash.edu.au/info/ecdefn.htm

The protocol of the resource is hypertext transfer protocol, the server is www-cec.buseco.monash.edu.au and the path of the resource is /info/ecdefn.htm.

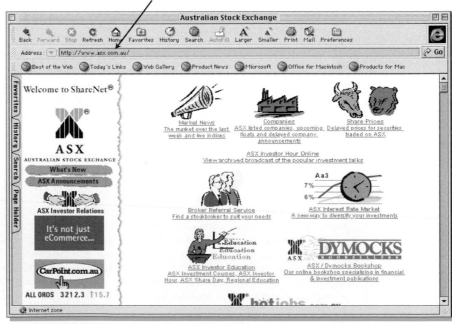

**FIGURE 3.6:** Web page shows the uniform resource locator of the Australian Stock Exchange (www.asx.com.au). © Australian Stock Exchange Ltd — 2000

## Architecture of the World Wide Web

The Web is based on a three-part architecture:

- Hypertext markup language describes the contents of web pages on the Internet.
- Hypertext transfer protocol provides the language that allows servers and browsers to communicate.
- A **common gateway interface (CGI)** is used by a web server to run a separate program that contains dynamic information, format it into HTML and send it on to the web server. For example, a web user at a virtual bookstore might enter some data, such as a book title, into HTML form on a web site. This data is sent to the web server, which uses the CGI interface to get the appropriate book title from the database and return the information, formatted appropriately, back to the user.

The modern Internet results from the interaction of a number of levels of providers and individuals. As can be seen from figure 3.7, individuals can connect (directly or via an intranet) to an ISP. The ISP is connected to an Internet access provider, which is connected to a national access provider. The national access provider is connected to a **very-high-speed backbone** (or spine) **network service** (VBNS), the fastest communication lines on the Internet.

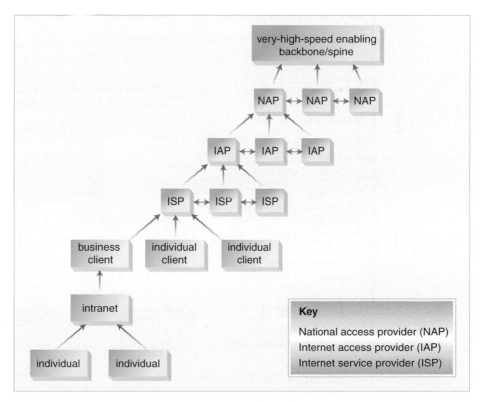

**FIGURE 3.7:** Architecture of the World Wide Web

These links use passwords and security protocols to allow access to the Internet. Access can be achieved in a number of ways, as shown in table 3.1.

In a more simplistic way, the structure of the Web allows a user to interact with various databases, collect information, and search for identity-specific and defined knowledge and information (see figure 3.8). This structure enables users to access the Web for recreation purposes, for communication and, perhaps more importantly, for electronic commerce. This structure can support business-to-business electronic commerce in the exchange of data (EDI), the billing and sending of accounts, the payment of accounts, electronic funds transfer and banking. The Web also provides companies with access to electronic catalogues for the supply of parts or complementary products.

The Web's structure also supports consumer-business electronic commerce by providing companies with an opportunity to display their products, their services or their databases. They can sell data and, more importantly, sell processed information and knowledge. Consumers can advertise and market products to other consumers.

However, a major attraction of the Web for business and consumers is the ease of access. The consumer is not particularly concerned about which method of contact over the Internet is used. The purchase of a modem and a relatively cheap contract with an ISP enables electronic commerce to begin.

| TABLE 3.1 | COMMON INTERNET ACCESS TECHNOLOGIES | |
|---|---|---|
| **TYPE OF INTERNET ACCESS** | **PROTOCOL** | **SPEED** |
| dial-up (shell account): easy and inexpensive, but cannot use Netscape | terminal emulation | 9.6, 14.4 Kbps |
| dial-up IP: full access to Internet, but more complex to configure and set up | SLIP, PPP, CSLIP (compressed SLIP) | 14.4 Kbps 56 Kbps |
| digital dial-up (ISDN): not widely available, and has problems with procurement and installation | PPP | 64, 128 Kbps |
| leased line: high-speed dedicated link, but can be expensive if not used frequently | IP | 56 Kbps 1.544 Mbps (T1) |
| cable modems | — | up to 10 Mbps (customers share so throughput will be lower) |
| satellite (e.g. Satnet) | — | 128 Kbps — may go up to 4000 Kbps |
| DSL (digital subscriber line) | — | 2 Mbps (high bitrate DSL) |
| wireless (e.g. Bluetooth, Airport) | — | 720 Kbps — 1 Mbps |

*SOURCE:* Adapted from R. Kalakota and A. Whinston 1997, *Electronic Commerce: A Manager's Guide*, Addison-Wesley, United States, p. 55

Internet Commerce: Digital Models for Business

For small business, access is similarly relatively cheap, although the motivation for these companies to actually join up is somewhat more complicated. Even with the ease of access to the Internet for small business, there are other hurdles to overcome if effective progress in this area is to be made.

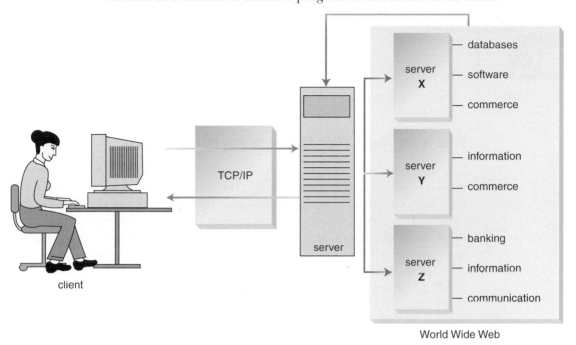

World Wide Web

*FIGURE 3.8:* Structure of the World Wide Web

## Common gateway interface

The architects of the Web wanted to ensure that HTTP could be used to move information and data around the Web, that is, that it would perform as the transfer protocol. HTTP and now XML were not designed to process the knowledge or data being transported. This is the role of a common gateway interface (CGI).

CGI provides a standard way for a web server to communicate with a script, which is a program that negotiates the movement of data between a web server and an outside application, such as a database. CGI can be developed using several languages, including the following:

• Visual BASIC, Visual C++ and PowerBuilder, which are used on NT-based servers

• C, C++, Tcl and Perl, the most commonly used languages on Unix servers.

The client environment is independent of the CGI environment, although CGI scripts are not necessarily platform-independent. Scripts written in Visual BASIC, Delphi and Visual C++ can run only on Windows platforms (such as Windows 3.1, Windows '95 or NT), whereas scripts based on Unix shell scripts will run only on Unix servers. However, CGI's performance is somewhat limited in that there has to be an individual program started for each CGI request. The way CGI works is shown in figure 3.9 on page 62.

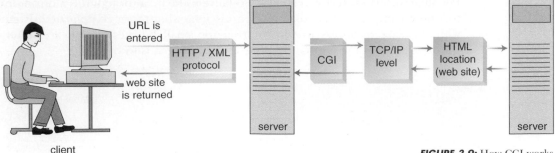

FIGURE 3.9: How CGI works

## Why is the World Wide Web becoming more popular?

The development of simple hypertext protocols has allowed those people connected to the Internet to use it easily. The interface between the user and the information on the Internet is a friendly one that encourages extended use. The hypertext protocols allow the content located at the various sites on the Internet to be easily developed and enhanced, which is continually occurring on the Internet. Search engines are being developed which allow the user to work through the Internet and find the information or data they require (see figure 3.10). These engines enable businesses or individual users to enter a key word or phrase that defines the information being sought. The most used search engines include Netscape Search, Yahoo!, Metacrawler, Altavista and Excite.

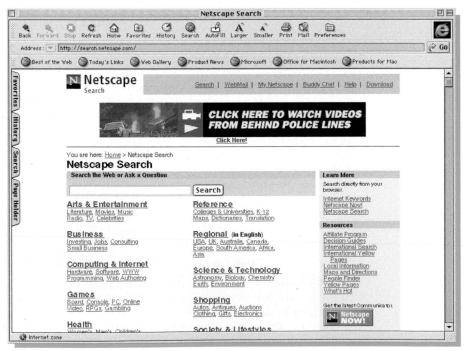

FIGURE 3.10: Netscape Search — one of the most commonly used search engines (http://search.netscape.com/).

Large corporations have been developed which allow 'front door' access to the Internet. They have the attributes of the search engines and focus the activities of the user within an environment that allows commercial development, advertising and access for any user. The two largest of these providers are Netscape (see figure 3.11) and Microsoft (see figure 3.12).

**FIGURE 3.11:** Netscape's web page provides links to information and support for its various products (http://home.netscape.com/).

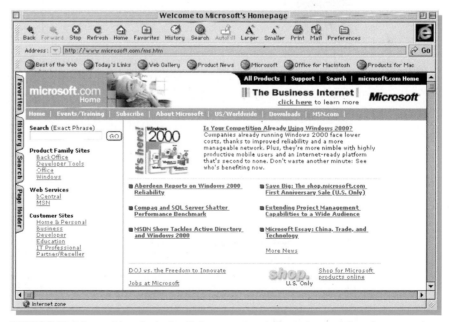

**FIGURE 3.12:** Microsoft's web site has links to product information and free demonstrations (www.microsoft.com) © Microsoft

In the past two years the search engines have evolved into large sites offering long lists of free services such as email, personalisation features, chat rooms, and a variety of content such as stock quotes, local news and weather. These directories have now further evolved into Internet '**portals**' — communication centres, service centres, virtual shopping malls, town centres and news hubs all rolled into one. The NineMSN home page (www.ninemsn.com.au/) is a portal into a large number of other services and products (see figure 3.13). How many can you find?

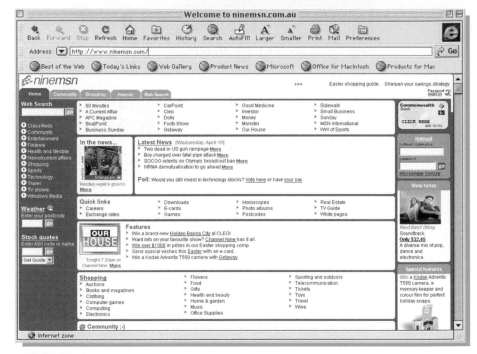

**FIGURE 3.13:** The NineMSN portal (www.ninemsn.com.au). What products can be found on this site?

Portals have attracted a great deal of attention in terms of advertising revenue and have been one of the driving forces for the boom in Internet stocks on the New York Stock Exchange. Portal site companies are injecting millions of dollars into marketing efforts hoping to attract new Internet users needing direction and guidance in cyberspace. The intention of a portal is to capture the users and take them to a vast range of products and services. The intent is to keep the web user online as long as possible increasing exposure to the sponsors working through and linked to the portal. A portal is essentially a one-stop location for a variety of products, services and information. Portals then are linking deals with Internet service providers to deliver the packaged browsers. For example, web access provider and telecommunications giant AT&T has signed deals with three portal sites: Lycos, Excite and Infoseek. Yahoo! and MCI Communications have joined forces to provide a web-based online service.

Another reason for the Web's popularity is that it is inexpensive to access. In the past decade ISPs have been established to provide businesses and individuals with access to the Internet. They link computers in a business or in the home to the Web for a small cost on a 'user-pays' system (see figure 3.14).

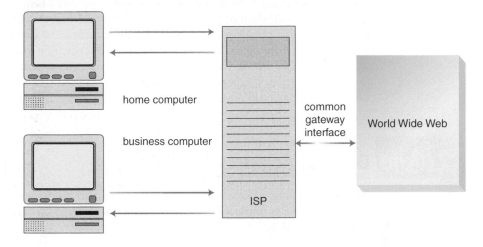

**FIGURE 3.14:** How an ISP links home and business computers to the Internet

Given the ease of use and low cost of access, the Web has become increasingly popular as potential business uses become apparent. These include:
- selling gifts (see www.violet.com)
- electronic publishing (see www.ibooks.com and www.infocus.com)
- banking and establishing digital cash and modes of exchange (see WingSpanBank at www.wingspan.com)
- selling pharmaceuticals (www.tradegate.org.au/).

The Web is also gaining populatiry because there are now millions of people and businesses throughout the world who own computers. Most of these computers have been sold with web-enabling software and inducements to link with commercial ISPs. For electronic commerce to be viable and attractive, businesses must have access to hardware. There is also a need for appropriate software to be available, to be financially competitive and to provide businesses with value for money. Some web browsers and search engines are free and become available when any business or individual joins up and pays an access fee to an ISP. In a commercial context, web servers are not expensive and have allowed the proliferation of many ISPs throughout the world.

For businesses, electronic commerce must be secure. Payments and data exchange must be protected from intrusion. The development of better firewall technologies (to protect against unauthorised access) and better encryption languages and processes (coding information in ways that make translation and capture very difficult) allow businesses to feel more secure about doing business electronically. The development of a new standard or protocol for electronic payments, secure electronic transaction (SET),[6] has ensured that further protection in a standardised form is available for businesses. Large businesses will engage in more electronic commerce when such protocols are well proven.

The major unresolved issue in electronic commerce is government regulation. Governments throughout the world have been increasingly reticent about establishing regulations or laws about Internet access and use or about security and confidentiality issues. There is also a need to gain a clearer understanding of the taxation and economic implications of electronic commerce and the use of digital cash methods and smart cards. For example, at this time it is not possible to use electronic receipts to support tax claims in Australia.

From this discussion it has become obvious that there are a number of specific technologies that affect the operations of the Internet and the Web. In the next section, each of the most important technologies is discussed separately.

# Gateway Accessory Store

The Gateway Accessory Store (www.gateway.com/accessories/) is one of the world's major shopping sites on the Internet. This site advertises and sells computing goods.

### EXERCISES

1.  Investigate this site to find out how the site was developed, where it is located and how the technology of the Internet enables the user to find the site.
2.  What can be bought at the site?
3.  How does the technology involved provide the consumer with easy access?

# BUSINESS TECHNOLOGIES FOR THE WORLD WIDE WEB

The technologies that allow business use of the Internet to be more effective include databases, multimedia and new programming languages designed for Internet use. It is important to note that the following discussion is simply an introduction to this subject.

## Database integration

In traditional inter-business online commerce, databases are shared in structured formats. Electronic data interchange (EDI) is an example of how databases can be linked. On the Web it is difficult to maintain the capture and sharing of data derived from existing databases. The protocols that drive the Web exchange data in semi-structured forms. This has the effect of making the transmission of transactional type data very difficult using traditional databases. This data includes items as diverse as invoicing, payroll systems and employee personal details. The Web operates systems that are designed to distribute more complex material such as software or operations manuals that are more correctly designated as semi-structured.

On the Web the interaction of databases can be facilitated with **middleware**. This form of software acts as a middle operations gateway between the client and the servers operating the web sites. Middleware operates as the translator of structured data, enabling structured data to be reprocessed and then transmitted in a semi-structured format via the Web. At this time there are a number of software/middleware packages that permit small-scale exchange of structured data, such as inventory systems, between databases. These include packages such as Oracle and mSQL (DBperl).[7] One of the most effective middleware packages is Sybase, which accepts **structured query language**[8] **(SQL)** commands, embedded within HTML forms. This enables structured data to be exchanged through a CGI system and then displayed in HTML form at the client end. The way these processes occur is shown in figure 3.15.

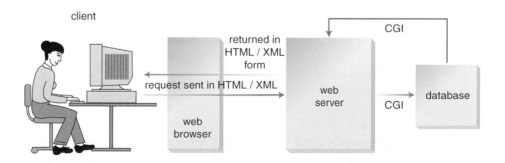

**FIGURE 3.15:** Database integration

Further developments in database integration and use on the Internet include object request brokering (ORB). This software acts as a broker which finds, retrieves and delivers data and information. More commonly, software developed for the Internet relies on simplicity and ease of use. (See www.corba.org for details).

The **thin client system** is a PC on a local-area network that does not have its own hard disk. Files are stored on a network file server. A **fat client system**, on the other hand, stores applications and files on the desktop. Thin client systems operate in a more cost effective and business efficient way. The server is the one location where software upgrades are performed, where all processing is done and where all files are stored. There is no PC box at each station, reducing costs. There is only one large disk for the system, reducing the cost of having smaller disks in each workstation. Security should be easier as there is only one access point to be protected, reducing costs. However, perhaps the most cost-effective argument about thin client systems is that PCs don't become obsolescent. Only the server needs to be upgraded.

One such application of client server technologies has been developed by Citrix in the United States. Citrix is a server-based computing system with software for Microsoft Windows NT Server 4.0, and there is also a Terminal Server edition. Citrix has also developed WinFrame® 1.8. This integrated server-based software is a commercially developed solution for deploying, managing and accessing business applications across the enterprise and provides access to virtually any application, across any type of network connection to any type of client.

# Java Beans

**Java Beans** is a portable, platform-independent component model written in the Java programming language. Java Beans was developed in collaboration with industry. Java Beans allows web developers to write reusable components of web pages of Internet software once and run them anywhere because of the platform-independent power of **Java** technology. Java Beans' components are reusable software components that can be manipulated visually in a builder tool. Beans can be combined to create traditional applications or their related smaller web-oriented relatives, applets.

Java Beans are becoming very popular with web developers to free themselves from large, slow and inflexible software applications. Java Beans are used to build up a portable, reusable code base. These application/components allow developers to quickly meet new market opportunities. Java Beans-based products include Corel, EnterpriseSoft, Gemstone, IBM, K & A Software, KL Group, Lotus development, Novell, ProtoView Development, Rogue Wave, and Stingray Software among many others.

# Multimedia and the World Wide Web

Further development of the Internet and Web has encompassed more than new programming languages such as Java. The Web enables transmission that utilises both audio and video. This attribute of the Web has led to the development of prototypes and languages that enable three-dimensional representations — **virtual reality modelling language (VRML)**. This language allows graphical representations and models generated by computers to be broken into smaller components and transmitted across the Internet. One example is Pathfinder.[9] The development of such a complex structure and the loading process results from the small packages being transmitted independently in some structured order. VRML is the most commonly adopted protocol used across the Web to enable three-dimensional graphical representation and transmission. To enter the domains of VRML, it is essential to have a VRML browser, that is, a three-dimensional web browser.

In addition, more recently developed software enables the delivery of on-demand audio and video across the Web. The process of audio and/or video streaming allows clients to order and be delivered pictures, video and audio associated with objects compressed to hold the digitised audio and video. Products such as StreamWorks, VDOLive and CU-SeeMe are all software packages that enable transmission and electronic commerce on the Web. CU-SeeMe allows real time video-video transmission which is suitable for face-to-face communications and negotiations.[10] Audio and video streaming have revolutionised software developments. One of the most popular forms of web-based audio streaming is the use of MP3 to listen to music or radio. MP3 is a form of compression for audio which is supplied through access to the Web. It allows a high level of compression with little loss in quality. However, MP3s are only *near* CD quality. The hardware and software requirements for MP3 include at least a Pentium, Power Mac or comparable processor, and a sound card and speakers. Users also need to download an MP3 player according to the OS platform being used (e.g. Windows, Macintosh or Unix/Linux). The most common software programs available include: RealPlayer G2, Quicktime 4WinAmp, MusicMatch, X11 Amp, Xaudio and Napster (www.napster.com).[11]

In terms of electronic commerce, the use of three-dimensional graphics and audio and video streaming will provide better opportunities for quality and effective advertising, catalogue development and allow for more effective home pages to promote consumer-to-business and business-to-business electronic commerce. These technologies will also facilitate the development of intranets within organisations and better communications in environments where the intranet is accommodating and user-friendly.

## SUMMARY

Electronic commerce offers businesses the opportunity to improve their access to markets, to increase their inter-organisational and intra-organisational efficiency and to complete business tasks more effectively. How these outcomes are achieved depends on which technologies that provide

Internet access are available to businesses. The technologies are designed to support the structure of the Internet and the way this physical structure enables ease of access. The Internet works using the various telecommunications networks established throughout the world, including public telephone systems, private cable networks, public and private microwave networks and satellite networks.

The technologies that make electronic commerce work include design elements that have enabled the development of intranets and extranets for businesses operating within the Internet. The development of the Web has enabled better and more creative use of the Internet, increasing potential for improved and more effective marketing, advertising, data exchange and communications. The Web has been enhanced with the development of software that provides better communications, more effective data exchange and transmission of information, and better communication between the Internet and individual clients or businesses. New and emerging technologies will continue to improve the effectiveness of the Internet for business. These developments will ensure that electronic commerce and Internet commerce occur more frequently in the global and local business environments.

**key terms**

common gateway interface (CGI)

electronic data interchange (EDI)

ethernet

extensible markup language (XML)

extranet

fat client system

hotlink

Internet protocol (IP)

intranet

Java

Java Beans

local area network (LAN)

middleware

multipurpose Internet mail extensions (MIME)

point-to-point protocol (PPP)

portal

post office protocol (POP)

protocol

search engine

serial line Internet protocol (SLIP)

simple mail transfer protocol (SMTP)

standard generalised markup language (SGML)

structured query language (SQL)

thin client system

transmission control protocol/Internet protocol (TCP/IP)

very-high-speed backbone network (vBNS)

virtual reality modelling language (VRML)

# THROUGH THICK AND THIN

## Thin client technology is helping Macquarie Bank expand its business into new markets.

BY MANDY BRYAN

Mergers, teleworking, business process outsourcing, and overseas ventures — sound like a typical portfolio of late-1990s business challenges? A local investment bank is tackling all four using a thin alternative to its client/server architecture.

The first opportunity to leverage Windows-based thin client technology came suddenly at Macquarie Bank late last year when its Private Client Investments, the stockbroking arm of Macquarie's Equities group, merged with Queensland stockbroker, Nevitts.

The Nevitts merger is the first of a number of mergers designed to put Macquarie on the national stock-broking map. With e-trading shaking up an already crowded market, Macquarie has identified technology as [the] key to further growth and differentiation. As such, the tech-nology delivery a Macquarie merger could offer Nevitts oiled the wheels of the deal significantly, says division director of global equity services at Macquarie, Michael McCarthy.

'Nevitts had very few standard applications across the business and instead had a plethora of small applications on their own PCs,' says McCarthy. 'One of the big advantages for them was that Macquarie Bank could make its sophisticated infrastructure available to them.'

### Fast rollout

Speed of implementation was vital. 'I guess the key to these acquisitions is to have the transition run as smooth as possible with pressure to have the environment online ASAP,' says McCarthy.

This meant Macquarie's Infor-mation Service Division suddenly found itself on the end of a very short time-frame to integrate eight offices of Nevitts, says Anthony Davoren, associate director of the bank's information services division.

## The thin advantage

**Thin client technology is helping Macquarie Bank overcome a series of business challenges**

■ Tactical adoption of thin client technology is helping Macquarie Bank tackle diverse business challenges.
■ A merger with a regional Queensland stockbroker has sped up Macquarie's thin client adoption.
■ Business process outsourcing, teleworking and overseas ventures will also benefit from the technology.
■ Sociability issues make it impractical to scale thin clients across the whole bank.

While Nevitts' Brisbane head office could adopt Macquarie's standard client/server operating environment and Macquarie Advanced PC System (MAPS) front-end, the cost of delivering the same to its seven regional offices, each employing just three to five people could not be justified. Furthermore, there was a risk that some of its more chatty client/server applications would be too slow running over a WAN, says Davoren.

As such, the Nevitts merger provided a compelling opportunity to capitalise on the bank's thin client development work which offered a solution one-third to a quarter cheaper than the standard server desktop model.

Having followed developments in thin clients over the years, the bank had only recently identified teleworking as a specific business driver for the Windows Terminal Server and Citrix Metaframe multi-user NT environment. 'We had 20 people running the teleworking pilot and we actually had to freeze this while we did the work for Nevitts,' says Davoren.

With a very tight timeframe of about three months, the need to get it out there and get it out there very quickly was asking almost the impossible, says Davoren. 'Before Nevitts, if I'd been asked how I felt about delivering a full production Metaframe environment in that timeframe I would have felt pretty uncomfortable about it — but we didn't really have a choice.'

Rollout started at the end of November last year and by early February, one user was pilot testing it. By the second half of February, rollout

was complete. The rollout itself took just two weeks by one person. 'All the work was done here so the people who developed the solution didn't have to leave head-office, and the thin client was implemented onsite by the guy that looks after hardware logistics,' says Davoren.

'This was brand new for Macquarie and there was risk associated with it,' says McCarthy, 'risk we were prepared to accept from a business perspective. Macquarie Nevitts now has access to front-end marketing systems, client contact and marketing management systems, plus online research. Macquarie Equities has 40 analysts sitting in offices around the works and it now has access to research published by those analysts.'

## Platform

The applications run on Metaframe servers in Sydney, all the data resides in Sydney and only screen and keyboard strokes move between the Sydney and regional office locations.

Initially toying with the idea of using older PCs, Macquarie opted for Windows Terminals at A$1300 apiece to ensure complete control over the environment. 'I don't believe you get hardware savings in this environment. Because everything you've taken out of the PC you've put into the server,' says Davoren.

The savings, he says, come in other areas such as reduced support and improved performance. 'This architecture provides an enormous degree of control for IT without taking away any functionality — except users can't introduce a floppy disk in the environment, which is not necessarily a bad thing.'

Metaframe also allows Macquarie to shadow a session and see exactly what the user is seeing if a help desk takes a call from someone in one of the outlying offices.

Furthermore, if the Windows Terminal dies, it will ship one out and they'll ship one back — it's a small box, no moving parts so it can be easily packaged up and couriered.

This environment also makes global upgrades much easier. 'Looking down the track at the cost of supporting this environment, we don't want to be visiting these offices everytime we change a Netware client or a bios upgrade on our PCs,' says Davoren.

Macquarie Nevitts also shares data between the offices and within the equities group generally. In that respect, he says, it's a lot more efficient to move data between them when they are sharing the same server. 'If we were shipping data out to these outlying offices, particularly large spreadsheets, it can have a fairly heavy impact on the link and if they happen to be trying to run a client/server application at the same time, it can have a disastrous effect on the link.

While Davoren describes this as 'almost a passive infrastructure', some outstanding issues with integration of the Netware technology have meant Macquarie has had to put more support in than that it would like, particularly in interoperability between Metaframe on an NT and Netware platform. Davoren also says support from Citrix and Novell on those issues is good.

Also proving a little unreliable is a Sydney-based NT print server that prints over a WAN to network printers in each of the Nevitts offices — a temporary solution hooked up to meet the tight rollout. Macquarie is looking to replace this with Novell's Distributed Print Services (NDPS) for IP printing. Overall though, despite being sent over a WAN, Nevitts' regional print jobs are normally quite satisfactory and users notice no delay, says Davoren.

## Teleworking

With the dabbling stage now well and truly behind it, Macquarie will again forge ahead with its suspended teleworking pilot in the form of a significant scale rollout this year, says Davoren.

Up until now, complex support issues and inconsistent performance of business applications over a modem line have limited the take-up of teleworking over traditional client architectures. Although he says thin client technology can overcome these hurdles, it also has its limits.

'We have to be careful in terms of selecting a group with a minimal applications set and a real need to do teleworking.' For instance, if someone uses 50 applications, IT would have to ensure their applications were scripted and sociable before putting them together on a server, he says.

Teleworking gives people a lot more flexibility generally, says Davoren, and with many people leaving organisations for lifestyle reasons, 'instead we can give you a day a week to nurse your sick father or balance a career and a family'.

Another group benefiting from a home connection would be IT support who receive callouts of an evening.

'I love using it myself and try to do at least a day a fortnight. The performance is fantastic — I use it at home over an ISDN line and it's as good as sitting on a PC on a LAN,' says Davoren.

### Business process outsourcing

Along the way Macquarie has also discovered some other enticing business applications for thin client technology.

In line with the reduced competitive advantage able to be squeezed out of discrete back office operations, Macquarie is reviewing its back office business process outsourcing offerings.

Its ability to share its back office systems — in the form of a hosted application that resides on the Metaframe server — works to amortise the costs of developing those systems and procedures.

In fact, one Macquarie business unit has already commissioned the IT services division to develop such a service and already has a client earmarked.

'We have put their application through it and it works and we have shown we can deliver it to an external client quite happily and with excellent performance,' says Davoren.

With Metaframe, the firewall just has to accept the Metaframe client software, the Independent Computing Architecture (ICA) protocol. It doesn't matter what application runs over that because it is only concerned with letting the screen and keyboard go through, therefore saving on ongoing firewall customisation.

### OS ventures

Exporting a financial service to Hong Kong for delivery via a single Macquarie operative is also well positioned to leverage the thin client.

Given that the business application in question doesn't work well over a WAN, and the prospect of supporting and upgrading a single remote operative would also be 'downright painful', says Davoren, the thin client option offers another welcome solution: 'We've actually built ... production servers to deliver this application in Hong Kong. We know the application runs just fine in Sydney so it will never actually leave Sydney,' he says.

### Total cost of ownership

So what's stopping the bank rolling out thin client architecture beyond these tactical pockets? Sociability issues, says Davoren. A high number of applications for a comparatively small number of users are not well matched to this architecture, and Macquarie has around 1000 applications spread across 2800 staff.

'This technology scales wonderfully up to an enormous number of desktops — the area where we are having difficulty is scaling the number of applications.'

If you find a conflict where some applications won't run with other applications on the client, the desktop may fall over — but on a server, the whole network goes down, says Davoren.

If you were embarking on a greenfields development, he says, you may look at the thin client and say the TCO figures stack up favourably. 'We are not a greenfields site — we have an enormous amount of intellectual capital already invested. If we were to turn around now and say gee there's this technology that seems to be wonderfully cost effective, let's roll it out, we've gained nothing and are just adding an additional cost.'

## Avoiding the pitfalls

*Recently pioneering Windows-based thin client applications tactically in the business, Macquarie Bank has learned its share of lessons. Macquarie Bank's Anthony Davoren shares these.*

■ If you have a pure Microsoft environment it's a lot easier. If you have a pure Netware environment, that's been pretty well sorted out now too. If you have both a Microsoft and Netware environment, as we and a number of other organisations do, it works but it's a lot harder in the implementation.

■ Everyone cites fantastic examples of using a DOS 286 but this isn't really the issue. The reality is the PC you use does make a huge difference. It's very graphics intensive so you do want a platform that has very good graphics support. We used Windows Terminals as a deliberate cost choice that said we are going to wear $1300 per terminal and I think we would recover that in just reduced support costs.

■ In terms of terminals, we found the market was a little immature. We found when we first started looking at them that they all seemed to be fairly buggy but we did eventually settle on a platform we are happy with — an NCD. I suspect this will be something that will be open for review — they will probably leapfrog each other in terms of development.

**SOURCE:** *MIS Australia*, May 1999, pp. 44–8

### QUESTIONS

1. What advantages does the thin client computer system deliver to the Macquarie Bank?
2. What is teleworking? How does it deliver business advantage to the bank?
3. Why does this thin client architecture provide an 'enormous degree of control for IT'?
4. What are the pitfalls of thin client computers in organisations?
5. Why is there an increasing use of outsourcing in businesses to gain advantage from IT?
6. Why are thin client computer applications seen as the best option for 'greenfield' developments?

**QUESTIONS**

1. Log into www.time.com/ and trace all of the site's paths by clicking the hyperlinks. Develop a tree diagram of all of the hyperlinks allowed from the site. Each of these are developed in HTML language. How do you know this?

2. The URL for one of the world's best examples of Internet commerce is www.public.iastate.edu/~PremCourses/dutchauc.html. Find the site and undertake the following exercises to gain some practical understanding of Internet commerce.
   (a) Read about the Dutch Flower Auction and how it works.
   (b) Why was the auction site developed?
   (c) How does the flower trading operate?
   (d) What are the advantages and disadvantages of the Dutch Flower Auction?
   (e) When was the IT form of the flower auction developed?
   (f) How does the IT site work?
   (g) Complete the case questions on the site.
   (h) Write an evaluation of the assessment of the Dutch Flower Auction site.

3. Choice Mall is a shopping centre in cyberspace.
   (a) How many merchants are there on this site?
   (b) How effective is the site as a network provider of goods and services?
   (c) Which sector of the suppliers' market is the site aimed at?
   (d) What are the establishment costs involved in using this site?

4. Visit www.isworld.org/isworld/ecourse. This site contains a wealth of research material.

**SUGGESTED READING**

Baker, R. H. 1997, *Extranets: The Complete Sourcebook*, McGraw-Hill, New York.

Benett, G. 1996, *Introducing Intranets*, Que Corp, United States.

Department of Foreign Affairs and Trade 1999, *Creating a Clearway on the New Silk Road*, Commonwealth of Australia, Canberra.

Department of Foreign Affairs and Trade 1999, *Driving Forces on the New Silk Road*, Commonwealth of Australia, Canberra.

Kalakota, R. and Whinston, A. 1996, *Frontiers of Electronic Commerce*, Addison-Wesley, United States.

Kalakota, R. and Whinston, A. 1997, *Electronic Commerce: A Manager's Guide*, Addison-Wesley, United States.

Kosiur, D. 1997, *Understanding Electronic Commerce*, Microsoft Press, United States.

Liu, C., Peek, J., Jones, K., Buus, R. B. and Nye, A. 1996, *Managing Internet Information Systems*, O'Reilly and Associates, United States.

Maddox, K. 1998, *Web Commerce: Building a Digital Business*, John Wiley and Sons, Ltd, New York.

McKeon, P. and Watson, R. 1996, Metamorphosis: *A Guide to the World Wide Web and Electronic Commerce*, John Wiley and Sons, New York.

 **END NOTES**

1. The following web site will provide additional information on PPP: www.cisco.com/univercd/data/doc/cintrnet/ito/55168.htm.

2. Further details on POP and post office software can be found at www.groupweb.com/email/es_soft.htm.

3. The development of the Web and of these protocols is available at www.w3.org/hypertext/www/History/1989/proposal.html.

4. The concept of a web browser is defined later in this chapter.

5. You can view such a file by opening www.mastercard.com/press/970718a.html.

6. The SET protocol agreement process and details are available at www.set.org.

7. Software packages that use object oriented programming techniques to develop programs and objects for display on the Internet or on PCs.

8. SQL is a language that enables object-oriented programming. Further details can be found at www.jcc.com/sql_stnd.html.

9. It would be worthwhile at this point to return to the Time site and examine the way the home page for Time actually loads onto a computer (www.time.com/).

10. The development of CU-SeeMe can be found at the following URL: http://goliath.wpine.com.au/cu-seeme.html

11. More detailed information can be found by starting a search at www.mp3.com/help/.

# CHAPTER

# 4

# World Wide Web commerce

## LEARNING Outcomes

You will have mastered the material in this chapter when you can:

- understand how to apply marketing strategies to Internet commerce
- know the old five P's and new five P's of marketing and their application to Internet commerce
- know how to plan, organise, control and monitor an Internet commerce site
- appreciate the use and potential of intelligent agents
- understand the importance of developing a community for products in Internet commerce.

*'Because communication — which in the end is what the digital technology and media are all about — is not just a sector of the economy. Communication is the economy.'*

K. Kelly 1998, *New Rules for the New Economy: 10 Radical Strategies for a Connected World,* Viking, United States, p. 5

# INTRODUCTION

The Web makes doing business cheaper and facilitates opportunities for manufacturers to sell their goods and services directly. In the computer industry we have seen major player Compaq adopt a **'clicks and mortar' approach** to selling its products, much to the chagrin of the tradition resellers. Compaq has been forced to go to online selling to compete with Dell and Gateway but has also elected to open physical retail shops as well. Intel has adopted what it calls a **'clicks and bricks' model**. It is vital to look at the various options that are available if a person or business wishes to set up an Internet commerce site. In this chapter we will examine various strategies to create a commercial site and keep it running successfully. In the early 1990s most companies wanted to create a web site so that they could be seen as being technologically 'with it'. In the late 1990s companies need to set up a site that is capable of allowing online business. In this section we will examine how to do this using a combination of the old five P's of marketing[1] and the new five P's of marketing.[2]

| TABLE 4.1 | THE OLD AND NEW FIVE P'S OF MARKETING |
|---|---|
| **OLD FIVE P'S** | **NEW FIVE P'S** |
| product | paradox |
| price | perspective |
| place | paradigm |
| promotion and people | persuasion |
| packaging | passion |

# STRATEGIES FOR SETTING UP A WEB SITE USING THE OLD FIVE P'S

## Product

It is vital that the company that wishes to go into online commerce has a **product** that consumers will require. If a company has had a successful business selling via catalogues, it is likely that such products will also sell well over the Internet, particularly if they involve finance, travel or automobiles. Online commerce is also excellent for selling services. A complete range of products should be available as consumers are frustrated if they believe they can buy a product in store but not online. However, as pointed out by Douglas Adams, we must remember that we still can't deliver a fridge by email.[3]

The cyber entrepreneur must look at the product and determine if it is user-friendly, if it is likely to be wanted or if there is a new way to market the product. The product should also be examined in terms of its life cycle: introduction, growth, maturity and decline. Dell Computer is doing US$40 million worth of business a day in Internet commerce and, in Australia, Dell is attracting small, medium and large enterprises, government, education and private consumers with its full range of enterprise solutions.

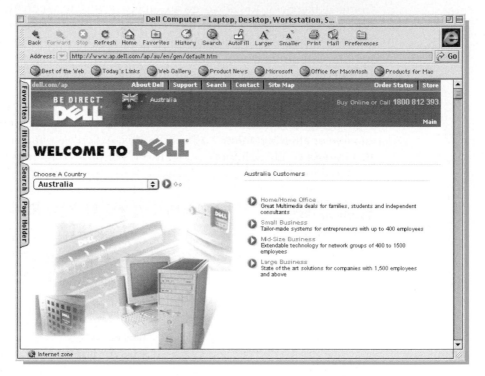

**FIGURE 4.1:** Home page of Dell Computer of Australia (www.dell.com/ap/au/index.htm). Reproduced with permission by Dell Computer. Copyright © 2000.

# Price

The product must be affordable to the target market. One of the great advantages of the Web is that products can be sold more cheaply because the large infrastructure of a physical shopfront is not necessary. Australian consumers have been attracted to web sites in the United States that sell CDs (e.g. CDNow) and books (e.g. Amazon.com) for far less than the retail **price** in Australia even after paying postage and handling costs. It is also necessary to consider special offers and incentives when using the Web to sell a product. Using the Web means the cost of advertising and communicating is reduced. Web ordering is efficient, quick and less prone to errors as the customer is doing the work of filling in the forms.

## Place

This is no longer such a vital consideration as the cyberbusiness can be on a server in a garage or in a home study. However, the business must realise that the market is now potentially a lot larger than if the business was setting up a real store. The CD and bookstore examples in the previous paragraph are graphic examples of this. Internet commerce transcends geographic and possibly even political, legal and cultural boundaries, so true globalisation is possible for even the smallest business. This globalisation of the marketplace has advantages for Australia, which has such a small local market, but also opens up the potential for more competition. Much global infrastructure for dealing on a world scale is already in place. In the province of Manitoba in Canada, the fledgling cyberbusiness ManGlobe approached Canada Post for assistance with customs requirements and the Royal Bank of Canada for assistance with payment options. Once ManGlobe had these major companies onside, it was able to use their expertise to the benefit of the cyberbusiness. Australian cyberbusinesses would benefit from such an approach.

Other items that normally need to be taken into account, such as shelf location, are no longer an issue. However, the category of **place** could also include the number of other sellers of the same type of product and the strength of the competitor's cyberbusiness. Place, therefore, could be considered to include actual cyber presence. Is it a large and clear presence that is easily found and identified? Does it offer a range of services (the cyber equivalent of a large department store)? Is it a small, less noticeable and harder-to-find site with few services (the cyber equivalent of a corner store)?

## Promotion and people

How to be seen on the Internet is a challenge. The business may decide to advertise on normal marketing channels as most people are accustomed to seeing URLs on advertisements on buses and trains. Radio and television advertisements often give the web address of businesses so people are becoming used to the 'double ewe, double ewe, double ewe, dot cyber business, dot com, dot a ewe' either in spoken or written form. If the business name is the same as the web address name (e.g. David Jones' web address is www.davidjones.com.au), this is a subtle form of advertising in itself. Failure to be as innovative as the competition and to use technology for strategic advantage means that a company may lose **promotion** opportunities. Failure to match competitors' unit costs is another strategic challenge. The Web allows businesses to promote using online advertisements such as banner ads, online catalogues, product information, competitions and electronic feedback.

The cyberbusiness must not forget that people are a vital part of any business, including the people who run the business and the **people** who interact with the business. (Customer relations will be dealt with fully in chapter 8.) Harris Technology of North Sydney is an example of how a small business set up shop on the Web and involved each and every member of the staff in the venture.

**FIGURE 4.2:** Home page of Harris technology (www.ht.com.au)

Harris Technology, a retail store in North Sydney, sells a wide range of computers and computer-related products. Harris Technology went into online commerce on the Internet in September 1996. By February 1997 it had generated $190 000 worth of business. By 2000 Harris Technology anticipates generating one million dollars per month. In 1999 Harris Technology was acquired by the large retail group Coles Myer.

Some other key points:

- All staff (100) have full access to the Internet and the Web. They are all involved in the way the web site is designed and run.
- The QUIDS (quotations, inventory, distribution and sales) database, written in Microsoft's FoxPro, lists 34 000+ products and 20 000 customer entities; tracks all sides of Harris Technology business, including sales, profitability, serial numbers and bills of materials; and allows the electronic transfer of stock and ordering information from manufacturer to distributor to reseller to the final customer via a web page.
- The web site runs live from the QUIDS data so that customers see the same information (pricing, stock availability, images and text) as seen by Harris Technology staff.
- The pages are compiled 'live on the fly' by Microsoft's Visual FoxPro program. All the images, downloadable drivers, text and web-site links are

attached to the product item in QUIDS. The Visual FoxPro program assembles them into pages when the customer requests the page.

- The company fields 1400 incoming and approximately 1400 outgoing telephone calls per day. It has call monitoring to ensure that all calls are dealt with.
- Tech Pacific, Harris Technology's main supplier, shares its stock availability and pricing with QUIDS each day via the Internet.
- Harris Technology's customers interact with the QUIDS inventory in the same way as its employees query the database to check availability and stock quantity.
- The web site has product overviews, pictures, links to press reviews, sites for downloading demos and software drivers, and an online ordering system.

| TABLE 4.2 | TECHNICAL SPECIFICATIONS OF THE HARRIS TECHNOLOGY WEB SITE | |
| --- | --- | --- |
| ITEM | TYPE | DETAILS |
| database | QUIDS | written in Microsoft FoxPro |
| network file server | MS Backoffice | IBM Infinity 5500 with dual Pentium processor and Raid 5, 25 gigabytes storage |
| workstations | 160 plus Windows 95/NT workstations | Pentiums 166+ MHZ, 100 Mbps network |
| QUIDS Internet Server | NT Server IIS 4.0 and Microsoft Visual FoxPro | Compaq Proliant 1600, dual processor, Raid 5 |
| bandwidth | dual 512 K, DDS Fastway links to Telstra and Internet | direct connection |

*SOURCE:* Ron Harris of Harris Technology 1999, www.ht.com.au

### EXERCISE

Write a short report outlining how the Harris Technology web site adheres to the five P's of marketing.

# Packaging

Shopping is considered by some as a form of entertainment or social event so the business has to engage in **packaging** the cyberproduct as such. Doing the shopping online has to appeal to the potential consumer. At Harris Technology, online buying is made attractive by offering discounts on certain goods and ensuring that the consumer is a member of their PC Club. FAI Insurance has developed a web site that offers a 10 per cent discount on its insurance premiums if the consumer buys the insurance via the Internet.

# STRATEGIES FOR SETTING UP A WEB SITE USING THE NEW FIVE P'S OF MARKETING

Tom Patty, a worldwide Nissan account director, believes that the old five P's were based on a world dominated by stability, a fast-growing economy and a much less competitive environment. He has proposed a replacement set of P's for the new world, where chaos has replaced stability, economies have slowed and global competition has increased.[4]

## Paradox

The *Oxford English Dictionary* defines **paradox** as:

> *A statement or proposition which on the face of it seems self contradictory, absurd, or at variance with common sense, though, on investigation or when explained, it may prove to be well founded …*

**SOURCE:** *Oxford English Dictionary* 1989, vol. xi, Oxford University Press, Oxford, p. 185

Patty gives an example from his own field to explain the meaning of the word: 'All cars are the same; all cars are different.' He then shows how to master this paradox by:

- exploiting the differentiation; for example, Altima is the 'first *affordable luxury* car'
- creating a unique identity, such as a well-known brand name that suggests that that particular brand name is somehow better than the others, although essentially 'all cars are the same'
- becoming the 'first of something' in order to highlight a product that is essentially the same as its competitors.

In the cyberbusiness it is very easy to exploit paradox. For example, Advance Bank (now St George Bank) was able to market itself as the first Australian Internet bank. Another example of paradox is Amazon.com, which has created a unique identity as a bookshop with over two and a half million titles on offer that does not have a physical shop.

The Australian Broadcasting Commission (ABC) is primarily viewed as a radio and television broadcaster. However, in 1996 the ABC established ABC Online as a new network in its own right. The ABC creates and packages content for an online audience rather than just value-adding for radio and television audiences. The ABC sees the online audience as a unique entity, which it aims to attract. ABC Online is consistently in the top five most-visited media web sites.[5] Online Coaching Colleges are providing virtual teachers to help students prepare for their final examinations.

Worldschool.com aims to charge students $A1 a minute for tutoring in a wide range of primary and secondary subjects. Parents could find such a service useful as they would not have to drive their children to tutoring lessons.

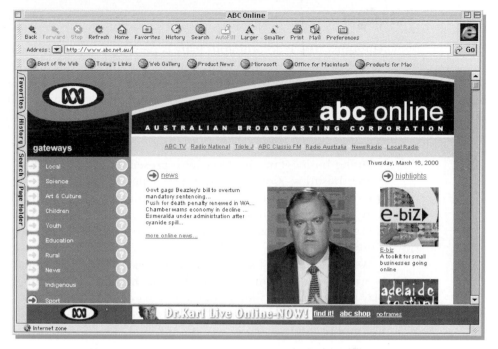

**FIGURE 4.3:** Home page of the ABC's Australia Online (www.abc.net.au)

# Perspective

Patty believes it is vital to view the products from the consumer's **perspective**. The cyberbusiness must determine:

- the consumer requirements that the product or service satisfies
- how its product satisfies those requirements differently and better than its competitors.

St George Bank targets executives and women in its advertisements. It appeals to these busy people by stating that it understands how difficult it is to do domestic business during a frantic lunch hour: how much more convenient it would be to do your banking at home via computer, where there is no more queuing, no more rushing? The web shop www.greengrocer.com.au offers a wider range of products than most physical fruit and vegetable shops. It also provides added value as follows:

- Products are rated according to the season.
- Value for money items are marked with a star.
- Items are delivered to the door.
- There is a money back guarantee if not satisfied.
- There is no delivery charge.
- Customers save time by not going to the shops.[6]

Online trading has satisfied a need for investors to do their own trading from home. Software such as Business in a Box has helped entrepreneurs set up their own webshops quickly (e.g. www.vetshoponline.com).

# Paradigm

The third new P according to Patty is **paradigm**: a pattern example, a model way of doing things. In this new world, paradigms shift and we have to start anew. In chapter 1 the example was given of how retrenched executives have had to reinvent themselves from company people to individual consultants. Encyclopædia Britannica had to change its mode of presentation from paper to CD-ROM. It is vital to identify the proper paradigm, and position the business accordingly.

Doing business on the Internet represents a paradigm shift in methods of doing business. Computer software sellers realised that selling over the Internet represents a major paradigm shift in the way they distribute their software. They can now download software directly to the customer's hard disk. In Netscape's Californian headquarters orders for its software used to come in at a rate of 1000 a day.

Web sites may hold audio and video files that can be listened to or watched by web users. Streaming technologies, such as audio streaming, allow users to play the multimedia files as they are being downloaded.

The ABC uses time shifting, an offshoot of audio streaming, to allow people to listen to ABC programs over the Internet, now that audio over the Internet is comparable to AM quality.[7]

# Persuasion

All businesses try to persuade people to buy their product or service. As Internet commerce is a new medium, companies are attempting different ways to persuade people to visit their site and get them to buy. Patty states that in order to master **persuasion** it is essential to concentrate on:

- credibility
- content
- involvement of the listener.

Obviously, well-established physical businesses will have no trouble with the credibility angle in the virtual world.

Start-up businesses, however, will need to establish credibility quickly. Content needs to be addressed in an online environment as too much content bores the online reader.

Speed of loading is vital to keep the potential client interested. In a web business there are many ways to involve the audience — after all it is an interactive medium. Some of the methodologies include:

- allowing the consumer to see a demonstration of your products and services
- allowing visitors to email your staff directly or order online
- letting people see how many others visit your site
- running contests
- providing value-added services; for example, the Sofcom site allows the visitor to search the Australian Internet Directory, which is a full directory of Australian web sites.[8]

# Libragirl

A site that has been built to ensure a high level of interactivity is Libragirl (www.libragirl.com.au). The site designer, Martin Lindstrom of Zivo, believes it is essential to keep people at the site for more than two minutes. The interactivity means that visitors spend more time there as they have opportunities to win prizes and ask for free samples of company products.

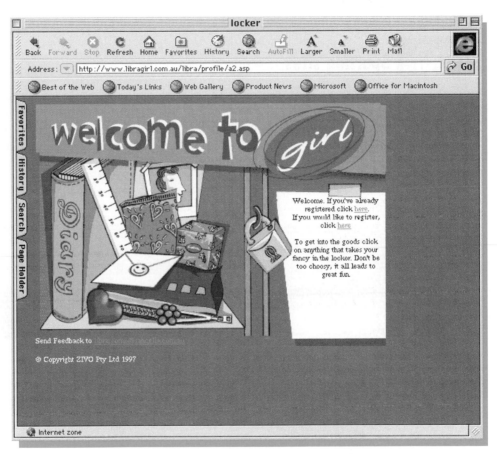

**FIGURE 4.4:** Home page of Libragirl — an interactive web site (www.libragirl.com.au)

## EXERCISES

1. Visit the Libragirl site and outline the ways in which it addresses the issues of interactivity. How would you rate it for credibility, content and user involvement?
2. Locate a commercial site (some of the car sites are excellent for this; for example, Ford, Volkswagen and Mercedes-Benz) that you believe has a high rate of interactivity. Report on its credibility, content and user involvement.
3. Visit the site www.napster.com which is being used by so many college students to download MP3 files that it is causing a bandwidth crisis at some sites. Debate the proposition that such sites should be off limits at universities and colleges.

## Passion

Patty states that he is passionate about his business objective — to develop exciting communication that persuades a consumer to visit a Nissan dealership. This **passion** could also be extended to the Internet commerce site. Remember that the Internet is an exciting communication channel, a brave new frontier in commerce and the business needs to persuade the consumer to visit the web site. The web site CyberHorse, www.cyberhorse.com.au, caters for hundreds of followers of horse racing. Subscribers pay a monthly fee to access its Virtual FormGuide, which allows punters to obtain comprehensive racing form guides for all Australian TAB meetings.

## Sporting sites

Because Australians are passionate about sport it makes sense to have a sporting web site. Greg Norman markets his golf and casual apparel line from the Greg Norman Collection via the Web at the Shop@Shark.com Store (www.shark.com). Tips, articles and the marketing of his golf-course design company are also found on the site. Patrick Rafter has an online tennis site at www.oncourt.com/. Centrebet uses the Internet to host sites in Australia, Denmark, Norway and Finland; conduct bets with clients; illustrate dates, times and locations of events for betting; and to conduct offshore banking.

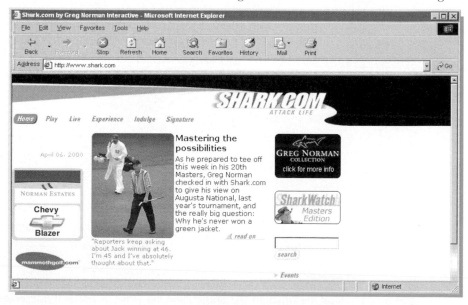

**FIGURE 4.5:** Home page of Shark.com (www.shark.com)

### EXERCISES

1. Locate commercial web sites that exploit Australians' love of sport. How have these sites used passion to ensure that they attract clients to the sites?
2. Select two sporting sites. Discuss the use of paradox, perspective, paradigm, persuasion and passion in these sites.

## CREATING A COMMERCIAL WEB SITE

### Planning

Any type of work involves planning, organising, controlling and monitoring activities.[9] Creating a commercial presence on the Web involves all of those, but with important variations. The traditional paradigm of 'gather data, evaluate alternatives and select plan' does not work with the Web and companies need to adopt an evolutionary and flexible approach for setting up a web site.[10] Because many companies have 1950s work philosophies, they react to the Web by setting up large committees to discuss policies, content and implementation strategies. They often lose strategic advantage by taking too long to get a web site online. It is better to get some web experience and projects online quickly and constantly improve them instead of spending months arguing over policies and content. Rather than setting up large committees, companies should participate in strategic planning workshops, which should be conducted by professional web consultants and should assist interested participants, including senior management, to become aware of the potential of the medium. It is vital to have a senior person on side if the web site is to get approval quickly. The first step in achieving quality excellence is the decision to make quality leadership a basic strategic goal. One half day could be spent training the participants in the Web and the next day working out strategies for how the company could create its commercial presence on the Web. It is essential to build quality into the page at this early design stage to conform to the principles of total quality management.

An Internet commerce strategist begins by considering all aspects of the current business, its process, people and customer base. The transition to e-business may involve many staff from within the organisation and potentially many from outside the organisation. Members of the information technology department must be involved in the successful execution of the strategy.[11] Some important aspects must be considered:

- new ways of doing business through technology
- evaluation of the organisation's response to customer needs
- ways to decrease cost and increase competitive advantage
- assessment of the customer base and its capacity to trade online
- assessment of products and services and how these may be marketed to the customer
- outsourcing requirements
- estimations of timing into the digital market, schedules for development
- assessment of the potential effects of disintermediation and reintermediation
- creation of a detailed partnering strategy
- financial requirements of the Internet business
- objectives for the first six months
- keeping up to date.

# Organising

The commercial web site should be thought of as a continually growing and informative picture of the company. As such it is essential that it is updated and constantly improved as part of total quality management. There must be some hook to get people to return to the site, otherwise it will not be revisited. This can be done by running contests, offering incentives, etc. Some companies are now adding in small advertisements for their own products and for the products of other companies. It is also vital to organise training sessions for all members of the organisation who are interested in the Web. The more people involved and enthused by the Web the better, as they will be able to provide new ideas for running the online business. Harris Technology is a good example of this approach where every staff member is involved with the web site design and implementation. The online business is seen as just another way of serving the clients. Training covering all aspects of server operations and web presentations should be provided because such good training will contribute significantly to standardisation and 'corporate image'. This idea is in line with company-wide commitment and company-wide introduction of total quality management principles.

# Controlling

In many large organisations control of the web site can become a power tool for a division or department. Office or organisational politics may cause serious conflicts over who has ultimate control. In some companies, divisions that have been downsized may see control of the web site as a way to get back into favour in the organisation. Other divisions, such as computing services, may see the web design and maintenance as just another chore that they have to do on top of their already busy schedule. A SPIDER (Strategic Planning for Internet Dissemination, Evaluation and Retrieval) team can assist in such ventures.[12] If different departments of an organisation want to become involved in the commercialisation of the organisation's web site, they need support in doing this but not complete control of every page that is added. **Templates** and guidelines can be circulated. Templates are useful as they assist the different departments to quickly add a page and it helps if they feel that they are not starting from scratch. The guidelines need to set out who has formal authority to approve pages. Change control documentation is important when considering a large project.

# Monitoring results

Once an organisation has a commercial web site it is a simple matter to gather statistics on the site. The online orders will provide the statistics but some companies favour visitor books or interactive forms. There is a danger of overkill on statistics. Web users tire of filling in large forms unless there is some incentive for doing so. It is possible to allow a daemon, a background process that runs on a Unix machine, to measure the number of hits. Each week, the service provider for Cyber.Consult emails the number of visits, or hits, to the Cyber.Consult home page. These figures are broken down into the countries of origin of the hits and the domain names. Obviously if a company needs more information, interactive forms and visitor books will be necessary. These forms do help a business build up a profile of their customers and after all not all visitors to the site will buy. It is handy if the cyberbusiness knows why the potential client has not followed through with an order. In attempting to adhere to the principles of total quality management, the gathering of information from the customers who visit the organisation's page can be used as a tool to ensure that the customer requirements are incorporated into the design and continual development of the site.

Creating and sustaining an Internet commerce site means being prudent with external companies, Internet service providers (ISPs), network integrators and Internet specialists.

## Creating a commercial web site quickly

One of the quickest ways to set up a business online is to go to a company that makes it easy for you. In Australia, Sofcom allows potential clients to set up a business for $250 using a series of **wizards** that help you design the commercial site. If you want to set up your online business from scratch, you may have to spend between $7000 and $12 000, with some businesses spending as much as $100 000. Companies and individuals buy templates for online catalogues and databases. InterWorld produces a software product called Commerce Exchange, which allows users to build up corporate catalogues and online malls, and manage accounts with multiple billing options, purchase ordering and invoice processing.

## Internet commerce technology review

In this section an overview of technology needed for a commercial web site is provided. (Refer to chapter 3 for more details.) The method of connecting to the Internet is the first decision to be made when establishing a web site. A commercial web site must be available to customers 24 hours a day, seven days a week. This is the major advantage that web buying has over physical shopping. The cyber business must have a dedicated connection to the Internet. In Australia there are many ISPs who will assist in setting up your communication link. They will also assist in making sure you have a domain name, which should reflect the company name. Melbourne IT is one company that registers commercial domain names for Australia (refer to the case study at the end of chapter 1). NetRegistry is another company that registers commercial domains but it is important to be aware that it is possible to register in other countries as well. Some of the items that need to be considered when choosing an ISP are:
- cost
- performance
- terms of service contract.[13]

The ISP might charge a flat rate fee, a set-up fee and a charge for hosting the electronic web site. Make sure that the ISP is able to support its customer base and that you have a disaster recovery plan in place if your ISP does not survive. Set-up costs for a virtual web server can vary from free to $450 (which includes domain name registration). Ongoing costs for a virtual server vary from $20 per month to several hundred dollars a month. Some ISPs also create web sites and prices vary from $70 to over $100 per hour. Alternatively you might decide to buy package deals such as a fully scalable solution as offered by InterWorld or e-business packages from IBM. The cyber business must also decide on whether to connect to the Internet via fast modem or via ISDN (integrated services digital network). A 28 800-bps-fast modem will support up to 20 000 hits per day whereas an ISDN line can support up to 80 000 hits per day. The business will also need a network device to connect the computer to the TCP/IP-based Internet — either a modem for a dedicated voice line or a terminal adapter for an ISDN connection. Some ISPs have their own overseas backbone link and avoid the congestion that may occur on Telstra's backbone. The cost of setting up a permanent modem connection varies from $150 to over $650 with ongoing fees of between $120 to $650 per month. The permanent ISDN connections are much more expensive and may cost from $150 to $2000 to set up and ongoing costs for such a fast connection may run from $120 to $1050 per month. Make sure you study the terms of the service contract to ensure you know what you are signing and what rights you have. In Australia disputes with ISPs should be referred to the Telecommunications Industry Ombudsman. The cost of setting up permanent web server hardware that has a lot of memory should also be remembered. Below is a table that sets out some typical hardware configurations for large- and medium-sized enterprises.

**TABLE 4.3** HARDWARE CONSIDERATIONS IN LARGE- AND MEDIUM-SIZED ENTERPRISES

| WORKSTATIONS CONNECTED | SERVER OPERATING SYSTEMS | SERVER HARD DISKS | SERVER MEMORY | PROCESSORS |
|---|---|---|---|---|
| 3000 workstations: 1000 Windows 98, 1000 Windows NT, and 1000 Macintoshes | Windows NT and Novell Netware, MacOs | 70 Novell servers, 40 NT servers, 20 Unix servers, 100 Macintosh servers with average hard disks of 4 gigabytes | up to 128 RAM | Pentium & Alpha Processors, Power PC processor, SUN, IBM, HP & Silicon Graphics, Unix processors |
| 80 | Windows NT | 2.5 gigabytes | 64 RAM | Pentium 233 |

*SOURCE:* E. Lawrence 1998, 'Setting up a shopfront', *Hands-on Solutions: E-Commerce*, CCH Australia Ltd, p. 35

The software that is required to operate web servers includes the following:
- directory indexing software to open uniform resource locators (URLs)
- audit log files to track every request for a file from your server, host name, date, time and type of request

- access control software that allows user access to be restricted by requiring a user name and password
- common gateway interface (CGI), which allows different types of networking software to interact with one another.

The following tables show the results of a survey of web server software usage on Internet-connected computers.

**TABLE 4.4** NETCRAFT WEB SERVER SURVEY 1999 — TOP DEVELOPERS

| DEVELOPER | NO. OF COMPUTERS IN AUGUST 1999 | PER CENT | NO. OF COMPUTERS IN SEPTEMBER 1999 | PER CENT | CHANGE |
|---|---|---|---|---|---|
| Apache | 3 928 112 | 55.50 | 4 078 326 | 55.33 | –0.17 |
| Microsoft* | 1 556 956 | 22.00 | 1 632 440 | 22.15 | 0.15 |
| Netscape** | 531 714 | 7.51 | 557 498 | 7.56 | 0.05 |

\* Microsoft is the sum of sites running Microsoft-Internet-Information-Server, Microsoft-IIS, Microsoft-IIS-W, Microsoft-PWS-95 and Microsoft-PWS.
\*\* Netscape is the sum of sites running Netscape-Enterprise, Netscape-FastTrack, Netscape-Commerce, Netscape-Communications, Netsite-Commerce and Netsite-Communications.

**SOURCE:** Netcraft Web Server Survey 1999, www.netcraft.co.uk/survey

**TABLE 4.5** NETCRAFT WEB SERVER SURVEY 1999 — TOP SERVERS

| SERVER | NO. OF COMPUTERS IN AUGUST 1999 | PER CENT | NO. OF COMPUTERS IN SEPTEMBER 1999 | PER CENT | CHANGE |
|---|---|---|---|---|---|
| Apache | 3 928 112 | 55.50 | 4 078 326 | 55.33 | –0.17 |
| Microsoft-IIS | 1 552 083 | 21.93 | 1 627 651 | 22.08 | 0.15 |
| Netscape-Enterprise | 432 481 | 6.11 | 457 716 | 6.21 | 0.10 |
| CnG | 172 257 | 2.43 | 183 276 | 2.49 | 0.06 |
| Rapidsite | 121 223 | 1.71 | 134 622 | 1.83 | 0.12 |
| thttpd | 117 135 | 1.65 | 123 487 | 1.68 | 0.03 |
| Zeus | 90 670 | 1.28 | 92 974 | 1.26 | –0.02 |
| WebSitePro | 89 648 | 1.27 | 90 169 | 1.22 | –0.05 |
| Stronghold | 82 719 | 1.17 | 78 340 | 1.06 | –0.11 |
| WebSTAR | 61 975 | 0.88 | 63 595 | 0.86 | –0.02 |

**SOURCE:** Netcraft Web Server Survey 1999, www.netcraft.co.uk/survey

## Internet commerce software

There are off-the-shelf e-commerce software packages available ranging from partial to total software solutions. In Australia, Open Market has taken a large slice of the market and is seen on the Telstra's Shopsafe site (previously known as Surelink) as well as Jadco's SecurEcomm site and the Interactive Knowledge Organisation (www.iko.com.au).

Shopping cart software may be integrated into your web shop — one solution is provided by Cart32 Shopping Cart (www.cart32.com). Large integrated total solutions are provided by such companies as InterWorld (www.interworld.com) and IBM e-business solutions.

Other software developments include e-commerce merchant systems connecting to telecommunications. NETcall Telecom and iCat Corporation are incorporating NETcall's Hyperphone links (the telephone equivalent of hypertext links) into e-commerce web shops.

This will enable web shoppers to browse, shop, click a button and be automatically connected to the desired merchant, enabling them to complete the transaction by phone.

Other useful software for e-commerce sites includes email-filtering software, which is able to analyse queries sent by email and quickly generate a reply from a database of responses.

# ELECTRONIC SHOPPING AGENTS

Electronic shopping **agents** are software tools that assist users to search the Internet for product items. Users interact with a shopping agent by submitting agent requests.

The agent then searches relevant online shops for items matching the search criteria. The agent returns to the user with:
- a detailed description of the items found
- the price of the items
- a direct link to the virtual store where the user can purchase the items.

The agent formats the information, perhaps by price or use, to help the shopper compare products. Several agent-based systems have been developed for electronic commerce systems (e.g. PersonaLogic, Firefly, BargainFinder, Jango, Kasbah, AuctionBot).

# BUILDING AN INTERNET COMMERCE COMMUNITY

As shown in the Shark.com site, building an Internet commerce community is helpful in ensuring the success of the cyberbusiness. Some of the areas that could be classified as Internet commerce hotspots in Australia are discussed on the following pages.

# Internet banking

In December 1995 Advance Bank (now St George) began offering banking on the Internet and immediately took on the leader position as the first Internet bank in Australia. By June 1996 it was on second place in the *Money Page*'s Cyberspace Top Ten Banks, immediately behind Security First Network Bank of the United States. In the United States, the virtual bank Wingspan-Bank.com (www.wingspanbank.com) opened for business in 1999. It advertised that in the 60 seconds it takes to find a parking spot at your old bank, you could get an answer on your loan application from WingspanBank. At the Commonwealth Bank in Australia, figures showed that of the 216 000 Internet banking customers, 110 000 used NetBank, 26 000 use Quickline, the bank's Internet business service, and 80 000 use Commonwealth Securities, the bank's online stock broking service.[14]

# Service-selling sites

Originally it seemed that cyber shopping malls would be the most effective way to get noted on the Web. Large department stores have not joined malls — they have set up their own sites. Retail shops that have succeeded have thrived by turning their customers into a community. The bookshop Amazon.com encourages community feeling by getting people to write reviews of books they have read, by encouraging the buyer to interact with the authors via email, and by getting customers to register with Eyes, a service that notifies customers of new books that are likely to interest them. Harris Technology enrols Internet clients in the Harris PC Club and offers special benefits, such as discounts on certain products, to the PC Club cardholder.

> *A general rule of thumb is that online consumers are interested in making better informed purchases more quickly, rather than getting the lowest price. The more tiresome a purchase is in the physical world, the more likely consumers are to try an online alternative. Because shopping for a mortgage is difficult and tedious, a site offering straightforward and easy-to-understand comparisons could be a hit. Because buying a CD is easy, (online music stores) must offer far more than a physical music store to draw in the shoppers.*[15]

In the service area Qantas builds community identity on its web site by allowing members of its Frequent Flyer club to buy tickets and to check their points online. If customers have sent packages via Qantas, they can trace the progress of consignments using the web site.

# Online publishing

This is an exciting area of Internet commerce. The major newspapers of Australia are now online, and so far their offerings are free. They are making money from advertising. The *Sydney Morning Herald* accepts classified advertisements over the Internet (see the case study at the end of the chapter). Publishers are extending their field of interest and joining with others in joint ventures as seen in the following Business insite.

# Downloadable music, video and books

The real power of the Internet lies in the user's ability to download finished products such as music, video and books digitally. For songs there are sound files that use a new compression technology called MP3, which can shrink a 60-Mb-sound file to less than 5 Mb by eliminating all the information the human ear cannot detect.

In October 1999, Yahoo! introduced an Internet broadcast service to position itself as a global distribution network for music, video and books online.[16] Yahoo! has identified four ways of making money from broadcasting over the Internet:

1. charging music labels to turn songs into streaming media and distribute them to the Yahoo! user base
2. seeking a percentage of the transaction fee when consumers pay for music online
3. building a series of super-sized music databases
4. aggregating content and posting advertisements.

Chaos Music in Australia sells mail-order CDs, and Sanity.com launched in Australia in late 1999. MP3.com distributes CD-quality music via the MP3 format and turned over $1 million in revenue in 1998–99. MP3 launched a new listening service at the beginning of 2000 called My.MP3.com, where customers can download their CDs onto the MP3 server and listen to them at any time on their computer by logging into the MP3 web site. Since launching the service, music companies represented by the Recording Industry Association of America (RIAA) have begun legal proceedings to stop the service, arguing that MP3 is breaking copyright laws. MP3 argues that their service is 'nothing more than a virtual CD player' and intends to fight the action.

Digital books such as SofBook by Virtual Press, RocketBook by NuvoMedia and Everybook by Everybook, Inc., have also made their appearance.[17] A new medium called electronic paper has been developed at the MIT's Media Laboratory. It is a flexible durable electronic paper and ink combination. An electronic current is passed through a stack of the new 'pages' and tiny electronic ink capsules within the paper rearrange themselves into words. They remain there using no extra power until the user wishes to erase or rearrange them. The paper can change the image on a page as often as 20 times a second and points the way for books that can display video clips also.[18]

## EXERCISES

1. What are the advantages and disadvantages of downloading music over the Web?
2. Write a short report on the types of portable player that may be used for storing downloadable music in MP3 format.
3. Write a short report on the current position of one of the following:
   (a) downloadable video clips
   (b) music
   (c) books.
4. The Web is revolutionising electronic publishing. Write a report on one of the new book devices.

## Business-to-business transactions

**Business-to-business** e-commerce refers to any transaction between two parties who are commercial in concept such as proprietary companies or partnerships. Also, if a seller enters into the transaction to make a profit and the buyer enters into the transaction as part of the means by which he will ultimately profit, then the transaction is business. Finally the nature of the transactions often defines 'business', for example, by looking at the following:

- frequency of the transaction
- dollar value of the transaction
- quantity of items purchased in the transaction
- role of the transaction in the supply chain.[19]

Coca-Cola Amatil Australia (CCAA) now uses eProcure, an Australian software product that connects requesters to approvers and buyers to suppliers, automating the functions from order making, sending and receiving the product. The self-service web interface ordering model has a level of access to the catalogue and is used for ordering IT equipment, stationery, travel, entertainment, contract and project-based services. GartnerGroup research has shown that online procurement can save companies up to 20 per cent in costs (or an average of 7 per cent to 10 per cent).[20] Examine the case study at the end of this chapter for an example of business-to-business e-commerce.

## SUMMARY

This chapter has outlined the techniques and methods that are useful for making Internet commerce a reality in the business environment. The old five P's and new five P's of marketing have been used to illustrate the ways in which Internet commerce can become a profitable business proposition. The cyber businessperson needs to consider product, price, place, promotion and people, and packaging in establishing an Internet commerce site. However, it is vital to take into account the five P's of marketing as set out by Tom Patty. These are paradox, perspective, paradigm, persuasion and passion. In this chapter we have looked at examples of Internet commerce sites that have shown attention to these new five P's of marketing. Finally, we have reiterated the need to plan, organise, control and monitor the web business. Examples of successful sites that have concentrated on building a community have been given. Business-to-business e-commerce has been examined and an overview of setting up an e-commerce web site has been given.

**key terms**

| | | |
|---|---|---|
| agents | paradigm | place |
| business-to-business | paradox | prices |
| 'clicks and bricks' model | passion | product |
| 'clicks and mortar' approach | people | promotion |
| comparison shopping | perspective | templates |
| packaging | persuasion | wizards |

# —ADONLINE: A PUBLISHING EXTRANET

**Case Study 1**

*This case study adds to information in the Business insite in chapter 1 on page 11. Please read that insite before attempting this case study.*

John Fairfax Holdings Ltd is a publishing house that produces high-quality broadsheet newspapers in Sydney and Melbourne, including the *Sydney Morning Herald*, the *Age* in Melbourne and the national tabloid-sized, *Australian Financial Review*. The company employs approximately 5000 people and has six main production sites in New South Wales and Victoria. It began online publishing of the *Sydney Morning Herald* in 1996. The classified call centre of the *Sydney Morning Herald* handles about 13 000 calls per week, with the greatest number being received on Thursdays (Payne, et. al., 1998). The company has been in the forefront of electronic commerce in that it has offered its online publications for free but has attracted high-profile advertisers to its site. It established the 'Trading Room' and a subscription model for researchers who wish to search the online archives of the publications. Researchers are able submit credit card details, for amounts up to $A50 and as articles are found for downloading, $A2 amounts are subtracted from the $50 stake. This model enables the use of credit cards for small transaction amounts.

## Background

AdOnline is a suite of software modules developed by internal information technology staff and some contracted third-party developers. AdOnline allows selected and favoured clients, who are regular advertisers in either the *Sydney Morning Herald* or the *Age* in Melbourne, to place advertisements into these publications directly from their own back-end systems via the Internet. AdOnline was conceived almost two years ago so that Fairfax could increase its efficiency, could be seen as a 'leading edge' force in the electronic media and e-commerce as well as maintaining the reputation as a dominant player in the print media.

Advertisements are entered into the two Fairfax proprietary, back-end, legacy systems without having to liaise with the call centres (known as the 'phone room' in the industry). AdOnline leverages the Internet substantially as the medium of transfer of information between the advertiser and the company's two main publishing systems. This project has seen the potential of the World Wide Web being realised by Fairfax to the extent that every advertisement that appears in the printed products now also appears on the Fairfax web sites. The New Business Development Manager identified the key business drivers as:

- being closer to the customer
- the flexibility in cost reductions, therefore improving service levels (e.g. fewer people ring through their ads at the peak time, Thursday. The longer waiting time had been causing people to hang up.)
- the shorter time taken to register an ad on AdOnline (about 10 to 40 per cent of the total time currently taken to log a call via phone)
- the additional material (e.g. multimedia information) that can be provided via AdOnline.

The actual budget for the project was $A100 000 for equipment plus $A250 000 for internal and external development costs. It is predicted that this investment will amount to saving for Fairfax of $A900 000 from inaccurate telephone logging.

The software client that is delivered to any user's personal computer was developed in both Visual Basic and Java scripts. The two application program interface (API) modules that interface with the back-end systems (Sii in Sydney, and Atex and Cybergraphic in Melbourne) were developed as PERL scripts running on the Unix server. There is also software that allows the client software, when it is offline, to render an advertisement as if it were already in either of the two back-end systems. They emulate the text composition languages from two different major publishing systems on a standard Windows 32 platform.

**Advantages**

There has been positive feedback from customers. Company A sends in between 30 and 40 text-based classified advertisements per week and it compliments some of the ads on the web site with images taken with a digital camera (supplied by Fairfax) of the same property. The peak time for uploading advertisements is Thursday afternoon between 2.00 p.m. and 5.00 p.m. Company B sends in between 5 and 10 ads per week on a Tuesday. Both representatives felt that the system was a boon and that Fairfax was good at listening to feedback. Company A felt the system was of 'great benefit' in that it allowed them to 'gang send' the ads when they were ready and they were able to see the ads *before* they are published. A whole week's work can be delivered to Fairfax for the cost of a single phone call. Company B liked the ease with which they could edit ads and send the ads at a time to suit them and not wait in long telephone queues. Both Company A and Company B said staff training was accomplished in a few hours.

**Disadvantages**

The New Business Manager identified the threat of unreliable technology and the fear of denial of service from the Internet. As with any extranet, the possibility of sharing information demands that attention be paid to appropriate security measures. The Classified Call Centre manager felt that the product needed further development and promotion. The issue of trust was a major issue in the setting up of such an extranet — some clients would be completely trustworthy whilst others would need to be checked all the time. There is definitely a need to ensure that call centre staff are encouraged to see this technology as a benefit rather than a threat — in fact this could be a major challenge for the industrial relations staff.

**SOURCE:** C. Payne and E. Lawrence 1999, 'Extranet, Extranet: Changing Publishing Paradigms. A Case Study of Extranets in Advertising', *Proceedings Volume 2 of the 10th Australasian Conference on Information Systems (ACIS)*, Wellington, New Zealand, 1–3 December 1999, pp. 725–35

## EXERCISE

This case study has shown how a large publishing company has re-engineered its business processes to align them with electronic commerce. Examine this case study from the following viewpoints:

- new ways of doing business through technology
- evaluation of the organisations' response to customer needs
- ways to decrease cost and increase competitive advantage
- assessment of the customer base and their capacity to trade online
- assessment of products and services and how these may be marketed to the customer
- outsourcing requirements
- estimations of timing into the digital market, schedules for development
- assessment of the potential effects of disintermediation and reintermediation
- creation of a detailed partnering strategy
- financial requirements of the Internet business.

# Case Study 2 —PORTALS: NEW PUBLIC UTILITIES

According to Power and Jerjian, portals are web sites that are used as launch-pads by customers looking to surf the Web. The most prominent examples are AOL (America Online), which joined Time Warner in 2000, Yahoo!, MSN (Microsoft Network), Lycos, Disney/Go and Excite. Power and Jerjian believe that the strategy of the portals is to become global supermarkets, providing everything for an individual at home, at work and on the move. They call portals the new public utilities and believe that portals put customers first. This customer relationship is what the stock market considers to be the most important asset of these Internet companies. The table below summarises the customer relationship valuations as reported at a seminar by Power at Temple University in Philadelphia on 4 February 2000.

| TABLE 4.6 | CUSTOMER RELATIONSHIP VALUATIONS | | |
|---|---|---|---|
| COMPANY NAME | ELECTRONIC CUSTOMER RELATIONSHIPS | MARKET CAPITALISATION (US$) | VALUE OF EACH RELATIONSHIP |
| AOL | 50 million | $100 billion | $2000 |
| Yahoo! | 40 million | $40 billion | $1000 |
| Amazon | 13 million | $26 billion | $2000 |
| eBay | 5 million | $20 billion | $4000 |

Power and Jerjian also believe that these portals perform the function of 'info-mediaries' or agents that will surf the net the find the best deal for the customer. They will not jeopardise the relationship because so much depends on it.

**SOURCE:** adapted from T. Power and G. Jerjian 1999, *The Battle of the Portals*, The Ecademy, www.ecademy.com

## RESEARCH QUESTIONS

1. Write a report on portals covering such items as: the history of portals, the strengths and weaknesses of portals and the future of portals.
2. Visit the Ecademy site at www.ecademy.com and report on the '12 Ecommandments of Ecommerce'.

## QUESTIONS

1. In this chapter it has been stated that service industries are likely to profit from Internet commerce. Prepare a marketing plan for getting a service industry business ready for Internet commerce.
2. Prepare a discussion paper to outline the benefits of Internet commerce for a particular business of your choice.
3. Research the development of intelligent agents. Discuss why they are unpopular with online shops. Try to develop a method to sell the idea of intelligent agents to online businesses.
4. Select one of the businesses outlined in this chapter and critique the commercial web site they have developed.

## SUGGESTED READING

Bayles, D. 1998, *Extranets: Building the Business-to-Business Web*, Prentice Hall, United States.

Hill, T. 1993, *The Essence of Operations Management*, Prentice Hall, United Kingdom.

Kalakota, R. and Robinson, M. 1999, *E-Business: Roadmap for Success*, Addison-Wesley Longman, United States.

Kalakota, R. and Whinston, A. 1997, *Electronic Commerce — A Manager's Guide*, Addison-Wesley, United States.

net.Genesis Corporation 1996, *Build a World Wide Web Commerce Center*, John Wiley & Sons, New York.

Pfaffenberger, B. 1998, *Building a Strategic Extranet*, IDG Books, United States.

## END NOTES

1. Teliatnik, R. 1997, *Small Business Marketing*, www.rimart.com/idignews/mark24.html.
2. Patty. T. 1997, *Mastering the new Five P's of Marketing*, www.chiatday.com/raw_materials/insights/5ps/5p_mkt.html.
3. Campbell, V. 1996, 'Promises, promises', *Information Age*, May, p. 40.
4. Patty, op. cit.
5. Survey by Top 100 Australia (www.top100.com.au), 26 March 2000, and survey by www.wheredidwego.com.au, 24 March 2000.
6. Lawrence, E. 1998, 'Setting up a shopfront', *Hands-on Solutions: E-commerce*, CCH Australia, p. 25.
7. Creedy, S. 1997, 'Aunty casts Net to catch up with PC generation', *Australian*, 12 August, p. 33.
8. Sofcom 1997, *Sofcom Australia's Premier Internet Publisher*, www.sofcom.com.au.
9. Hill, T. 1993, *The Essence of Operations Management*, Prentice Hall, United Kingdom.
10. Newton, S. 1999, 'Electronic business: factors for success', MA thesis for School of Computing Sciences, University of Technology, Sydney.
11. Lanfear, K. 1995, private e-mail on strategies for implementation of World Wide Web, Networks Information Products Coordinator of United States Geographic Services.
12. ibid.
13. Lawrence, op. cit.
14. Nicholas, K. 1999, 'Net banking expected to take off', Biz.Com, *Sydney Morning Herald*, 31 August, p. 25.
15. Anderson, C. 1997, 'In search of the perfect market', *Economist*, 10 May, p. 9.
16. Needham, K. 1999, 'Yahoo broadcast tunes in Web's absolute power', Biz.Com, *Sydney Morning Herald*, 28 September, p. 32.
17. Silberman, S. 1998, 'Ex Libris: The joys of curling up with a good digital reading device', *Wired*, July, pp. 98–104.
18. Austin, K. 1999, 'Sign of the tomes', Icon, *Sydney Morning Herald*, 29 May, pp. 4–5.
19. Macpherson, A. 1998, 'Business-to-business transactions', *Hands-on Solutions: E-commerce*, CCH Australia Ltd, p. 7.
20. *E-Commerce Today* 1999, 'Coca-Cola Amatil embraces online procurement', issue 61, 23 September, www.ecommercetoday.com.au.

# 5

# Electronic payment systems

## LEARNING Outcomes

You will have mastered the material in this chapter when you can:

- explain the various types of electronic payment system
- define electronic purchasing, explain the benefits and list the forms of transactions that can be used to transact electronic purchasing
- explain the importance of the supply chain–customer relationship
- identify the security needs of offline and online electronic purchasing systems
- define EDI and demonstrate how invoicing and payments can be made
- explain the advantages and disadvantages of EDI relative to other forms of electronic payment systems
- describe and explain the value of various e-cash systems and smart cards.

*'Banks can dramatically reduce the cost of transactions using the Internet and converging technologies. The average cost of making a banking transaction in developed countries ... halves to $0.52 using telephone banking, $0.27 per ATM transaction, $0.015 cents for PC banking, then drops to $0.01 using the Internet — a saving of 99 per cent compared to traditional arrangements.'*

Department of Foreign Affairs and Trade 1999, *Creating a Clearway on the New Silk Road: International Business and Policy Trends in Internet Commerce*, Commonwealth of Australia, Canberra, p. 41

# INTRODUCTION

With rapid technological development, changing technologies and business re-engineering, there is a specific need for managers to be able to identify appropriate new technologies and to use them in the successful operation of their own business. This chapter concentrates our attention on how electronic commerce, specifically **electronic payment systems (EPS)**, can work effectively in Australia and internationally in a range of organisational and institutional settings. Better supply chain–customer relationships and **electronic purchasing** are developed when the electronic mechanisms are well understood and implemented in business in ways that add value to businesses and improve effectiveness, efficiency and profitability. An EPS is a process that describes how value (usually **money**) is exchanged for goods, services or information. In some contexts, the EPS will be part of a value-adding process, while in others it can be a direct payment with no value being added to the good or service. An EPS can be designed to enhance business operations and ensure better customer–supplier relationships.

When you purchase groceries at a supermarket or buy milk from the local convenience store, or buy a large item like a washing machine or perhaps even a car, do you use the same form of exchange? Many people now use a credit card or debit card or cash to buy groceries. They will invariably use cash to purchase the milk. With larger items such as the washing machine or a car, customers will arrange other forms of payment. Some will pay cash (usually as a cheque) and others will use a credit loan or hire-purchase agreement to buy the car.

Purchasing is the process of exchanging currency or value in the form of money for goods, services or information. Electronic payment systems involve that same exchange process but use an electronic intermediary to facilitate the exchange. Instead of paying for the groceries with cash, it is now common for customers to use an electronic transfer of funds system using the same cards they utilise for their personal banking. The electronic system validates the value of the exchange, debits the customer and credits the supplier, all electronically. These systems eliminate cash and eliminate the need for frequent banking just to obtain cash. It is worth thinking about all the forms of transaction that can occur using EPS. They range from small-scale and individual buying of groceries and household items at one end of the scale to large-scale exchange of products and components, valued in millions of dollars, using **electronic data interchange (EDI)** processes at the other end.

In the global trade in services (including software, entertainment and information products and professional services), which now accounts for well over $40 billion of US exports alone, electronic purchasing has the potential to revolutionise trade by lowering transaction costs. It will also assist in increasing the potential implementation of just-in-time manufacturing processes, improving delivery time of component parts and facilitating new types of commercial transaction. Real-time ordering of and payment for supplies, components, services or information must facilitate greater efficiency and induce the potential for expanded trade at regional, national and international levels.

# FROM TRADITIONAL PAYMENT SYSTEMS TO EPS

Throughout recorded history we have engaged in the exchange of value in many ways. In earlier times goods and services were exchanged by barter or by tokens of various sorts. Some two or three millennia ago, the first forms of symbolic tokens with specific values emerged. These primitive coins and tokens formed the basis of the modern forms of exchange, which derived their value from societies' recognition of the value of precious metals such as gold. In the immediacy of the twenty-first century, the value of coinage and paper money is found in the comparison of one currency against another. Coinage and paper (plastic in Australia and Thailand) notes now have their own intrinsic value and an acceptance in society that generates and maintains that value. If a currency is overvalued because of government policy or because of economic conditions, governments can now devalue the currency relative to the currencies of other countries as Thailand did by 18 per cent in July 1997.

No matter which form money takes, it performs four functions.
- Money is a medium of exchange.
- Money is a means of account (stating how much is owed and by who to who).
- Money provides a standard of deferred payment.
- Money is a defined store of value.

Any asset that performs all four of these functions can be defined as money. The question we are confronted with in discussing electronic forms of money or exchange is: Do the various types of electronic purchasing perform all four functions? This question needs to be considered as this chapter is read and discussed.

Today we also have the added impact of exchange processes that allow us to exchange the value of goods and services in ways other than by using coin or paper money. For many decades bills of exchange, gems and precious metals have been used as alternative forms of exchange. In the 1990s, the emergence of EPS has further revolutionised the way we buy and sell goods and services. Traditionally we exchanged value in a process that engaged us in a multi-step process (see figure 5.1). Today that multi-step process has been significantly changed to reflect the electronic exchange of value (see figure 5.2).

In Australia and most other nations, central or reserve banks play a key role in the exchange of value, control of the money supply and control of payment systems. Through monetary policy these central banks attempt to control the level of inflation in an economy and impact on growth rates of **gross domestic product (GDP)**. In recent times, currency problems have forced the Malaysian central bank (Bank Negara) to set policy to affect the nature of money and the way banking systems exchange value in Malaysia.

> *This move towards consolidation is in line with the Government's policy not to bail out weak companies but to rationalise businesses towards higher productivity. Business consolidation through merger is indeed a common practice globally to achieve economies of scale and higher productivity.*[1]

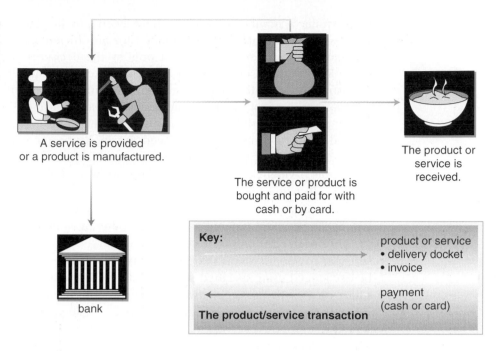

**FIGURE 5.1:** Paying for goods and services in the traditional way

A service is provided or a product is manufactured.

The service or product is bought and paid for with cash or by card.

The product or service is received.

bank

Key:

→ product or service
• delivery docket
• invoice

← payment (cash or card)

**The product/service transaction**

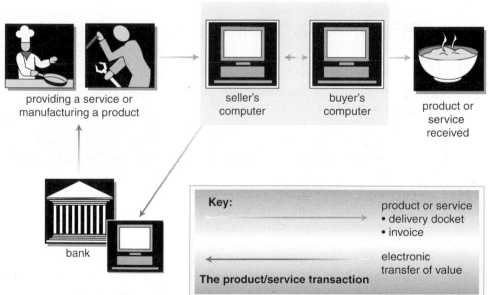

**FIGURE 5.2:** Paying for goods and services using electronic technology

providing a service or manufacturing a product

seller's computer

buyer's computer

product or service received

bank

Key:

→ product or service
• delivery docket
• invoice

← electronic transfer of value

**The product/service transaction**

Thailand, where the crisis had a greater impact than in Malaysia, is drafting a new Bank of Thailand Act that will explicitly identify price stability as the main objective of monetary policy, as well as legislate for a Monetary Policy Board and its procedures and responsibilities.[2]

In Australia a number of policies have been put in place to facilitate a process where payments can be facilitated for an efficient exchange process. Australian businesses are affected not only by the decisions of governments and the Reserve Bank on exchange processes, they are required to report to the Australian Securities and Investments Commission about the nature, extent and impact of their payment systems and business activities.[3] To facilitate efficient clearing of payments lodged electronically, there have been systems developed to improve the speed at which transfer payments can be verified to support better cash flows in business.[4]

Electronic payment systems operate in various ways. The ways that exchange can occur electronically include:

- electronic financial payment systems (where value is exchanged using a system where a card is debited with some value or where a card allows value to be transferred from one account to another)
- Internet payment systems (where systems are in place which allow value to be exchanged using specified protocols on the Internet)
- **smart card** payment systems (where a silicon chip is used to transfer stored value from a card to a business system in exchange for goods and/or services).

The first half of this chapter deals with the first two systems and the latter part with smart card systems of exchange.[5]

# ROLE OF EDI IN ELECTRONIC PAYMENT SYSTEMS

Within large-scale agricultural, manufacturing or service organisations, the processes of exchange are more complex and perplexing in terms of exchange of value.

Electronic data interchange (EDI) is the transfer of organisational or business data in a structured electronic format, from one computer system or application in one business to another computer system or application, using an electronic link.

For two decades or more now EDI has facilitated the transfer of data, invoicing, information, ordering and now payments in complex supply-chain situations where there could be many suppliers to a single organisation or many purchasers of an organisation's goods or services (see figure 5.3).

In the real complexity of the business world the linkages between suppliers and consumers can be exceedingly complex (see figure 5.4). EDI allows some simplification and order in this complexity and the adoption of an EPS in conjunction with the EDI process allows the transfer of value to be speedily resolved and thus enable the maintenance of cash flow that is so important for large- and small-scale business operations. The banker's role in the exchange of value generated by EDI has developed into electronic exchange mechanisms that can be used within the complex situations of EDI or the simple purchase of groceries or petrol.

**FIGURE 5.3:**
EDI links
between
suppliers and
purchasers

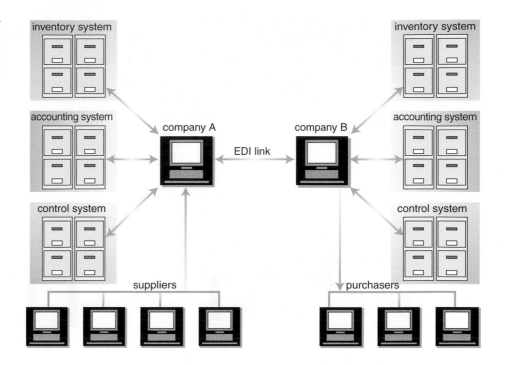

**FIGURE 5.4:**
Complex
relationships
in business

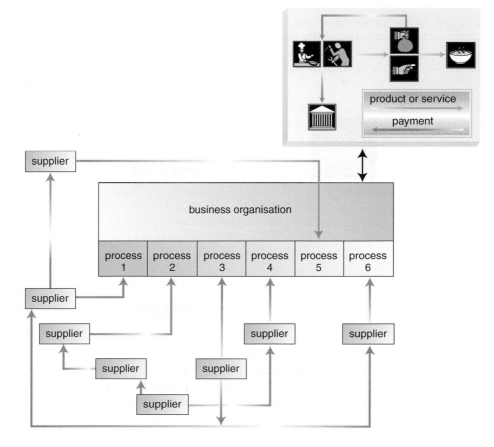

# EFT AND EFTPOS

Electronic funds transfer (EFT) and electronic funds transfer at point of sale (EFTPOS) are electronic tools currently in use to effectively transfer the value of exchange process for goods or services or information. EFT is any transfer of funds initiated through an electronic terminal, telephone, modem, computer or magnetic tape so as to order, instruct, or authorise a financial institution to debit or credit an account.[6] EFT utilises computer and telecommunication components both to supply and to transfer money or financial assets (see figure 5.5).

**FIGURE 5.5:**
EFT and shopping

shopping process

shop's bank

EFT

customer's bank

This transfer process is information based. EFTPOS is a form of EFT where the purchaser is physically at the point of sale, such as the checkout in a supermarket or in a petrol station. EFTPOS operates either on credit or debit cards, where the value of the exchange is immediately debited against an existing bank account. On credit cards, EFTPOS systems check the validity of the card status and then credit the value of the exchange against the credit card account for future payment by the card holder (see figure 5.6).

**FIGURE 5.6:**
EFTPOS, payments and shopping

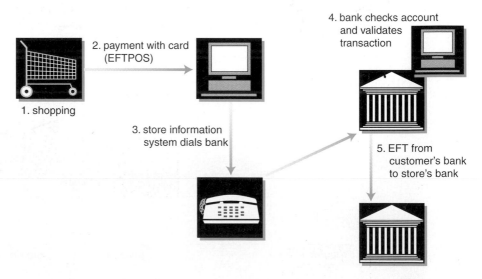

1. shopping

2. payment with card (EFTPOS)

3. store information system dials bank

4. bank checks account and validates transaction

5. EFT from customer's bank to store's bank

The roles of EFT and EFTPOS in electronic payment systems will form an important part of a discussion later in this chapter of **e-cash** and the ways we can generate exchange value in electronic commerce.

# EPS IN A SIMPLE BUSINESS ENVIRONMENT

In a simple trader relationship between supplier and customer, goods and services are exchanged for cash payment. This process is complicated by the role of banks and other financial institutions where the cash is stored. The banks become an intermediary in the transfer of value across a merchant/trading system (see figure 5.7).

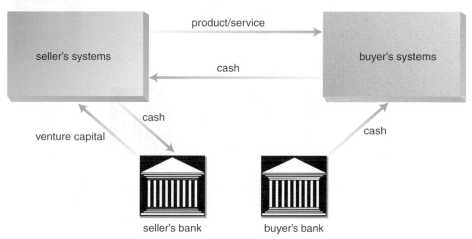

**FIGURE 5.7:** Banks as an intermediary in the trading system

If payment for goods and services is made electronically, this trading relationship is altered. And it is altered according to whether the exchange of money value for the goods and services is made online or offline. An online system is one where the business transactions are occurring in real time between two computers and/or servers. People are not an essential component of online transactions. Processing is automatic (see figure 5.8).

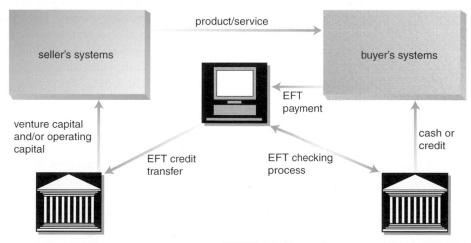

**FIGURE 5.8:** The trading system with an online EPS

Offline trading refers to systems where the electronic or any other component acts as an intermediary in the system between the customer and the supplier. The process is not direct. It doesn't happen automatically. There has to be intervention by a person in at least one stage in the process. We have now become more used to using magnetic stripe cards, ATMs, EFT and EFTPOS. But we are also beginning to see the more effective use of automatic, real-time exchange of data in EDI systems or purchasing goods on the Internet (see figure 5.9).

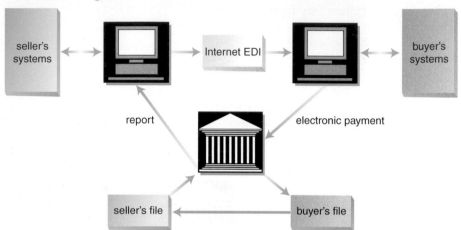

**FIGURE 5.9:** A trading system with an offline EPS

# Requirements of an online trading system

When you purchase a washing machine in an electrical goods store and use a MasterCard or Visa or your bank debit card (EFTPOS) or a stored value card, what happens? There is firstly a requirement that the supplier of the goods has the required equipment to facilitate processing of the card you present. That process represents a cost to the supplier not only in terms of hire of the machines but also cost in terms of time delays that might occur in the transfer of the money you pay through the EPS. Some would rightly argue that such time delays are very rare and, in fact, real-time transactions are more efficient as it saves the retailer spending/wasting time in the physical banking process in queuing up and counting cheques, cash, etc. Using the Internet at home to purchase goods or services can also incur a delay for the supplier as there are new requirements involved. These include the time taken to read the Internet orders, the time taken to process those orders and, because nearly all Internet selling sites use credit card transactions as their form of EPS, there is time involved in transferring information to the credit card process.

As a customer you also have requirements of an EPS. You need to know that the information you are allowing to be transferred electronically is safe and secure from entrapment by others. You need to be able to trace orders if there are delays and you need to be able to audit all of your purchases if you use EPS on a regular basis. Banks, as the intermediaries in trading systems using EPS, usually provide an audit or record of all transactions on a monthly basis that is then the responsibility of the supplier on one side and customers on the other side to audit for themselves.

McKeown and Watson argue that some products are better than others in maintaining the appropriate customer–supplier relationship in an online situation.[7] **Supply chains** have to be efficient throughout. For their marketing of an end product to be effective in an online context, there are some principles that need to be adhered to:

- They must be high in information content.
- They must be readily ordered in an online context.
- They must be accessible to customers.

From the supplier side, products, services and information need to meet these criteria to be sellable products in an online situation. However, these are reflections of only one side of the process. Customers have to want to buy. In terms of the simple electronic trading model used in this chapter, customers will purchase goods using various payment systems such as an EFT system or EFTPOS only when they are satisfied that the goods meet the required quality, are value for money and that their transaction is secure. Clarke suggests that there are a number of other issues that must be addressed in terms of customers' willingness to use EPS to trade electronically. These are:

- user needs and product features, which have already been discussed above
- corporate processes and structures — will companies have to employ more or less staff? Will administrative procedures have to change?
- corporate strategy — will market share and the opportunities for organisational development and growth change?
- regulation — will all companies have equal access in a business world where payments are made electronically? How will governments regulate the exchange processes and control the economic effects of this type of trading?
- economics — will electronic trading affect the supply of money and the level of economic activity throughout the country? Will such trading result in more or less taxation?
- social processes and structures — will trading and transaction activity need to be monitored or traced? Will electronic payments decrease transaction anonymity?
- political governance — what effects will EPSs have on the levels of government interference in supplier and consumer behaviours?[8]

It is important not only to understand how simple transaction processes work in an electronic context. We must also have some understanding of what happens in a complex supply–customer relationship with large organisations.

# EDI — TRADING AND PURCHASING IN COMPLEX BUSINESS ENVIRONMENTS

## EDI and how it works

Throughout the past century, physical distribution channels of goods and services in businesses have been established. These distribution channels (or supply chains) were based on getting the raw materials of a product to a manufacturing plant, processing those raw materials and then establishing ways or channels of warehousing, distributing and moving the finished products to market. Part of the process was the appointment of intermediaries who took responsibility for redistribution of goods, invariably from warehouses. However, there were always dilemmas about how best to manage the process as there were inventories, transportation, warehousing, order communications and best utilisation of floor space to be managed. The problem was how to integrate the management process. This led to the development of distribution managers in large organisations whose responsibilities were about managing the logistics of goods from production to market.

There are various activities that have to be integrated into the information flow and physical distribution process in any supply chain. Part of these processes are the establishment and operation of various intermediaries who also need to be part of the scheme of management of the primary organisation and who themselves have management problems to resolve with their information flows and physical channels of operation (see figure 5.10).

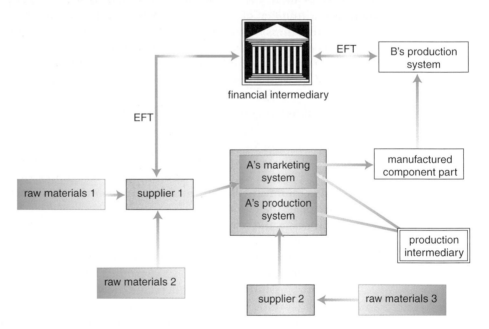

**FIGURE 5.10:** Intermediaries in the supply chain and EFT process

In a more complex environment, these activities can include:
- *manufacturing*
  - supply of raw materials
  - manufacturing processes
- *distribution and intermediations*
  - transportation
  - storage
  - utilisation of space

- *marketing and intermediations*
  - advertising
  - promotions
  - market research
  - market testing
  - forecasting
- *retailing*
  - merchandising
  - inventory management
  - re-ordering management
  - forward planning.

How can all of these be integrated into a supply chain model and assist in understanding the trading process? Figure 5.11 is a theoretical example of how organisations might put these various activities together.

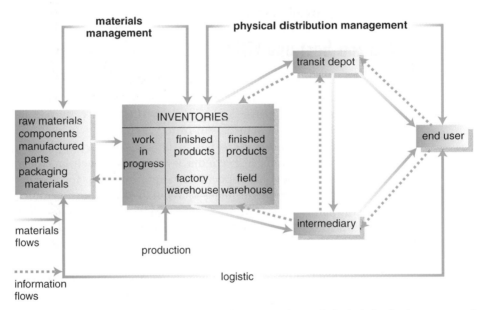

**FIGURE 5.11:** Integrating activities into the information flow and physical distribution process of a supply chain. **SOURCE:** J. Gattorna and D. Walters 1996, *Managing the Supply Chain: A Strategic Perspective*, Macmillan, Great Britain, p. 10

This diagram suggests that supply chains begin and end with customers. Customers determine what needs to be produced and in what quantities. EDI is an electronic process that is designed to supplement and improve the nature and operation of the supply chain process. This process arose with greater access to and use of computers in business, with improvements in tele-communications, and with the needs of companies geographically distant both locally, regionally and internationally. Other factors that have encouraged the development of EDI include the demands of new management techniques introduced and developed with the development of manufacturing in Japan in the 1960s and onwards. These new techniques, such as total quality management (TQM) and just-in-time (JIT), demand a level of responsiveness and efficiency that is customer rather than supplier driven. Such responsiveness requires constant and immediate recognition of the demands that a computer-to-computer system can meet most effectively.

EDI is a structured computer-to-computer transfer of information. EDI allows the transfer of business information or business transactions between companies (large and small) or between companies and government agencies or between companies and banks. EDI processes must have the following characteristics:

- the exchange of information must be in a structured format so that the data is placed and found in predetermined places in the electronic message
- the format or structure of the information must be agreed upon by both the receiver and the sender
- the data must be machine readable. EDI does not involve the sending of data by fax from one organisation and then the re-keying of that data in the new place of operation.

## Who can best use EDI?

The following types of company can best use EDI:

- companies where there is a large volume of supplies and suppliers (e.g. the Coles Myer organisation or Woolworths, where there can be hundreds of suppliers/manufacturers supplying their products to those companies)
- companies where there has to be careful tracking of supplies because of dangerous goods (e.g. chemical companies, such as Hoechst) or where the goods may perish in specific time periods (e.g. food such as dairy produce or eggs or fresh fruit juices or vegetables or pharmaceuticals)
- companies where there is a large volume of paperwork involved (e.g. import/export companies where customs and excise controls in various companies require detailed documentation and audit)
- companies where the manufacturing process relies on just-in-time practices (e.g. automobile manufacturers in Australia, such as Ford, GMH, Toyota and Mitsubishi, where JIT is used to precisely demand delivery of very large numbers and precise amounts of components in a specific order or at a specific time).

EDI requires a connection to be made between trading partners. Therefore, there is the need to ensure that both trading partners have compatible software so that the electronic communication process will actually happen. The EDI communication process can be simple or complex depending on the requirements of the supply-chain relationship and depending on whether the communication is direct or part of a network process. Such supply-chain processes include value-added networks or VANs. A VAN is a network where data is transmitted and accepted by businesses in various formats that are converted on acceptance to formats that can be used by the business receiving the data. This process adds value to the raw data that was originally sent. In addition, VANs also perform other tasks. VANs are capable of holding information in electronic storage until it is required by a business. This process adds value to the management of information through management of time, enabling businesses to conduct business in frameworks that suit their production or servicing schedules. This is very important in international exchanges using EDI where there are significant time differences in the working day.

VANs operate independently of businesses and as an intermediary in the EDI process. They store and send on information and data in forms that are acceptable by the businesses receiving the data. VANs act as intermediaries for large numbers of businesses, acting as a focal point in the multi-transactional, multi-nodal nature of most businesses. VANs act as a router of data, and act as a consultancy point for new business. The most important VANs in Australia include Tradelink and T-Net, which are run by Telstra, and EXIT, which is run by OTC, Australia. The network processes used in an EDI transaction are shown in figure 5.12.

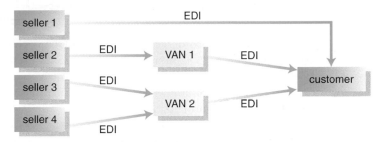

**FIGURE 5.12:** How EDI works

# EDI standards

The EDI communication process illustrated in figure 5.12 depends on the existence and acceptance of specific EDI standards and protocols that have to be adopted by each user in both simple and complex EDI relationships. Linking a customer with a supplier in an EDI relationship involves a hierarchy of communication levels, each of which has different accepted standards and protocols.

## Communications infrastructure level

This is the system level that permits communication to happen — telephone lines, satellites, electronic exchanges, etc. These are the conduits through which information flows. In Australia, the major owner of this infrastructure is Telstra. However, new operators such as Cable & Wireless Optus, Hutchinsons and Foxtel now have the capacity to use other forms of infrastructure to exchange information electronically.

## EDI messaging/communications level

The majority of standards and protocols used in EDI communications are derived from the International Consultative Committee for Telephony. EDI standards for messages usually involve the data being broken down into smaller packages for transmission of information and sent to a receiver where they are reassembled into a coherent message (see figure 5.13).

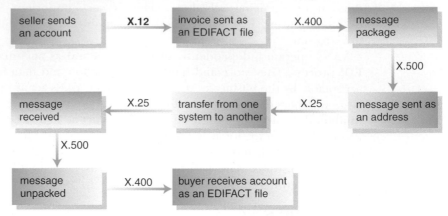

**FIGURE 5.13:** EDI process protocols

The exchange protocols used in the EDI process above perform different functions. The X.25 standard allows electronic messages to be broken up into specific packages of information (packets), which are sent to the receiving PC and enable reassembling of the original information sent. The **X.25 protocol** controls the EDI process at the communications level. At another level, the **X.400** and **X.500 protocols** enable the message to be handled by the sending and receiving PCs. They are not concerned with content but, in the case of the X.400, with how the data can be broken up and packaged and, in the case of the X.500, with addresses and directories used in the EDI process.

As a result of the need for specific standards for successful EDI processes, a number of standards have been established throughout the world including **TRADACOMS** in Great Britain. In Australia **EDIFACT** is the standard used in EDI.

EDIFACT (electronic data interchange for administration, commerce and transport) is the United Nations-agreed standard for EDI transmission. This protocol is recommended within the framework of the United Nations. The rules of EDIFACT are approved and published by UN/ECE in the United Nations Trade Data Interchange Directory (UNTDID) and are maintained under agreed procedures. The details of EDIFACT syntax, message structures and specific protocols can be found at www.unece.org/trade/untdid/texts/d422_d.htm.

## Advantages and disadvantages of EDI

There are a number of advantages and disadvantages of using EDI within the supply chain. The advantages are:
- an ability to maintain control over the movement of materials
- an enhancement of an organisation's ability to participate in JIT
- a reduction in labour costs
- a reduction in routine tasks that can often cause errors
- a reduction in stockholding and accounts receivable
- an increase in cash flow due to the effective management of trade creditors

- an increase in customer service
- a move to one-time entry and elimination of superfluous administration.

The disadvantages are:

- personal contact between vendor and customer staff is reduced
- problems with those staff who refuse to use technology and are resistant to change
- the need for cooperation within transaction and physical distribution channels may be difficult to get.

Internet EDI is an extension of EDI adopted for the more recent technology of the Web. Electronic data interchange is the precursor of today's business-to-business electronic commerce. Traditional EDI usually uses proprietary networks, VANs and operates in a manner that is similar to emails (store and forward). In many industries there are industry-wide networks that use traditional and non-traditional networks to link services and products together. One of the best examples is IVANS,[9] which provides electronic communications services to insurance and health-care companies and related organisations in the United States and Canada. An industry-owned organisation, IVANS works to supply the most cost-effective, efficient technology solutions to all parties in the insurance distribution system. IVANS' mission focuses on helping members find value-added electronic commerce solutions that improve their ability to compete and provide quality services to their customers.

Today's EDI (Internet EDI) goes beyond exchanging electronic documents, giving trading partners access to product specifications, availability, price, delivery tracking, payment details, and even the delivery of digital products. Internet EDI does not rely on proprietary networks, but on public networks like the Internet and its derivations, extranets and intranets. Organisations benefit from having a common standard for information sharing and exchange. The outcome will mean shifting the business model from a supply chain to a supply web. The common standard being adopted is **Open Buying on the Internet (OBI)**.

OBI is a freely available standard that contains an architecture, detailed technical specifications and guidelines, together with compliance and implementation information. The OBI standard provides buying and selling organisations with an easy-to-use, standards-based solution that achieves interoperability through a flexible, technology product-neutral architecture. The OBI standard is for Internet business requisitions that combine web technologies, such as digital certificates using **X.509 protocol**, with legacy systems or back-end systems, such as EDI.

Using open standards for trading and open financial exchanges like the Bank Internet Payment Systems (BIPS) project [10] developed by the Financial Services Technology Consortium (FSTC) (see figure 5.14) will enable better business-to-business electronic commerce. BIPS is a project to develop an open specification for bank customers to securely negotiate and communicate payment instructions to bank systems over the Internet. This project, which began in 1996, is supported by a number of large banks, including Citibank, and is closely linked with existing EFTPOS payment systems like SWIFT, which is used across Australia.

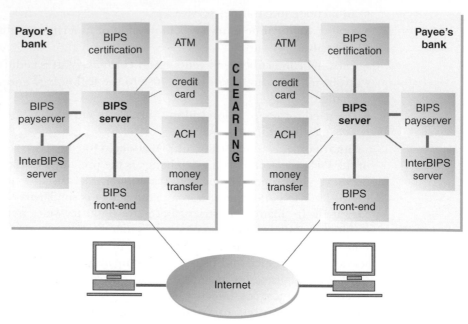

**FIGURE 5.14:** The Bank Internet Payments Systems project

Business-to-business electronic commerce shortens product cycles and business cycles. Organisations can respond to customers more rapidly and change their offerings to satisfy customers. Business-to-business electronic commerce enables the exchange and sharing of information of high content, hence organisations can micro-market, that is, provide customised products to suit customer requirements.

# BHP and EDI implementation

## ELECTRONIC COMMERCE: YESTERDAY, TODAY AND TOMORROW

BY RENAE ADAMS

THIS paper summarises a current research project in the 'Development of Electronic Commerce: Yesterday, Today and Tomorrow'. The research primarily comprises... a case study of one of Australia's largest companies, BHP Pty Ltd and their use of various forms of electronic com-merce...

**Electronic commerce today**

The need for electronic commerce stems from the demand within business and government to make better use of technology, to simplify business procedures and to increase efficiency. Electronic commerce brings important benefits to both buyers and sellers and hence, more and more businesses are looking to electronic commerce to facilitate their business needs. Banks and businesses can now be connected by international networks which enable the transfer of documents, money, pictures and images, and even video, using various forms of electronic commerce . . .

BHP's involvement in electronic commerce began with EDI in September 1988 with a pilot study involving twelve partners on a PC-based system (Rommel, 1997c, p. 3). The pilot concluded in January of 1989, was declared a success by all and eventually led to further developments in April 1990 when Steel Group Management approved the Electronic Trading Project to develop an Electronic Trading Gateway. The Gateway was commissioned in December 1991 and now provides a common approach for BHP Divisions and Trading Partners, minimising costs and duplication of effort (BHP Information Technology, 1994, p. 2). The Gateway essentially manages the exchange of EDI messages between BHP businesses and their trading partners (BHP Steel, 1993, p. 6) . . .

The Electronic Trading Project represented the first measurable step towards achieving a fundamental change in the way BHP conducted its business. Currently the Electronic Trading Gateway processes approximately 1.7 million documents per annum (Meakins, 1997, p. 7). The proposed long-term strategy is for BHP to be able to offer a variety of value added electronic trading services on an international standard communications basis to customers, suppliers and other trading partners.

Consistent with this approach to electronic commerce, BHP have developed a solution for financial electronic data interchange, i.e., an instrument for the settlement of invoices, payments and reconciliation using the process of electronic

exchange (O'Hanlon, 1993, p. 31). BHP divisions are able to connect their finance applications via the BHP Electronic Trading Gateway (ETG) and ANZ bank to complete the business cycle using EDI.

The ETG also provides the ability to transfer a document from a BHP application to a customer's facsimile machine. This is particularly useful for smaller trading partners where the use of EDI is not appropriate. Steel test certificates are another document transmitted to customers from BHP's Electronic Trading Gateway through either EDI or facsimile and the Gateway also has a large test certificate database for the storage of these documents. If customers are EDI capable, they can send in a request for another copy of the test certificate to be sent.

BHP Steel Group have also introduced a barcoding project that is intended to facilitate the seamless transfer of data between EDI applications and barcoding systems which support materials transfer and storage (BHP Steel, 1996a, p. 1). This involves the use of barcode scanning when a product is despatched from a BHP plant which automatically triggers the transmission of a EDI despatch advice message to the customer's computer . . .

When the product reaches the customer, they can scan the barcode and all the necessary information relating to that product is available to them, as it will have already been received in an EDI message. It is hoped to achieve significant savings in the cost of materials and product handling for both BHP and their customers. One aim of the research project is to determine if these savings are being achieved.

### Electronic commerce — tomorrow

BHP are committed to the continuing adoption of electronic commerce initiatives. This had led to the development of a five year plan (covering 1997–2002) for the management of electronic commerce. Central to the electronic commerce management approach will be continued support for BHP Divisions in enabling their improvements to business, manufacturing, service and other key applications (BHP Steel, 1997, p. 1).

Projects being undertaken by BHP include:

- Web site development — BHP are looking at putting technical information on the Internet with the intended audience being architects and engineers (Rommel, 1997b).
- steel test certificates on the Web — when final product is despatched from a BHP plant, they are accompanied by a test certificate stating quality information and test results. These test certificates may now be placed on an external managed Web service. The test certificate will be sent in an EDI message from BHP's Electronic Trading Gateway to a Web server that will be managed by a value added network (VAN). Customers can then pick up these documents using a Web browser and the Internet, or by receipt of an EDI message (Rommel, 1997b).
- EDI across the Internet — BHP's Integrated Steel Division, in conjunction with one of their trading partners, have recently conducted a pilot study to investigate the possibility of using the Internet as a transmission medium for EDI documents. The pilot study involved the sending of the purchase order document from BHP's Electronic Trading Gateway to an Internet service provider, via an X400 EDI message. From there, the trading partner connects, via the Internet, to the service provider's network to receive their purchase order. This is downloaded into an Electronic Form (E-Form) supplied by the service provider. The pilot study was successful, showing no data loss over the Internet, acceptable delivery performance, as well as a friendly interface for the trading partner involved (ETG Support, 1997, p. 5).

### Current status of research

… EDI and EFT using a VAN have been in use and accepted for several years and their method of transmission permits both secure and standardised trading between organisations. EDI caters for large volumes of transmissions at significant cost and time savings for the trading partners involved (compared to paper based trading).

On the other hand, the Internet and other global online networks are creating new commercial opportunities for networked commerce. Global access provides organisations with a cheaper alternative to EDI and it is an affordable option for all sized organisations, not only for the large players. However, to date, development and use for electronic commerce has been limited by the lack of a secure infrastructure and the concerns associated with sending sensitive information over the Internet. BHP Corporate have made a decision that the Internet will not be used for financial transactions, their reasoning behind this being security concerns. Karl Rommel (1997b) of BHP Steel's Electronic Commerce Group believes there will be no changes in this decision for at least the next two years. The review of literature so far

suggests that the creation of more secure Internet systems has already begun and will provide opportunities for completely new sets of global and national trading relationships. Issues such as security and reliability are being constantly addressed.

The next step is to undertake a SWOT analysis of the use of the Internet as a transmission medium for EDI, as opposed to the current use of value added networks (VANs). It is hoped that the SWOT analysis will show whether the Internet is a viable medium for transmission of documents, both financial and non-financial. This may show that BHP's reluctance to use the Internet for EDI, and in particular for financial information, may be unjustified with decisions made in haste and by the wrong people. The results may provide BHP with the benefits, or lack of, to using the Internet to facilitate their electronic trading. The results may also dispel common and often unfounded beliefs that the Internet is not a secure transmission medium and restore some confidence in doubtful users who are considering using the Internet for their business needs.

**SOURCE:** paper presented at the Proceedings of the First Annual CollECTeR Workshop on Electronic Commerce, Adelaide, 3 October 1997

**QUESTIONS**

1.   What is an electronic trading gateway?
2.   How does the gateway integrate VANs, communications systems suppliers and business applications?
3.   How might use of the Internet improve the EDI processes used by BHP?

EDI is about information and data exchange and represents a system that allows an efficient form of communication between companies. As Adams suggests in the Business insite above, there are other newer forms of exchange and communication that will either enhance or replace EDI in the exchange of information, especially in the financial sector. One of these developments includes the use of smart cards and digital-cash systems.

## BUSINESS-TO-CONSUMER EPS: STORED VALUE CARDS AND E-CASH SYSTEMS

### Smart cards (stored value cards)

Smart cards are a form of EPS that uses a plastic card with a microchip that stores information, usually about value. Value is stored on the card and acts as a substitute for cash. Smart cards, or more correctly **stored value cards (SVCs)** where it is the value of money that is stored, can store more information and perform more functions than the magnetic stripe cards that are more commonly in use throughout the world. It is estimated that there are over 600 million smart cards in operation throughout the world, either as magnetic stripe cards or as SVCs with microchips. They are used to store information about people's health, they are used as identity cards and security cards, and form the electronic signature in digital mobile phones. Australian and European trials of smart cards as substitutes for cash by companies such as VISA and Mondex suggest that smart cards will eventually replace the common magnetic stripe cards now used in EFTPOS and banking transactions using ATMs.

FIGURE 5.15: A magnetic stripe card

Smart cards are really microcomputers that rely on another medium or reader to supply the power source to make them work. Smart cards have a small chip embedded, usually in a plastic card. This chip acts like a microcomputer with a typical input/output device, a microprocessor, and ROM and RAM memory (see figure 5.17).

Smart cards or SVCs can store everything found in a wallet or purse. They operate mostly by transfer of data/value from the card to a business system, usually without verification, which make them different from online payment systems. The protocols used in this process are:

- the programming of cards, assigning serial numbers and loading keys to increase and decrease the value of cards. This is called personalisation.[11]

- the allocation of transaction reload capability, which enables the stored value on the card to be added to when desired

- a debit transaction process facility that enables a business system to download value and debit the loading system for the value of a transaction.

FIGURE 5.16: A stored value card (SVC) — the front and back of one of Telstra's Phonecards

Smart cards can also store university transcripts, personal records, medical information, hospital files, social security information, employment records, in fact any personal or organisational information that needs to be stored and be portable. It is not beyond the realms of thinking that in Australia an SVC could be developed that would be our driver's licence, Medicare card, Bankcard, bank debit card and contain our medical records and personal CV. The limitations to this development have to do with privacy and other legal, social and political issues, which are discussed in the next chapter of this book and which can be more fully explored in Tyree (1997) (see the list of suggested reading at the end of this chapter).

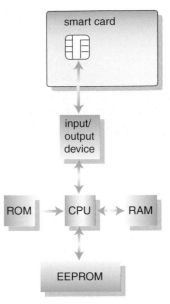

**FIGURE 5.17:** Components of a smart card and internal communication flow. **SOURCE:** A. Furche and G. Wrightson 1996, *Computer Money: A Systematic Overview of Electronic Payment Systems*, dpunkt, verlag für digitale Technologie GmbH, Heidelberg, FDR, p. 65

**FIGURE 5.18:** In the future, it is possible that an SVC could contain all of these elements.

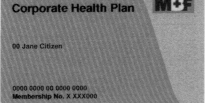

In Thailand, Lenso has developed an SVC for international telephone calls that operates at Lenso telephone points. In this case, the consumer buys a card for either 250 baht or 500 baht (A$10 or A$20) and then uses the value stored on the card to make international telephone calls. The value stored on the card is downloaded at the conclusion of the telephone call. This is a closed system. The cards are manufactured by Lenso, who receive payment when they are purchased. The business system, the international telephone point, downloads the value, capturing the payment just as a coin-operated telephone captures coins. This SVC is non-reusable and is discarded after the value is used up. A similar smart card system is used in the Melbourne Central car park under Melbourne Central. On entering the car park, the customer is given a smart card that can then be used to store/record the value of purchases made throughout this very large shopping complex. The system is designed to give the exiting customer a 50 per cent discount on car-parking charges for every $10 spent in the shopping complex. The system also recognises each additional $10 unit of purchases as a credit for further discount at future use of the car park.

The Microbus public transport system throughout Bangkok, Thailand, has recently introduced an SVC that is purchased from the bus driver and then given value by the consumer passing bank notes into a machine either on the bus or at a number of offices throughout metropolitan Bangkok. Each trip is then debited against the card when it is put into the card reader in the bus. In this case, the SVC is reusable and can be 'topped up' at any time.

In China reusable SVCs are being used to activate electricity meters and in Singapore a tourist card (SVC) is being developed to eliminate the need for moneychangers. Already there are banks in Asia that have electronic reader machines that change currency from one to another by reading the currency electronically, eliminating the human interface in the transaction. These are true EPSs as each eliminates the intermediary process of human handling. Stored value is transferred from a card to another organisation's account. This is then adjusted through an electronic banking system.

## Types of stored value card

Closed-system stored value cards are smart cards where the intrinsic value of the card is fixed. Such cards include fixed price, pre-paid telephone cards or pre-paid transport tickets. In this case, the owner of the card and the provider of the service are the same. Open-system stored value cards are smart cards where the intrinsic value of the card can be changed. These cards can be recharged in value. They can be described as an electronic wallet where the value on the card can be increased each day or at any regular interval. Most commonly, the owner/issuer of such open-system stored value cards is not the service provider. For example, a bank can issue an open-system SVC (e.g. Thai Danu Bank's SMART Cash card) and this card can then be used in any store or for any purchase or transaction where there is a card reader.

With both closed- and open-system stored value cards there will be an impact on the transaction process and the accounting of money throughout the economic systems they engage. In effect, they complicate the value exchange process (see figure 5.19).

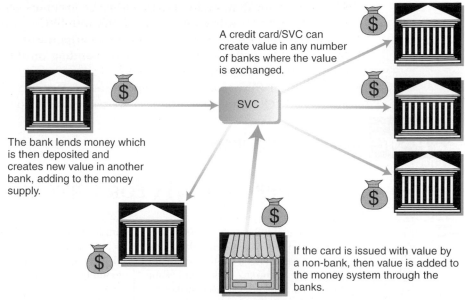

**FIGURE 5.19:**
Stored value cards
in the exchange
process

A credit card/SVC can
create value in any number
of banks where the value
is exchanged.

SVC

The bank lends money which
is then deposited and
creates new value in another
bank, adding to the money
supply.

If the card is issued with value by
a non-bank, then value is added to
the money system through the
banks.

## Advantages and risks of SVCs in business

In a very detailed evaluation of smart cards in Australia, the Centre for Electronic Commerce at Monash University has concluded that:

- Smart cards will have a significant impact on the banking system and the way it operates.
- Smart cards will affect the way money is exchanged.
- Smart cards may erode the traditional role of banks in the payment systems, although the Australian banks and others, such as in Thailand, are at the forefront of the development and issue of SVCs and other smart cards to maintain their traditional roles.
- Smart cards have the potential to allow institutions other than banks to issue value and thus create money that has been the traditional role of banks. For example, a company could issue smart cards for transactions in its own stores or enterprises which could be developed and issued on credit and thus create money. This could impact on the supply of money and the level of inflation in an economy.
- Smart cards and SVCs are expensive to establish and the potential profitability of the new value and service created by the stored value cards will be lessened at least in the short run.
- SVCs should improve the efficiency of electronically transferring funds for low-value, high-volume transactions.
- SVCs should offer a range of choice in payment methods and improve convenience.
- SVCs and smart cards will probably increase the cost to consumers by the need of suppliers to cover costs.
- SVCs may not be affordable by all consumers thus raising equity issues in society.

- The protections that are in place to protect consumers when using existing payment systems/cards do not always apply with SVCs.
- Smart cards are more secure than magnetic stripe cards.
- SVCs could be more secure than cash, depending on the card design and the method of recording stored value.
- The trials on SVCs currently in operation in Australia (VISA, Transcard, MasterCard, Quicklink and Mondex) are technically incompatible!

## Making digital money

# REAL OPPORTUNITY FOR VIRTUAL CASH

BY JOHN FOLEY

When I'm going through a train station or airport, I don't hesitate to plop down $5 for a magazine at a newsstand, a buck or two for a cup of coffee and some change on anything else that strikes my fancy as I move along.

Would I still buy those items if I had to pull out a credit card at each stop?

Probably not — and there's the rub for businesses that are selling on the Web.

It's becoming increasingly clear that, in the world of electronic commerce, it sometimes makes sense to give customers alternatives to credit cards when it comes to payment options.

Credit cards have gained wide acceptance and they still account for the vast majority of purchases made on the Web. But credit cards are also limiting, and that means there are opportunities for companies that come up with imaginative new ways for conducting online transactions.

Credit cards, for example, aren't well suited for impulse purchases or for buying items that cost, say, under $10. In this respect, surfing the Web isn't unlike a walk through an airport or train station.

Consumers are probably willing to spend the money on things of interest —

music, video clips, photographs, news articles and other digital content — but chances are they would rather not want to fumble with their credit cards to do it.

A growing number of companies are finally figuring this out. Visa International is working with a handful of merchants to test smart cards as a way of making payments online.

Starting in June, CDNow will let America Online users pay for music using digital wallets. Even the *Wall Street Journal* has begun using micropayment technology to let visitors to its web site get daily subscriptions for 75 cents.

Others have introduced online bartering systems. Just last week, I was invited to participate in a program that offers 'points' in exchange for visiting select web sites and responding to email solicitations. The points can be exchanged for name-brand merchandise.

Successful e-commerce efforts will require the right products, business models and payment options. I spend lots of time online and I don't mind spending money for something I want or need.

But I've never spent a penny on a web site. Make it easier to do, and you may find some willing customers. ■

**SOURCE:** *InformationWeek*, 21 June 1999, p. 65

## QUESTIONS

1. What is virtual cash?
2. Will virtual cash resolve problems with people not wanting to use credit cards on the Internet for small purchases?

# Properties of digital payment systems

At a more experimental level, the increasing use of the Internet and the Web for commerce is creating a need for another type of EPS — digital cash. When digital currencies first appeared, many bankers feared that they might become obsolete. However, digital cash has had a difficult time: its issuers either went bankrupt (**DigiCash**), dropped the product (**CyberCash**) or moved into another business (First Virtual Holdings' product is now being sold by MessageMedia). A tutorial on Ecash is found at www.ecash.net.

Digital cash consists of a small string of encrypted digits, or electronic tokens, that can be used as a substitute for money to purchase various goods and services in an electronic environment, usually the Internet. For example, token or exchange value certificates can be used on the Internet or on private networks such as SITA (Société Internationale Transportation Aéronautiques), which provides a private network that supports the booking processes and traffic planning of most of the world's airlines. Digital cash replaces money in the transaction but depends on an institution, such as a bank, to provide the monetary value for the digital transaction (see figure 5.20). Ecash is issued by the St George Bank in Australia.

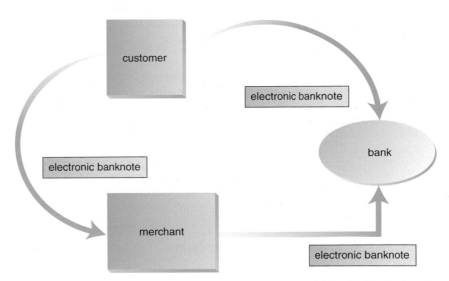

**FIGURE 5.20:** E-cash: how it works

One of the problems of using digital-cash systems is the need to ensure the security of the payment being made. Three major protocols have been developed to try and ensure that all electronic payments made over the Internet are secure. These protocols are:

- *STT*. Developed by Microsoft and VISA, STT uses a two-keyed authentication and encryption system that enables purchases to be completed using credit cards in a method similar to offline credit card usage. Each person is authenticated as a user by an electronic certificate or credential that is unique to them. Any transaction must be verified by this credential.

- *SEPP.* This protocol was developed by IBM, MasterCard, Netscape, Verisign, RSA, Terisa Systems, SAIC, GTE and CyberCash using existing credit card procedures. However, SEPP differs from STT in that SEPP uses other forms of communication and other existing and private networks, as well as the Internet, to process the exchange of value involved in the transaction. In effect, it uses existing EFT infrastructure to operate.
- *SET.* This protocol was developed by both of the major credit card providers VISA and MasterCard to establish a uniform, secure communication standard for Internet commerce and is designed to become the standard for Internet commerce. SET trials began in 1997. SET uses the Internet rather than existing EFT infrastructure. On 4 June 1998 SET Co awarded the right to use the SET trademark to the first four vendors of SET-compliant software: GlobeSet Inc., Spyrus/Terisa Systems, Trintech and Verifone. These companies' wallet applications were determined to be compliant with the SET 1.0 protocol. Check www.set.org for SET protocols.

## CommerceNet

One global organisation that has an interest in EPS is CommerceNet (www.commerce.net) which has its Australian office in Adelaide. CommerceNet has put in place portfolios that deal with five initial areas:
- infrastructure (EDI, robustness, network management and related infrastructure services)
- financial service (payments, Roselta Net, eCheck)
- trust and security (public key infrastructure (PKI), security showcase and encryption)
- information access (catalogues, directories, agencies and search interoperability)
- architecture and markets (eCo framework, iMarkets, vertical markets).

CommerceNet issues an email newsletter on electronic commerce matters. To receive it, send an email to buzz-request@lists.commerce.net. In both the subject line and in the body of the message, type the word 'subscribe'.

## New digital currency products

The second wave of digital cash is now starting for various reasons. Many people like the anonymity of digital cash as opposed to credit cards. Access to credit cards can also be a problem for some consumers: many people (from developing nations) do not have credit cards and some people are too young to qualify for a credit card. Auctions and consumer-to-consumer e-commerce have also created a need for online payment between individuals other than via a credit card. Merchants may also find digital cash more convenient as credit card costs cut into merchants' revenue and sites selling small items such as a single song need to be able to accept micropayments ranging from one-tenth of a cent to $10. Millicent is an account-based micropayment scheme originally developed at DEC's System Research Center in 1995 (see www.millicent.digital.com).

Some of the new digital cash techniques include the following.[12]

- Consumers can now store value in an online account and deduct from it the price of small purchases. This technique was pioneered by iClickCharge. IBM and Compaq use a similar technique, as does Fairfax for its archived article.
- Qpass makes no initial charge but accumulates payments and deducts the final amount from a credit card.
- Trivnet and Ipin use ISPs to track customers' online spending and add it to their bill.
- Flooz issue gift certificates. The giver uses a credit card to pay money into an account. The recipient of the gift certificate can then spend the money in the account at a participating online merchant. At the beginning of 2000, there were US$5 million worth of flooz certificates.
- Consumers are being paid in 'beenz' to be online to visit web sites, fill in forms or go shopping. They can then spend the 'beenz' at participating sites.
- CyberGold allows consumers to convert 'cyberdollars' into real money.
- PayPal have been developed by Confinity to enable people to open an account at the web site and then email dollars to other people (can be transferred via Palm Pilots).
- E-Gold allows clients to fund their accounts by purchasing gold or other metals and then transfer units of those metals (measured by weight) by entering a recipient's account and a password.
- Various online bartering schemes exist such as BarterTrust, BigVine and LassoBucks.
- A British firm called Oakington has developed software that allows for the automatic payment of taxed and 'time escrow' so that a transaction does not clear until the goods arrive.

Another digital cash product is the wallet, a small software program that is used for online purchase transactions. It allows for several methods of payment to be defined within the wallet. It may take several different kinds of credit card. Microsoft offers its Passport wallet to store credit card details and shipping addresses. This information is sent over a secure connection to online merchants. Using a mobile telephone to pay for items and do banking is discussed in chapter 11, page 287.

Research on digital cash has concentrated on trying to resolve the difficulties that exist technically and socially. As a result, a number of new alternatives are being developed. For example, in 1995 at the University of Newcastle, the Monetary Systems Engineering Group developed Millicent, an account-based transaction protocol for low-value transactions that allows a vendor to verify a transaction without contacting a central authority and without expensive encryption. Millicent uses brokers and scrip. Brokers look after account management, billing and establishing accounts with merchants. Scrip is electronic cash that is valid only for a specific vendor.

A more detailed discussion of digital cash systems is to be found in Furche and Wrightson (1996) (see suggested reading list at the end of this chapter). Developments in the design and use of digital cash in Australia can be viewed at www.cs.newcastle.edu.au/Research/pabloins/mseg.html.

# FEDEX BETS ON INTERNET2 FOR PURCHASING TOOL

BY ANDREW NACHISON

THE FASTER, more secure and more reliable next-generation Internet is still somewhere in the future. But enough progress has been made on an experimental version of that network, dubbed Internet2, that Federal Express is building a global purchasing system that will take advantage of it when it arrives.

'A year ago, if I'd have said: "Look, I want to go buy some great backbone software to manage procurement everywhere around the world", [anyone else would] say: "Are you out of your mind? Where's the bandwidth? Where are you going to get the software?"' said Toby Redshaw, vice president of global supply-chain integration at FedEx.

But now, 'given what we think the future looks like, we really believe you can do that', he said.

The first version of the FedEx system, due to launch this summer, will eventually allow more than 100 000 employees in 90 countries to purchase everything from ballpoint pens to truck parts. In its initial phase, the application will use the existing Internet infrastructure and expand its features, as Internet2 — which will boost the performance and security of the Web — becomes a reality. The application will replace a hodgepodge of private networks and paper-based processes that waste time and make it hard for FedEx to take full advantage of its buying power.

The new system will allow financial, legal, technical and business managers to review spending plans at the same time, rather than waiting for one another's decisions before evaluating a purchase.

Redshaw declined to disclose the precise cost of the system, which he said is in the millions of dollars, but estimated that if FedEx can cut 10 per cent from its annual purchasing costs, 'that's $US500 million. You're talking about huge shareholder value'.

PeopleSoft purchasing and inventory systems provide back-end financial capabilities, while Hewlett-Packard will host the data — another sign of Redshaw's faith that Internet2 will be more secure and reliable than today's Web.

'I would be stupid to [host critical data] outside our firewall on somebody else's machine if I thought... we were moving towards a more chaotic, more unstable environment in the network world,' Redshaw said.

Michael Rabin, who manages AT&T's involvement with the Internet2 project, said he expects Internet2 advances to make their way into the commercial Internet within three years.

Some corporate information technology managers are reluctant to develop systems based on IP standards because of problems with scalability and reliability, said Matthew Kovar, senior data communications analyst at The Yankee Group.

Richard Shoenthaler, manager of compliance systems at Ecolab, a cleaning products and services company, is one example. He said the next-generation Internet 'could become an important mechanism for online meetings, to distribute advice and data efficiently and in real time'. Still, 'we're not making decisions' until he sees the actual improvements, Schoenthaler said.

**SOURCE:** *ComputerWorld*, 28 May 1999, p. 32

## QUESTIONS

1. What is Internet2?
2. Why might the next generation of Internet enable better electronic purchasing?

Electronic payment systems are becoming an increasingly important part of business-to-business and business-to-consumer payment transactions and the exchange of value. The Internet has enabled consumers to have access to many products and services that can be shopped, ordered and paid for electronically. Electronic catalogues are being developed that will allow businesses and consumers to order anything from automobile components to pizzas and wine. Electronic payment systems using smart cards, online EFTPOS-type systems and digital-money systems enable businesses and consumers to pay electronically.

Electronic payment systems can vary from simple transactions using magnetic-stripe cards, where the customers' details are exchanged for goods or services and an account is sent, to more complex systems where an online purchasing system can debit existing bank accounts of the purchaser and credit bank accounts of the seller. This new form of purchasing has reduced the importance of cash or money as the only form of transaction or exchange of value. Traditional forms of exchange, money, are being replaced by these new methods of exchange, which are effectively diversifying the nature and complexity of business-to-business dealing and consumer-to-seller transactions both in terms of cost and convenience. In a more complex way, business-to-business transactions of data and exchange of value have increasingly been used in many industries, especially in retailing and the automobile industry. EDI transactions enable more efficient allocation of resources for production and servicing and enable better planning and inventory control in businesses. Financial uses of EDI through VANs enable more efficient transactions and monitoring of manufacturing or service provision.

Electronic purchasing enables more cost effective and time effective transactions to occur. However, in this process there are security demands that have to be both recognised and addressed by both businesses and consumers. The nature of these security issues as they affect online, electronic commerce and electronic payment systems is discussed in detail in the next chapter.

## key terms

| | | |
|---|---|---|
| CyberCash | electronic payment system (EPS) | supply chain |
| DigiCash | | total quality management (TQM) |
| e-cash | electronic purchasing | |
| EDIFACT | gross domestic product (GDP) | TRADACOMS |
| electronic data interchange (EDI) | just-in-time (JIT) | value-added network (VAN) |
| electronic funds transfer (EFT) | money | X.12 protocol |
| | Open Buying on the Internet (OBI) | X.25 protocol |
| electronic funds transfer at point of sale (EFTPOS) | | X.400 protocol |
| | smart card | X.500 protocol |
| | stored value card (SVC) | X.509 protocol |

# UNIVERSITY OF ILLINOIS SELECTS SCHLUMBERGER TO HELP PROVIDE FIRST SMART CARD-BASED SOLUTION FOR SECURE DISTANCE LEARNING OVER THE INTERNET

**Pilot program paves way for new generation of smart card-based campus applications built on PKI infrastructure**

SAN JOSE, California, August 30, 1999 — Schlumberger, the world's leading provider of smart card-based solutions, today announced that it is providing the first public key (PKI) smart card-based network security solution for distance learning and other business and service related applications. Schlumberger, in conjunction with the University of Illinois, is launching a pilot program designed to enable students and other authorized university personnel based either inside or outside the campus environment to securely access course materials and other University of Illinois developed applications via the Internet using PKI smart card-based technology.

'The Schlumberger network security solution allows the University of Illinois to expand its student population through a borderless, worldwide virtual campus,' stated Gary Brinkley, director, business systems analysis for the University of Illinois office of cash management and investments. 'The University expects nearly a tenfold increase in their distance enrollment (UI On-Line) while at the same time achieving a drastic reduction in unauthorized access to valuable information and course materials

by utilizing this revolutionary new smart card system.'

Brinkley noted that the smart card pilot is expected to expand the present all-university multi-application I-card to a much more versatile and secure card. He stated, 'The innovative Schlumberger multi-application smart card will allow the University of Illinois to interface many existing systems with a reduction in development and production cost.' Brinkley hopes to prove this as part of the pilot on their Springfield campus.

**Smart card-based network security reduces risk of fraud**

Within the university environment, digital signatures reduce the risk of fraud and allow for authorization of virtual students as well as better data security and improved access to sensitive information such as class schedules, registration information and medical records campus-wide. The University of Illinois smart card ID system will be used by students in remote locations to access a virtual campus via a secure web site operated by the University. The system initially allows secure e-mail, and Internet/extranet access, while providing the flexibility to fit into a university-wide security solution in the near future.

Scheduled to begin in early September 1999, the pilot will be initially launched on the University of Illinois' Springfield campus. The pilot utilizes Schlumberger smart card-based network security technology, including a Cryptoflex card with a public key certificate that enables identification and authentication of students, a Reflex card reader and software. RSA security mechanisms inside the smart card make fraud or virus attacks impossible, and signature operations cannot be launched without a user PIN code. Additionally, confidential information stored inside the card cannot be read by other applications, eliminating the risk of compromising data.

**Smart card-based integration allows for multi-application expansion**

In the next planned phase of the pilot, the Schlumberger campus offering will enable the University of Illinois to realize a significant reduction in costs by bundling together secure Internet/extranet access and physical campus access with other services on a single smart card. The expanded pilot will take advantage of the Schlumberger integrated networking solution by extending the existing university-wide ID card with built-in stored-value applications. This enhancement will enable software developers, value-added resellers (VARs) and retailers to roll out exciting new programs for the University's students, faculty and administrators.

**About Schlumberger**

Schlumberger Campus Solutions is North America's only single source provider of total smart card-based solutions for closed and semi-closed environments, such as college campuses, corporate campuses, hospitals, municipalities and resorts. Schlumberger provides a complete solution from concept development and planning through implementation and maintenance. The Schlumberger offering includes cards, readers, POS terminals, software, application development, installation, project management, training, service and other support.

Schlumberger is the leading provider of smart card-based solutions worldwide. Drawing on 20 years experience in pioneering smart card innovations, Schlumberger is continuing to evolve the new generation of smart cards, parking terminals, ticketing machines, payphones, banking terminals, servers, software, applications and systems integration that will play a key role in the 21st century's digital age. Additional information is available at http://www.slb.com/smartcards.

Schlumberger Test & Transactions provides smart card-based solutions; semiconductor test, metrology and handling systems and services; and corporate Internet and network solutions to customers across the globe. It is a business unit of Schlumberger Limited, a $11.8 billion global technology services company.

*SOURCE:* Schlumberger press release, 30 August 1999, www.slb.com/ir/news/set_illinois0830.html

# QIANFLEX: SCHLUMBERGER TAKES THE LEAD IN THE LARGEST SMART BANK CARD PROJECT IN THE WORLD

**The challenge**
- Modernize China's financial infrastructure by implementing chip-based cards and terminals.
- Issue electronic means of payment based on the People's Bank of China (PBOC Integrated Circuit (IC) Card Specifications).
- Ensure card interoperability in China and conformity with ISO and Europay-MasterCard–Visa (EMV) standards.

**The solution**
- A complete front-end system including cards, Point-of-Sale (POS) terminals, and personalization package.
- Local expertise in marketing and technical development to support the People's Bank of China Working Group

**The results**

Qianflex is a complete solution that provides a convenient means of financial transactions for China's more than one billion citizens. The commercial banks in China now have the ability to implement secure interoperable debit transactions systems and electronic purses. The system is easy to upgrade and Schlumberger is working closely with the People's Bank of China and its member banks to introduce Qianflex products, exploiting the card's infrastructure to create value-added services for customers.

Qianflex includes:
- SmarT 1000$^{TM}$ EFTPOS (Electronic Funds Transfer Point of Sale) terminals
- Security Access Modules (SAM) for the POS terminals
- a personalization solution that is a complete tool for introducing Qianflex cards in the marketplace.

The solution not only provides for the issuing of chip-based cards but also magnetic-stripe cards and SAMs. Qianflex thus addresses the complexity of migrating from a magnetic stripe card environment to a modern chip-based card system.

Schlumberger has played a leading role in the development of global standards for smart cards. In its effort to modernize the country's banking system, the People's Bank of China (PBOC) invited Schlumberger to cooperate with the PBOC Working Group to jointly develop and formulate the China Bank IC Card Specifications, which were released in 1997. The Qianflex payment system is the result of that collaboration.

**SOURCE:** Schlumberger web site, 9 May 1999, www.slb.com/smartcards/news/qianflex/html

## REFLECTION AND REVIEW QUESTIONS

1. How do the two experiments using smart cards differ?
2. What is the strategic importance of each experiment?
3. Which system has proven to be the most effective? Why?
4. How do these systems work?
5. Draw a diagram to illustrate the exchange mechanism using the smart cards.
6. What will the introduction of such systems do to the money supply?
7. What are the advantages and disadvantages of each system?
8. Are such systems better than EFT or EFTPOS or VISA/MasterCard-type systems?

**QUESTIONS**

1. (a) How useful are the following sites in terms of their relationship with you as a potential customer?
    - (i) www.asiandevbank.org/
    - (ii) www.fv.com/
    - (iii) www.internet.net
    - (iv) www.yahoo.com/business_and_economy/ electronic_commerce/
    - (v) www.yahoo.com/Entertainment/Automobiles/ General_Motors/
    - (vi) www.southwire.com/wgta/mempages/cemc/cemcover.htm
    - (vii) www.interaccess.com:80/users/numusic/
    - (viii) www.lubricants.dupont.com:80/

   (b) How did each of these sites establish a supplier–customer relationship?

   (c) Which of the sites provides the best access for the customer? What criteria did you use to make those judgements?

   (d) How effective do you think these organisations will be in maintaining an effective supplier–customer relationship? How good are these sites as shopping centres?

   (e) Identify other organisations that could effectively use the Internet or an online context to market their products as part of an effective supply chain utilising an effective supplier–customer relationship.

2. Go to www.microsoft.com/indonesia/EVENTS/SLIDES/ TrackC-3_files/frame.htm#slide0108.htm. Examine this site in detail. What do the providers of this information suggest are the best business e-commerce solutions for Indonesia? What might you add?

3. Find out as much as you can about the following EDI standards and protocols: WINS, IDI, CCITTX25, CCITX.400, CCITX.500, ANSI X.a2, EDIFACT, TRADACOMS, EANCOM, Financial EDI, Hybrid EDI.

4. (a) Visit the DigiCash web site (http://digicash.com) and collect detailed information about how it works and make an evaluation of its potential.

   (b) Now investigate another digital cash system called CyberCash, which was developed in the United States, at www.cybercash.com. Do the various types of electronic purchasing perform all four functions of money?

5. (a) Examine these sites on SET:
    - (i) www.mastercard.com/set/
    - (ii) www.zdnet.com/zdnn/content/inwo/0323/296952.html
    - (iii) www.idg.net/new_docids/transaction/electronic/internet/ vendors/secure/even/popularizing/ implementednew_docid_9-48998.html.
   Suggest some apparent advantages and disadvantages of SET.

6. Undertake a search at the Bank Negara in Malaysia (www1.bnm.gov.my/). Why has Malaysia rejected SET?

## SUGGESTED READING

Centre for Electronic Commerce 1996, *Smart Cards and the Future of Your Money*, Report for the Commission for the Future, Monash University.

Churchman, P. 1987, *Electronic Payment Systems*, Basil Blackwell, Oxford, United Kingdom.

Emmelmainz, M. 1990, *Electronic Data Interchange: A Total Management Guide*, Van Nostrand, New York, United States.

Furche, A. and Wrightson, G. 1996, *Computer Money: A Systematic Overview of Electronic Payment Systems*, dpunkt, verlag für digitale Technologie GmbH, Heidelberg, FDR.

Gattorna, J. and Walters, D. 1996, *Managing the Supply Chain: A Strategic Perspective*, Macmillan, Great Britain.

Hammond, R. 1996, *Digital Business: Surviving and Thriving in an On-line World*, Hodder and Stoughton, London.

Kalakota, R. and Whinston, A. 1996, *Frontiers of Electronic Commerce*, Addison-Wesley, United States.

McKeown, P. and Watson, R. 1996, *Metamorphosis: A Guide to the World Wide Web and Electronic Commerce*, John Wiley and Sons, Inc., United States.

Tran, V. G. 1995, 'EDI: good for what ails the healthcare world', *EDI World*, September, pp. 28–30.

Tyree, A. 1997, *Digital Money*, Butterworths, Sydney.

## END NOTES

1. Quoted from a Bank Negara statement in an extract from the Malaysian newspaper *The Star* at http://mir.com.my/lb/econ_plan/contents/press_release/110899merge.htm. Further details of this process can be found at http://mir.com.my/lb/econ_plan/index.htm.
2. See www.bot.or.th/bank/public/findata/Mbpolicy/MonetaryPolicy.htm for more information.
3. The Australian Securities and Investments Securities web site is www.asic.gov.au/.
4. See the Australian Payments Clearing Association's web site where the schemes in operation in Australia are set out: www.apca.com.au/Paymentsystems.htm#Financial.
5. After reading the detail in this chapter, further information and more detail on each system can be obtained in Furche, A. and Wrightson, G. 1996, *Computer Money: A Systematic Overview of Electronic Payment Systems*, dpunkt, verlag für digitale Technologie GmbH, Heidelberg, FDR.
6. Kalakota, R. and Whinston, A. 1996, *Frontiers of Electronic Commerce*, Addison-Wesley, United States, p. 298.
7. McKeown, P. and Watson, R. 1996, *Metamorphosis: A Guide to the World Wide Web and Electronic Commerce*, John Wiley and Sons, Inc., United States, p. 127.
8. A fuller evaluation of these issues can be found at: www.anu.edu.au/people/Roger.Clarke/Electronic Commerce/EPMIssues.
9. For more information about IVANS see www.ivans.com/about/index.cfm.
10. A description of this project can be found at www.epf.net/PrevMtngs/Jan97Mtng/Presentations/Odell/index.htm and www.neology.com/portfolio/fstc.cfm.
11. Furche, A. and Wrightson, G. 1996, *Computer Money: A Systematic Overview of Electronic Payment Systems*, dpunkt, verlag für Technologie GmbH, Heidelberg, FDR, p. 68.
12. *Economist* 2000, 'E-cash 2.0', 19 February, pp. 69–70.

# 6

# Security issues, networks and electronic commerce

## LEARNING *Outcomes*

You will have mastered the material in this chapter when you can:

- list the major security issues that underpin networks and their application to electronic commerce
- describe how confidentiality, integrity, availability and authenticity issues can be addressed in Internet commerce/electronic commerce
- define and explain how firewalls and proxies are used in securing networks running electronic commerce applications
- explain how viruses affect the security and integrity of online and electronic communication and electronic commerce.

*'In terms of security, computing is very close to the Wild West days. Some installations recognise computers and their data as a valuable resource and have applied appropriate protection. Other installations are dangerously deficient in their security measures. But unlike the Wild West bankers, some computing professionals and managers do not even recognise the value of the resources they use or control ... Worst yet, in the event of a crime, some companies do not investigate or prosecute for fear that it will damage their public image.'*

C. P. Pfleeger 1997, *Security in Computing*, Prentice Hall, United States, p. 2

# INTRODUCTION

Electronic commerce is concerned with doing business using electronic technologies. It can involve the transmission of data, transactions and payments, or marketing and value adding to existing products or databases. That data can be as simple as an invoice or an order form in an EDI exchange. Electronic commerce can also involve the exchange of tokens that represent value or the exchange of credit card numbers that represent purchases by a consumer from a retailer. In all of these cases there is an acceptance that the integrity and safety of the exchange has been secure from capture or interference from **hackers** or others wishing to gain information illegally. Data transferred across networks needs to be protected and it needs to be confidential. In this chapter, we will review those issues relating to the **security** of business done in an online context or business that uses other electronic methods.

From the time a business installs a web server or hires space on a commercial web server from an Internet service provider (ISP), there is the potential for the business systems in the organisation to be exposed to breaches of security and **confidentiality** across the entire Internet. Any link to the Internet exposes businesses to tampering (Internet graffiti) where data can be altered or covered with meaningless scribble, pictures or electronic junk in the same way that a graffiti artist scrawls on walls. Links to the Internet also expose the business to the theft of data. Databases can be captured whole and transferred for other uses such as industrial espionage very easily. Almost as big a problem is the deliberate alteration of data that might influence decision making or change the ways business decisions are made. The TCP/IP protocol developed to run the Internet was not designed with security in mind. This protocol, the basic system running Internet communication, is vulnerable to interception. Any movement of data from browser to a server or back is vulnerable to eavesdropping.

Web site security is about keeping strangers out but at the same time allowing controlled access to a network. Sometimes achieving both of these elements can be very difficult. However, this raises the question of whether there is any real difference between security in a paper-based business organisation and an electronic-based business organisation. The security of data and information is just as important in both cases. What is different is that the electronic-based business is exposed to very fast capture of large volumes of data. In the paper-based organisation, it would take considerable time to capture and transcribe large volumes of data. Even the process of theft of files is not really a quick process. Special security measures have to be taken in an electronic environment to prevent access to confidential data.

There is one more question that needs to be raised. Are the security issues of networks any different from other security issues? There is a great deal of debate about security on the Internet. However, there can be as much concern about security of transmission using other electronic forms. When a fax is sent from one machine to another, what certainty is there that the fax reached its original destination or that the fax had not gone to another location, been altered and then sent on again? There is concern by consumers about sending their credit card details over the Internet. They fear that their transaction information will be intercepted and used by someone else. On the other hand, people now readily telephone their credit card details when paying accounts. Is there any more security on a telephone network than on the Internet? Probably not! However, all security issues revolve around resolution of business risk. Business risks can be associated with products that may or may not sell, with services that people may or may not want, and can also be generated by inadequate legal provisions as in most parts of the world where the law does not adequately address the needs of Internet commerce. This includes a lack of recognition of digital signatures and a lack of application of consumer protection laws for goods purchased outside the country. However, where attention to the details of the protection of data and the protection for trading has been considered, as has occurred in Singapore,[1] there is always a greater chance that risk will be reduced and business made more secure. In addition, risk can result from poor reliability of trading partners, from staff behaviour within organisations and as a result of problems with ISP security.

For businesses to be established and run effectively it is imperative that as much attention as possible is paid to information and security risks as is given to financial risks. Risk analysis 'entails identifying ways in which the confidentiality of data, the integrity of data and systems, and the accessibility to data and systems can be compromised, as well as identifying other loss-related outcomes and their probable impact'.[2] Such a risk analysis needs to take into account:

- the financial significance of data
- the impact on competitive advantage of the firm
- the exposure to fraud
- confidentiality
- privacy.

## Cybercops and business protection

### E-FRAUDSTERS ON NOTICE AS ASIC APPOINTS CYBERCOP

BY CASS WARNEMINDE

MELBOURNE — Looking to turn up the heat on Internet fraudsters, the Australian Securities and Investment Commission (ASIC) has established a dedicated electronic enforcement division.

In creating the new unit the organisation has appointed Tim Phillipps, previously NSW director of enforcement, to front its attack on electronic corporate crime.

Phillipps said ASIC has formed the Electronic Enforcement unit in a bid to leverage emerging technologies as the spearhead of its surveillance activities and will especially rely on automated search tools to keep on top of Internet-enabled financial fraud.

'It's more about positioning, it's more about creating a very particular presence. That's really what it's about. We're trying to build our technical capacity to conduct surveillance and awareness work on the Internet, to do some more automated searching of Web sites and bulletin boards and so on,' he said. 'The other side of it is actually [to put] some policy together on when we will litigate, when we will take enforcement action, when is it appropriate to prosecute, how do we actually go about doing that, do we need legislative change, and that sort of thing.'

Citing ASIC's recent Federal Court Action against a local online investment advice site (www.chimes.com.au) as an example, Phillipps said ASIC is looking to the new business unit to cement its position on the technological, legislative and enforcement issues surrounding online fraud.

'[The case against www.chimes.com.au] really brought home that there needs to be a level of expertise in dealing with these issues. While we can cope with the technological issues and we have, we believe, adequate legislation to make all these things happen, the question is physically making that happen in a practical enforcement environment. How do you go about capturing all these things? How do you go about convincing a court how the Internet works and why providing investment advice on a bulletin board is the equivalent of distributing flyers on the street?

'That's the issue, and I think we've demonstrated the need to build that expertise in-house and focus on it,' he explained.

'Part of the challenge for us is to determine how big the problem really is and to make the technological tools work in that way as well.'

Six people will initially staff ASIC's Electronic Enforcement unit, with a mixture of technical, legal and investigation skills.

**SOURCE:** *ComputerWorld*, 30 April 1999, p. 8

**QUESTIONS**

1. What role does ASIC play in the control of Australian business?
2. Why did ASIC develop the Electronic Enforcement Unit?

Security of data and transmission of information in an electronic form, whether online or not, is a fundamental issue for businesses and individuals engaged in electronic commerce. All businesses must ensure that the security and integrity of their data and of transmission of sensitive information is protected from bugs and misconforming system interference, from graffiti and data alteration, from browser-side interference and corruption of data and from interruption from telecommunication infrastructure problems.

# SECURITY ISSUES IN NETWORKS RUNNING ELECTRONIC COMMERCE APPLICATIONS

Security issues in online and electronic forms of business can be classified in various ways. The issues to be addressed by businesses have been classified by Kalakota and Whinston,[3] who suggest that the concerns are of two broad types: client–server security, and data and transaction security. The World

Wide Web Consortium (W3C) (www-genome.wi.mit.edu/WWW/faqs/wwwsfl.html) propose that there are basically three overlapping types of risk:

1. bugs or misconfiguration problems in the web server that allow unauthorised remote users to:
   - steal confidential documents not intended for their eyes
   - execute commands on the server host machine, allowing them to modify the system
   - gain information about the web server's host machine that will allow them to break into the system
   - launch denial-of-service attacks, rendering the machine temporarily unusable

2. browser-side risks, including:
   - active content that crashes the browser, damages the user's system, breaches the user's privacy, or merely creates an annoyance
   - the misuse of personal information knowingly or unknowingly provided by the end-user

3. interception of network data sent from browser to server or vice versa via network eavesdropping. Eavesdroppers can operate from any point on the pathway between browser and server including:
   - the network on the browser's side of the connection
   - the network on the server's side of the connection (including intranets)
   - the end-user's ISP
   - the server's ISP
   - either ISP's regional access provider.

It is important to realise that 'secure' browsers and servers are only designed to protect confidential information against network eavesdropping. Without system security on both browser and server sides, confidential documents are vulnerable to interception.

The following discussion highlights the major issues involved with network security and suggests how these issues might be addressed. In this chapter, security issues are treated individually as many of the issues can apply to all types of security issue classifications like those referred to above.

# Confidentiality of data

Confidentiality of data in e-commerce is concerned with the notion of protection from intrusion, that no-one can access the contents of data or information being sent and that no-one can identify who is sending or receiving a message. This is especially important where highly sensitive documents such as strategic plans, business plans and marketing strategies are exchanged electronically. Such confidentiality is also important in the transmission of data where credit-card users and the operators of business can be identified or where their own security card or electronic payment system (EPS) is involved.

Confidentiality is very closely linked with the issue of privacy for individuals and businesses using the Internet or using any form of electronic business communication. One of the problems with maintaining privacy lies with the protocols actually used in electronic commerce. Almost all servers log every access and record the IP address and/or host name, the time of the download, the name of the user (if obtained by user authentication or by protocol), the URL requested, the status of the request, and the size of the data file(s) transmitted. Immediately this occurs there is a chance the privacy of the user can be affected. In addition to the capture of this information, browsers can also provide the URL that the client came from, and the user's email address. Browsers maintain a record of all users of sites and of any browsing patterns. In terms of privacy, a network manager or 'the web police' may investigate the use of the Web inside any organisation. This collection of data can be used to build a user profile that might contain information that may affect the individual's position within any organisation.

# Integrity of data

Integrity of data requires that data transmitted electronically cannot be altered, defaced or lost during transmission. Integrity relies as much on ensuring that data is not lost accidentally as it does on ensuring it is not lost intentionally. Ensuring **data integrity** involves the operators of business systems understanding that data is protected at all levels in the operation, from the operator (the human element) to the systems being used (browsers, systems, networks, servers, and communications infrastructure).

The process of ensuring data integrity must include an auditing process. Some would argue that with no auditing there is no security. The data trail of transactions and transmissions must be secure to ensure data integrity. In traditional practice it is common for responsible managers to check data for accuracy.

In addition, business managers will check for the reliability of the source, for the accuracy of any figures and charts, for the standing of creditors and suppliers and for an assessment of credit limits where those form part of that business transaction. This process is slow and often requires a number of people to manually check every element of the transaction/data that is supplied in paper format. This process is shown in figure 6.1.

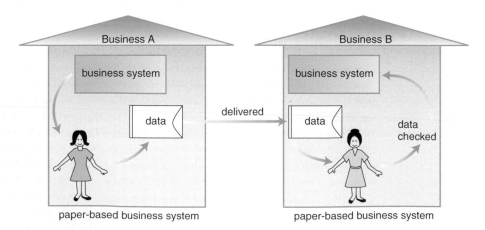

**FIGURE 6.1:** Traditional checking process for data integrity

With a change to electronic business practices, the data is often transmitted from machine to machine. Therefore, new controls must be developed and implemented to check the validity of the data and to check for errors, processes that were previously done manually. Electronic checks need to be built into the system. Key data needs to be electronically matched. This could for example be a simple process of electronically matching data from invoices with delivery dockets and purchase orders. This electronic checking system needs to be under constant review and subject to continuous scrutiny to maintain appropriate levels of data integrity (see figure 6.2).

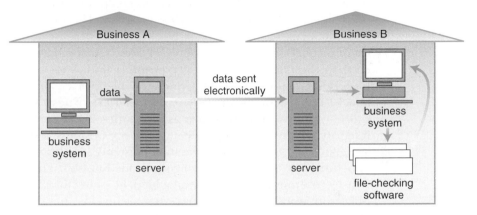

**FIGURE 6.2:** Checking data integrity in an electronic environment

The interaction/transactions must be authorised and authenticated by the business. In addition, there must be constant vigilance in searching networks for **viruses** as these are probably one of the major causes of destruction of data integrity.

## Viruses

The fear that viruses can affect business operations, business systems and transactions and communications between businesses and between business and customer can cause as much, or more, damage than the actual virus. The management problem for businesses is to develop and enforce controls to trap and eliminate computer viruses, and to disseminate information about appropriate software so that a distinction between normal control structures and viruses is available to users of business systems. Online and electronic commerce is very susceptible to virus damage because of the complexity of the Internet connections network and the **availability** of sites for hackers and virus creators to hide and load their software. The oldest forms of interference are called **worms**. Worms propagate and exist independently. They do not have to attach to another program or part of the operating system, distinguishing them from viruses.

A computer virus is defined by its ability to replicate itself. A computer virus cannot replicate itself independently. It requires some form of carrier or 'host'. A computer virus creates damage to the computer system 'infected', either accidentally or deliberately. Computer viruses can occur everywhere in a personal computer's software, as boot blocks, in file allocation tables, in EXE and COM files, and in ordinary files masquerading as functional files. Computer viruses come in all sizes and shapes. These are programs' that seek out unused resources and use them to resolve master programs' problems or tasks. Cracks are programs that have been copy protected, and have been illegally broken.

Computer viruses are classified by their mode of infection, the path used to replicate the virus and the type of system infected. Boot viruses infect the boot block on a floppy or hard disk. These computer viruses usually replace the boot block with all or part of a virus program. The virus files hide in memory and the virus moves the boot block on the disk to another location. File viruses infect ordinary EXE or COM files. Usually they just attach the virus code to the file. Multipartite viruses infect both boot blocks and executable files. Being opportunistic, they find available files at random. A systemic virus attacks the system files necessary to run DOS. These files control the allocation of system resources such as directories. Polymorphic viruses attack the integrity of the operating system used in business system computers and servers. Whilst trying to conceal their existence, stealth viruses can modify file structures to conceal additional codes added to files. The newer viruses, meta viruses, use meta languages embedded in powerful modern programs like Microsoft Word to create damage to existing files and potential files as they are created.

Virus infection is not always very obvious in business organisations. Computer viruses behave in an exponential way. They initially spread and multiply quickly until saturation is reached and they slow down. Any infection can go undetected for months. In most cases damage caused by the virus will be widespread before the problem is recognised. In business organisations it is essential that infection is detected as early as possible after infection. The earlier it is detected, the easier it is to stop. Another problem for businesses engaged in electronic commerce is that the origin of the infection can source multiple infections all with different paths of infection. The importance of virus detection becomes more and more important in organisations as they rely more and more on computer systems for their management and operations and for trading. The more reliant a business is on computer systems, the more vulnerable it becomes to damage caused by computer viruses. A strong company policy against any illegal software is the simplest step in preventing virus infection. In the Business insite on the following page are the responses of 219 employees of computer and information systems (IS) departments in business organisations. The level of responses indicating that illegal or unethical action is acceptable indicates that a well-defined and enforced policy is needed in all business organisations.

Useful resources from the Internet are the Users' Security Handbook (http://info.internet.isi.edu:80/in-notes/rfc/files/rfc2504.txt) and its companion site The Security Handbook (SSH) (http://info.interact.isi.edu:80/innotes/rsc/files/rfc2196.txt. Tips on how to protect systems from viruses are found in these publications.

# COMPUTER CRIME AND ABUSE BY IS EMPLOYEES: SOMETHING TO WORRY ABOUT

BY SUSAN J. HARRINGTON

MOST information systems (IS) managers have long been aware of the need to maintain system security, particularly against computer fraud and sabotage. However, IS managers may not consider their own programmers and analysts as possible perpetrators of computer fraud and sabotage. In addition, programmers and analysts may be in prime positions to initiate other forms of security problems, such as computer cracking (sometimes called hacking), viruses, and software copyright violations. Yet it is tempting for managers to believe that most such security problems come from outside the organization.

Unfortunately little is known about whether IS employees pose a serious threat to an organization's information systems. The facts previously available to IS managers usually include descriptions of individual incidents (e.g. 40-year-old programmer deletes 168 000 sales commission records), highly summarized estimates of costs to organizations nationally (e.g., cracker attacks cost U.S. organizations $160 million), or generalized trends (e.g., 'internal crime is on the rise'). Such lack of facts related to IS employees leaves IS managers to wonder how vulnerable they are within their own organizations.

Even so, IS managers must make critical decisions on whether to spend money on internally-focused security measures. Making such decisions often leaves the IS manager in a quandary: i.e., how much of a threat is there from one's own IS employees who are in trusted positions, and is there a sufficient threat to the organization's systems that warrants sometimes significant additional expenditures?

In order to better understand IS employees' propensity to commit computer crime or abuse, this study obtained the computer-related ethical views of 219 employees, all of whom worked in the IS departments of their organizations.

**The study**

The IS employees studied included 80 programmer analysts, 78 analysts, 17 technical specialists, 15 managers or supervisors, 12 project managers, 7 programmers, 6 security administrators, and one information center specialist. The average age was 37, with the minimum age 22 and maximum age 62. Average time working in information systems was 11 years. Average educational level was a bachelor's degree. The IS employees were randomly selected from 9 organizations in northeastern Ohio.

**Table 1** IS employees' responses (N=219)

| Statement | Number agreeing | Percentage agreeing |
|---|---|---|
| 1. (The person in the vignette) is justified in making (illegal) copies of the software package. | 11 | 5% |
| 2. I would copy software (illegally) for my use or for my friends, too. | 75 | 41% |
| 3. The computer user was justified in accessing and using the services (of another company's computer) to his advantage. | 6 | 3% |

| | | |
|---|---|---|
| 4. I would do the same thing (crack into a company's computer) if I knew how. | 15 | 7% |
| 5. The programmer did nothing wrong in writing a virus program to output the message 'Have a nice day'. | 21 | 10% |
| 6. Management can be so unfair at times that a person can be justified in erasing files. | 2 | 1% |
| 7. I would do the same thing (program a small adjustment to a bank account system to avoid a service charge) if I knew how and knew I wouldn't get caught. | 15 | 7% |
| 8. The manager did nothing wrong in (cracking into another company's computer and) identifying other customers so that her company could try to sell to them. | 13 | 6% |

**FIGURE 1:** Open-ended employee responses related to the question, 'I would copy software for my use or for my friends, too'.

| Response | Reason |
|---|---|
| Agree | I do not feel that making copies for my personal use of software I own is wrong. Giving it to a friend is wrong but I might do it. |
| Agree | I do not agree with copyright laws. |
| Agree | I'm not sure why, but it just doesn't seem as wrong; if the company wanted to, it would find a way to prevent copying. |
| Disagree | I know this is a true violation of the right this company has to profit from its work. |
| Agree | (I) often only need (it) for only one occasion. |
| Undecided | I feel this is stealing, but for financial reasons I may sometimes copy software I couldn't afford. |
| Agree | Software is expensive — it's easier to share. |
| Disagree | My values do not permit me to do so. |
| Strongly Disagree | It is illegal and not worth getting caught. |
| Agree | Occasionally I don't do the right thing. |

**FIGURE 2:** Employee responses to 'The computer user was justified in accessing and using the services to his advantage'.

| Response | Reason |
|---|---|
| Disagree | The services were not for the user; he violated security and privacy standards. |
| Strongly Disagree | It is stealing. Stealing something is wrong even if a lot of cleverness is employed. |
| Strongly Disagree | He was cheating the company of usage fees and setting up another person to take a fall. |
| Strongly Agree | It let him. If they were concerned about this, they would have tighter security. If they can't do that, they should not offer the service at all. |

**SOURCE:** *Journal of Information Systems*, March/April 1995, pp. 8–9. Reproduced by permission.

## QUESTIONS

1. What do the responses in table 1 suggest about the integrity of IS employees?
2. Which responses stand out as significant problems?
3. Are responses from three, six and seven per cent of respondents really problems?
4. How might such activities be controlled?
5. Do the responses justify the actions taken in copying software or accessing data?

It is impossible for a computer virus to be created accidentally. They are invariably introduced into business systems by contact with virus-infected disks or from downloaded information from web sites or from Internet commerce transactions. Software bugs that cause virus-like damage can be created accidentally but such bugs are not viruses as they are not created specifically to do malicious damage; they do not propagate and they can be easily tracked and rectified.

Virus infections must be dealt with quickly and with expert knowledge. A lack of understanding about the location of the virus or the nature of the virus can be catastrophic for a business. Properly designed computer virus repair software must be used as it is often the case that attempts to clean up viruses that may, or perhaps may not, exist can create far more damage than could be caused by the viruses themselves if inadequate repair software is used. Therefore, businesses engaged in electronic commerce must ensure that their networks are secure from external or internal accidental or deliberate damage caused by computer viruses.

# Availability issues

Availability requires that the communications infrastructure and the network systems in place can receive and send information and data and enable electronic transactions in business. There is a requirement that the actual electronic business process gets through. Systems and networks have to be secure enough to ensure that there is no blocking. For the business this must mean that the computer systems, the network, the servers and the software are reliable. It is also essential that the engineering supporting the systems and networks are both sound and reliable and therefore that no technical hitches occur which affect the quality or speed of any transactions or transmissions. Common gateway interface (CGI) scripts are essential software programs. CGI scripts link servers and software and servers and other resources such as databases. These scripts are themselves small servers and this can create problems in making information too available. The problem with CGI scripts is that each one creates opportunities for exploitable bugs. CGI scripts may leak information about the host system that will help hackers break in. These leaks may be either intentional or unintentional. CGI scripts that process remote-user input, such as the contents of a form, may be vulnerable to attacks in which the remote user tricks them into executing commands. Therefore, it is essential that business organisations ensure the security not only of servers but also of the CGI scripts that link their servers to other resources used in the business. Therefore, there must be a well written, precise and coherent policy established in each business to ensure that all possible traps and leaks are covered.

To ensure availability, it is essential that business organisations, ISPs, network managers and telecommunication infrastructure companies have a well-formed and implemented security policy. Such policy has to affect not only action plans in cases of emergency and the requirements of quality delivery and service, but also ensure that the sending or receiving system is set up to do what is intended. In some cases the system could be set up to block everything except some specific tasks. In a purchasing/ordering system transactions using a VISA or MasterCard can be allowed through and all other transactions blocked. Such policy is essential not only to make the system do what it is intended to do but also to ensure that any fraud can be detected. Security policy of all forms requires that the developers of the systems understand the nature of the organisation they are working for. Organisational knowledge is essential to ensure that systems do not do too much or handle tasks that are extraneous to the core function of the business. It is generally accepted in networks that 'knowledge is power' — the more a hacker can establish about a system, the more chance there is for the hacker to find loopholes and break into the system. Denial of service attacks on major e-commerce sites such as Yahoo!, Ebay and Buy.com in February 2000 illustrate the fragility of the Internet. Site spoofing involves masquerading as another web site.

# Authentication issues

**Authentication** of data and information transmission in online and electronic form requires that the message sent must reach the intended recipient and only that recipient. The receiver also needs to be sure that the identified sender is really the one sending the message and that there has been no intermediary sender involved in the process. The simplest means of authenticating data and information transmission is with a name and a password. This is one way of establishing a trust relationship in business-to-business or consumer-to-business electronic links. The most common ways business organisations can establish authentication is with an Access Control List. The platform on which network systems are most usually operating (Unix, Banyan, Windows NT, Novell) all have established protocols built in which enable read, write, print and execute functions. More sophisticated access barriers for authentication use **encryption** or coded messages that operate on a dual system of codes or 'keys' (see figure 6.3).

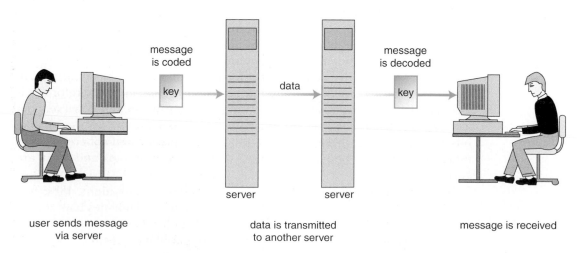

*FIGURE 6.3:* Keys and codes for authentication

# GOVERNMENT STARTS OVER ON SIGNATURES

**Both the Federal and Victorian governments have had to modify plans for the public sector to oversee electronic authentication.**

BY PAUL MONTGOMERY

THE FEDERAL GOVERNMENT has dropped its previous attempt at proposing a peak body to oversee digital signatures in Australia for a new council that will not control operational aspects of the authentication regime, causing the Victorian Government to wait for a uniform national approach.

The National Electronic Authentication Council (NEAC) replaces the National Authentication Authority (NAA), which was proposed last year but never officially created. The NAA proposal attracted some specific criticisms in submissions to the National Office for the Information Economy (NOIE). These have been addressed in the NEAC model.

Senator Richard Alston, Federal Minister for Communications, Information Technology and the Arts, admitted at the launch of the electronic company registration service for the Australian Securities and Investments Commission that the pace of change in technology had made government strategies obsolete in less than a year.

'You can move too quickly on regulation, and the corporate sector is quick to develop its own solutions,' he said.

The NEAC proposal has also affected plans by Victoria for its own policy organisation, called the Electronic Signature Recognition Body (ESRB). The ESRB was proposed in an issues paper released with the E-Commerce Framework Bill, which itself has been superseded in some respects by the Commonwealth Electronic Transactions Bill in constructing a legal basis for purely electronic transactions.

Robert Clarke, Victorian parliamentary secretary for Treasury and Multimedia, told *Image & Data Manager* the Multimedia Ministry had been 'very pleased' with the Federal Government's approach.

'We're proposing to have a close look at the detail of how the NEAC is set up and what it's going to do,' said Mr Clarke, stating that the Victorian Government would amend its policy on the ESRB 'once we've had that look, in light of how NEAC is composed, and what it will be covering'.

**Victoria defers**

Mr Clarke echoed Multimedia Minister Alan Stockdalc's public statement in May that the Victorian Government would defer official discussion of its Bill until spring.

'The Electronic Transactions Bill will be reviewed by the Standing Committee of Attorneys-General in hope of getting an agreement on the content of it. I expect we would proceed with whatever comes out of that,' he said.

Terry O'Connor, spokesperson for Senator Alston, said the NAA discussion paper had been useful in its role of 'kick-starting industry and internal government discussion' and that it 'focused minds on which way we wanted to go'.

'The proposal had [either] a government agency that was responsible for the regulatory environment, or a laissez-faire approach,' he said.

'There is no need for government to be doing something that industry itself can be doing. But we also rejected the laissez-faire approach because there's a standard that has to be maintained.'

Mr O'Connor said the role of NEAC would be 'several-fold', with its primary job being to act as a policy advisor to the Federal Government in conjunction with Standards Australia.

'There is a need to make sure industry does the right things itself,' Mr O'Connor said. 'We don't expect the Australian industry to do anything other than ensure standards [are enforced].

**SOURCE:** *Image and Data Manager,* July/August 1999, p. 20

## QUESTIONS

1. What is the problem with different jurisdictions trying to deal with the authentication problems?
2. How might you resolve the problems?

## Security writing and encryption

Encryption is the process of enabling information/data/knowledge to be coded in such a way that it cannot be read without a decoding system or key. In an authentication system everyone owns a unique set of codes (keys). In one type of authentication both the receiver and the sender own the same encryption key to transmit and read transmissions. This is often called symmetric encryption. In another form of encryption one of the keys is a public key that is widely distributed and owned by all people using the system. The second key is a private key that is kept secret. With this system a message is sent with the public encryption key but can be read only by the recipient with the private key. This is an asymmetric or public form of encryption. In this process the person sending the message 'owns' a certificate, digital signature or identification file, which ensures that the person sending the message using the public key is who they say they are. The most commonly used public key encryption system presently is RSA.[4]

Using this form of authentication is very important in web-based communications as the TCP/IP protocol is very easily tapped into. There are devices called packet sniffers that can listen to TCP/IP traffic on any network and pull down any files, codes, documents, or data that is passing across the network. It is therefore vital that any measure that avoids this form of detection must be implemented in a business organisation committed to doing business electronically.

Restricting access to servers and therefore to files, documents, data, plans, or business operations in an electronic commerce environment means restricting access in three ways: specifying access, specifying user names and passwords and using codes and encryptions to restrict access.

## Specifying access

Access can be restricted to specific IP addresses, sub-nets or domains that are defined by the business organisation at their server. This process will prevent 'noise' — that random hacker or nosey investigator who is seeking easy access. However, such a process will not prevent the determined, well-organised and structured hacker. With the proper equipment and readily available software, hackers can make it seem as if they are connecting from a location different from their real one. This act of an intermediary hacking into the message process is called 'spoofing'.

There is no guarantee that a person contacting a server from an authorised host is in fact the person the receiver or the web manager thinks. The remote host may have been broken into, tampered with and being used as a hidden access route. To ensure proper authentication, IP address restriction must be combined with something that checks the identity of the user, such as a check for user name and password.

## Specifying user names and passwords

A password is only good if that password is chosen carefully. Many people choose their names, their middle names, their birth dates, their office phone numbers, their children's names or even QWERTY![5] Each of these types or forms of names can be randomly found by clever hackers who send random search messages over the Internet hoping to break into sites where simple passwords of this form have been used. A patient hacker can work for hours trying to get into a server as some servers do not impose a limit on the number of attempts at access. The hacker can try over and over to get in. This is very different from access to bank accounts using ATMs. In this case the ATM has been programmed to take only three attempts. After the third error the ATM captures the card and disables any more attempts until the card is retrieved from within the bank itself.

Passwords have to be clever and randomly developed. If the business sells a certain type of car such as a BMW, it would be very sensible *not* to include these three letters in the password. Numbers rather than letters are also not a good idea as there are many software packages that can generate large volumes of random number series which can be applied to access attempts at Internet sites. Some combination of letters and numbers that make sense only to a person creating them or make no sense at all are safer. However, it must be noted that any use of letters and numbers is never really safe. The longer the password the better for safety and perhaps the use of other characters from the keyboard such as '$', '&' and '^' can help.

## Using codes and encryptions to restrict access

In encryption protection both the request and the document being sent are coded in such a way that the text cannot be read by anyone but the intended recipient. At this stage there are no universal solutions to the problems of security and encryption. However, there are some newer developments with software becoming available to ensure that electronic commerce can be done in a more secure way.

# Recent developments in security

The newer schemes for Internet security include SSL (secure socket layer) proposed by Netscape Communications. This is a low-level encryption scheme used to encrypt electronic commerce communications and transactions in higher-level protocols such as HTTP, NNTP[6] and FTP. The SSL protocol can authenticate servers (verifying server's identity), encrypting data in transit, and verifying client identity. SSL is available on several different browsers, including Netscape Navigator, Secure Mosaic, and Microsoft Internet Explorer.

This software is also available on a number of servers including those from Netscape, Microsoft, IBM and Quarterdeck. SSL uses public-key encryption to exchange a session key between the server and the client accessing the server. This session key is used to encrypt the HTTP transaction. There is a different session key used for each transaction. Therefore, if a hacker manages to decrypt a message or a transaction, it does not mean that the key protecting all of the data has been discovered. Decrypting another transaction will require the same amount of effort in trying to decrypt the first message or transaction.

Another security protocol has been developed which operates with HTTP, the highest level protocol most commonly used on the Web. SHTTP (secure HTTP) works only with the HTTP protocol. However, with more advanced encryption techniques becoming available, there is a demand for governments to take a more regulatory role in the further development of electronic commerce.

One new exciting development in security protocols is with **Cryptolope**. Cryptolope is IBM's trademark for its *crypto*graphic enve*lope* technology. Cryptolope objects are used for secure, protected delivery of digital content. They are similar to secure servers. Both use encryption to prevent eavesdroppers from stealing or interfering with content. Both use digital signatures to offer the end user a guarantee that the content is genuine. However, IBM argues, cryptographic envelopes go further:

- A single envelope can incorporate many different, but interrelated, types of content — for example, text, images, and audio – and keeps the package intact.
- A Cryptolope object is a self-contained and self-protecting object, and can be delivered any way that is convenient. For example, Cryptolope objects can be placed on CD-ROMs, can be mirrored to different FTP sites, or even passed casually from user to user, all without breaking the underlying security.
- A Cryptolope object ties usage conditions of the content to the content itself; for example, the price or specifications that viewing the content can only be done with a special viewer or specifications that data can be delivered only to a system that is capable of applying a digital watermark. Because the Cryptolope object is digitally signed, usage conditions cannot be tampered with without invalidating the cryptographic envelope.

The Cryptolope components are all written in Java and the 'envelope' is nothing more than a JAR (Java archive) file. The opener is simply a program that causes the Cryptolope object to begin execution. This allows the maximum flexibility in applying Cryptolopes to an application.

## Non-repudiation issues

**Non-repudiation** requires that the sender and recipient of messages can validate their role in the transmission of data. The sender and the recipient must not deny their role in the transmission of a message of the electronic transaction using credit cards or digital cash.

## ADDRESSING SECURITY ISSUES IN ELECTRONIC COMMERCE

## IT audits

In operating a business in an electronic environment it is essential that companies ensure that a proper audit of all of the factors leading to the issues referred to in the previous sections of this chapter are addressed. The process of an **IT audit** will ensure that those factors creating an insecure environment are addressed.

Figure 6.4 illustrates a framework that encompasses all of the processes necessary to implement an effective IT audit to ensure secure and effective electronic commerce.

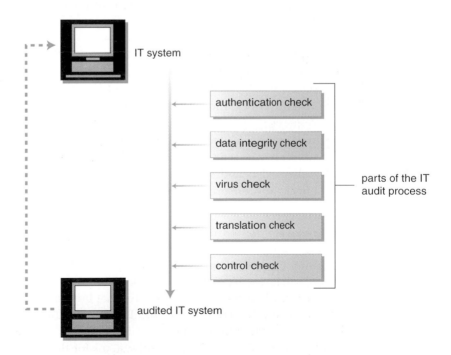

**FIGURE 6.4:** An IT audit for secure and effective electronic commerce

This audit trail requires a 5-step process:[7]

1. **Authentication check**

   Systems checks need to be made to ensure that:
   - secure passwords are allocated within the organisation
   - documented and delegated levels of authority are established and are reflected in the password structure
   - all unused passwords are deleted
   - login attempts are monitored, controlled and limited
   - the number of login accounts available on the machine is limited
   - control systems are established to ensure that the sender of any message can be verified
   - customers and trading partner agreements are in place
   - established and agreed protocols for communication are in place
   - controls systems are established which will automatically generate verified receipts for all electronic communications
   - agreements and legal documents exist which will assure acceptance and non-repudiation of electronic communications with or without electronic signatures.

2. **Data integrity check**

   The implementation of electronic and online trading necessitates the development of new controls to detect invalid data and to check that data sent matches data requests and is aligned with data already processed in similar transactions. To implement data integrity in an online system, it is important that:
   - systems and software are in place to enable data matching electronically
   - exception reports are checked and verified according to previously sent data
   - systems check the accuracy of data in data communications involving requests
   - systems are in place to check previous documents exchanged and follow up on requests at regular intervals
   - policy exists and systems are developed and implemented to review edit checks and ensure continued data integrity.

3. **Virus check**

   Viruses are the most common form of corruption of data in online and electronic commerce environments. Internet viruses are becoming more common and the ease of download of secreted viruses necessitates that checks are both immediate and continuous on all servers and on all machines linked to servers. It is therefore imperative that businesses establish:
   - virus check systems and install virus detection and repair software on servers and all linked PCs
   - a process of daily checks of all systems for delayed virus impact
   - an immediate reaction policy to detection of viruses in engaging in online or electronic commerce.

4. **Translation check**

   In many instances of electronic commerce and online commerce there is a need to enable the translation of data from one form to another which allows access to existing databases and files within a business organisation. This is especially important in old and newer versions of EDI where data files are translated out of the sender's server and into the receiver's server. Therefore, it is important that:

   - any translation process implemented is tested
   - quality control procedures are in place to ensure that the quality of data received is compatible with the needs of existing business databases and processes
   - shells and interpreters not absolutely needed have been removed
   - a policy and appropriate software is in place to direct and alert operators when translation failures occur
   - there is a system check that ensures that only information designed to be processed has been sent
   - systems are in place that report data that is incompatible or not processed.

5. **Controls check**

   In electronic commerce it is essential that the data was correct and whole when sent and received by the intended parties. To achieve this goal it is important that all businesses operating in an electronic environment have established control systems where:

   - all data is received by using sequence checks which check data trails, check for errors and which constantly monitor the audit process
   - communications between clients and the host business are immediate and reliable to ensure there are no delays in transmission
   - data sent on each occasion is filed within correct data files and over-writing of previous data does not occur
   - appropriate archiving of all sent and received data is achieved to enable checking where there are disputes
   - all unused servers are turned off.

   In response to typical business practice, many organisations outsource their IT, electronic commerce and sometimes security processes. **CERT (Computer Emergency Response Team)**[8] and **AusCERT (Australian Computer Emergency Response Team)**[9] provide a comprehensive process to support security in organisations. AusCERT provides a single, trusted point of contact in Australia for the Internet community to deal with computer security incidents and their prevention. AusCERT aims to reduce the probability of successful attack, to reduce the direct costs of security to organisations and lower the risk of consequential damage. Secure communications are facilitated on request. AusCERT is a member of the international Forum of Incident Response and Security Teams (FIRST) and has close ties with the CERT Coordination Centre, with other international incident response teams (IRTs) and with the Australian Federal Police. AusCERT also:

   - provides a centre of expertise on network and computer security matters
   - centralises the reporting of security incidents and facilitates communication to resolve security incidents

- provides for the collation and dissemination of security information including system vulnerabilities, defence strategies and mechanisms and early warning of likely attacks
- acts as a repository of security related information, tools and techniques.

There is one other method that will facilitate higher levels of security in organisations undertaking electronic commerce using the Web or to other networks. This is the implementation of **firewalls** and proxies within the system servers.

# Server security, firewalls and proxies

Most commercial servers are constructed as an intermediation process between the Internet and database and other servers behind the network they support. These network servers tend to store various software packages which enable mail, FTP, newsgroups, network operating systems, the Web, CGI scripts and telnet. With such an array of software, the server is vulnerable to attack. Security policy and the technology practices an organisation adopts must address these vulnerabilities.

**Server security** can be flawed because of intrusion either from in front or behind the server. It is imperative that security checks are made on networks servers and regular tests are made on a server's operation and on the security of each of the component software packages it operates. This involves not only implementation of a security policy and security audit; it also requires the use of additional features to ensure screening and repetitive testing.

Firewalls are pieces of software or hardware that allow only those users from outside a system with specified characteristics to access that system. Firewalls can protect a system or a network or a section of the Internet from unauthorised use both from outside and from within. Levels of access to various parts of a system can also be protected when an internalised firewall system is implemented. Firewalls are devices that can enable secure access and communications between intranets which have been secured and levels of trust ensured, and the Internet and external networks where the level of security and trust is not well established.

Firewalls are part of the audit strategy that has already been discussed. All of the checks and controls referred to in that audit process can be made more effective with a policy that stipulates implementation of a firewall. To enable the types of protection the audit process would enable, firewalls are located at an access point into or out of a system or network (see figure 6.5).

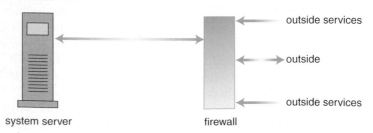

**FIGURE 6.5:** Firewall and security from the outside world

If a firewall is placed inside an existing network server, an internal site is created that is insulated from the outside and is accessible only from within the local area network (LAN). Such a firewall might be one that is suitable for the development and implementation of an intranet in a business organisation. These types of firewalls can enable businesses to control access to various levels of information within an organisation and ensure that there is internal security of the operations of that organisation (see figure 6.6).

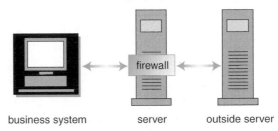

business system      server      outside server

*FIGURE 6.6:* Firewall and internal protection

If the business organisation wants its business server to have access to an external network or wants its server to be accessed by the outside world and other users of the Internet, there is a need to place the business network's server outside of the firewall (see figure 6.7).

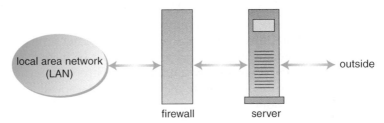

firewall      server

*FIGURE 6.7:* Firewall allowing external access

Firewalls can provide three levels of security depending on the levels of security desired by a business organisation. Firewalls can:
- simply log traffic into and out of a server
- screen or filter information passing through the firewall by using various protocols that can establish which IP addresses (in and out), domains, names or passwords are acceptable. This operation can effectively block undesired or unrecognised incoming traffic and limit the extent and routing of outgoing traffic
- control all traffic with strict protocols and include levels of access, which include information hiding, or maintain regular audits of all data trails and/or communications (e.g. email). This level of firewall security is the most developed and when strictly enforced can maintain a strict level of control of and knowledge about the use of a business' server.

However, there is a danger in the overdevelopment of firewalls. As with all servers and the software loaded on them, the more things that run on the server and the firewall, the more things that can be cracked open by a hacker and, thus, the more difficult it is to maintain and ensure security.

One of the more common forms of firewall is the use of a **proxy**. A proxy is a small program that is able to read messages on both sides of a firewall. Requests from outside users for information, files, transactions or communications from the web server are intercepted by the proxy, checked and then forwarded to the server machine. The response is eventually forwarded back to the requester (see figure 6.8).

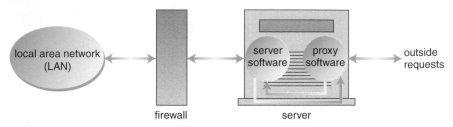

**FIGURE 6.8:** Role of the proxy in firewall security

Proxies increase network security because they can strictly control authentication processes and check all logins to the server. Proxies can support high-level protocols that can enable and deny access to the server and thus to the business organisation's business systems. Proxies also enable better network management because they provide an intermediary in the transaction process that increases the potential for checking and adds another level to the transaction process that will also enable a higher level of security. However, one disadvantage of the use of proxies is that by having an additional level of activity in the business systems interacting with the Internet there is a greater chance for viruses to infiltrate the system and escape detection until some damage has been done.

## SUMMARY

Security of networks and systems operating in business organisations is of paramount importance to all businesses engaged in electronic commerce and online commerce. This needs to be done in a well-organised and systematic way. Bernstein et. al. (1996) (see the suggested reading list at the end of this chapter) suggest that there are three critical paths to maintaining and managing a security audit trail to ensure business security in Internet commerce. These paths are shown in figure 6.9.

Systems can function very effectively and improve the efficiency of businesses to a significant degree. However, if the confidentiality of the data transacted, communications sent or the files stored cannot be assured then the system is of less value to the organisation. Business done electronically relies on the integrity of the data being sent. If data is corrupted by poor systems, poor system management, inadequate or incompatible software and hardware, or by viruses, then the business transacted is of no value whatsoever. Business organisations need to be able to protect the goodwill and value of their business. They need to be assured that their data and their files are not stolen or made accessible to those who have no right of access. Network systems must be made secure from prying computers and the eyes and intelligence gathering of hackers. Business systems must ensure that the identity of both senders and receivers of information, data or communications is correct and appropriate for the information or transaction desired. It is only with the development and implementation of proper IT policy and the establishment of an IT audit for security that businesses will gain proper and thorough security in their operations of their networks.

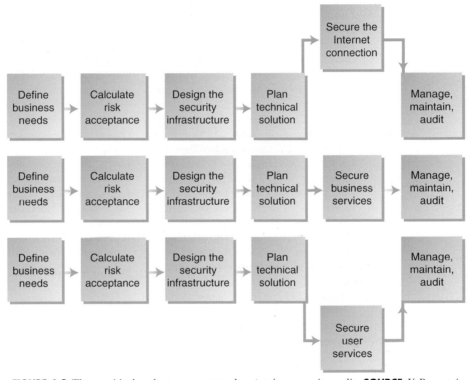

**FIGURE 6.9:** Three critical paths to manage and maintain a security audit. **SOURCE:** Y. Bernstein, A. Bhimani, E. Schultz and C. Siegel 1996, *Internet Security for Business*, John Wiley and Sons, Inc., New York, p. 80

| key terms | | |
|---|---|---|
| AusCERT (Australian Computer Emergency Response Team) | Cryptolope | proxy |
| | data integrity | security |
| authentication | encryption | server security |
| availability | firewall | virus |
| CERT (Computer Emergency Response Team) | hacker | worm |
| | IT audit | |
| confidentiality | non-repudiation | |

# BETTER SAFE

## BY DAVE TAYLOR AND ROSALIND RESNICK

AT this moment, thousands of Internet shoppers are innocently typing their credit-card numbers into e-mail messages and zapping them to online vendors. Others are entering credit-card information into Mosaic forms at Internet cybermalls. Happy merchants, meanwhile, are ringing up sales from an internetworked world.

But is it safe? Ah, there's the rub. Credit information is an acceptable risk on the network — but a significant risk just the same. Although in the nine months since we finished our book, *The Internet Business Guide*, some important new software has appeared that promises to make Internet commerce safer, Internet security still has a way to go.

As of this writing, Secure HTTP (HyperText Transport Protocol), the so-called secure Mosaic being developed by Enterprise Integration Technologies (EIT), is being beta-tested ... and a cross-platform security standard has yet to emerge. However, there are a variety of technological solutions now available that give Net buyers and sellers a measure of security that was lacking earlier.

### Danger lurking in every wire

What makes the Internet so vulnerable to electronic mischief? Unlike centralized networks operated by commercial online services such as CompuServe and Prodigy, the Internet is a decentralized system spread out across millions of computers worldwide. Each of these machines has its own passwords and security procedures — or lack of them. In some cases, the Internet is only as strong as its weakest link, and intruders who break into one part of the system can rapidly gain access to much of the rest of it.

The Internet's rapid growth has aggravated its security problems. With more than 20 million potential users throughout the world, the small-town ethos that members of the network once enjoyed has given way to modern big city problems that need commensurate solutions.

Dain Gary, manager of the Computer Emergency Response Team, reports that his group logs three to four security breaches on the Internet each day. For 1994, Gary expects a 50 percent increase over last year's 773 reported intrusions. The real numbers are probably even higher.

### Dealing with the problem today

As Internet commercial services become increasingly popular, so does the risk of credit-card theft. One company that has had to address this issue is Cyberspace Development, a cybermall operator in Boulder, Colo.

'Although the Internet is not a "secure" system as the term is used in defense and financial circles,' said Andrew Kurrie, president of Cyberspace Development, 'many people believe that using credit-card numbers on the Internet is an acceptable risk — on a par with giving out credit-card information to telephone merchants or paying a restaurant tab with a credit card, where the credit-card number on the receipt is clearly visible.'

However, Currie has reason to minimize the risk. Cyberspace Development, like many Internet cybermall operators, encourages shoppers to transmit their credit card information once over the Internet, then to sign up for a special customer account for future transactions.

A firm with a more secure approach is Internet Shopping Network, a Menlo Park, Calif.-based firm recently purchased by the Home Shopping Network. 'Even the initial transmission of credit-card information over the Net is an unacceptable risk,' said Bill Rollinson, vice president of marketing. 'We give our customers membership codes after they've given us their credit information by calling our 800 number or faxing us. It's a simple system that works.'

**Secure lanes on the highway**

Many experts believe the real answer to credit-card security on the Internet is encryption. That's where Secure HTTP comes in. With ordinary Internet e-mail, merchants cannot prove that customers are whom they claim to be, that a message received was the one originally sent, or that a message wasn't read along the way. Moreover, a customer could deny that he or she sent a message or placed an order.

With Secure HTTP, a customer browsing an online catalog on the World Wide Web can select a product by clicking on a 'secure submit' button. This causes the client program to generate a session key to encrypt the order form's contents, which safeguards the credit-card data from prying eyes. The online merchant's public key can then be used to encrypt the customer's session key; both encrypted components are delivered to the server. (Of course, even Secure HTTP can't protect Internet merchants from credit-card fraud.)

Although Secure HTTP's developers — EIT, NCSA, and RSA Data Security — have begun releasing the software to members of CommerceNet, a California high-tech manufacturing consortium ... and are planning to let NCSA distribute it for free on the Internet, Secure HTTP is not yet in widespread use on the Net. Meanwhile, other developers are rolling out proprietary products that ultimately will support the Secure HTTP standard.

In September 1994, Spry, developer of Internet in a Box, rolled out Secure Encrypted Transactions (SET), a software architecture that permits credit-card transactions to be conducted safely through the Web's Mosaic browser. SET supports a variety of security standards, including the DES and RSA public-key encryption systems. Recently, Spry announced that it would support Terisa Systems' Secure HTTP and would release a system called Mosaic Express.

Not to be outdone, Netscape Communications Corp., the commercial spin-off of the team that developed the original Mosaic at the National Center for Supercomputing Applications (NCSA), released several Internet security tools. The Netscape Web browser provides encryption based on the RSA public-key algorithm, while Commerce Server, a Unix-based server application, includes both encryption and authentication capabilities.

MCI Telecommunications Corp. just announced an Internet shopping service called interMCI that will use Netscape's secure software in its front end for customers' credit-card transactions. The Netscape software will be integrated with client software from ETP Software Inc.

Many Internet merchants and cybermall operators are making do with ad hoc security solutions. Popular encryption programs like ViaCrypt's version of RSA's PGP (Pretty Good Privacy), Kerberos, PEM (Privacy-Enhanced Mail), and the public-domain versions of PGP ... are being used to secure transactions. Sled Corp. introduced a service that lets users download discount coupons using ViaCrypt's software. More recently, NetMarket, a small Internet services provider, bundled PGP into X-Mosaic, allowing customers to order products securely from one of the merchants on its server.

There are also a variety of off-line solutions incorporating toll-free phone lines and faxes. Internet Shopping Network, a Web-based catalog retailer, requires new customers to submit their credit-card information by fax. First Virtual also has introduced a service that allows buyers and sellers to perform transactions online, with sensitive credit-card data handled off-line after they have set up an account by phone ...

A new Web-based cybermall called Downtown Anywhere uses a Personal Payment system that eliminates the need for transmitting sensitive credit-card numbers over the network. In minutes, an online shopper with a credit card and a touch-tone phone can acquire a Personal Payment Password that can be used for online purchases in Downtown Anywhere and at other participating sites.

Although the technology for secure Internet transactions may not be perfect, it's come a long way in a short time. And merchants who stay on the sidelines waiting for a fool-proof solution to Internet security may well miss a chance at one of the hottest markets of the decade.

### Tokens and PINs

To safeguard your privacy and protect valuable information, the first line of defense is to shield your account with a password. The face of modern banking transactions has changed dramatically since the introduction of automated teller machines (ATMs), and the simple idea that really made the ATM system work was the secret personal identification number (PIN). The PIN, like a password, is typically a secret four-digit number that users key in along with their ATM cards to verify that they are authorized to use the card. If someone steals your card, it's useless without the PIN.

Computer systems can be protected similarly via account passwords. Unlike an ATM system, however, users can choose not to have a password or to use a password that is simple to break (for example, 1234).

There are a number of password security products on the market that generate new passwords every 60 seconds or so ... These solutions, called token authentication systems, consist of a token or card carried by the user that is synchronized with the code generator. Some of these products offer fixed and changeable passwords in combination; this is called two-factor authentication.

## Keeping e-mail private

When sending e-mail messages, it's a good idea not to post anything on the Internet you wouldn't want to see on the front page of the *National Enquirer*. This goes for chat rooms, too.

Recognize that a bulletin board manager or system operator has the legal right to read all e-mail messages — even if they are intended to be private. Many sysops periodically screen public and private e-mail just to protect their BBSs from being shut down by the police.

The surest way to protect your e-mail privacy is through encryption. If this sounds like spy stuff, it is. Encryption software programs like PGP ... and RIPEM (available online by sending e-mail to rsares@rsa.com) break down ordinary e-mail messages into unique codes, allowing only those with special keys to unlock them. A digital signature at the end of the message verifies the sender's identity.

You also can use an anonymous mailing service to protect your privacy. You can get an account on an anonymous server on the Internet to shield your online activities from public view. Any messages sent to your anonymous e-mail address get rerouted to your real e-mail address. Replies are handled the same way. Probably the most popular anonymous server is anon.penet.fi, run by Johan Helsingius of Finland. For more information, send e-mail to julf@penet.fi.

Dave Taylor (taylor@netcom.com) and Rosalind Resnick (rosalind@harrison.win.net) are co-authors of *The Internet Business Guide: Riding the Information Superhighway to Profit* (SAMS Publishing, 1994).

## EXERCISES

1. How do the issues raised in this case study of Internet shopping help both sellers and customers engage in secure Internet commerce?
2. Use the classification systems given at the start of the chapter and arrange the various security issues discussed in the chapter into the categories given.
3. Try to develop a better classification of the security issues based on your evaluation of the security needs of businesses engaged in electronic commerce.
4. Undertake a review of any business organisation's security needs and try to develop the elements of a security policy that would meet the needs of that business. It is important that you tackle this problem with some discretion. You should be concerned to find out the needs not specifics about databases or systems operations in that business.
5. Undertake a search for web sites that provide detailed information on security that would be useful for business organisations wanting to improve their security.
6. Develop a list of existing and proposed software packages that enable proxy development and evaluate the potential of each to meet the security needs of a business engaged in online commerce.
7. Prepare a report on advances in security techniques since this article was published.

# Case Study 2 — INTERNET ETIQUETTE

'Uncivilised' behaviour is becoming increasingly more noticeable on the Internet as more people, including the unscrupulous, log on. Bill Joy, Sun Microsystems' chief scientist and an early Internet architect, offers some ideas to ensure more civilised behaviour on the Internet ('Report from the cyberfront', Newsweek, 21 February 2000, p. 42). He believes that just as we might add caller ID to our telephones to help stamp out obscene telephone calls, we might also have to put in similar facilities on the Internet.

Joy's ideas include the following:

- Attackers are able to send junk mail free of charge. If they had to pay for each email they sent, there would be fewer attacks. There would be a lot of opposition to this idea as it punishes everyone for the bad behaviour of the minority.
- Email could be priced by introducing several classes of service for email. For example, a first-class service might require you to identify yourself and pay a fee; a free, anonymous service would have no guarantees for delivery. This idea has merit as it does not make everyone suffer for the actions of some badly behaving persons. It is similar to paying for express snail mail — something that businesses are often willing to do.
- Ownership marks could be required for email. This is analogous to putting number plates on cars to identify the owners and enforce road rules. Cryptolopes could be useful in this context (see page 152).
- PCs were not designed with security in mind. More secure Internet appliances and Internet-enabled mobile phones are on their way. These 'personal communicators' will use tamper-resistant identity chips protected by password or by biometrics, and will be suitable places for keeping digital money. Hopefully, with the introduction of Internet2, levels of security will be much better. This is further discussed in chapter 11, page 300.

Other suggestions include to improve behaviour on the Internet include:

- universities and colleges stressing ethics in their computing, information technology and business courses
- penalties for unlawful actions on the Internet should match the severity of the crime.

## EXERCISES

1. Debate the pros and cons of the four ideas put forward.
2. Prepare a report on secure Internet access appliances and Internet-enabled mobile phones.

## QUESTIONS

1. What are the major security issues affecting network security?
2. How can the authenticity of messages be verified on the Internet? How does authentication affect Internet business?
3. Why is government policy for security so important?
4. Should all governments attempt to develop an international agreement on information law? Why?
5. How and why are firewalls and proxies so important?
6. How do viruses affect the security and integrity of online and electronic communication and electronic commerce? What can businesses do to protect themselves from security breaches by viruses?
7. Prepare reports on:
   (a) site spoofing
   (b) denial of service attacks.

## SUGGESTED READING

Ahuja, V. 1997, *Secure Commerce on the Internet*, Academic Press Ltd, London.

Bernstein, Y., Bhimani, A., Schultz, E. and Siegel, C. 1996, *Internet Security for Business*, John Wiley and Sons, Inc., New York.

Chapman, D. B. and Zwicky, E. D. 1997, *Building Internet Firewalls*, O'Reilly and Associates, United States.

Ford, W. and Baum, M. 1997, *Secure Electronic Commerce*, Prentice Hall, United States.

Furche, A. and Wrightson, G. 1996, *Computer Money: A Systematic Overview of Electronic Payment Systems*, dpunkt, verlag für digitale Technologie GmbH, Heidelberg, FDR.

Garfinkle, S. and Spafford, G. 1997, *Web Security and Commerce*, O'Reilly and Associates, United States.

Ghosh, A. K. 1998, *E-Commerce Security*, John Wiley and Sons, Inc., New York.

Kalakota, R. and Whinston, A. 1996, *Frontiers of Electronic Commerce*, Addison-Wesley, United States.

Kalakota, R. and Whinston, A. 1997, *Electronic Commerce: A Manager's Guide*, Addison-Wesley, United States.

Liu, C., Peek, J., Jones, K., Buus, R. B. and Nye, A. 1996, *Managing Internet Information Systems*, O'Reilly and Associates, United States.

Pfleeger, C. 1997, *Security in Computing*, 2nd edn, Prentice Hall, United States.

Rubin, A., Geer, D. and Ranum, M. 1997, *Web Security Sourcebook*, John Wiley and Sons, Inc., United States.

## END NOTES

1. See www.ec.gov.sg/policy.html for further information.
2. Bernstein, Y., Bhimani, A., Schultz, E. and Siegel, C. 1996, *Internet Security for Business*, John Wiley and Sons, Inc., United States, p. 59
3. Kalakota, R. and Whinston, A. 1996, *Frontiers of Electronic Commerce*, Addison-Wesley, United States.
4. A detailed discussion of RSA can be found in Furche, A. and Wrightson, G. 1996, *Computer Money: A Systematic Overview of Electronic Payment Systems*, dpunkt, verlag für digitale Technologie GmbH, Heidelberg, FDR.
5. QWERTY are the first letters on a keyboard from the top left across. They have been commonly used as a password.
6. NNTP is the network news transfer protocol designed to enable newsgroups to run supporting Windows 95 and Windows NT.
7. The thin IT audit process was developed from work carried out by G. Behrendorff from the Centre of Electronic Commerce, Monash University.
8. See www.cert.org for more information.
9. See www.auscert.org.au/Information/Auscert_info/whatis.html for more information.

# CHAPTER 7

# The **Internet customer**

## LEARNING *Outcomes*

You will have mastered the material in this chapter when you can:
- define the Internet customer
- understand the effect the World Wide Web has on marketing
- provide examples of different approaches to Internet marketing
- understand the various methods of interacting with the Internet customer
- understand ways of marketing to the Internet customer
- understand database marketing
- know the difference between direct and database marketing
- appreciate the issues of customer relationship management.

*'E-commerce has increased customer expectations, and customer expectations have raised the bar on service levels ... if companies fail to leap over it, they're out of the game.'*

R. Kalakota and M. Robinson 1999, *e-Business: Roadmap for Success*, Addison-Wesley Longman, United States, p. 109

# INTRODUCTION

The Internet and Web create some distinct challenges for those who wish to find, develop and interact with **customers**. The Internet consumer could be thought of as a different breed to the traditional consumer. The Internet has enabled them to access information on products and services from a variety of competitors, from across the globe. Customer acquisition is the name of the game on the Internet and companies have to adapt by paying attention to them and providing better levels of service. Research has shown that Internet customers are:

- brand loyal (but within limits)
- take to new concepts easily
- accept risks
- are averse to rules (Why can't I do that?)
- willing to pay (but demand value)
- want to customise their own solutions quickly and easily.[1]

# DEFINING THE INTERNET CUSTOMER

At first, defining who is and who is not an Internet customer seems easy: an Internet customer is anybody who makes purchases via the Internet. From this perspective the Internet customer is anybody who engages in a transaction with a vendor. Such a definition focuses on those people who browse the Internet and make a purchase (perhaps using a credit card) from a vendor of some product. This definition, however, is unnecessarily narrow. Perhaps a better definition of 'customer' might be to borrow from the Quality movement and view the customer as any consumer of goods and services, regardless of the type of financial transaction. This definition can be modified to include any consumer of content on the Internet, where content can include tangible goods, as well as services and information.

With this shift in mind the focus has moved from purchasers of things to the wider community of those who use the Web. This large and nebulous group becomes a somewhat unruly mass to understand and an even more difficult one to interact with. Included in this broad category of Internet customer are:

- readers of company web pages
- recipients of company emails
- online subscribers to newsletters
- direct purchasers of goods (e.g. software and graphic art)
- indirect purchasers of goods (e.g. books and CDs).

With this view in mind, there are many Internet customers, only some of whom are involved in traditional transactions with a vendor.

Other subtleties exist when thinking about who is the customer. Some have suggested that not only are there external customers, but internal customers too. Intranets serve as content providers for employees of a given organisation. Silicon Graphics provides an excellent intranet for its employees, or internal customers.

# Just who is the Internet customer?

Are you having trouble finding Internet customers? Look in the office next door and you will find one. A survey by Boston Consulting found that 10 to 15 per cent of all shopping in Australia will be conducted online within three to five years. For products such as computer software this will be closer to 80 per cent.[2] According to IBM's E-Commerce Assistant page,[3] the success or otherwise of a product on the Internet depends on six overall factors:

1. The target market should preferably be one that consists of:
   - computer users
   - technology early adopters
   - people with above-average levels of income
   - people with above-average levels of education
   - a mix of men and women now that the balance is getting to be 50/50.
2. Preferably, the product should:
   - be computer-related
   - not need to be touched or tried on before purchase
   - be simple and easy to understand
   - be easy to ship to a customer
   - be standardised
   - be innovative
   - have global appeal
   - occupy a niche market.
3. The product needs a known brand so that customers will be more trusting.
4. To be an attractive product on the Internet, the product:
   - should be easy to distribute globally
   - should not have local, non-Internet distributors competing.
5. An attractive Internet product will:
   - not be too expensive or too inexpensive
   - have a price that can be changed frequently
   - be able to leverage off existing publicity and advertising
   - have a lower cost structure on the Internet
   - not have too much competition to drive prices down.
6. The market environment should:
   - allow anonymity for purchase
   - be in growth rather than depression
   - be in a developed region or country.

There are several sites you can use to check out the types of people who use the Web. The **Hermes Survey**, which is carried out by Georgia Tech in conjunction with the University of Michigan, contains such useful information as the output of an online survey of Internet users as to their reasons for not making purchases on the Internet. The user survey (1998) highlights a range of significant factors that include not only security concerns, but privacy, comfort with existing shopping processes, and other technical and marketing issues. The analysis of these results by location does not highlight any huge variations on a global perspective.[4]

According to a survey of 3000 United States consumers with Internet access, Greenfield Online found that Generation X is doing the most buying online. The table below highlights some of the findings.

| TABLE 7.1 | FREQUENTLY PURCHASED PRODUCTS | |
|---|---|---|
| **ITEM** | **1998 (PER CENT)** | **1999 (PER CENT)** |
| books | 10 | 26 |
| CDs | 10 | 24 |
| computer software | 11 | 21 |
| computer hardware | 7 | 13 |
| airline tickets | 5 | 12 |

**SOURCE:** Greenfield Online 1999, *Generation X Buy More Online*, October 5, www.nua.ie/surveys

Consumer purchasing increased by 11 per cent over 12 months, nearly 75 per cent of the participants buy online and 82 per cent buy more than one item per session.

Clearly, the Web is an important place in which to find out about products and services, and it is a slowly growing forum for more traditional transactions.

The issue of culture cannot be ignored. The first Chinese/English e-commerce product of its kind to be released onto the market for bilingual merchants is being offered at no cost over the Internet. The software from Hong Kong can be downloaded from www.inter-Merchant.com.[5] In traditional face-to-face, or even traditional distance-based, customer interactions, the cultural identity of the customer could be rather easily known. On the Web, culture is expressed through a keyboard. This creates new difficulties and challenges. Subtleties of language may become easily lost on the Web, potentially creating communication barriers. It is important to be aware of cultural difference when operating within the Web.

# REACHING INTERNET CUSTOMERS

Getting to customers is a central problem in Internet commerce. In more traditional times business proprietors could rely upon such simple activities as physical proximity to ensure that customers were reached. Putting up a billboard sign over the highway assured that local shoppers knew about products. Now, however, the Web has exploded physical proximity as a variable in the customer relationship. Steering the customer to a given product is a much more difficult and complex process. In fact it has been suggested that rather than see the customer passively awaiting the marketer, the customer and marketer should work together in developing the Web marketplace.[6]

Very early attempts at facilitating the meeting between customer and provider were found in hotlists. Lists of providers, organised around themes or products, were available on such services as Yahoo!. A natural progression from the hotlist was the **Internet shopping mall**, which is a more highly structured and organised form of hotlist. For example, The Internet Mall solicits businesses, without charging an access fee. The mall makes money through corporate sponsorship and **advertising**. The Internet Mall differs from the CyberMall in New Zealand where a small monthly charge is levied. Such malls, however, are targeted towards small and often new businesses. Sofcom, an Australian Internet publisher operating the Sofcom mall, bills at a rate of $40 per month.

Trying to pick the next web trend is important and a Deloitte Consulting report released in September 1999, picked vertical portals. The Business insite below also mentions other ways of getting close to Internet customers.

## Special interest, vertical portals, 'Delling' and zShops

A Deloitte Consulting report has predicted that vertical or special-interest portals could be the next 'hot' trend in the world of web commerce. One example used is a portal for the outdoor lifestyle, where people could access information and buy camping, climbing or fishing equipment.[7] Another name for this is the specialised portal such as one devoted to a specific industry. Content focus shows up in the level of categories that are considered important. PikeNet[8] has a directory entry on the top level of its **ontology** or directory categorisation scheme called 'REITs and Institutions'. This is a specialised corporate form used by a number of large apartment building owners and investors. Only a specialist site would have the knowledge that this should be a high-level category. Such specialised portals are a rich source of information and traffic for many industries.

Proctor and Gamble has set up Reflect.com as an attempt to follow the Dell model. According to consultant, Ed Tazzia, the consumer-products giant will sell customised products like cosmetics over the Internet. Proctor and Gamble believes this will give them the insight to craft both marketing and sales relationships with consumers. Tazzia said 'Once you can figure out how to get into somebody's home, who needs Wal-Mart?'[9]

Amazon.com has also opened a new consumer mall. Jeff Bezos states 'Amazon.com seeks to be the world's most customer-centric company, where people can find and discover anything they may want to buy online'. Its new mall, called zShops, enables any retailer — large or small — to sell products from a personalised page for a small fee. In other words, the mall will help Amazon.com customers find almost anything without ever having to leave the Amazon.com web site.[10]

### EXERCISES
1. Locate and critique a vertical portal on the Web.
2. Visit PikeNet or a similar specialised industry portal and examine the ontology to see if it is using categories that might appeal only to specialists.
3. Debate the pros and cons of the statement: 'Once you can figure out how to get into somebody's home, who needs Wal-Mart?'
4. Discuss the zShop model as a type of portal.

# Advertising to reach customers

More sophisticated methods of reaching customers are evolving, such as advertising. **Banner advertisements** are passive advertisements that are encountered by simply visiting a web page. These banner advertisements have not proved as popular as advertisers had hoped as many web surfers do not click through. One solution to this is the live banner, which lets a user get more information about the product without leaving the current site. The problem with live banners is they work slowly (especially with slower modems) and are expensive to develop.[11] **Target advertisements** are active. These advertisements are those on which a user must click in order to visit; they invite the user to act. Target advertisements are appearing more often on the Web, encouraging would-be customers to visit pages. Sponsorship of search engines is a way of gaining high visibility and contact with customers. For example, IBM ecommerce carries a banner advertisement on the search engine Web Wombat. Clicking on the advertisement directs the customer to the IBM ecommerce site.

There, customers can read about new products, register products or discover more about the company. By positioning an advertisement on a search engine, US Robotics — Australia ensures that its message is seen by a wide number of web users. Search engines are a favoured place for advertisements, because they offer the marketer an important advantage.

As searchers enter their searches, the key words are used to determine what type of advertisement will come up on the screen. For example, if you were to search using the key word 'car', the page that appears listing the web sites containing that key word would also feature advertising from businesses such as car dealerships. For example, a search using the key word 'telephone' will result in an advertisement by Optus.

DoubleClick is a major international online advertising company that both sells and manages web advertising. It provides a service called DART to send online advertisements to specific web pages. DoubleClick has come under attack from privacy groups in 1999 and 2000 over its advertisement serving and data collection practices and has decided to hire a chief privacy officer and retained Price Waterhouse Coopers to do regular privacy audits.

Commercial vendors of other products may also carry advertising. For example, Traveland sponsor advertisements on the *Sydney Morning Herald* web page. Readers of the *Sydney Morning Herald* simply click on the Traveland advertisement, which advertises cheap travel fares, and are taken to the travel agent's site.

Advertising is sold using three different methods.[12] First, is **flat-fee advertising**, which simply charges a set fee for the advertisement over a time period. In this arrangement no assurances are made concerning who sees the advertisement, or its effectiveness. In many ways the flat-fee model harks back to the days of a simple billboard sitting by the roadside.

Slightly more sophisticated than this model is the **CPM** (cost per thousand presentations model) **advertisement**, which calculates the number of times the advertisement is viewed. Thus, the higher the bill for the advertisement, the greater its visibility. The average cost of the CPM advertisement is about US$40, with advertisements appearing on soap operas, mysteries and dramas peaking at an average of US$250.[13] A third model of advertising billing is **'click-through' advertising**.

This model bills on the basis of the number of times the advertisement is clicked on, taking the viewer to the advertising page. Thus, billing is on the number of times somebody actually undertakes an action.

**FIGURE 7.1:** Advertising on the Web: home page of DoubleClick (www.doubleclick.com)

## Satisfying customer needs

Thus far, these approaches to guiding customers to the desired site have been replications of very traditional advertising plans. Technically, they are increasingly sophisticated, but they rely upon some very tried and true methods.

Use of the Web, however, has led many to interact with customers in much richer ways. For example, the NRMA provides membership services via the Web. Customers can access the NRMA's survey of new car prices, a technical hotline and other motoring news using their membership number and membership expiry date.

In providing these services, the NRMA attracts customers to its site. It has now released its first online sales facility allowing customers to purchase travel insurance over the Web. Users can obtain a quote online and before departure secure the transaction using a credit card. Obligation-free quotes are available and to attract new users NRMA is offering a discount of 25 per cent for any travel insurance purchased over the Internet. Following an equally sophisticated tack are the organisers of the Fourth International Symposium on Quality Function Deployment. Symposium organisers ask visitors to visit the web page to register their interest in the conference.

From then onwards, registrants receive emails outlining new symposium events, speakers and topics. Using such interactivity, symposium organisers attract customers to the site, making the site an important and useful link in keeping would-be attendees informed of important events.

## Satisfying your online customer

Many online shoppers are 'time poor' and like the convenience of shopping online. Outlined below are some of the reasons people are using online grocery stores:
1. to avoid the crowds at supermarkets
2. to avoid the trouble of finding parking spots
3. to avoid the overhandling of goods — for example the in-store shopper has to handle the items up to five times, picking the items off the shelf and placing them into the trolley, taking them from the trolley onto the cashier's station, lifting them from the cashier's station back into the trolley, from the trolley to the car boot, from the car's boot to the kitchen shelf, from the shelf into the cupboards. By contrast the online shopper handles the goods only once — from the kitchen shelf into the cupboards.
4. to avoid wasting Saturday mornings doing shopping
5. to cut the grocery bill as online shopping limits impulse buys
6. to be able to shop from the comfort of your home, in the middle of the night and with your hair in rollers
7. the delivery of the items can be set to your convenience.

For the online shopper the most time-consuming part is setting up the initial order. Once the master order has been established, it is easier as only about a quarter of the average supermarket order changes each week.[14]

### EXERCISE

Select two online supermarket sites and write a critique on both addressing such issues as:
(a) the appearance of the opening page
(b) the speed of loading
(c) the use of advertisements
(d) how easy is it to set up a master list
(e) the payment options
(f) the delivery options
(g) the search engine on the site.
(h) how the supermarket makes the customer feel comfortable with the site.

# CUSTOMER RELATIONS

**Customer relations** is a vital subject in the evolution of Internet commerce. Developing that affinity between providers and customers is crucial for successful online commerce. In Australia there are roughly 100 000 businesses online. The unfortunate reality is that most of those businesses fail to maximise their use of the Web. Ideally, relating to and interacting with customers is more than simply putting up a web page. Elaine Rubin, Senior Vice-President of Interactive Marketing of iVillage and one-time head of the highly successful interactive services group 1-800-Flowers, has advice on customer relations.

> *The power of online marketing, she says, comes from one-to-one communications between retailers and manufacturers and their customers. Used right, the technology can actually build affinity and relationships. Unfortunately, many corporate web sites are nothing more than repurposed advertising and use the Internet simply as a way of lowering costs...*[15]

Refer to 'Sites to search' on page 216 for sites to assist online customers. Some advances in helping consumers manage their digital identity are taking place as seen in the following Business insite.

## Your digital identity

Novell and Microsoft have entered the arena to assist online customers build their individual digital identities.

The Microsoft offering is called Passport, which attempts to centrally manage consumers' online relationships. Users of Hotmail may enter their credit card details and shipping information details from a Passport entry site on the Hotmail web site.

Novell has launched digitalme™, a personal data repository that allows users to create virtual online identity cards. This new technology is aimed at e-commerce businesses, including portals, ISPs and retail companies, that want to provide their customers with a way to control their identities on the Web and enjoy conveniences such as 'single-click buying'. (See the web site at www.digitalme.com.)

Why would the digitalme technology be useful? At its most basic level, digitalme saves consumers from having to manage a number of passwords for multiple sites and from having to re-do registration forms to buy online goods and services.

The Novell product promotes exchangeable customer profiles called meCards. The cards could include a shopping card with credit card number, colour preferences, clothes size, etc. Some cards might be used for visiting sites anonymously; other cards might be used to send to friends when the user's address or telephone number changes.

Novell also plans to allow users to withdraw their meCards from sites and directories if there is any abuse of personal information.

**SOURCE:** adapted from *Wall Street Journal*, 'A card that says it all', in *Sydney Morning Herald*, IT Internet, 12 October 1999, p. 4c, and Novell 1999, 'Novell debuts new digitalme 'in-the-net' service', 5 October, www.novell.com/lead_stories/1999/oct05/index.html

## EXERCISES

1. Investigate the usage of Passport, meCards and digitalme to ascertain their level of popularity. If other systems have come into use since this article was published, comment on their adoption or lack of adoption by the online consumer.
2. Report on how the digitalme service works and why it might be useful for e-commerce consumers.

Perhaps the most basic way of relating to customers is through email, which is an efficient and simple way of interacting with customers. Assisting customers in interacting through email serves the interests of everybody. For example, Amazon.com communicates extensively with its customers via email. Each book order that is placed with Amazon.com receives an acknowledging email containing the specifics of the order and the order number. The signature of the email contains a hypertext link back to the Amazon.com web page. Further facilitating the ease of communication are simple directions for sending a return email, which is routed to the appropriate department automatically.

To follow email best practice, consider the following:

- Offer email facilities only if you are prepared to support them at a high level.
- Every email deserves a response.
- Answer the questions posed by the email sender.
- Match the medium's expectations (i.e. people who send email expect a rapid response).
- Implement a staffing model that matches your customer's needs.
- Treat every email as a sales opportunity (but with care).[16]

Providing a web-based form for communication may enhance email use. This makes communication easier for the customer, who does not need to create a structured reply but rather supply only specific answers to questions. It also allows the content provider to classify responses by field. So, for example, customers may be asked to give demographic details such as age. The customer might click only on an age category, rather than give an exact age. The content provider can simply classify responses to categories, which are then automatically logged into a database (e.g. FileMaker Pro). No data entry need be done in order to compile a database.

Of course, some may wish to combine both fields with specific questions and open comment fields. Ansett, for example, allows visitors to its site to combine both specific feedback as well as open-ended commentary (see figure 7.2 on the following page).

Establishing relationships beyond the simple buyer–seller relationship can be accomplished by providing information of interest to customers. For example, Morgan and Banks has compiled a comprehensive web page providing visitors to the page with a wealth of information about employment. While the Morgan and Banks mission is to trade in employment services, its site may be used by anyone interested in employment issues. Not only does the company provide information, but it also solicits participation in various surveys and questionnaires. Morgan and Banks surveys often are reported on in the news, thus enhancing the sense of participation.

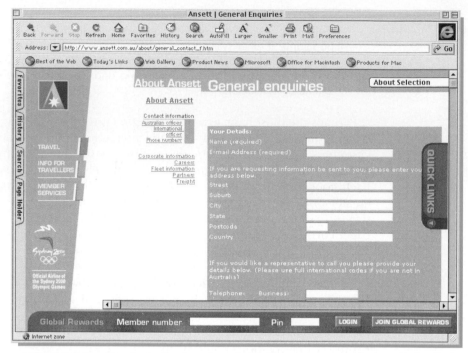

**FIGURE 7.2:** Provision for feedback on Ansett's site (www.ansett.com.au/contact/index.htm)

The Morgan and Banks experience, however, is a not a common one. Most web pages are designed with little or no consultation with customers. In fact, according to a recent GartnerGroup report, 90 per cent of the companies surveyed had created their web sites without ever asking what their customers wanted on those sites![17] This, once again, supports the conclusion that most businesses on the Web fail to work with customers in an effort to meet their needs. Developing methods of consulting with customers is vital to web site success. Ideally, customers are consulted not just once, but repeatedly, in order to better ascertain their needs over time.

Generating repeat business from customers is essential for successful online and offline trading. It hinges on developing a positive relationship between client and seller called customer relationship management. The goals of such a framework are set out in table 7.2 on the opposite page.

Sometimes, however, customer relations break down. Responding to customer complaints in a quick and speedy fashion is vital. Standards Australia has outlined the essential steps to handling **complaint resolution** in developing the Australian standard **AS 4269**. The essential elements are:

- possess a commitment to efficient and fair resolution of complaints
- commit resources necessary to handle complaints
- have a visible process for handling complaints
- ensure the complaints handling process is accessible
- provide assistance for the lodgement of complaints
- be responsive to complaints
- ensure that remedies for complaints are available

- ensure that data is systematically collected
- account for complaints and classify them to allow their later analysis
- review complaints handling annually.

Ideally, a web-based form should be available so that complaints can be lodged. If not a web-based form, then at least a hypertext email address inviting customers to comment and provide feedback should be used. Following these guidelines ensures that customer interactions, when and if things go wrong, result in building relationships and not breaking them down.

**TABLE 7.2** CUSTOMER RELATIONSHIP MANAGEMENT

| TACTIC | METHODOLOGY | EXAMPLE | WEB EXAMPLE |
|---|---|---|---|
| use existing relationships to grow revenue | identify, attract and retain the best customers | maximise relationship via up-selling and cross-selling | www.barnesandnoble.com |
| use integrated information for excellent service | use customer information to save customers' time and ease their frustration | don't make them repeat information | www.aol.com |
| introduce repeatable processes and procedures | improve consistency in account management and selling | make sure the different employees know the customer | www.CDNow.com |
| create new value and instill loyalty | make this your point of difference | offer discounts for buying online | www.nrma.com.au |
| implement a more proactive solution strategy | use a customer-focused business solution across whole enterprise | eliminate issues before they reach crisis point | www.amazon.com |

*SOURCE:* based on R. Kalakota and M. Robinson 1999, *E-business: Roadmap for Success*, Addison-Wesley Longman, United States, pp. 111–12

# DATABASE MARKETING STRATEGIES

Database marketing is the storage and retrieval of customer and client data, such as name, address and purchase history, for the purpose of better understanding customer and client needs and delivering goods and services that satisfy these needs in a manner that achieves organisational objectives.[18] This is particularly important on the Web where it is vital to encourage existing customers to buy more and to buy more frequently.

Direct marketing differs from database marketing in that direct marketing focuses only on promotion because it relies on advertising to generate a measurable response and/or transaction. Database marketing focuses on four elements of the marketing mix, namely targeting, tailoring, tying and tapping.

The table below outlines some of the strategies that are vital in database marketing.

| TABLE 7.3 | THE FOUR T'S OF DATABASE MARKETING |
|---|---|
| **THE T'S** | **EXAMPLE** |
| targeting | micromarketing and fine-tuning of customer segments to find out who should be targeted in promotions, which customers should be retained, etc. |
| tailoring | adapting the offer to suit the customer's needs — communicating the right message to the right person |
| tying | building permanent customer relationships by developing trust and satisfaction, e.g. using frequent-buyer programs |
| tapping | tapping into increased profits by using satisfied customers as sources of references for prospective buyers, e.g. giving away gift certificates to customers encourages them to recommend the site to their friends |

*SOURCE:* C. Perry and H. Master 1999, *Strategies for Database Marketing, Model 3*, study book for e-Business Strategy, University of Southern Queensland, pp. 3.6–3.7, adapted from K. Rohner 1998, *Marketing in the Cyber Age: The Why, The What and The How*, John Wiley and Sons, Inc., New York

Some issues that need to be addressed in developing a database marketing system include:

- What will it be used for (e.g. list management, identifying segments) and will its use be legal and ethical?
- Who will be using the database (e.g. marketing or other departments)?
- How will the database be used (e.g. are clear and precise applications noted)?
- What further data is required from external sources (e.g. census data or Internet behaviour data)?
- Who will be responsible for implementing and maintaining the database (e.g. onsite or outsourced)?[19]

# CUSTOMER SECURITY

**Customer security** remains the most problematic issue for commercial transactions. Surveys consistently cite security as the main reason for not engaging in online transactions. Yet, most customers poorly understand threats to security. Security threats fall into two groups — those threats against individual accounts and those that threaten whole databases. Industry is more concerned, obviously, with the latter, whereas individuals more so with the former. More often than not, however, newspaper headlines fail to make these distinctions. There have been cases of databases being broken into and credit card details stolen. These are security issues of great relevance, but have little or nothing to do with the individual customer. The holder of credit card data on the database is responsible for ensuring that the data is protected. In this case, there is no way for the user to personally guarantee that his or her credit card is protected from unwanted use.

Instead, most customers worry about the actual transaction in which they are involved. Most believe that their credit card details are being stolen or can be stolen during a transaction. Few, if any, cases exist where this has occurred. Even more troublesome for individuals involved in commercial transactions is the misunderstanding concerning liability. Credit card holders are liable for only the first $50 of stolen credit card transactions; the banks carry the majority of risk. Yet, it seems that most credit card holders fail to make this observation. Some Internet customers keep an Internet-only credit card (with a low credit limit) for online purchases.

In an effort to overcome security concerns and allay customers' worries, credit card companies in conjunction with banks are working to develop encrypted transactions, thus protecting the entire transaction. In August 1997 the ANZ Banking Group became the first of the major Australian banks to employ a secure mode for Internet banking. Credit card holders with the ANZ Bank used **virtual wallet software**, which was loaded on their PCs. These virtual wallets used **Secure Electronic Transaction (SET)** encryption to protect transactions. However, it appears as if secure socket layer (SSL) has become the de facto security standard, particularly with Australian banks.

Of course, commercial transactions are not the only sorts of transactions to occur on the Web. Other data can be accessed via the Web, such as personal records. This data must also be protected from unwanted examination. Recent experience in the United States suggests that security concerns stop at financial matters. American citizens wishing to access their social security records could do so briefly via the Web. Reality outweighed expectations when thousands of people accessed their social security information. The experiment was closed in less than a week, when demands outweighed expectation and after concerns were raised that insufficient security safeguards might allow unwanted access to private files.

# SUMMARY

The customer relationship on the Web is fraught with possibilities and challenges alike. It is not a traditional customer relationship as might have existed in other commercial contexts. Rather, it is one that demands a high degree of participation from all parties. It is important that content providers respond to customer needs and ask what those needs are on an on-going basis. It is also important to guide the customers to information you wish them to have. Establishing this on-going two-way relationship will greatly enhance the business-to-customer relationship.

<table>
<tr><td>advertising</td><td>customer</td><td>ontology</td></tr>
<tr><td>AS 4269</td><td>customer relations</td><td>Secure Electronic</td></tr>
<tr><td>banner advertisements</td><td>customer security</td><td>Transaction (SET)</td></tr>
<tr><td>'click-through' advertising</td><td>flat-fee advertising</td><td>target advertisement</td></tr>
<tr><td>complaint resolution</td><td>Hermes Survey</td><td>virtual wallet software</td></tr>
<tr><td>CPM advertising</td><td>Internet shopping mall</td><td></td></tr>
</table>

**key terms**

# Case Study 1 — BUILDING CUSTOMER RELATIONSHIPS ON THE WEB

## SECOND WAVE IN E-COMMERCE
### Marketing

BY KATE CRAWFORD

A second wave of e-commerce arrived in 1999, forcing businesses to develop more sophisticated marketing techniques to retain customers online, according to a leading US Internet analyst.

Mr Gene deRose, the 35-year-old chairman and chief executive of high-profile Internet research company Jupiter Communications, said e-commerce this year had moved beyond a simple 'land grab' for consumers to become a more sophisticated process of brand building and developing customer relationships.

'The first stage of Internet development, which is still continuing, is about grabbing as many customers as possible, but overlapping this is this new phase which emphasises the retention of customers and developing loyalty to brands,' he said.

Mr deRose cites the acquisition of Hotmail, the free e-mail service, by Microsoft as an early example of companies buying up databases of customers that can be used for marketing purposes.

'It's about how you use the information. The new development in Internet business is not just about getting customers but about the sophisticated ways you can turn that customer base to your advantage. This is why Amazon is good at selling things regardless of whether it's books, CDs or toys. They have built a brand loyalty,' he said. But while e-commerce has reached a new level, many companies have rushed to the Internet without being completely ready, resulting in a lower quality of service for customers.

'The irony is that although the e-commerce market has doubled in size this year, customer service has worsened. The race to put commerce online has been faster than the capacity to manage [Internet sales] well. The service threshold will be another opportunity for businesses to make or break in this game.'

Mr deRose, who is visiting Sydney this week for the Internet World 99 conference, says Australia is well placed to take advantage of e-commerce opportunities. 'This is a market that is surprisingly advanced. Australia has some similarities with the Nordic countries in that there's a remoteness from the cultures it has a strong connection to, such as the US and the UK. Hence, there is a rapid uptake of technology as a way to bridge that gap. That means there is great promise for the market to grow, as long as there are no barriers caused by the dominant telecommunications player.'

Handing out opinions about Internet commerce may make Mr deRose a very rich man, if all goes to plan with the public float of Jupiter on the Nasdaq exchange.

The float was announced on Monday, with the company planning to raise as much as $57.5 million.

The number of shares to be sold and their price is yet to be announced.

Mr deRose holds a 21.8 per cent stake in the four-year-old research company, which opened an office in Australia in February but is yet to produce local research.

Jupiter claims $21 million in revenues and boasts a client list of more than 600 companies.

## Internet research from Jupiter Communications

- Two-thirds of Internet users have used the Web to research or book travel arrangements.

- Teens and children will account for $US1.3 billion of e-commerce in 2002.

- Online households in Western Europe will triple by 2003 to 31 per cent.

- More than 15 million US households will receive their bills online by 2002.

- 44 per cent of US online households shopped online during Christmas 1998, spending $US3.14 billion ($4.8 billion).

- 80 per cent of online consumers trust Internet news outlets as much as they trust newspapers, broadcast television and pay TV news outlets.

**SOURCE:** *Sydney Morning Herald*, 4 August 1999, Biz.Com, www.smh.com.au, p. 25

### EXERCISES

1. In what ways has the online environment changed traditional marketing? Provide examples of these changes on the Web.
2. Search the Web to find other examples that illustrate the web site as an investment and not a cost. Upon what basis did you choose your sites?
3. Find examples of marketing of web services through traditional media and analyse their similarities and differences.
4. Discuss the quote 'although the e-commerce market has doubled in size this year, customer service has worsened' and suggest ways in which customer service on the Web can be improved.
5. Go to Jupiter Communications' web site to update the statistics presented in the box in this case study.
6. Find examples of generic sites and sites marketing specific items. What are the differences? Do generic sites do poorly? Why?

Keynote Systems is a Californian company that tracks the reliability of e-commerce sites. They have concluded that the big online brokerage firms, such as Schwab and E*Trade, are the most technologically demanding sites on the Web and are accessible more than 90 per cent of the time; Schwab states its site is accessible 99 per cent of the time. Gene Shklar, the vice president for marketing of Keynote Systems says these reliability figures are a mind-boggling technological feat but notes that when customers have their own trading dollars on the line, they expect perfection.

The Schwab web site was designed to accommodate 264 000 users simultaneously; the peak was 60 000 on 26 April 1999 when the system crashed. Customers accessing Schwab's site actually link up with the Schwab data centre in Phoenix where 152 web server computers (mainly IBM gateway servers) store and serve up the main Schwab web pages. Load-balancing software evenly distributes the incoming traffic. Customers who want to trade stock are sent from these gateways to one of 84 IBM 'middleware' computers, which convey incoming trading data over ultra-high-speed internal lines to one of seven multi-million-dollar IBM or Hitachi mainframes. These mainframes store and process most of the crucial data in the transactions.

On April 26, 1999 the mainframe hit a snag and the software dialled the east coast office of the software maker. The computer technician entered a command that was supposed to fix the problem but it caused the program to freeze and the web site was offline for more than 45 minutes during trading hours. In January 1999 the site crashed as a result of the failure of the data centre's own technicians to configure the software correctly when trying to shift some of the workload from one mainframe to another. IBM and Schwab are now planning to develop jointly load-shifting technology for the online brokerage industry.

*SOURCE:* adapted from M. Richtel 1999, 'What causes those online trading glitches', *Business Review Weekly,* 9 July, pp. 58–9

### EXERCISES

1. Do some research on high-profile e-commerce web site outages. (For example, you might look at examples from the auction sites such as eBay or tax sites such as Web Turbo tax.) Discuss how web-site owners might recover customer confidence after such a problem.

2. Online trading has become a growing area in Internet commerce. Prepare a report on the uses of the Internet for share trading, using at least one online share trading web site as a case study.

## QUESTIONS

1. Assume that your manager has asked you to recommend whether your company should or should not start marketing its products or services on the Internet. What factors about Internet marketing would you include in your report?
2. Investigate whether or not there is a difference between direct marketing or database marketing. Access an e-commerce site, decide which model the site uses and explain your decision.
3. What sort of customer-based issues might you need to consider when designing a presence on the Web?
4. What are the strengths and weaknesses of the various methods of advertising on the Web?
5. How can commercial vendors address customer concerns over transaction security?
6. How can companies on the Web enhance their relationships with customers?
7. What are some methods you can use to identify and attract customers to a Web site?

## SUGGESTED READING

Department of Foreign Affairs and Trade 1999, *Driving Forces on the New Silk Road: The Use of Electronic Commerce by Australian Businesses*, Commonwealth of Australia, Canberra.

eMarketer, *eMarketer Weekly Newsletter*, www.eMarketer.com.

Hanson, W. 2000, *Principles of Internet Marketing*, South Western College Publishing, Thomson Learning, United States.

Kalakota, R. and Robinson, M. 1999 *e-Business: Roadmap for Success*, Addison-Wesley Longman, United States.

Maddox, K. 1998, *Web Commerce: Building a Digital Business*, John Wiley and Sons, Toronto, Canada.

NUA, *NUA Internet Surveys*, www.nua.ie.

Rohner, K. 1998, *Marketing in the Cyber Age: The Why, The What and The How*, John Wiley and Sons, New York.

## END NOTES

1. Maurice, D. 1999, *Trading in Cyberspace: Satisfying the Internet Customer*, E-commerce and the Internet, KPMG seminar, 31 August 1999.
2. Bullock, G. 1999, 'Send an email to a worldwide e-tailer', *Sun Herald*, Shopping Online, 10 October, p. 63, www.sunherald.com.au.

3. Perry, C. and Sweeney, A. 1999, *Module 2, Internet Marketing, Unit 75707, e-Business Strategy, Study book*, University of Southern Queensland, pp. 2.13–2.15, based on E-Commerce Assistant program on IBM site at http://advisor.itnernet.ibm.com/inet.nsf.

4. Hermes Consumer Survey of World Wide Web Users, www-personal.umich.edu/~sgupta/hermes/.

5. *E-commerce Today* 1999, 'New no cost bilingual ecommerce solution released', issue 10, October, p. 16.

6. Hoffman, D. and Novak, T. 1996, 'A new marketing paradigm for electronic commerce', *The Information Society*, www2000.ogsm.vanderbilt.edu/novak/new.marketing.paradigm.html.

7. *E-Commerce Today* 1999, 'Vertical portals the next web trend', 30 September, www.ecommercetoday.com.

8. Hanson, W. 2000, *Principles of Internet Marketing*, South Western College Publishing, Thomson Learning, United States, p. 270.

9. *Washington Post* 1999, 'Proctor & Gamble attempts to "Dell" its industry', www.washingtonpost.com, in *eMarketer*, newsletter no. 40, www.emarketer.com.

10. *eMarketer* 1999, 'Amazon builds one-for-all mall', newsletter no. 40, www.emarketer.com.

11. Capron, H. L. 2000, *Computers tools for an information age*, Prentice Hall, United States, p. 250.

12. Novak, T. and Hoffman, D. 1996, 'New metrics for new media: toward the development of web measurement standards', *Project2000*, www2000.ogsm.vanderbilt.edu/novak/web.standards/webstand.html.

13. Focalink Communications 1997, *Focalink Reports Web Serial Sites Charge an Average CPM of US$250, The Highest Web Ad Rate*, www.focalink.com/home/fc/fc26ad.html.

14. Bullock, G. 1999, 'Tap into your supermarket', *Sun Herald*, 10 October, p. 64, www.sunherald.com.au.

15. 'Content is still king, says the queen of online marketing' 1996, OtR, www.hotwired.com/market/96/15/index1a.html.

16. Maurice, D. op. cit.

17. Kline, D. 1996, 'Memo to the boss: your web site is useless', *Hotwired*, http://hotwired.lycos.com/market/96/15/index1a.html.

18. Schoenbachler, D., Gordon, G., Foley, D. and Spellman, L. 1997, 'Understanding consumer database marketing', *Journal of Consumer Marketing*, CD-ROM, vol. 14, no. 1, pp. 5–44, http://www.mcb.co.uk/jcm.htm.

19. Perry, C. and Master, H. 1999, *Strategies for Database Marketing, Model 3*, study book for e-Business Strategy, University of Southern Queensland, p. 3.9.

# 8

# Organisational communication

## LEARNING Outcomes

You will have mastered the material in this chapter when you can:
- define organisational communication
- understand the effect the World Wide Web has on organisational communication
- provide examples of different approaches to organisational communication
- understand the various methods of interacting within and between organisations.

*'In a sea of economy buzzwords, network-effects (part economics, part strategy, part ideology) may be the defining business mindflip of the twenty-first century.'*

Eric Ransdell 1999, 'A good idea is spread like a virus', *Sydney Morning Herald*, 21 September, p. 30

# INTRODUCTION

The Internet is changing the way organisations do business. Not only is the Internet creating new and more efficient ways of doing things, but it is also providing new opportunities for entirely novel work practices. Today, the dream of the paperless office is closer than it has ever been before. The new workplace, filled with electronic forms, databases and web pages, also brings with it all the benefits of the information age. Not only are offices now potentially less cluttered by paper, but communications can now be governed by formal rules of logic.

Organisations are now seeing that the next wave of customer-centric innovation requires business integration of processes, applications and systems on a new and grander scale. Sue Bostrom of the Cisco Internet Business Group suggests that businesses should 'develop an e-culture mind-set by looking at the Internet across the entire system of their business'.[1]

This chapter focuses on the impact the Internet is having on organisational communication. It will focus on both intra-organisational communication, via an intranet, and extra-organisational communication, via the Internet. Before focusing on these topics, however, we should examine some broader themes of the Internet and organisational communication.

# HOW THE INTERNET IS CHANGING ORGANISATIONAL COMMUNICATION

The Internet is changing the dynamics of organisations in many ways. Three primary points of focus are the new publishing paradigm, the Internet and work, and just-in-time information.

##  The new publishing paradigm

The problem of creating, printing, using and storing information has long plagued organisations. Consider the daunting task of creating, printing, using and storing information that the Commonwealth Government faces. Whole legions of public servants spend hours collating, distributing and searching for information. It is a monumental task. The number of hours it takes to generate publications or look for old ones is huge. Under the old publishing paradigm labour was intensively used to create, print, use and store information. Research officers collected data, analysts created information, public affairs specialists distributed it and librarians collected it. Under the new publishing paradigm, however, creating, printing, using and storing information is no longer as labour intensive. Equally important is the fact that organisations no longer have to plan for long lead times in order to get information out to their stakeholders. Instead of creating a newsletter in a fortnight, Internet publishers can create and distribute newsletters in as little as a few hours. Consider the changes wrought by the new publishing paradigm in table 8.1.

| TABLE 8.1 | CHANGES WROUGHT BY THE NEW PUBLISHING PARADIGM |
|---|---|
| **OLD PUBLISHING PARADIGM** | **NEW PUBLISHING PARADIGM** |
| publishing control centralised | publishing control decentralised |
| long lead time to publication | very short lead time to publication |
| labour intensive | not labour intensive |
| once published, almost impossible to change | easily changed and altered |
| static medium with little interaction | dynamic medium with a high level of interaction |

The new publishing paradigm provides many new changes and challenges for organisational communication. It has the potential to create a far more fluid, and perhaps even chaotic, publishing environment. This will create new challenges for managers in the years to come. Two professors from the Harvard Business School formulated what is known as the Law of Digital Assets.[2] Unlike physical assets, digital assets are used but not consumed, which means that digital assets can be used over and over again. The organisation can create more value by continually recycling its digital assets through a large, nearly infinite, number of transactions. However, it is still vital to revise, enhance, improve and repackage these digital assets. Many newspaper firms, such as the *New York Times* and the *Sydney Morning Herald*, allow web surfers to read articles online for free but charge for archived material.

Bertelsmann Online (BOL), a German bookseller, plans to launch downloadable books that can be read by the Rocket eBook, which can display 36 000 pages from its battery powered memory. The German book wholesaler Libri has launched a service digitally printing single copies of hard-to-find books.[3]

# The Internet and work

Donald Tapscott, in his book *The Digital Economy*, argues that networked organisations are changing not only how they do things, but their very structure as well. He writes that a '... radical rethinking of the nature and functioning of the organization and the relationships between organizations' is occurring.[4] Large organisations have long had the advantage of being able to draw on economics of scale and resources. The smaller companies who can adapt to change more rapidly, however, are quickly overcoming the advantage held by the larger organisations. Small companies can use the Internet to tap into pools of information previously unavailable, partly because the Internet overcomes the tyranny of distance. Previously, organisations were constrained by distance and time in use of resources. Now with the Web, such problems of distance and time are largely overcome.

An example of how the Internet is changing the very nature of the organisation is best illustrated by **teleworking**. Teleworking simply refers to the process of working remotely from home via a network connection. (It may not necessarily involve the Internet, but for our purposes here we will focus on the Internet connection.) For example, it is estimated that there are over ten million teleworkers in the United States. In Australia there are relatively few teleworkers, despite the increased attention, but one in four employees is likely to work from home within the next ten years, many running their own business or consultancy.[5] Teleworkers need not go to the office, may communicate with their managers only via the Internet, and may interact with customers only through the Internet.

# Just-in-time information

**Just-in-time (JIT) information** was an important change in inventory control. Personal computer manufacturers were often stuck with a large inventory of yesterday's PCs stuck on warehouse shelves. Aiming to accelerate delivery speed, while reducing inventory and costs in the PC supply chain, Intel established an extranet or private Internet to communicate real-time inventory levels and demand to suppliers and customers.[6]

An extranet is a specialised and customised online information service provided by a company to its valued clients (individuals or organisations). Its platform is Internet connectivity and web technology. A business needs to look at its suppliers and customers as strategic allies. The business is part of a group providing high-quality products and best possible services and needs to design its extranet with that in mind.[7]

JIT inventory control meant that the size of an inventory was controlled to match current production as closely as possible. The same principle now applies to information because of the Internet. No longer are organisations slaves to traditional methods of information collection and dissemination. Instead, JIT information now provides organisations with the capacity to create, acquire and disseminate information in a much more efficient fashion. Corporate newsletters, intranets and email now make JIT information a real possibility.

Consider a simple example of a sales meeting. A meeting scheduled for 2.00 p.m. is cancelled. Before network solutions were available someone had to first call around to those who were supposed to attend the meeting and let them know it had been cancelled. In addition, considerable effort was spent in trying to set up a new meeting time convenient to all involved. By linking offices together via an intranet, a meeting can be cancelled with ease. Broadcast emails further facilitate schedule changes, as do online calendars. The amount of time wasted in inefficient communication is significantly reduced if the networked solution is used effectively.

JIT information allows organisations to more quickly focus their energies on things that matter. Thus, as organisations become more efficient in their use of information, they gain important competitive advantages.

# ORGANISATIONAL ISSUES

Organisational issues that affect businesses include:

- building infrastructures for sharing information
- managing knowledge
- using intermediaries
- maintaining flexibility
- flattening the organisation.[8]

A comprehensive communications capability should be a fundamental part of the infrastructure, such as usage of email or setting up a Lotus Notes database. The organisation should not keep two separate systems for customer service (e.g. one via the telephone and one via the Internet) — they should be converted to a common data platform. The organisation should share the information among everyone who might benefit from the information.

## Survival of the best connected

According to Randy Whiting, CEO of CommerceNet, two vital attributes of Internet survival are agility and adaptability.

Agility, he cautions, is not just being able to do something quickly, because this can often create high costs in terms of dollars, people and operational disruption. Agility is the ability to react and change directions quickly, with minimal effort. He believes that agility needs to be integrated into all levels of the organisation, not just implemented by large amounts of overtime and exhausted employees.

The second component, adaptability, allows companies to dynamically reconfigure their organisations to meet changing conditions. Many strong and stable organisations are being severely challenged by smaller and weaker firms that are more agile and adaptable. The classic example is that of the Amazon Book store, a startup business that rapidly gained 12 million customers worldwide, and Barnes and Noble, the established bookstore chain in the United States that reacted slowly to the Internet.

Whiting states that once companies have mastered agility and adaptability, they are in a position to take advantage of the real power of the Internet: its unique ability to support unstructured and interactive relationships. This new phase, says Whiting, is marked by the emergence of business interoperability — or using the Internet to create new ways for businesses to work together.

CommerceNet is the embodiment of how these principles are being put to work. In addition to providing research on e-business innovation, it helps collaborative companies around the world link together with the Internet as the foundation. These members use this ability to link with partners to identify, create and exploit new business opportunities. However, CommerceNet realised that one of the challenges stems from the wide variety of ways in which e-commerce is carried out. To this end, CommerceNet established eCo, a common, interoperable framework within which the diverse

Chapter 8: Organisational communication **189**

world of e-commerce can be represented. The aim of eCo is to set the stage for establishing global networks of businesses and marketplaces, which should provide a catalyst for an explosion of global entrepreneurial activity.

Whiting believes that agility and adaptability will be the defining attributes of companies that are able to participate effectively in these new interoperable and collaborative environments. Companies that can cooperate with other organisations to exploit new opportunities will be in the best position to survive and flourish. He states that to be successful in e-commerce, the key characteristic may be in the end 'not the survival of the fittest or the best adapted, but survival of the best connected . . .'

**SOURCE:** based on a four-part series by R. Whiting 1999, 'Letter from Randy Whiting', in CommerceNet, *Buzz*, vol. 4, nos 8, 9, 10 and 12, www.commerce.net

### EXERCISES

1. Research the history of the growth of Amazon.com. Some questions that might be worthwhile investigating include:
   - How was it possible for it to become such a major player before the established booksellers caught on?
   - What is the situation now with Amazon and its 'bricks and mortar' rivals?
   - How has Amazon changed its business model over time?
   - Does Amazon illustrate 'survival of the best connected'? If so how? If not, why not?
2. Investigate the eCo framework and write a critique of this framework.

## INTRA-ORGANISATIONAL COMMUNICATION

The Web has affected **intra-organisational communication** in a variety of ways. It also has the potential to completely revolutionise intra-organisational communication, but that potential is yet to be realised. The three primary vehicles of change have been the use of email, the development of the intranet concept and the use of graphical browsers as the front-end for other applications.

## Email

Email has dramatically affected intra-organisational communication. Forty per cent of Australia's adults (nearly 5.5 million) accessed the Internet in the 12 months to 9 May 1999, a 54 per cent jump from May 1998.[9] Forty-three per cent of small businesses and 84 per cent of medium-sized businesses in Australia use email to do business with clients, customers and business contacts.[10] Billions of messages are sent around the world each day and email has become a key driver behind the explosion of electronic commerce.

It is used to transfer company data orders, invoices, word-processed documents, spreadsheets and CAD files between business partners saving time and the expense of sending paper communications.[11]

Michael Dertouzos, Director of the Massachusetts Institute of Technology's Laboratory for Computer Science, underscores the importance of email, writing, 'Email is a basic function on all information infrastructures.'[12] Email provides a number of benefits to intra-organisational communication, including:

- efficiency
- speed
- accountability (the receipt of an email can be electronically monitored)
- automation
- embedded HTML (allowing text, graphics, images, sound and video in an email)
- visibility (email makes it easier to find people, especially if they are overseas because they will be listed in an email directory somewhere on the Internet).

The disadvantages of email for intra-organisational communication include:

- people stop talking to one another
- people spend too much time emailing each other
- communication is inappropriately targeted
- email readers become bogged down in a sea of email
- mind dumping (where people send emails on subjects that they might not otherwise have written a letter about).

A survey conducted by Price Waterhouse Coopers in 1998 found that 13 per cent of Australia's top 100 companies regularly monitor email and about 6 per cent read messages. About 15 per cent of companies that monitor do not tell their employees. In the United States about 27 per cent of companies monitor workers' email.[13]

Email is becoming an essential element in virtually any information infrastructure. Sending emails to multiple recipients will distribute the message to an almost infinitely large number of people. This is an effective way of broadcasting important information to a wide spectrum of employees. Of course, email can also be targeted to specific individuals as well. **Attachments** may be added to email, allowing the inclusion of documents created in a number of word processing, database and spreadsheet packages. A sales presentation can be prepared in one part of an organisation, reviewed by another, and modified by yet another, before being presented. All of this may take place in a large geographical area, and may occur easily within hours. The **interactive mail access protocol (IMAP)** allows for better control over the way messages are delivered. Instead of having all the new email messages delivered from the email server onto the user's computer in one go, IMAP gives the user greater flexibility in interacting with the inbox. The user may choose to download only the subjects of the new email messages, then select and only download relevant messages. It also allows the user to see what files are attached to an email and then decide which ones to download. Obviously, this is ideal for users receiving email over slow connections such as a laptop computer connected to the Internet via a mobile telephone.[14]

Companies should ensure that they have an electronic communications policy that expressly categorises certain conduct as prohibited and outside the scope of employment contracts. Further details on email are found in chapter 10, page 252.

# Communication convergence on the Web

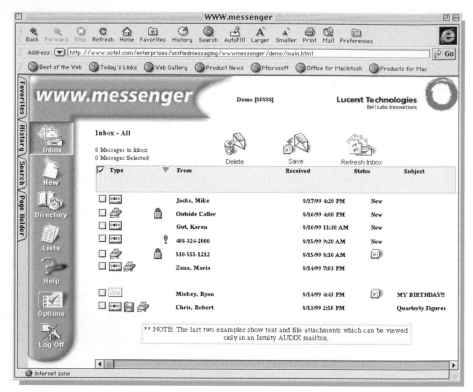

**FIGURE 8.1:** Demo page of the web-based message management tool, www.messenger™

Organisations are becoming increasingly dependent on email. In fact, research shows email is the killer application of the Internet — it has gradually taken the place of written communications in the business world. Lucent Technologies have developed a web-based message management tool that offers a mobile, unified application for voice, fax and email services via the Internet.

Users can view all types of messages in the mailbox. Other useful features are:

- voice message playback, creation, reply and forwarding via telephone or multimedia computer
- fax message viewing, printing and forwarding with voice messages
- messages addressed by mailbox number, user name or distribution list
- administrative functions such as creating greetings, editing distribution lists and changing passwords through a telephone or computer
- viewing, creating, forwarding and replying to email.

News Ltd is moving towards various methods of electronic delivery of its publications, including the transmission of news content to mobile telephones

through its alliance with One.Tel. It will use the new **wireless application protocol (WAP)**, which enables Internet and intranet content to be delivered to mobile telephones.

There are 300 million mobile telephone subscribers around the world and that number is predicted to increase to one billion by 2003 and 2.5 billion by 2015 mainly as a result of the new mobile Internet data delivery capabilities.

**SOURCE:** based on information from Lucent Technologies, 1999, www.octel.com, and D. Hellaby 1999, 'Read all about it — on your mobile' Computers/News Features, *Australian*, 5 October, p. 53, www.news.com.au

## QUESTIONS

1. What are the main advantages and disadvantages of communication and computer convergence?
2. Investigate the uptake of web-enabled mobile telephones in your country. If possible, interview users of such mobile telephones to ascertain the advantages and disadvantages of these appliances.

# Intranets

Another change in intra-organisational communication has come from the development of the intranet. An intranet is simply a smaller, local version of the Internet. Whereas the Internet is accessible and accesses information from around the globe, an intranet is accessible and accesses information locally. Douglas Cruickshank explains:

> *Intranets employ the same information-organizing principles as the World Wide Web, a graphically-oriented, highly flexible approach that can be tailored to the existing structure of virtually any organization or project. Yet unlike the Internet, an intranet can only be accessed by individuals within an organization, and by outsiders who've been given passwords to allow them in. A special network security device known as a 'firewall' keeps out all others.*[15]

Intranets give organisations the capacity to provide JIT information to any part of an organisation. In addition, intranets act as a resource to employees; for example, John Wiley and Sons Australia has a useful intranet for staff (see figure 8.2 on the following page). Staff can download all forms used in general business, check the schedules for projects, read updated information about the company and company social events and find links to useful web sites.

Intranets have been adopted quickly by a wide range of organisations throughout the world. Some of the features of an intranet include:

- the ability to transmit timely, important information rapidly throughout the organisation
- web browser software capable of browsing the Internet as well as the intranet (e.g. Netscape Communicator)
- high bandwidth, assuring speedy communication
- security
- front-end access to other internal software applications (e.g. databases).

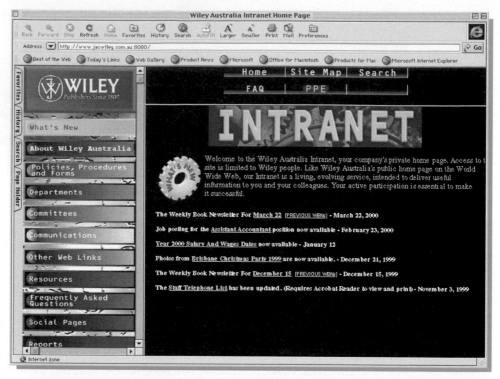

**FIGURE 8.2:** The intranet home page of John Wiley and Sons Australia (www.jacwiley.com.au:8080)

Useful downloadable software applications can also be linked to intranet pages so that employees need only download and configure software to their local machine. For example, human resource managers may wish to electronically support the assessment of employee performance. Software is available that supports the performance appraisal process by keeping track of employees and their key performance indicators. The **Performance and Assessment Results 4 (PAR4)** software can be linked through an intranet. Managers can then download and configure PAR4 to their local machines as needed. Human resource managers can use the intranet to provide managers with software that makes their job of assessing employee performance more manageable.

Intranets ensure that information can be disseminated quickly throughout the organisation, that everybody has the same information, and that those important tools and resources are universally available.

Software from companies such as Allaire™ and Cold Fusion makes it easier for companies to build web applications to handle e-commerce, business process automation and dynamic information publishing on intranets, extranets and the Internet. Macromedia has a series of software applications that assist in the production of sites that deliver high-impact, low-bandwidth web sites to browsers. These include Flash 4, Fireworks, Shockwave and Dreamweaver. Visit www.macromedia.com and www.allaire.com to see sites using some of these applications.

# Online education is the way of the future

The article below shows how universities are using the Internet to deliver courses. Note that the students have to log into the RMIT intranet.

## WEB STUDENTS PASS INNOVATIVE COURSE

JENNIFER FORESHEW
❏ Education

RMIT has claimed a world first by graduating students from its Web-delivered Master in Innovation Information (MBII) course.

Three students of RMIT's School of Business Information Technology have graduated from the course, which is believed to be the only one of its kind offered internationally on the Web.

Students have already graduated from RMIT's Web-delivered Graduate Diploma in Document Management.

Both courses began in 1997 and have attracted about 130 students from Australia, Europe, North America, Canada and New Zealand.

They deal with document technologies, the Web, workflow and knowledge management, and their effects on business.

Course co-ordinator John Kerrisk said the demand for Web-delivered study was growing and had resulted in better student performance.

'The people who enrol tend to be fairly high achievers, so if anything, the standard is better than in a normal classroom,' Mr Kerrisk said.

Most students are in middle to senior management and take the courses part-time.

All lecture and tutorial material is published on RMIT's Web site and accessed by students using a password.

Mr Kerrisk said some people still had reservations about studying on the Net.

'Some people fear you will lose the human interaction between teaching staff and participants, but we haven't found that,' he said.

'In fact, the communication level is far higher than if we were teaching in class.'

*www.greenweb.com.au/rmit/*

**SOURCE:** *Australian*, Computer section, 12 October 1999, p. 45, www.news.com.au

## EXERCISES

1. Many organisations are turning to the Web to deliver courses. Debate the advantages and disadvantages of this method of course delivery.
2. Cisco has set up a worldwide network of Cisco Academies to deliver training in 'Internetworking'. The course material and examinations are online. Visit the Cisco site at www.cisco.com and prepare a report on what the program offers, the global reach of the program and the target audience, and comment on the idea of commercial companies entering the education sphere.

# Using graphical browsers as front-end interfaces

Another change in intra-organisational communication is in the use of graphical browsers as front-ends, or access points, for other software applications. Within organisations financial information and customer databases may be accessed remotely using a graphical browser interface. For example, the Macquarie Graduate School of Management has trialled handling queries through online forms. Prospective students fill out the form and send it. The data is used to update a FileMakerPro database and a copy is emailed to the university marketing group. The customer helps both build the database and initiate the process of sending out marketing information. While this application starts with an external user initiating communication, it results in a change in how the organisation communicates internally. No longer is data entry required. Equally important, updated figures can be generated about online marketing.

Remote tracking of mailed packages is fast becoming an important web application. The application was originally pioneered by Federal Express. Other companies now using a web interface to track packages include Qantas, DHL Australia and TNT.

The final change brought about by graphical browsers is the use of video-conferencing and Internet telephone calls. Videoconferencing and Internet telephones have been available, in varying quality, for a short period on the Internet. Telephone calls within an organisation but outside of the existing telephone network can also be made via the intranet. Videoconferencing is also available, linking a number of intra-organisational sites together by way of a video camera and web-based software. As web technology improves, it is becoming increasingly possible to engage in a live videoconference through a corporate intranet, linking people within a single company who are geograph-ically dispersed.

Equally appealing for intra-organisational communication are groupware applications, such as Lotus Notes, which allow users to interact remotely with one another in a structured environment. Such groupware is ideal for group meetings, brainstorming sessions or other such applications. Groupware brings to group meetings the immediacy of videoconferencing, with the logical structures found in many software applications.

# Cyber orders: physical deliveries are a potential logistical nightmare

According to Forrester Research, e-commerce retailers will deliver about 230 million packages this year, mostly over the Christmas holiday season. Etoys ships 1000 packages daily and Amazon ships 10 000 a day. Jupiter Communications predicted that the busiest sites such as Amazon, CDNow and Barnes and Noble could reach 58 000 transactions a day during November and December.

As customers become demanding, web shops can no longer afford to antagonise them by not shipping the ordered goods on time. To ensure

efficiency in shipping, some of the web entrepreneurs are starting to build their own warehouses near major shipping hubs. However, this takes time so now the scramble is on to find third parties to handle distribution. The United States company Hanover Direct's Keystone Fulfilment handles distribution for Mercata, KBkids and Dress Barn. Federated's Fingerhut Business Services hands Wal-Mart, Levi Strauss and Etoys.

The Internet customer demands real-time inventory, which includes access to information about product availability and shipping status. If a customer orders a book from an online bookshop there is an expectation that the customer can click on delivery companies such as FedEx or DHL and track the parcel delivery. The distribution warehouses must be closely wired to the merchant's web operations.

*SOURCE:* adapted from B. Tedeschi 1999, 'First the orders, now the chaos', Biz.Com, *Sydney Morning Herald*, 7 October, p. 28

### EXERCISES

1. How might a remote or client-based web tracking facility affect the workplace?
2. Can you think of other similar applications that might be used by businesses?

## EXTRA-ORGANISATIONAL COMMUNICATION

**Extra-organisational communication** is also changing. Extra-organisational communication is that which occurs between the organisation and some group or individual outside the organisation.

Many of the same tools that are changing intra-organisational communication are also changing extra-organisational communication. Two primary examples of how extra-organisational communication is changing are found in modifications to the supply chain and the recruitment of employees.

## The supply chain

A simple example of the ways in which the Web facilitates extra-organisational communication is found on the web page of Freedom Furniture. This site allows businesses to register with Freedom Furniture and download the software package **GENTRAN** in order to set up online payment and ordering. The supply chain in this example is streamlined by removing buyer–seller voice communication.

Another example of the electronic supply chain is found at Woolworths. The Woolworth web page, unlike that of Freedom Furniture, provides instructions on how to establish an electronic supply chain. Freedom Furniture provided no options in how to establish the supply chain — users are locked into using the GENTRAN software. Woolworths, on the other hand, makes no software prescriptions. Rather, they help would-be suppliers to understand the electronic supply chain.

**FIGURE 8.3:**
Easy to follow
instructions from
Woolworths on
the electronic
supply chain
(www.wool-
worths.com.au/
vendorguide/
index.stm)

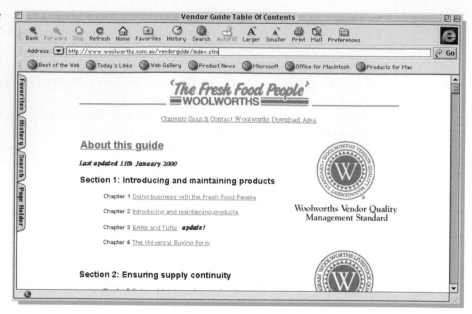

General Motors has set up the e-Gm online service division to tighten its
supply chain and retail sales processes. General Motors, Ford and Daimler
Chrysler are driving forces behind the Automotive Network Exchange (ANX)
— an initiative to force auto-industry suppliers to communicate via the
Internet. The e-GM system will provide the car maker with a worldwide web
configuration and ordering platform in the first quarter of 2000. Since
November 1999, Ford has accepted customised web orders on a limited range
of vehicles.[16]

**FIGURE 8.4:**
Ford's home
page. Notice the
'Shop for New
Vehicle' link
(www.ford.com).

# Recruiting employees

The recruitment of employees is also changing dramatically via the Web. Traditionally, recruitment has been limited to a few methods — newspaper classifieds, bulletin boards or recruitment agencies. Time and control limit all of these methods. Newspapers come only at a given time of day, space is limited and they cannot be updated. To add something to a newspaper one must wait for the next edition. Bulletin boards and recruitment agents both take control away from the prospective employer and place it in the hands of another.

Monster Board Australia, an offspring of Monster Board in the United States, provides employers and prospective employees with greater functionality than a simple classified advertisement. Monster Board solicits and touts jobs, but also provides assistance to job seekers through the use of an online résumé engine. It also contains a 'virtual interview' as well as feature articles, user polls and a résumé posting service. Also available are employer profiles that can be surveyed by job seekers at any time and job seekers are able to register their job preferences on some sites and have job listings emailed to them daily.

Companies, of course, need not depend upon the services of an intermediary at all. Job postings are a common occurrence in organisations. Often, nobody knows about the job posting except those who happen to read it in the coffee room or wherever it may be posted. The Web takes the in-house posting and makes it globally available. For example, InterWorld, an electronic commerce consulting firm, advertises directly on its web page rather than publishing their job announcements through some third party.

The web site www.employment.com.au offers jobseekers a user-friendly site.

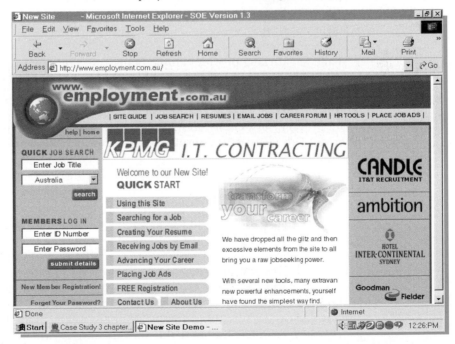

**FIGURE 8.5:** Australia's longest running employment site (www.employment.com.au)

There can be little doubt that the Web affects extra-organisational communication. We have seen two ways in which that impact is realised. The supply of goods, services and people is greatly affected by the Web. What other impact will the Web have on organisational communication?

# THE HUMAN FACTOR

There can be no doubt that the Web is affecting organisational communication. In so many ways organisations can win huge efficiencies by its intelligent use. There are, however, some human factors that need to be acknowledged. For example, consider the human issues that are present in teleworking. Some of the positive benefits from teleworking are:

- increased worker autonomy
- enhanced worker control over their own schedules
- reduction in family/workplace conflicts
- increased morale and enhanced trust
- higher productivity
- fewer occurrences of workplace bullying and confrontations between employees and their bosses.

Yet, Lamond, Standen and Daniels also observe problematic areas in teleworking, including:

- decreased opportunities for development and promotion
- increased conflict between home and work
- less time in face-to-face contact with fellow employees
- reduced job security
- social isolation
- increased hours of work.[17]

While teleworking provides ample benefits to both the organisation and the worker, one should not forget the downside. Considering how human problems will be addressed and handled remains a vital challenge for any organisation, no matter what technological advances are made. On-going training is certainly one answer to developing and maintaining mastery over the Internet. Other areas to consider when reflecting upon the management of the human factor include:

- recruiting and selecting employees with appropriate Internet experience
- assessing Internet skills and abilities during performance appraisals
- maintaining a fair and equitable Internet environment
- ensuring occupational health and safety (e.g. repetitive strain injury)
- planning future Internet uses and needs
- developing organisational policies on use and misuse of the Internet.

Even with the best planning in place, however, the technology that drives the Internet will continue to change. At what pace this change will occur is anybody's guess. Just think about the impact that information technology has already had on organisations. In 1997 Reuters commissioned the report *Dying for Information*, which outlined the various ways in which information technology like the Internet is impacting on organisations. The report found that roughly two-thirds of surveyed managers found that information overload resulted in stress and lowered job satisfaction.[18] One spokesman from Reuters commented, 'Information has truly become a bit of a liability.'[19]

We are caught in a dilemma. On the one hand, we need more and better information to stay competitive. Yet on the other hand, too much information leads to stress and even organisational dysfunction. The challenge is to try and manage this dilemma. Dertouzos reflects on the human factor, writing:

> Human emotions and foibles have a huge effect on all professional exchanges within an organization. Solid bonds or rifts among employees, the boss's mood, motivation or lack thereof to achieve goals, passion, greed, jealousy, and altruism are all at play in any human organization. The Information Marketplace will have greater impact on organizations if it can effectively handle these subtle links among humans along with the more straightforward exchanges of information.[20]

The Web creates a myriad of new interactions between people. Managers must account for the many ways in which people will react to these new interactions. One cannot forget the human factor.

## Teleworkers

In Australia, the 400 000 teleworkers/telecommuters with agreements make up just over five per cent of the work force. One method adopted by some high technology companies is called **'hot desking'**, whereby employees work from home and on the days they need to come into the office they sit wherever they can find a desk.

A Morgan and Banks survey found that 92 per cent of workers gave this system a definite 'thumbs down'. These employees wanted to telecommute but still wanted a permanent space to call their own.

A **telecommuting** scheme has been operated by the New South Wales Road and Traffic Authority since the early 1990s. In 1997 the RTA produced a training manual providing information for businesses and the community at large on how to set up a telecommuting program. In 1998 the Queensland University of Technology completed a study on telecommuting that listed numerous potential legal and physical obstacles.

The study found that if the employer provided the telecommuting equipment the employee was obliged to ensure the equipment's safety by providing such equipment as security locks and fire extinguishers. Such employees were also obliged to ensure that the computer being used at home was protected from viruses and that passwords were secure. Software security was also a responsibility of the teleworker.

TeleTask is an organisation set up in New South Wales to provide people with employment they can do from home or from a telecentre. The services range from virtual call centres to application programming, editorial and secretarial services and a wide range of contracting.

**SOURCE:** adapted from D. Hellaby 1999, 'Jobs put on line in interests of success', Mobile Office, *Australian*, 26 October, p. 1, www.news.com.au.

**EXERCISES**

1. Check out the following sites for more information on teleworking/telecommuting: www.rta.gov.au and www.teletask.com.au.
2. Research teleworking/telecommuting statistics in your home country.
3. Write a report on 'hot desking', outlining its origin, the companies who use it and the pros and cons of such a system.
4. Draw up a chart outlining the advantages and disadvantages of teleworking.

## SUMMARY

In this chapter we have examined the ways in which the Web impacts upon organisational communication. Generally, the Web is creating a new set of dynamics in which organisations are operating. Two of the key changes highlighted were in teleworking and just-in-time information. Teleworking allows employees geographically distant to interact with the central organisation. Just-in-time information emphasises the rapid nature in which information can be collected, processed and distributed via the Web. This chapter also focused on both intra-organisational communication and extra-organisational communication. In intra-organisational communication it was seen that email, intranets and the use of the graphical browser as a front-end for software are the key influences. In extra-organisational communication it was observed that the Web is changing the ways in which supply chains operate as well as where future employees are located.

Finally, the human factor was emphasised. No technological change or solution stands apart from human issues. The key to benefiting from the Web will ultimately be found in matching human requirements with technological solutions.

**key terms**

| | | |
|---|---|---|
| attachments | intra-organisational communication | telecommuting |
| extra-organisational communication | just-in-time (JIT) information | teleworking |
| GENTRAN | | wireless application protocol (WAP) |
| 'hot desking' | Performance and Assessment Results 4 (PAR4) | |
| interactive mail access protocol (IMAP) | | |

# THE BATTLE OF CALL CENTRES AND EMAILS

## E-MAILS EAT INTO CALL CENTRE SAVINGS: EXPERT

SIMON HAYES

❑ Call centres

LARGE businesses that allow call centre staff to answer e-mails themselves were wasting the cost savings gained in using the Internet as a sales channel, vendor executives have warned.

Steve Redman, general manager at Rockwell Electronic Commerce, said the figures often used to sell Internet interaction with customers overlooked the cost of managing sometimes complex interactive inquiries.

Mr Redman said many customers were sold on figures that showed face-to-face contacts cost between $150 and $300, branch contacts at $12, telephone contacts at $6 and Internet contacts at between 10 cents and $2.

But research from GartnerGroup showed costs could blow out to around $17.50 if e-mails and multimedia chat sessions were handled manually, he said.

There were other reasons to avoid manual answers of queries, he said. 'Can all your agents read? Do they all have perfect grammar? Do you want to give your agent legal empowerment in answering your e-mails?'

Mr Redman was promoting Rockwell's latest automation answers, Internet Communications Studio and Email Management Solution.

The products link a company's Web site to a call centre for real-time chat, voice or video interaction with customers, as well as managing the way e-mail is answered.

Mr Redman said the company's products could also suggest appropriate responses and let the agent choose.

Some call centres answered up to 80 per cent of e-mails automatically, he said.

'Gartner says the cost of a contact can be as high as $17.50 if you ask an agent to read an e-mail and decide on a response,' Mr Redman said. 'If you let agents take e-mail without auto-response, you push the cost up.'

CCR managing director Martin Conboy warned that call centres would become overwhelmed unless they address multimedia contacts.

'At the moment, most call centres are flat out dealing with the volume of telephone calls,' he said.

'The call centres are not keeping up, and unless they consider how they are going to deal with new types of media, they'll fall over backwards.'

*www.ec.rockwell.com*
*www.callcentres.net*

**SOURCE:** S. Hayes 1999, *Australian*, 19 October, p. 51, www.news.com.au

## EXERCISE

Prepare a report on the use of automatic answering systems for call centres and help desks.

**QUESTIONS**

1. Visit the site of the trade journal Datamation (www.datamation.com) and browse through Datamation's Workbench for articles on extranets and intranets. Write a case study illustrating one company's use of an extranet or an intranet.
2. Prepare a report on Recruitment web sites covering such issues as:
   - growth of recruitment web sites
   - relationship of recruitment web sites and paper job-recruitment advertisements
   - control of out-of-date advertisements on recruitment web sites
   - advantages of online recruitment over paper-based recruitment
   - disadvantages of online recruitment over paper-based recruitment.
3. What sort of organisational communication issues might you wish to consider when designing an intranet?
4. What are the strengths and weaknesses of using the Web for organisational communication?
5. How can organisations implement an electronic office strategy and replace the traditional publishing paradigm with the new publishing paradigm?
6. How can organisations use the Web to change the way they undertake their missions?
7. What are some of the ramifications of teleworking on the office and on society?
8. How might information overload be controlled within an organisation?

## SUGGESTED READING

Bayles, D. (1998) *Extranets: Building the Business-to-Business Web*, Prentice Hall, United States.

Department of Foreign Affairs and Trade 1999, *Driving Forces on the New Silk Road: The Use of Electronic Commerce by Australian Businesses*, Commonwealth of Australia, Canberra.

Kalakota, R. and Robinson, M. 1999, *E-Business: Roadmap for Success*, Addison-Wesley Longman, United States.

Kosiur, D. 1997, *Understanding Electronic Commerce: How Online Transactions Can Grow Your Business*, Microsoft Press, United States.

Lamond, D., Daniels, K., and Standen, P. 1997, 'Virtual working or working virtually? An overview of contextual and behavioural issues in teleworking,' *Proceedings of the Fourth International Meeting of the Decision Sciences Institute*, Decision Sciences Institute, Sydney, Australia.

Lamond, D., Standen, P. and Daniels, K. 1997, 'Contexts, cultures and forms of teleworking', *Proceedings of the ANZAM conference*, Melbourne.

Pfaffenberger, B. 1998, *Building a Strategic Extranet*, IDG Books, United States.

Phillips, M. 1997, *Behind Australia's Most Successful Websites*, Bookman, Melbourne.

**END NOTES**

1. Newton, S. 1999, 'Electronic Business: Critical Success Factors for Implementation — A Case Study of ACME Connectors', Collecter99 Conference, Wellington, New Zealand, 29 November.

2. Kosiur, D. 1997, *Understanding Electronic Commerce: How Online Transactions Can Grow Your Business*, Microsoft Press, United States, p. 229.

3. Grimming, R. 1999, 'Booksellers buy the digital title', Computers/Cutting Edge, *Australian*, 26 October, www.news.com.au.

4. Tapscott, D. 1996, *The Digital Economy*, McGraw-Hill, New York, p. 54.

5. Potts, D. 1999, 'Home alone is all the rage', Getting into business, *Sun Herald*, 17 October, p. 4.

6. Kalakota, R. and Robinson, M. 1999, *E-Business: Roadmap for Success*, Addison-Wesley Longman, United States, p. 225.

7. Pfaffenberger, B. 1998, *Building a Strategic Extranet*, IDG Books, United States, p. 70.

8. Kosiur, D. op. cit., p. 229.

9. Australian Bureau of Statistics 1999, 'Use of the Internet by Householders, Australia', May.

10. Yellow Pages 1999, *Yellow Pages Survey of Computer Technology and E-commerce in Australian Small and Medium Business*, May.

11. Braue, D. 1999, 'E-mail features that make every post a winner', Jargon, *Sydney Morning Herald*, 28 September, p. 32.

12. Dertouzos, M. 1997, *What Will Be*, Harper Edge, New York, p. 89.

13. Lowe, S. 1999, 'This mail may knock twicc', *Sydney Morning Herald*, 23 September, p. 11.

14. Braue, D. op. cit., p. 32.

15. Cruickshank, D. 1996, *The Intranet Reinvents Business*, www.sigraf.co.yu/sigraf/oblasti/sgi/www/intmain.html.

16. Tebbutt, D. 1999, 'E-commerce to save General Motors $18 bn', *Australian*, Computers/Net News, 12 October, p. 49, www.news.com.au.

17. Lamond, D., Standen, P. and Daniels, K. 1997, 'Contexts, cultures and forms of teleworking', *Proceedings of the ANZAM conference*, Melbourne.

18. Lowe, S. 1997, 'Information technology — overload control,' *Sydney Morning Herald*, 30 September, p. 6.

19. ibid., p. 6.

20. Dertouzos, G. 1997, *What Will Be*, Harper Edge, United States, p. 204.

CHAPTER

# 9

# Taxation of Internet commerce

## LEARNING Outcomes

You will have mastered the material in this chapter when you can:

- appreciate the impact of Internet commerce on the administration of the Australian taxation system and the implications for Australia's tax base

- find out the quantity, value and type of goods entering Australia under the duty and sales tax-free limit and the commercial entry thresholds, which are administered by the Australian Customs Service, and comment on their appropriateness

- assess the extent to which the Government's potential responses to the growth in Internet commerce are affected by international agreements or conventions

- research the policy approaches being taken by other countries and the scope for international cooperation.

*'The avid regulators of the European Union — who are prone to imposing uniform standards on practically everything from children's playgrounds to fish and chips — are moving towards imposing taxes and restrictions on international electronic commerce.'*

Chris O'Hanlon 1999, 'Cyberpirates stir things up, Net gain', Computers — The Cutting Edge, *Australian*, 9 February, p. 6, www.news.com.au.

# INTRODUCTION

In the closing years of the twentieth century, taxation authorities throughout the world have been placed in the unenviable position of trying to cope with many new issues of great complexity, including the nomination of a taxation regime for Internet commerce. Other examples of dominant issues include the growth of the black economy and profit shifting in a global economy. Since the publication of the *Discussion Report on Tax and the Internet* by the Australian Taxation Office (ATO) in December 1997, electronic commerce issues have been discussed in international forums. Many countries have carried out investigations and published their own analyses of tax issues involving the Internet. The Organisation for Economic Cooperation and Development (OECD) has conducted three major international conferences that have addressed Internet issues, including tax issues.[1] The 1999 *Tax and the Internet: Second Report of the Australian Taxation Office* delivers the results of discussions with business representatives, academics and government agencies. The resulting action plan outlines some immediate actions that can and should be taken to enable the ATO to meet the challenges and take advantage of the opportunities afforded by the emerging digital economy.

In July 1999, the Australian Government passed tax reform legislation that will mean Australian businesses will be issued with an Australian Business Number (ABN) as part of the **Goods and Services Tax (GST)** registration process. The new Australian GST tax package is due to commence in July 2000. Government departments will monitor these ABNs to ensure they are up to date.[2] A digital certificate will be issued with the ABN as part of the registration process and will enable all businesses to positively identify themselves to agencies such as the ATO.

In December 1997, the Australian Government announced a new tax exemption for goods delivered (i.e. downloaded) via the Internet and vowed not to introduce a tax on Internet usage. However, Australia's fragile tax base is under a lot of pressure and massive changes are being made to our taxation system. Many countries are grappling with what to do about taxing Internet businesses. There exists the possibility of individuals being able to set up accounts with cyberbanks in tax havens to circumvent the international banking system. In such a scenario, the transfer of currency could be completed directly between the cyberbanks and account holders through personal computers, leaving no traceable information trail for revenue officials. **Tax evasion** on a wide scale will be easier and more difficult to catch when carried out over the Internet.[3] The Australian Government wants to be seen to be encouraging innovation and improvement of our business infrastructure. However, certain businesses will see the Internet as a way of operating without bureaucratic red tape. Companies will be tempted to choose countries that offer them legal advantages such as bank secrecy and low or no tax. Australian and international taxation laws are being examined as they relate to corporate and individual residency, **tax avoidance** and evasion, **money laundering** and technology transfer.

Some of the questions that governments, including Australia's, are trying to answer include:

- If cyberbanks are set up, how will they be regulated so that the Australian Government does not lose potential taxation revenue?
- How will the jurisdictional issues be determined for the levying of taxes, with regard to electronic payment over the Internet?
- What will be the likely impact of offshore electronic credit facilities on government taxation revenues?

# AUSTRALIA AND TAXATION

Even before the electronic revolution, it has been apparent in Australia for many years that our tax system has needed reform. Unfortunately, experts have not been able to agree on how to achieve such reform. Australia has a reputation for having high marginal income tax rates because our top rate of 48.5 per cent, including the Medicare levy, applies to incomes of $50 000 and above. By comparison, in the United States the top rate is 39.6 per cent and it applies from incomes of $US260 000 or A$410 000 and above.

The GartnerGroup's white paper *Australia's IT and T Future* (1998) states that there is a perception that Australia's high taxes make it an unattractive location for investment. The two highly visible taxes are **income tax** and capital gains tax (CGT). Income tax (including the Medicare levy, which is a tax) is now a flat 50 per cent tax on marginal earnings for most people employed in the well-paid information technology and telecommunications (IT and T) sector. CGT is very high relative to other developed countries and the GartnerGroup believes it is the main disincentive for overseas investment.

To address these problems, the GartnerGroup advocates:

- immediate action on tax reform, particularly with regard to CGT and high rates of personal tax
- removing barriers to tax-free pension investment funds from the United States investing in Australia
- the development of electronic commerce laws (as countries like Singapore and Malaysia have already done)
- fostering the use of broadband cable networks for uses beyond cable television
- boosting funding to IT and T courses, for example, by reviewing the tax subsidy for research and development
- reviewing local regulations that could hold back Australian companies in the worldwide marketplace
- encouraging more people and companies to take risks
- promoting a more vibrant venture capital community
- promoting banks to be more aggressive in moving to support electronic business and to facilitate business-to-business and business-to-consumer trade financing, security and transactions online.

Many Australian politicians have found the issue of tax reform to be a 'poisoned chalice'. Joh Bjelke-Petersen advocated a flat tax in the 1980s and was spectacularly unsuccessful in his attempt to get into Federal Parliament. The then leader of the Federal Opposition, Dr John Hewson, advocated a GST in the 1993 election and was soundly beaten. In 1998, the Prime Minister, John Howard won his second term of government after advocating a GST of 10 per cent but was returned with a significantly reduced majority. The GST is due to be introduced in July 2000.

It is interesting to see the flat tax idea is now gaining some momentum. A leading Sydney taxation lawyer, Louise McBride, is an admirer of the work of the Stanford economists, Robert Hall and Alvin Rabushka who have spent 20 years modelling a flat tax of 19 per cent. Ms McBride advocates a flat tax, saying:

> *The current tax system has pushed nearly 20 per cent of all full-time employed persons into the top marginal tax bracket compared with about one per cent in 1954–55. A flat tax regime, combined with a complete overhaul of the current system would revolutionise the way we live.*[4]

It is within this framework that tax officials now have a new and potentially income-threatening business phenomenon to deal with, namely electronic commerce.

Australia's taxation policy receives much criticism in the press and indeed the Australian Taxation Office (ATO) is mindful that there are opportunities and pitfalls in the area of developing taxation policies for Australia in general and Internet commerce in particular. The Taxation Institute has formulated 10 principles that they consider a blueprint of the essentials for a good tax system. The institute believes 'the tax system should be designed so as to simply collect revenue in a way that encourages efficient economic activity and business profitability'.[5] The 10 principles are:

1. The system's design, legislation and administration should be such that ordinary taxpayers are able to comply, without resorting to professional assistance.
2. All taxes should be visible.
3. The system should be equitable.
4. The system should foster rather than detract from Australia's ability to compete internationally.
5. Changes to taxation law should be prospective not retrospective.
6. Indexation should apply to rates of tax and thresholds.
7. There should be parity of rates between taxes that are directed to the same end; for example, income tax, company tax and **fringe benefits tax**.
8. The system should operate such that, from a compliance cost and overall tax position, taxpayers are indifferent as to whether income is derived from a foreign or domestic source.
9. The tax collection mechanism should be adapted to business operations, rather than business operations having to be adapted to the collection mechanism.
10. The collection mechanism should be certain in its operation and not create any bias between different business relationships or parties.

It remains to be seen whether these principles will be taken into account in the reform of the Australian taxation system as a whole or, indeed, with regard to Internet commerce.

## insite Digital certificates

For more information on the Australian Business Number, see www.noie.gov.au.

### BUSINESS TO GET DIGITAL CERTIFICATES

In a move designed to boost business-to-business e-commerce and move government services online, the ATO will give each of Australia's 2.5 million businesses a number linked to a digital certificate for free. From November 1 companies can apply online for their Australian Business Number and an online certificate, which comprises a cryptographic public and private key. The number will be listed on a publicly accessible register to be hosted by the Federal Government's Business Entry Point web site.

The ATO hopes to have most businesses registered by June 2000 as part of its tax reform measures and implementation of the Goods and Services Tax, which will also help stem tax revenue leakage brought about by cross-border electronic trade. National Office for the Information Economy spokespeople said only 'tombstone' information would be registered — business name, registered address and the contact person for the tax office such as a company director/secretary.

'There's an opportunity to leverage it up and leverage the uptake of e-commerce to conduct secure transactions,' they said of the system expected to become a ready standard for e-commerce. Businesses with an annual turnover of $20 million will be the first to be issued with the number. They would save time and money by 'telling [government] once, using many times' any changes to their details. Even trusts, non-trading entities, superannuation trusts, sole traders, partnerships must register for the number, the spokesmen said. They expected the certificates would be kept as secure as are currently company seals.

**SOURCE:** *E-commerce Today*, 29 July 1999, www.ecommercetoday.com.au

### EXERCISES

1. Visit the publicly accessible register at the Federal Government's Entry Point web site (www.business.gov.au) and check out two of the businesses listed there. Debate the proposition that having a government entry point position makes potential online shoppers feel more secure.
2. Debate the proposition that the issuance of an ABN number and free digital certificate is a ploy by the ATO to ensure they do not lose any tax revenue via Internet commerce.
3. Debate the statement that this technique will encourage more Australian Internet businesses to host their web sites offshore.
4. What work has been done internationally to devise a universal business number?

# THE NATURE AND EXTENT OF INTERNET COMMERCE IN AUSTRALIA AND THE WORLD

An Angus Reid survey of 28 374 consumers in 34 countries gave the following statistics for adults shopping online: United States — 31 per cent; Sweden — 21 per cent; Switzerland — 19 per cent; Canada — 18 per cent; and Australia — 14 per cent. Banking, share trading and downloading digital music proved the most popular products.[6]  By August 1999, in Australia, 42 per cent of all PCs in business were Internet enabled, 65 per cent of Australian businesses had a web home page and another 20 per cent aimed to have one by December 1999.[7]

| TABLE 9.1 | BUSINESS COMPUTERS ON THE INTERNET* | |
| --- | --- | --- |
| **TYPE OF BUSINESS** | **1999** | **BY 2003** |
| medium to large businesses | 2 250 000 | 3 840 000 |
| small businesses | 900 000 | 3 210 000 |
| government organisations | 400 000 | 1 570 000 |
| educational institutions | 300 000 | 1 010 000 |

\* Includes all Internet-connected devices such as PCs and mobile phones

**SOURCE:** K. Nicholas 1999, 'Work access to net multiplies', Biz.Com, *Sydney Morning Herald*, 23 August, p. 37

There have been several crucial Australian Internet commerce initiatives established recently, including Telstra's SureLink, now called TheArcade. Telstra launched its SureLink electronic payment service in 1997. SureLink licensed Open Market's Transact system, which has US government endorsement for its high-level encryption standard. Telstra signed up retailers involved in travel, wine, music, books, insurance and computers and built a substantial new revenue base from the fast growing online economy. It earns a small transaction fee from merchants every time the service is used. In 1999, it launched its Telstra.com portal.

Australian Business Access has developed a Java-based secure Internet buyer-to-bank solution targeting retailers, online finance companies and insurers. FAI was the first to sign up and launched its site in June 1997.

Another software company, Sausage Software, announced its Java-based system for selling intellectual property over the Internet using eVend in March 1997. This system allows web site providers to charge users micropayments as small as one cent for their content on a per page basis. Both Intel and St George Bank invested in the Melbourne company in 1999.

# TAXATION IMPLICATIONS OF INTERNET COMMERCE — AUSTRALIA

In order to consider the impact of Internet commerce on the tax system, it is necessary to examine the nature of the liability imposed by a particular tax, whether it be income tax, **sales tax** or fringe benefits tax.

## Income tax

Income tax is an aggregate tax, whereby the liability is arrived at after adding up all items of assessable income and subtracting all allowable deductions. Income tax imposes a personal liability on the person who derives the income. Thus personal identity is extremely important. In cases of taxpayer defaults in payment of income tax, the identity, whereabouts and financial position of the taxpayer are all relevant.

## Sales tax

Sales tax is an example of transaction tax, whereby liability results from an imposed tax on particular types of transaction. A consumer buying a car, for example, is subject to a sales tax on that car and the advantage for the government is that the car dealer collects the tax for the government.

The following Business insite illustrates the impact of sales tax and duty payable on items. From this example you will see that:

- the Australian Customs Service collects duty and sales tax on behalf of the Australian Taxation Office
- the same rules apply to goods ordered over the Internet and those purchased by mail order.

## Internet purchases on overseas sites

### NET PURCHASE
**Sit back and relax. Let your fingers walk the Web.**
LEEANNE BLAND

It's a great idea. Being able to shop for goods from the comfort of your lounge chair (or at least from the comfort of your computer desk chair), browse through shops without sales assistants bugging you, compare prices and shop around for items, all at the click of a mouse button.

And with the Australian Bureau of Statistics figures showing almost 20 per cent of households have the Internet at home and more than 30 per cent of Australians have used the Net in the past 12 months, the Internet — and online shopping — can't be dismissed as a flash in the pan.

But although Internet research company www.consult believes shopping online will take off in a big way in Australia, it hasn't yet.

The company's research shows that more than 66 per cent of regular Internet users have tried online shopping in Australia more than once. But only 4 per cent have tried it more than 10 times.

Nevertheless the research found that Australian online shoppers spent about $139 million on the Net in the 12 months to July 1998.

So who are these intrepid surfers — shopping where no Australian has shopped before? According to www.consult, they are youngish — aged 25–35 — highly educated and in 'professional' occupations.

But Richard Sandlant, the director of Online Shopping Research with www.consult, says this is slowly changing.

'We are seeing new users,' he says.

More and more women, more younger people and more older people — 'the silver surfers' — are surfing the Net, he says.

Once these people start using it to shop — and Sandlant is sure they will — a big rise will be seen in the dollars being spent online.

When this happens, he says, the challenge will be for Australian retailers to provide the sites so that the shopping money doesn't go overseas. But more about that later.

Although many people aren't using the Internet to shop, they do use it to browse.

'The Internet is a great resource for comparison shopping. Instead of searching store after store, you can navigate between World Wide Web sites from the comfort of your home.

Before buying, use the Web to get price and product information and to find the items you want,' says the Internet shopping section of the Visa card Web site.

According to the Web site of the Department of Communications, Information Technology and the Arts (DCITA), the most popular item today for electronic commerce is software.

'[This is] followed by books, music, magazines, and then computer hardware.'

Flowers, tickets, travel, wine and food also made the list.

Surprisingly, however, people are not necessarily shopping for price savings.

Sandlant says, 'You can get a better deal [on the Net], but not necessarily by cost savings.'

He says the better deal comes from ing able to shop overseas and being able to shop from home at any time.

The really early adopters are using Internet shopping services like those offered by greengrocer.com and being trialled by Woolworths and, more recently, Coles, he says.

Twenty-nine per cent of these early adopters says they shop to save time, says Sandlant.

They are using the Woolworths service even though it does not discount the groceries and, in fact, charges a fee for delivery, he says.

But by far the most popular shopping site would have to be amazon.com, a huge book repository based in America.

'Amazon.com is a super brand,' says Sandlant. 'For a great many Internet users, particularly new Internet shoppers, they look at that brand first of all.'

'It provides a very sophisticated Internet shopping experience.'

But Sandlant predicts that books won't retain their position at the top for long. He says areas such as travel and Internet investment are likely to increase in popularity.

Clothes and shoes are other areas that he nominates for growth.

Already, he says, 'For socks and jocks, you can shop online at Gowings and Lowes.'

He thinks these types of sites will become popular for the sorts of things that you don't need to try on.

But although Lowes, Gowings and other Australian retailers are on the World Wide Web, Australians who are shopping online are doing it overwhelmingly in the US.

Information from the ABS shows that about 64 per cent of those who had shopped on the Net had shopped at overseas sites.

'People can go to a US site and buy clothes that you just can't get in Australia,' says Sandlant.

Of course, if you are buying from an overseas site, it means you need to take currency conversions and sales taxes and duties into account.

'Overseas purchases made through the Internet are subject to sales tax and duty, just like any other imported goods. You should know what the additional cost, if any, of tax and duty will be before you decide to buy from an overseas company,' says DCITA (see Buying goods overseas).

Another issue that arises when buying products from overseas is what happens if you are not happy with your purchase?

'When you buy over the Internet, you may well be dealing with a business in a different State, Territory or country. This can create problems with delivering goods, and returning them if they are faulty. You should make sure you know how your order will be delivered and under what conditions the company will provide a refund before you hand over your money,' says DCITA.

'You should think about what will happen if something goes wrong — such as the goods not arriving, or arriving damaged — and the supplier does not resolve the problem to your satisfaction.'

If the company is in Australia, 'then your local State or Territory fair trading/consumer affairs body may be able to help you. If, however, the company is based overseas, you may have great difficulty in finding an organisation in that country that will help you.'

These sentiments are echoed at the Visa site. 'Before completing an online transaction, read the delivery and return policies on the merchant's home page,' it says.

'Make sure you can return any unsatisfactory items and check to see if you can get your money refunded, or if you will receive a merchandise credit. Sales policies should cover the delivery methods and cost of delivery, currency accepted, taxes applied, return and refund policy, and a contact number or e-mail address.'

The need for these details is one of the reasons why sites such as amazon.com are popular. It is well-known and reputable, says Sandlant.

That reputation also appeals to those who are worried about security and privacy, both of which are genuine concerns.

'The security issue is real, but I still haven't come across a person being ripped off where they weren't foolish,' he says.

'When you shop online, you should check that the site has at least [SSL] level of encryption.'

As Visa explains: 'Using Netscape navigator version 2.0 (or later), or any version of Microsoft Internet Explorer as your browser provides you with an added level of security when shopping on the Web. These browsers use (Secure Sockets Layer) technology, a proven and easy-to-use system that lets your browser automatically encrypt, or scramble, your personal data before sending it to the merchant via the Internet.

'SSL shows you that a Web site is secure when an unbroken key or a lock appears in your browser window.'

If it has this, Sandlant says, it is at least as safe as giving a waiter your credit card in a restaurant and waiting for 15 minutes while it is taken out the back.

According to DCITA, 'Half of all e-commerce sites don't encrypt your details, so make certain that the company you're dealing with does. Look for an unbroken key or lock to appear at the bottom of your browser window.'

Privacy is another important issue.

'Many people are concerned that personal information they provide to businesses may be misused. You should think about what personal information you are willing to disclose and how it might be used. Thought should also be given to the disclosure and storage of the information by the business,' says DCITA.

'You need to know what the privacy policy of the site is,' agrees Sandlant.

'You really want to look for some sign that you are dealing with a responsible retailer.'

He says you should be pretty safe with all the well-known Internet site brands, such as Dymocks and greengrocer.com.

Dan Coyne, from the Australian Consumers Association (ACA), says it all boils down to knowing for sure that the Internet site you are dealing with is legitimate.

'Just because it is on the Internet doesn't mean it is a legitimate business,' he says.

'You need to know the company you are dealing with and the product you are buying.'

At the very least, Coyne says there should be a street address and a phone number on the Internet site.

DCITA says, 'There is also important information you should look for before you decide to trust a company with your money — for example, clear description of goods, clear company name and address, description of how they will handle your financial information, accurate and inclusive prices, clear delivery dates, and privacy, refund and return policies.

'Talk to friends about their favourite online stores and their suggestions for reputable companies.

'And start small — you can always add more goodies to your electronic shopping trolley after you're satisfied that the business can deliver the goods.'

But if you have never shopped on the Net before, it can be difficult to know where to begin.

Sandlant suggests first-timers try an Internet 'portal'. Although this sounds like a Star Trek term for being transported to another galaxy, it is simply an Internet site that acts as an entrance of sorts to lots of other sites.

He suggests sites such as yahoo.com.au and ninemsn.com.au.

'They give you links to banking, shopping and news,' Sandlant says.

Another useful site is www.storefind.com.au.

And whether you are unsure about the site you are dealing with or not, you should always keep records of transactions and monitor your bank statement.

The advice from Visa is the same: 'Just as you would save your receipt in case you need to return or exchange an item, you'll want to keep a record of all online transactions, including the merchant's URL [Internet address].

'That way, you'll have all the information at your fingertips in case a question about an order arises. Several computer software and browser providers now offer electronic wallets that can automatically log your Internet purchases. Many online merchants will e-mail you an order confirmation that summarises the price and quantity of a purchase. Print and save a copy of this information,' Visa advises.

ACA's Coyne says that if you notify your bank as soon as you detect any unauthorised activity on your card, you will usually be liable for only the first $50.

## SITES TO SEARCH

If you are thinking of shopping online, but are still a bit wary and want to know more, there are a variety of sites around that can help you.

Probably the most comprehensive source of information is the Department of Communications, Information Technology and the Arts, at its Web site: www.dcita.gov.au/shoponline

The department's series of six Net shopping fact sheets cover:
■ What are the benefits and risks of shopping online?
■ What type of information should I look for in a Web site?
■ How safe is it to use my credit card?
■ Do I have to pay sales tax or duties on imported goods?
■ What happens to my personal information?
■ What if something goes wrong with my purchase?

Because credit cards are the main form of payment for Internet purchases, credit card companies have a vested interest in ensuring you get the Internet shopping experience right. With this in mind, Visa has a useful section on online shopping on its Web site. Surf it at www.visa.com

The Australian Consumers Association is looking out for Web shoppers as well, and its Internet site at www.choice.com.au

contains some useful information to bear in mind when shopping on the Net. To find it, do a site search for 'Internet'.

For information on whether customs duty will apply to your purchase, the Australian Customs Service Internet site may be the go (www.customs.gov.au/bizlink/imports/index.htm).

And if you are wondering about the level of consumer protection you have when you shop on the Net, the Australian Competition and Consumer Commission has the answers.

It outlines where Net surfers can go for consumer protection advice, and it doesn't just talk about the operations of the ACCC itself.

It also lists the Australian Securities and Investment Commission — which is responsible for consumer protection in the financial services arena — along with information on consumer protection and the fair trading agencies in each State which administer each State's Fair Trading Act (which tend to mirror the Federal Trade Practices Act).

Contact details for each State's Consumer Association, the Australian Pensioners and Superannuants Federation and the Consumer Credit Legal Centre, among others, are also listed. Surf it at http://www.accc.gov.au/consumer/cons_advice.html

# BUYING GOODS OVERSEAS

With the majority of Internet purchases happening on overseas sites, it means sales tax or duty may become an issue when you get goods shipped or mailed to Australia.

People are finding that sometimes they have to pay sales tax or duty and at other times they don't, and this can be confusing, according to the Department of Communications, Information Technology and the Arts (DCITA).

'Whether you have to pay depends upon the goods that you've bought and the total amount of your purchase,' it says on its Internet site (www.dcita.gov.au/shoponline).

In short, if your purchase is being imported by sea and cost less than $250 ($1000 for items through the post), and any sales tax and customs duty levied is less than $50, the purchase is considered to be 'insubstantial'. Customs shouldn't be an issue, as you will be entitled to an exemption of sales tax or duty, says DCITA.

The DCITA Internet site provides some examples.

'If a consignment of toys worth $100 is imported into Australia, then no formal entry declaration is required because the value is below the $1000 and $250 thresholds. In addition, the duty and sales tax payable is $37.72, so the $50 free level is not exceeded. Therefore, the goods are "screened free".'

In the meantime, it says, if a parcel of toys worth $200 is imported into Australia, again no formal entry declaration is required because the value is below the $1000 and $250 thresholds. However, the sales tax amounts to $65.44, which means the $50 free level is exceeded. Therefore, the goods are not 'screen free' and the $65.44 is payable by an informal clearance document.

'If an imported postal consignment was valued at $1100, then a formal entry declaration would be required. The duty and sales tax, even if less than $50, would therefore be payable, and the goods would not be "screened free",' says DCITA.

Different products are subject to different rates of duty or sales tax.

The following table outlines examples of duty and sales tax-free limits and commercial entry thresholds.

## MINIMUM VALUE OF GOODS BEFORE DUTY OR SALES TAX IS DUE

| GOODS | DUTY RATE | SALES TAX RATE | COMBINED RATE | MIN. VALUE ($) |
|---|---|---|---|---|
| APPAREL | 34 | 0 | 34 | 147.06 |
| CAR PARTS | 15 | 22 | 45.36 | 110.23 |
| CASSETTES | 0 | 22 | 26.40 | 189.39 |
| CDS | 0 | 22 | 26.40 | 189.23 |
| COSMETICS | 5 | 22 | 37.72 | 152.81 |
| JEWELLERY | 5 | 32 | 45.32 | 110.33 |
| PHOTO. MATERIALS | 5 | 22 | 32.72 | 152.81 |
| TOYS | 5 | 22 | 32.72 | 152.81 |
| SPORTING GOODS | 5 | 22 | 32.72 | 152.81 |
| WATCHES | 0 | 32 | 38.40 | 130.21 |

*Source:* DCITA

**SOURCE:** L. Bland 1999, 'Net purchase', Money, *Sydney Morning Herald*, 2 June, pp. 16–19

1. The tax figures in the table will change after July 2000 as a result of the GST. Do some research to see what is the current status of these rates.
2. Do some research on the Web to see if you can find any online shops that have put up disclaimers to tell shoppers they may have to pay import duties in some countries.
3. Conduct a survey among your class group to ascertain how many have purchased via the Web, what they have bought, and whether they have paid tax or duty.
4. Check out each of the mentioned sites and write a short report on their usefulness.
5. These sites have been designed to put the potential online shopper at ease. Can you suggest any improvements to these sites?

## Fringe benefits tax

Some taxpayers seek to minimise their taxation burden by using flexible salary packages. In such a case, a person might have his or her children's school fees paid directly to a school or parking fees paid directly to the parking station. This money therefore does not appear as salary and lowers the person's tax burden. Obviously the ATO is interested in ways in which the Internet could be used to help minimise taxable income.

# INCOME TAX — INTERNATIONAL IMPLICATIONS

Most countries seek to tax residents on all income regardless of its source while non-residents are taxed only on income derived in the taxing authority's country of jurisdiction. Otherwise, such a situation could lead to inequities where residents are taxed on the same income twice. International treaties exist to cover these types of problem but these rules will have to be modified to take the Internet into account. International cooperation on allocation of taxing rights and **compliance** measures to secure those rights will be crucial.[8]

# SOURCING INTERNET INCOME — DIFFICULTIES IN ENFORCING TAX COMPLIANCE

The ATO maintains its interest in commercial transactions over the Internet, but it has recognised the following difficulties inherent in the commercial usage of the Internet.

• A web site can be moved quickly from one location to another, even to another country. Cheap hardware can be discarded or disposed of quickly.
• 'Stock on hand' can be merely a set of data files, which can be updated periodically and automatically from afar.
• Customer orders and payments can be handled by a back-end database system, with payments (electronic cash or credit card details) being channelled somewhere entirely unconnected with other parts of the site.

- A third party can deliver physical goods such as books or CDs on an agency basis.

The use of a web site allows for material values for items such as software, data and goodwill in a business to be both indefinite and mobile. The ATO may find it difficult to use their full powers under sections 263 or 264 of the *Income Tax Act* to assess the income of a commercial web site[9] because:

- components of the web site do not have to be physically co-located
- logically integrated business operations can be spread over a number of places.

Professor Tyree believes that international cooperation will be vital, but points out that it is a certainty that some small countries will establish 'computer money havens', just as they have established tax havens and bank havens.[10]

## GST AND ONLINE TRANSACTIONS

### ONLINE FINANCIAL TRANSACTIONS TO BE GST FREE

Online transactions involving the supply of financial services (e.g. transferring, lending or borrowing money) were one of the few Internet-based transactions that would not attract a GST, according to a Deloitte Touche Tohmatsu senior analyst. Kavita Panjratan, an e-commerce and GST specialist, said financial services were 'broadly defined' under the GST but, if a business was classified as a financial supplier, it would not be required to charge GST on its supplies.

For example, if a business outsources its credit card authorisation function to an IT company, not all of the services provided may be subject to GST. Part of this authorisation process may involve arranging the transfer of money which is a financial supply and consequently not subject to GST. This means that businesses should be aware of the services that are being provided to them and that they are providing. Generally the GST does not differentiate between doing business online or offline.

'It is a tax on the supply of virtually everything,' Panjratan told *ECT*. 'It does not really matter, for example, if someone receives something digitally rather than in the mail,' she said. A taxable transaction will remain taxable for e-commerce purposes. However, many goods themselves will be subject to GST. KPMG tax partner Mark Goldsmith previously told *ECT* that many goods which did not attract the old wholesale sales tax because they were in digital form — such as music, books or software — would attract GST because the GST applies to not only physical goods but also to services which may include sale of such goods.

**SOURCE:** *E-commerce Today*, 19 August 1999,
http://www.ecommercetoday.com.au/ecom/au/a5619.htm

### QUESTIONS

1. Discuss the assertion that GST does not differentiate between doing business online or offline.
2. In 1997 the Australian Government declared that downloaded articles would not attract tax. What is the Australian Government doing about this now?

# TAX REFORM AND TRADE POLICY

Many industry groups in Australia are worried about consumers evading custom duties and wholesale sales tax by making purchases through the Internet. Groups representing sporting goods, music and software companies see their business being eroded by Internet commerce. Anecdotal evidence collected by the Australian Fishing Tackle Association suggests that the Government could be losing 'hundreds of millions of dollars' in lost duty and wholesale tax collections.[11] The arrival of the GST in Australia has meant the total revamping of the wholesale tax structure.

# ELECTRONIC TAX PACK

Australian taxpayers were able to complete their first online tax returns in 1999 after the completion of a successful pilot in 1998 when 1200 personal income tax returns were filed over the Internet.[12] To participate, the tax payer must be using Windows and download the eTax application from the ATO's web site. The taxpayer must also enter his or her tax file number and any requested details about his or her previous tax assessment. The taxpayer then receives a password, which is generated when personal details are verified. The software security company Baltimore developed the security technology. Digital certificate technology is used to sign the data on the return to ensure authenticity. The data is then encrypted before being sent over the Internet.

# INTERNET GAMBLING

Australians are known to enjoy gambling. Indeed every November, the nation almost comes to a standstill to watch the Melbourne Cup. Over the past ten years, most capital cities have opened large casinos. Australian Bureau of Statistics figures show the states received $3.3 billion from gambling revenues in 1995/96 — revenue that is placed at risk by competition from Internet-based gambling sites. Representatives of the gambling industry have met with government bureaucrats to come up with a plan to ensure that Australia is in the forefront of Internet gambling, which is seen as inevitable. (See the Business insite on the opposite page). In 2000, the Federal Government set up an inquiry to investigate the feasibility and consequences of banning Internet gambling.

According to the president of Atlantic International Entertainment, Richard Iamunno, Australia could lead the world in home casino gambling. He put forward five major items that stand in the way of making Internet gambling politically and socially acceptable:

* prevention of consumer fraud
* coping with gambling addiction

- stopping underage gambling
- solving taxation issues
- preventing money laundering.

## Internet gambling

# PLACE YOUR INTERBETS PLEASE

BY ALEX MITCHELL

AUSTRALIA has been praised for legalising Internet gambling and giving it legitimacy among overseas punters and investors.

According to Wall Street analyst Sebastian Sinclair, Australia is helping to fuel the craze of cyberspace gambling and boosting the price of US-listed Internet gaming stocks.

'The legalisation of Internet gambling in Australia will forever change this industry,' said Mr Sinclair, of New York finance house Christiansen/ Cummings Associates.

'Australia is a real country, not a small republic with questionable credibility. Australia-based online gaming enterprises will overcome the greatest hurdle confronting at-home Internet gambling — legitimacy.'

Mr Sinclair said *Bloomberg News* recently reported that shares of companies that were planning to offer gambling online were among the biggest gainers on the US stockmarkets.

'Franky, we are not surprised by this turn of events,' he said.

'Thanks to the failure of anti-Internet legislation in the US and the legalisation of the technology in major overseas markets such as Australia, the future of at-home gambling via the Internet has never been brighter.'

Queensland, the ACT and the Northern Territory have all passed Internet gaming legislation but no licences have yet been granted to providers.

Victoria is the next State to embrace cyber-gaming, with Premier Jeff Kennett expected to introduce legislation this year. The first application for a licence will be lodged by Melbourne's Crown Casino, which this week became part of Kerry and James Packer's PBL empire.

In NSW, the Carr Government and Kerry Chikarovski's Coalition are opposed to legalising Internet gaming.

NSW Gaming and Racing Minister Richard Face is also opposed strongly to Net gambling, because it is virtually unpoliceable and can be accessed by minors.

He warned recently that computer-literate children could sign on to gaming sites and use their parents' personal identification numbers (PINs) to make bets on roulette, blackjack and other casino-type games.

Mr Face is also opposed to credit betting, the system used on the Internet, which allows punters to give their credit card details to place bets.

Mr Face and Opposition Gaming spokesman Richard Bull have been campaigning for the Federal Government to impose a national ban on Internet gaming.

Laurie Bowe, president of the NSW Council on Problem Gambling, said the Howard Government had 'missed a golden opportunity' to pass legislation to outlaw Internet gaming.

**SOURCE:** *Sun Herald*, 7 March 1999, p. 22, www.sunherald.com.au

**EXERCISES**

1.  Visit three Australian states' TAB sites and compare and contrast them with the New South Wales TAB site.
2.  Does the NSW TAB site take credit card information over the Internet? If so, how has the NSW TAB ensured the security of credit card details? If not, what are the plans for this?
3.  What effect has Internet betting had on the amount of overseas betting? Try to obtain up-to-date figures.
4.  Write a short report on interactive Internet games and gambling such as Fono.

# THE AUSTRALIAN TAXATION OFFICE'S ELECTRONIC COMMERCE PROJECT

## Background

In 1996 the ATO set up a project team to examine the effects, both risks and opportunities, of electronic commerce on income tax, sales tax and fringe benefits tax. The team consisted of a multi-disciplined group of ATO personnel and external consultants with expertise in large and small businesses, industry research, banking and finance areas, taxation (international, fringe benefit, withholding and general tax law) and information technology. The report's recommendations were released at the end of August 1997. By December 1997 the Australian Government announced a tax exemption for goods (such as CDs and books) downloaded via the Internet (i.e. not posted). It promised not to introduce a tax on Internet usage. Internet gambling is to be subject to State taxes. The Government recognised that its decision would create loopholes for taxpayers but this illustrates the difficulties inherent in trying to tax Internet transactions.[13]

Some of the issues in the report that concerned the ATO were as follows.

*   The Internet allows trade to be conducted in an environment that does not necessarily create independent audit trails.
*   Electronic entities on the Internet are not easily linked with their physical equivalents, making identification and recourse difficult.
*   The Internet lowers the cost of international trade, potentially increasing the number of participants and, therefore, the number of businesses engaged in profit-shifting activities.
*   Encryption systems that make electronic cash viable also impede the ability of the ATO to ensure compliance with the tax law.
*   Efficient collection mechanisms are under challenge because the traditional leverage points, the 'middlemen' in the distribution chain from producer to consumer, are under threat due to an effect known as '**disintermediation**'. This means that producers and consumers are connected directly, cutting out the middlemen such as wholesalers, distributors and retailers. Some of the most efficient collection mechanisms are those which make use of a leverage point. A common example is the group tax arrangements whereby employers remit PAYE tax instalment deductions on behalf of employees.

Under these arrangements the tax payable by more than six million employees can substantially be collected by concentrating collection activities on a much smaller number of employers. By eliminating 'middlemen', tax collection efficiency is reduced.[14]

Australia is already losing taxation revenue as a result of people purchasing CDs and books from the United States. However, Professor Tyree believes that these examples should cause little loss in tax revenue as the price of CDs in Australia is artificially inflated by regulations such as the *Copyright Act* and the subsidy of the local market allows book publishers to maintain prices that are substantially higher than overseas.[15] Furthermore, he does not feel overly pessimistic about lost taxation revenues from salary and other monies in off-shore accounts because he does not believe there is a strong enough incentive for business organisations to agree to such payments of unreported salaries or monies to foreign accounts.

## The report

The report on the ATO's Electronic Commerce Project, which was released in August 1997, was 140 pages in length and had taken ATO experts and consultants over a year to finalise. The report defined a business model to help them understand how various players make money from the Internet so they could work out how to assess and collect taxation from transactions on the Internet. The business model also makes explicit the base assumptions underlying the study so that they can be examined and critiqued.

# NATIONAL AND INTERNATIONAL RESPONSES TO INTERNET COMMERCE

Australia is not alone in trying to set up guidelines to cope with the impact of Internet commerce. In 1996 Australia, Canada and the United States jointly produced a paper for the Organisation for Economic Cooperation and Development (OECD) called *Implications of the Communications Revolution for Tax Policy and Administration*, ref. CFA (96) 46. In the *United States Framework Document,* issued by President Clinton in July 1997, the United States backed a tariff-free approach to the sales of electronic goods and services over the Internet. It does not apply to tangible products ordered and paid for over the Internet but delivered via conventional means.

The Australian Parliament's Joint Committee of Public Accounts examined the opportunities and challenges presented by electronic commerce.[16] The Australian Society of Certified Practising Accountants is supportive of **tax neutrality**, which rejects the imposition of new or additional taxes on electronic transactions. Neutrality requires that the tax system treat similar income equally, regardless of whether it is earned through electronic or existing means. Germany toyed with the idea of taxing business sites by way of a licence, much like a television licensing system as used in England. However, they rejected this taxation model in August 1997. Belgium's Ministry put forward a Bit Tax proposal whereby they would attempt to tax data travelling over

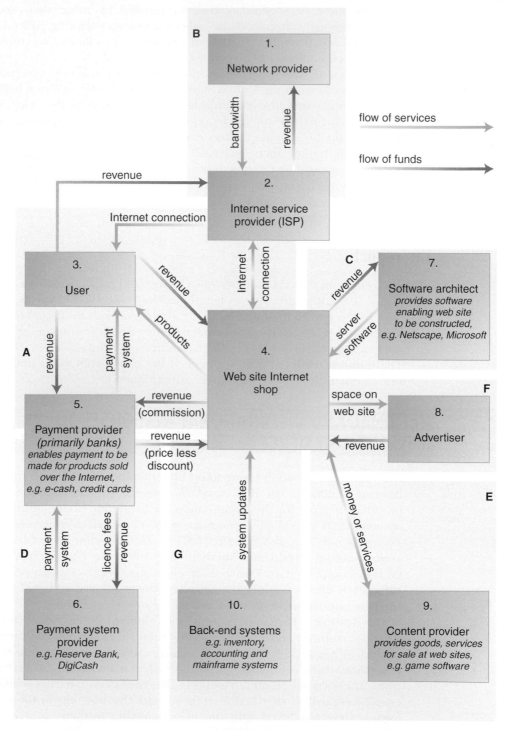

**FIGURE 9.1:** An Internet business model for taxation purposes.
**SOURCE:** Australian Taxation Office 1997, 'Tax and the Internet', *Discussion Report of the ATO Electronic Commerce Project*, Australian Government Publishing Service, Canberra, p. 13

their communication links. In Europe, Internet retailers are supposed to collect the value-added tax (VAT), which is similar to GST. The idea of a transmission tax has been put forward as preferable to taxing the 'value' of the almost intangible information. The Minister of Telecommunications in Belgium stated that the number of bits crossing Belgium's border annually is $10^{17}$ and, at $0.01 per MB, would yield $10 billion in annual tax revenue (about four per cent of Belgium's GDP).

## Tax on email

The United Nations has suggested the introduction of a Bit Tax on data sent through the Internet as a way to bridge the gap between the world's rich and poor.[18] The *United Nation's Human Development Report* (1999) proposes a tax of one US cent for every 100 lengthy emails transmitted. According to the report, this could generate US$70 billion per annum. The 'elite minority' who use the Internet, according to the report, are usually urban, high-income earning, university-educated males who are under 35 and speak English. (Fewer than one in 10 persons worldwide speak English.) Further, the report states that 'tighter control of innovations in the hands of multinational companies ignores the needs of millions'.

### EXERCISES

1. Debate the merits or otherwise of the proposal to tax emails.
2. Try to think of other original ways to raise money to assist bridging the gap between the world's rich and poor.

## The United States' response

According to Nicolas Negroponte, Director of the Massachusetts Institute of Technology's Media Lab, tax regulation is the biggest issue facing the Internet for years.[19] In the United States, the *Framework for Electronic Commerce (Framework Document)*, which was issued by the authority of President Clinton on 2 July 1997, looked at financial, legal and market access issues.[20] The United States supports a tariff-free approach to transactions involving electronic goods and services over the Internet, excepting tangible products ordered and paid for over the Internet but delivered via conventional means.

The United States proposes that Internet trading be placed under a universally agreed global framework, while many developing countries want the United Nations to control the Internet.[21] Ira Magaziner, President Clinton's top adviser on the electronic economy, outlined the US position at the Internet Industry Association of Australia (INTIAA) (now called the Internet Industry Association) annual conference in December 1997, namely:

- a tariff-free electronic commerce trading environment without new taxes
- minimally regulated secure electronic payment systems
- a common commercial code that accepts electronic signatures and other authentication procedures that has a dispute resolution mechanism, liability exposure rules and access to registries of Internet users.

Magaziner put forward two possible ways to tax electronic transactions:

- introduce a corporate profits tax similar to the US taxation regime
- develop a smart card to automatically deduct sales taxes or value-added taxes at the time of a trade. (This would require taxes to be internationally uniform.) The major advantage of this method would be that it ensures taxation authorities get 100 per cent of the sales tax revenue due compared with present sales tax revenue yields of about 60 per cent.[22]

The US position rules out any kind of new taxation of e-commerce transactions and no discriminatory taxation on the Internet; in other words no new taxes on Internet access or Internet telephony. Again, developing countries are opposed to this as they often use state-owned telephone monopolies as a source of foreign currency. The Internet is therefore potentially valuable to such countries. The United States has the following Internet commerce strategy:

- create a predictable environment for industry by securing international agreement that there will be no censorship of the Web nor will there be discriminatory or overly bureaucratic ways of taxing the Internet
- create a predictable legal environment for the Internet on an international scale so that, for example, digital signatures in one country would be recognised in another.[23]

The above gives the impression that all is working well in the United States but the reality is somewhat different. The United States' form of government, where government power is shared between the states and the national government, creates a legal environment in which businesses must deal not only with federal law but also with the law in each state in which they have customers. Standards for determining the constitutionality of state and local taxes have been set by the Supreme Court. To meet the constitutionality standard a state tax on interstate businesses must pass a four-part test (as seen in the Complete Auto Transit, Inc v. Brady, 430 US 274 (1977)). State taxation of interstate business must:

- tax only interstate activities with a sufficient connection to the taxing state
- be fairly apportioned to the taxpayer's activities in the taxing state
- not discriminate against interstate commerce
- be fairly related to the services provided by the state.[24]

Two well-known instances of imposing unconstitutional tax obligations are in the sales and use tax area. Twice the US Supreme Court has told states that tax collection obligations cannot be imposed on businesses that have no physical presence in their states. The states, led by the Multistate Tax Commission (an organisation of state tax administrators), engage in 'tax terrorism' according to Caldwell. This consists of states claiming that existing legal precedents no longer apply, revising state standards and then forcing the companies to litigate the case all the way to the Supreme Court again. Thus, state laws, be they tax laws or other laws, that discriminate against interstate commerce will have a negative effect on the ability of electronic commerce businesses to access nationwide markets. Caldwell believes that the United States needs to create a single market environment in which companies can thrive.[25] The growth of electronic commerce necessitates a more nationwide and indeed global marketplace, which will force 'badly behaving' states to drop policies that discriminate against interstate commerce.

### The US National Tax Association's Electronic Commerce Taxation Project

The original goal for the US National Tax Association's Electronic Commerce Taxation Project[26] was for industry and the states to develop a broadly available public report that identified and explored the issues in applying state and local taxes and fees to electronic commerce and that included recommendations to state and local officials regarding the application of such taxes and a model legislation designed to implement the recommendations of the project.[27] By early 2000 agreement had not been reached. It is expected that the moratorium on Internet tax will be extended another three years.

Caldwell believes that there are several remedies that Congress could implement to ensure that state and local governments do not impose unconstitutional forms of taxes on e-commerce companies. She recommends a remedy that works to prevent the collection of unconstitutional taxes such as denying attorney's fees in tax cases where the tax is found to be unconstitutional and ensuring the refund of taxes that have been declared unconstitutional.

Caldwell believes that in order for electronic commerce to develop to its fullest potential and provide consumers with the maximum benefit from the low-cost Internet marketplace, a national standard on state and local taxation of interstate businesses is required. Will state tax be 'roadkill on the information superhighway?'[28]

## Canada's response

The Canadian Government in its report *The Canadian Electronic Commerce Strategy*, emphasised that the private sector has the lead role in the development and use of electronic commerce in Canada and it is the role of governments to support the private sector. It recommends three ways to provide this support:

1. provide a supportive and responsive domestic policy environment for electronic commerce by ensuring consistent treatment of digital and paper-based commerce.
2. work with other governments and international organisations to establish a truly global regime that provides consistent and predictable global rules.
3. show leadership by acting as model users of new technologies to demonstrate the advantages of electronic commerce and build trust among businesses and consumers.[29]

Ottawa hosted the 1998 OECD Ministerial Conference 'A Borderless World: Realizing the Potential of Global Electronic Commerce'.

## Europe's response

Germany investigated the idea of taxing business sites by way of a licence, but rejected this taxation model in August 1997. Belgium's Ministry put forward a Bit Tax proposal, whereby they would attempt to tax data travelling over their communication links. This idea of a tax on each packet of data sent across the Internet where revenue is derived directly from Internet traffic on a volume basis was ruled out by the US Government when President Clinton announced there would be no new taxes on the Internet.

The President of the European Union agreed in principle to the Internet becoming a duty-free environment. He expressed support for the development of an internationally uniform, simple system of taxation based on the principle of tax neutrality, which requires that the tax system treat similar income equally, regardless of whether it is earned through electronic means or through existing means.[30]

At the Internet, Web, What Next? Conference in Geneva in July 1998, the prospect of large web income flows encouraged many governments to think about cashing in on the Internet boom by introducing taxes and tariffs. Ronert Verrue, Director General of the European Union's DG XIII demonstrated his case for World Wide Web legislation that would impose VAT on commercial transactions. The EU ruled that cross border retailers should collect tax at the rate of the state in which its products are consumed.

In contrast to the tax perspective, international trade opinion favours minimal intervention in the growth of electronic commerce, despite such insights as that of OECD Secretary General, Donald Johnston:

> *The emergence of electronic commerce — commercial transactions based on the electronic transmission of data over communications networks such as the Internet —heralds a major structural change in the economies of the OECD countries. Its impact may be as far-reaching as the invention of the printing press and the automobile. It will affect all aspects of the economic environment, the organisation of firms, consumer behaviour, the workings of government and most spheres of household activity.*[32]

The European Union's 1997 *A European Initiative on Electronic Commerce* established the EU policy and objectives on key issues relating to the implementation of electronic commerce in Europe.[33] Details are at www.ispo.ce.be/ecommerce/, and include:
- the need for access to infrastructure, products and services necessary for e-commerce to be as widely available as possible
- establishment of a coherent regulatory structure throughout the union based on its single market principles
- promotion of skills and awareness of e-commerce business opportunities
- coordination of EU regulatory principles with a compatible global regulatory framework.

The European Commission singled out taxation as an area of concern, asserting that no new taxes should be introduced in electronic commerce.

# The OECD's response

The Organisation for Economic Cooperation and Development has taken a leading role among international institutions on electronic commerce policy and analysis.[34] Details are at www.oecd.org/dsti/sti/it/ec/index.htm. The governments of the OECD countries have realised they needed to develop a common approach on how to respond to the challenges that the Internet and global commerce will place on their taxation systems.

In 1997 at the Turku, Finland, conference on e-commerce entitled 'Dismantling the Barriers to Global Electronic Commerce', organised by the OECD, the following issues were addressed:
- access to and use of infrastructure

- building user and consumer trust
- minimising regulatory uncertainty
- easing logistical problems.

The Turku conference concluded that the Committee on Fiscal Affairs (CFA) of the OECD was the international body that would be most able to coordinate and further the taxation matters of electronic commerce. This was primarily due to the work that the CFA did in developing and maintaining the Model Tax Convention. The CFA was given the task of developing the taxation framework conditions that are applicable to electronic commerce.[35]

The OECD 1998 Ottawa Ministerial Conference was entitled 'A Borderless World: Realizing the Potential of Global Electronic Commerce'. This conference had the active participation of a large cross-section of the stakeholders in electronic commerce. The OECD recognised the need for all the stakeholders to work collectively in order to find solutions. The participants included international organisations, business, labour, consumer and public interest groups.[36] This conference adopted three formal Ministerial Declarations on the subjects of:

- protection of privacy on global networks
- consumer protection in the context of electronic commerce
- authentication for electronic commerce.

The ministers also endorsed the OECD report on *Taxation Framework Conditions for Electronic Commerce*. In the area of international tax arrangements and cooperation, the OECD has agreed to undertake the following actions:

- clarify how concepts used in the OECD Model Tax Convention apply to electronic commerce in particular
- determine taxing rights, including the concepts of 'permanent establishment' and the attribution of income
- classify income for the purpose of taxation; for example, intangible property, royalties, services and, in particular, digital information
- monitor the effect that electronic commerce has on the application of OECD Transfer Pricing Guidelines
- improve administrative assistance to taxation authorities by the use of existing bilateral and multilateral agreements
- investigate the effect of electronic commerce on harmful tax competition in the context of the recommendations on geographically mobile activities, which accompanied the OECD's report *Harmful Tax Competition*.[37]

The following recommendations were formulated at the OECD Ottawa Conference in 1998:

- Small advisory groups from both the public sector and business should be developed rather than using large conferences.
- Clarification of how the concepts of the OECD Model Tax Convention apply to electronic commerce should be sought; namely, determining taxing rights and classifying income for taxation purposes.
- The effect that electronic commerce has on the application of OECD Transfer Pricing Guidelines should be monitored.
- Administrative assistance to taxation authorities should be improved using existing bilateral and multilateral agreements.
- The effect of electronic commerce on harmful tax competition in the context of the recommendations on geographically mobile activities should be investigated.[38]

# Ireland's approach to tax and electronic commerce

The intensity of the international debate underlines the importance of the taxation issues surrounding e-commerce and the need for Ireland's Revenue Department to be able to articulate Irish national interests on the issues arising. The national reports of Australia, Canada, Japan, the United States, New Zealand and the United Kingdom and the reports of the international bodies such as the World Trade Organization (WTO), EU and OECD stress the need for the implementation of an agreed international framework for the taxation of e-commerce.[39] International debate must move away from discussion of tax principles and focus on delivering practical arrangements for international e-commerce. Until practical tax arrangements are agreed and implemented, the free flow of global e-commerce will be impeded.

Ireland wants to be the centre of e-commerce in Europe. It has passed e-commerce laws and offers tax incentives to IT players. Its paper, *Electronic Commerce and the Irish Tax System*, was released in July 1999. (This can be found at http://www.revenue.irlgov.ie.) From a tax perspective, the Irish Revenue Department wants to ensure that tax rules do not stifle the development of e-commerce in Ireland. While it is vital that this policy goal remains central, the Revenue Department must ensure that the growth in business on the Internet is not at the expense of national revenues. The department wants to keep tax rules and tax compliance neutral between e-commerce and other forms of commerce. To work properly, tax rules may need to be tailored to cater for the technicalities of the Internet.

# International regulation

The *Model Law on Electronic Commerce*,[40] proposed by the United Nations Commission on International Trade Law in June 1996, hopes to offer national legislators a set of internationally accepted rules on how a number of legal obstacles may be removed and how a more secure legal environment may be created for e-commerce. It looks at aspects such as legal recognition of data messages, retaining data messages and attribution and acknowledgement of receipt of messages. In December 1996, the United Nations recommended that all governments, including Australia, give favourable consideration to the Model Law when they enact or revise their own laws pertaining to electronic commerce.

# The role of cypherpunks

Cypherpunks or 'crypto-anarchists' are dedicated to building anonymous systems. In the *CypherPunks Manifesto*, Eric Hughes states: 'We are defending our privacy with cryptography, with anonymous mail forwarding systems, with digital signatures and with electronic money'. By combining encryption technology with digital signatures and remailers people will be able to move funds in the form of anonymous digital cash without a trace. Governments will not be able to tax what they cannot see and even if they try to break the encryption, the resources necessary to decipher potentially millions of transactions would be beyond those available to taxation authorities.

Anguilla, in the Caribbean, has been marketed by Vince Cate as a tax effective jurisdiction in which to locate. His web server (www.offshore.com.ai) supplies businesses with their place of effective management and, hence, Anguillian residency. Cate believes that more than 50 per cent of pure Internet business will operate from tax havens within 10 years.[41]

What this means to taxation authorities is obvious. In *accounted* electronic payment systems, the issuer of the payments keeps a record of the flow of electronic money through the system; hence accurate identification of the parties involved is possible. In *unaccounted* electronic payment systems no records of the flow of electronic money are kept. With no audit trails, it is impossible to identify the parties involved.

Anonymous digital money will allow people to have instantaneous access to offshore banking facilities where there is no central body to control the issue and exchange of electronic cash. The growth of e-commerce will mean people will have the ability to avoid scrutiny of the taxation authorities.

## SUMMARY

Taxation of Internet commerce is a vexed issue. Governments throughout the world are examining their taxation laws as they relate to corporate and individual residency, tax avoidance and evasion, international taxation agreements, money laundering and technology transfer. Taxation reform for the entire system in Australia is an ongoing political debate and various special interest groups and politicians have proposed a radical overhaul of the system. The Australian Taxation Office has released two reports, one in 1997 and one in 1999. The ATO has also embraced the idea of using the Internet to carry out its business of processing taxation packs.

Gambling on the Internet is another area of special interest to the Australian Government as it is a high revenue earner for State and Federal Governments. Some states and members of the gambling industry have been cooperating with the government to ensure that Australia becomes a major player in online gambling. However, the Federal Government commenced an inquiry into Internet gambling in 2000.

Jean Baptiste Colbert, Louis XIV's treasurer, advised 'the art of taxation consists in so plucking the goose as to obtain the largest possible amount of feathers with the smallest possible amount of hissing'. It remains to be seen how the taxman will catch the virtual goose of Internet commerce.

**key terms**

| | | |
|---|---|---|
| compliance | Goods and Services Tax | sales tax |
| disintermediation | (GST) | tax avoidance |
| fringe benefits tax | income tax | tax evasion |
| | money laundering | tax neutrality |

**Case Study ①**

# NIGHTMARE RULING CHALLENGES WEB

TOM BURTON

In the early days of the Internet the *New Yorker* magazine captured the libertarian enthusiasm of the tyro Web users with a classic cartoon of a dog sitting in front of a personal computer telling his dog mate: 'On the Internet, no one knows you're a dog.'

The arrival of the marketeers with their tracking software, relationship marketing programs and cookies (devices which identify a particular PC) has rapidly destroyed the idea of the Web as a virtual cubby house where surfers were free to roam without fear of identification, scrutiny or regulation.

The regulation part suffered a major set back last week when the New York Supreme Court ruled a Caribbean Internet gambling business had breached a New York ban on cyber betting.

The judgment comes from the highest US court to consider the jurisdiction issue and has huge implications not just for the Internet gambling business, but for e-commerce in general.

Both the fact that 90 per cent of the world's e-commerce occurs in the US and the tendency of Australian Courts to follow US precedent in technology law — or risk judicial isolation — means the decision could easily flow on to local judgments.

The nub of the decision was the conclusion by Justice Ramos that 'the Internet gambling site creates a virtual casino within the user's computer terminal'. You don't need to be a lawyer to appreciate the implication of this judgment.

If the transaction occurs where the end user's PC is located, rather than where the company's computers are (in this case the servers were in Antigua) then it follows that any company offering gambling will be bound by the local laws of its customers.

If followed that could have a significant impact on Centrebet, Australia's biggest online gambling operator and according to the Productivity Commission's latest report, one of the top five gambling sites in the world.

Online gambling in Australia is still very new, with the Commission's survey suggesting a user base of around 86 000 in 1998–99. The main game for Centrebet is offshore gambling, with the Commission claiming 20 per cent of Centrebet's traffic is from the US — which is strange as the site specifically bans US residents from using the site.

In any case Centrebet — which was acquired late last year by the Gold Coast casino operator Jupiters — has clear international ambitions, which, as a result of Justice Ramos, have suddenly become much more problematic. Ditto for the two soon-to-be listed Net gambling floats, Centrebet's fellow Northern Territory gambling site, All Sports and the Coms21 spin off, Ebet.

A ruling which effectively attaches jurisdiction to the location of the user's PC is the judgment from hell for Web gamblers, as it means they have to comply with every different regulatory requirement of every country or state they operate in.

More profoundly, the judgment could affect the whole e-commerce industry. As Las Vegas gambling law expert, Tony Cabot, told CNET last week: 'This case is one in a continuous series of cases where the Attorney's General of various (US) states have successfully convinced the courts they have jurisdiction over persons offshore who use the Internet to reach citizens of their state.'

'Clearly, the principles being used to assert jurisdiction over the gaming sites are the same principles used to assert jurisdiction over an e-commerce site.'

If this principle is sustained it would require every e-business to comply with a myriad of laws and regulations in whatever territory they seek to do business in.

For the burgeoning e-commerce industry it would quickly prove to be impossible to do business if every provider needed to engage a local lawyer in any market it happens to sell into.

Attaching jurisdiction to the PC also has dramatic implications for other legal issues such as copyright, intellectual property, defamation and privacy. In Australia the whole area of jurisdictional reach is as yet untested with only a few cases and even less-established judicial principles.

But just as has been the case in the US, the gambling industry is where the issue of jurisdiction is most likely to be tested first. The State Governments have become concerned to protect the gambling taxes which are now so vital for their Budget and are now invoking various laws to control online gambling and provide some consumer protection.

The big risk for the local e-commerce industry is that a case-by-case approach could see a hotch potch of principles emerge before the issue of jurisdiction is settled, leaving a dog's breakfast and the industry vulnerable to civil and criminal action.

*Tom Burton is the Herald's Online Editor. tburton@access.fairfax.com.au*

**SOURCE:** *Sydney Morning Herald*, Biz.Com, 4 August 1999, p. 24, www.smh.com.au

## QUESTIONS

1. Why is this called a 'nightmare ruling'?
2. Debate the pros and cons of online gambling.

# GST HURTS E-COMMERCE

JEREMY HOREY

HAVE you ever heard of the Advisory Commission on Electronic Commerce? This is a group appointed by the US Congress to look at how the Internet is affecting government in the US.

The Commission is investigating how to deal with taxes and the Internet. This is becoming an urgent issue, which the US government is taking very seriously.

According to a study by the University of Texas, the Internet in the US is now the 18th largest economy in the world.

Another economist, Austan Goolsbee, this time from the University of Chicago, has estimated that the States of the US are missing out on $US300 million ($454 million) in sales tax on Internet transactions.

While this is a small sum compared with the total amount collected, it is going to grow.

The growth projections for e-commerce indicate that 10 to 20 per cent of all retail business could be transacted across the Web within five years.

Without adequate tax measures, the States of the US could find themselves with 10 per cent less revenue.

Some sales tax is payable now. Currently, if you are in the same State as the e-commerce site, you should pay tax.

But outside that nobody has come to grips with just how tax should be collected.

The difficulty is that sales tax is a State matter. This means that there are different rates and different items taxed in different States.

Most Internet transactions cross State borders, so it is unclear who should pay, and how much.

There is no simple answer. If tax is levied at the rate applicable in the seller's State, sellers in the higher tax States will move their servers to lower tax States, or offshore to places where no tax is payable. If the tax is payable at the rate applicable in the buyer's State, it is going to be impossible for sellers to administer.

Studies at *www.uchicago.edu/fac/ austan.goolsbee/research/intertax.pdf* have shown that customers are very aware of and sensitive to sales tax.

They will change their behaviour to avoid tax, so it is reasonable to conclude that retailers have serious motivation for getting the best tax break for their customers.

So far the States have let the matter ride. But as Internet commerce grows, it is harder and harder to ignore.

Even though enforcing sales tax on Internet transactions will slow the growth of e-commerce, the push is now on to get a uniform sales tax rate and a uniform set of taxed goods across all States.

This is going to require a lot of work, but it will make it easier to collect taxes on Internet transactions within the US.

While it may be possible for the US States to work together, there is a larger problem. This is the international issue. There are different rates of sales tax or GST or VAT everywhere. There are plenty of countries without any equivalent tax at all.

As well, there are many places that would be happy to give Internet transactions a zero sales tax rate so they could get businesses to host their sites in their country.

The benefit a small country could gain by hosting sites from countries with high sales tax regimes would outweigh the loss of income from tax.

And it is not just taxes on Internet transactions. As globalisation continues, tax across national borders becomes more of an issue. As transnational companies become more powerful and more adept at shifting their money around to take advantage of the different tax regimes in different countries, it becomes harder to tax these entities.

The international tax treaty system looks ridiculously cumbersome and slow in chasing after tax from these transnationals.

Finding an equitable tax system is becoming harder and harder, especially in smaller economies. It isn't just the Internet.

In fact, the Internet isn't even on most countries' tax agenda yet. Governments are under considerable pressure to provide a system that is attractive to multinationals. If they can't do that they may offer tax breaks to entice the multinationals to set up shop.

I am not suggesting there is anything like a crisis, but tax problems are becoming difficult to deal with at a national level.

There is a need for international bodies to take a more active role in tax matters.

It is ironic that Australia now has a new form of sales tax at just the time when this issue is becoming internationally important. Peter Costello's recent gaffe in Parliament — about goods arriving from overseas in small quantities avoiding the new GST — is evidence that the government has not thought this issue through.

The GST is going to generate an immense amount of confusion for Australian business.

Businesses will have to adjust the way they operate so they can either cope with the new demands on their cash flow or take advantage of the benefits flowing from an increase in cash flow.

A lot of businesses will go to the wall, and most of the ones that survive will be better run.

However, it would have been better to wait. There will have to be ongoing adjustments to Australia's tax regime.

Not only will politicians not leave the tax system alone, there will be changes forced by outside pressures. These will be large, and will involve changes to the rate and to the goods exempted.

If the Government had not been so driven by its ideological commitment to the GST, it could have deferred its introduction or phased in the new tax, making it easier for business to adjust.

Of course, phasing in the tax would not have given it the opportunity to provide such large income tax cuts.

As the world focuses on the need to provide a way of funding government activities that is sustainable in the face of globalisation and the Internet, we will pay the price for a hastily introduced and ill-conceived tax.

*Jeremy Horey is a senior consultant with Tech Talk Australia, a division of Com Tech Online. You can reach him at jeremyh@techtalk.com.au*

**SOURCE:** *Australian*, 6 July 1999, p. 7, www.news.com.au

1. Debate the author's claim that we will pay the price for a 'hastily introduced and ill-conceived tax'.
2. Debate the statement that 'As transnational companies become more powerful and adept at shifting their money around to take advantage of different tax regimes in different countries, it becomes harder to tax these entities'.
3. Use a brainstorming session to see if your groups can come up with innovative ideas that would ensure that governments raise enough money to pay for necessary infrastructure for their people.

# Case Study 3 — INTERNET GAMBLING OVERSEAS

## NET GAMBLING SITES EYE ASIA

SELINA MITCHELL AND COSIMA MARRINER

Although online gambling may present major social problems, Australian companies are poised to make significant investments in gambling systems, citing potential for major growth in Asian markets.

Without palliative measures and regulation, online gambling will pose significant new risks for problem gamblers, a recent Productivity Commission report, *Australia's Gambling Industries*, suggests.

More than 80% of Australians gambled last year (excluding raffles and sweeps), while spending has doubled compared to a decade ago. However, for the moment Internet gambling and other new access means such as cable are not very popular with gamblers. Only around 86 000 Australians, or 0.6% of the population, gambled on the Net in 1998 to 1999, the report notes.

Traditional gamblers' median age is 44 years, while Net gamblers are an average age of 33 years. Net gamblers also have a significantly higher income. As more Australians purchase home PCs, this profile is expected to change.

The report notes that online gambling offers potential benefits to some consumers (such as greater choice), and a mechanism for profits for some business. However, it also provides a 'quantum leap' in accessibility to gambling and will help generate an entirely new group of gamblers.

The risk to minors could be minimised with screening requirements and account monitoring, but the report suggests that some form of regulation is desirable. 'The Commission considers that, regardless of what regulatory approach is taken, there are strong grounds for governments to pursue palliative measures, such as warning people of the hazards of offshore online gambling; providing information on the Internet about gambling help services and gambling sites which meet consumer protection criteria; and making available or promoting software for providing consumers with greater control over online gambling,' the report states.

The report came out shortly after a study by analysts Merrill Lynch which suggests Australia could be a major player in the online gambling industry due to the introduction of regulations in some states and the expected ban on Net gambling in the US.

Some local companies are already looking to exploit that growth. Australian online casino Lasseters Online has committed more than half a million dollars to a Web advertising campaign. In a bid to attract more visitors to the online gaming site, Internet advertising company DoubleClick will be targeting 'specific geographies and cultures' with its campaign for Lasseters, according to DoubleClick Australia managing director Rod Bryan. The first target will be the Asian region.

'Online gaming is considered to be a good leisure pastime in those markets,' said Bryan. In addition, the US and Europe will also be targeted. The world's first regulated online casino, Lasseters is unavailable to Australians outside the Northern Territory. Internet gaming company eBet is planning to follow its parent company Coms21 into overseas markets such as Asia and North America.

**SOURCE:** *Australian Personal Computer*, September 1999, p. 24. Reproduced with permission.

## QUESTIONS

1. What methods could online gambling sites put in place to ensure minors are not using the sites?
2. What is the current position on Internet gambling for the following locations: Australia, the United States, Canada, Malaysia, Hong Kong, England? Try to find out what each place is doing regarding tax and Internet gambling.

## QUESTIONS

1. Select three countries and research their approach to taxation of electronic commerce. Compare and contrast their approaches with Australia's approach.
2. Study the business model presented in figure 9.1 on page 224. Explain how each entity gains revenue, using a specific example for each entity. For example, for entity 2, the Internet service provider, select an ISP and investigate how it raises revenue.
3. Visit the ATO's tax site (www.ato.gov.au) and find their e-tax area. Investigate how taxpayers obtain a 'digital signature'. What are the advantages and disadvantages of filing a tax return online?
4. Investigate the progress made by the taxation authorities in:
   (a) obtaining and putting into place the computer program that automatically deducts the appropriate tax from each online transaction
   (b) getting international cooperation to ensure that all computer programs match the tax needs of individual nations.
5. Investigate the idea that the tax office could use the Internet to monitor the number of transactions conducted over it without invading anyone's privacy.
6. Debate the statement: 'The e-tax system should allow the Australian Taxation Office to do its work with much less staff.'

## SUGGESTED READING

Deutsch, R. L. et. al. 1999, 'Residence and source', in the *Australian Tax Handbook*, Australian Tax Practice, Sydney, pp. 25–38.

*Economist 2000*, 'A survey of globalisation and tax: the mystery of the vanishing taxpayer — special report', 29 January, pp. 1–25 (special insert).

Ford, W. and Baum, M. 1997, *Secure Electronic Commerce*, Prentice Hall, United States.

Furche, A. and Wrightson, G. 1996, *Computer Money: A Systematic Overview of Electronic Payment Systems*, dpunkt, verlag für digitale Technologie GmbH, Heidelberg, FDR.

Goolsbee, A. and Zittrain, J. 1999, 'Evaluating the costs and benefits of taxing Interent commerce, *National Tax Journal*, September, vol. 52, issue 3, pp. 413–28.

Lawrence, E. 1999, 'Virtual tax reform', *Hands-on Solutions: E-commerce*, CCH Publications, Sydney, Australia.

McCouat, P. 1998, 'Taxation in cyberspace', *Hands-on Solutions: E-commerce*, CCH Publications, Sydney, Australia.

Pinto, D. 1999, Taxation issues in a world of electronic commerce, unpublished paper, Curtin University of Technology, Perth, Australia, pp. 1–67.

## END NOTES

1. Electronic Commerce Project Team 1999, *Tax and the Internet: Second Report of the Australian Taxation Office*, December, Australian Government Publishing Service, Commonwealth of Australia, Canberra, p. 4.

2. Davidson, J. 1999, 'Taking care of business on the net', *Australian Financial Review*, 23 July.

3. Muscovitch, Z. 1/996, 'Taxation of Internet commerce', *ILSA-Ottawa*, Papers Archive #1, www.globalserve.net/~zak/index.html.

4. Loane, S. 1998, 'A force in law, profile: Louise McBride/lawyer, Spectrum Features, *Sydney Morning Herald*, 21 November, p. 3.

5. Ilbery, J. 1996, 'Ten principles', *Taxation in Australia*, vol. 31, no. 4, p. 182.

6. Needham, K. 2000, 'Hey big e-spenders are Australian', *Sydney Morning Herald*, Biz.Com, 12 April, p. 27.

7. Nicholas, K. 1999, 'Work access to net multiplies', Biz.Com, *Sydney Morning Herald*, 23 August, p. 37.

8. Merrick, F. 1997, 'Ensuring taxation on electronic trading — first results from the ATO's investigations', *Proceedings of the Second Australian Computer Money Day*, University of Newcastle, Department of Computing Science and Software Engineering, Randwick, Sydney. (Frank Merrick, Assistant Commissioner, ATO, Electronic Commerce and Internationals).

9. ibid.

10. Tyree, A. 1997, 'Regulation of international electronic trading', *Proceedings of the Second Australian Computer Money Day*, University of Newcastle, Department of Computing Science and Software Engineering, Randwick, Sydney.

11. Dwyer, M. 1997, 'Tax reform entering cyberspace', *Australian Financial Review*, 10 June, p. 4.

12. Tebbutt, D. 1999, 'Net return to taxpayers', *Australian*, 6 July, p. 40, www.news.com.au.

13. Stott, D. 1997 'Internet purchases dodge the taxman', *Sydney Morning Herald*, 10 December, p. 5.

14. ibid., p. 50.

15. Tyree, op. cit.

16. *Australian Accountant* 1997, 'E-commerce — the way to go', October, p. 50, www.cpaonline.com.au.

17. Soete, L. and Kamp, K. 1996, *The 'BIT TAX': the case for further research*, www.ispo.cec.be/hleg/bittax.html.

18. *E-commerce Today* 1999, 'The global market', issue 8, August, p. 4.

19. Davidson, J. 1997, 'Holes in the tax net', *Australian Financial Review*, 18 October, www.afr.com.au.

20. United States Government 1997, *Framework for Electronic Commerce*, www.iitf.nist.gov/eleccomm/ecomm.html.

21. Lynch A. 1998, 'Tax office stems net evasion', Networking, *Australian*, 26 November, p. 8.

22. ibid.

23. Riley, J. 1997, 'US lobbies against Internet taxation', *Australian*, 16 December 1997, p. 42.

24. Caldwell K. 1999a, 'States behaving badly: the public policy report', *Electronic Commerce Core Series*, June, vol. 1, no. 6, p. 1.

25. ibid, p. 2.

26. See the project's web site at www.nhdd.com/nta/ntaintro.htm.

27. Caldwell, K. 1999b, 'Federalism: should Congress take a more active role in restraining the states from interfering in interstate commerce?', *Electronic Commerce Core Series*, vol. 1, no. 6, p. 12.

28. Bishop, M. 2000, 'The happy Eshopper: globalisation and tax survey', *Economist*, 29 February, p. 11.

29. Canadian Electronic Commerce Strategy, *Task force on Electronic Commerce*, http://e-com.ic.gc.ca and www.connect.gc.ca.

30. Riley, op. cit.

31. Bishop, M., op. cit., p. 15.

32. Johnston, D. J. 1997, 'Commerce goes electronic', *OECD Observer*, no. 208, p. 4.

33. Townsend, D. N. 1999, *Briefing Report on Telecommunications Regulatory Issues for Electronic Commerce, ITU Regulatory Colloquium No. 8: The Changing Roles of Government in an Era of Telecommunications Deregulation*, ITU, Geneva.

34. Townsend, op. cit.

35. Wilcox, C., MacKenzie, G., Grishenko, N., Fitzpatrick, P. and Hay, W. 1998, 'Case study: tax and Internet commerce', project for Internet commerce and commerce on the Internet, University of Technology, Sydney, November, p. 41.

36. Wilcox et. al., op. cit., p. 50.

37. Wilcox et. al., op. cit., p. 52.

38. Lawrence, E. 1999, 'Virtual tax reform', *Hands-on Solutions: E-commerce*, CCH Publications, Sydney, Australia.

39. Revenue Department 1999, *Electronic Commerce and the Irish Tax System: A Revenue Discussion Document*, Irish State, p. 17, www.revenue.ie/e-commerce/e-commerce.htm.

40. Lawrence, E. op. cit.

# 10

# Legal and ethical issues

## LEARNING *Outcomes*

You will have mastered the material in this chapter when you can:

- identify the problems associated with determining which legal jurisdiction applies to international transactions conducted via the Internet
- assess the differences between the establishment of a contract for goods or services in the traditional marketplace and a contract established via the Internet
- appreciate the potential for fraud and other criminal activities using the Internet
- understand how copyright and defamation laws may be infringed by making information freely available over the Internet
- understand how privacy of the individual and company records may be eroded by users of the Internet and what safeguards are required to preserve that privacy
- appreciate how the Internet may be regulated by government concerns over such matters as censorship and consumer protection.

*'The emergence of a truly global legal/regulatory framework for electronic commerce takes time — if it will ever happen.'*

Paul Timmers, European Commission, Directorate General XIII 1999, 'Think global — act local: the challenge of thriving in the global digital economy', *Twelfth International Bled Electronic Commerce Conference*, Bled, Slovenie, June 7–9, p. 12

# INTRODUCTION

Commercial transactions are subject to a comprehensive system of controls consisting of:
- the common **law**
- **legislation** at the State, federal and international levels
- industry codes of practice.

These controls have been established over time in an ad hoc fashion in response to the need to provide a high degree of certainty in contractual relationships and to give the consumer confidence that he or she will obtain a 'fair deal' in any spending decision. Both of these are necessary ingredients in the promotion of trade and commerce upon which modern economies depend. The controls have evolved and have been adapted to new technologies as they arise, although there is always a lag time before the controls 'catch up' with the latest technology.

We are still at an early stage in establishing controls over commercial transactions on the Internet despite the large volume of transactions taking place daily. Unique features of the Internet compared with earlier technological changes are:
- its rapid proliferation
- the multiplicity of communication channels
- the enormous volume of information and range of services available
- the ease and speed with which trans-border transactions can be conducted.

All of these pose a unique set of problems.

Although international agreements do exist for the regulation of international trade, they are not keeping pace with commercial realities. The principal problem is that existing agreements, and even those proposed, deal with only business or trade transactions. They do not deal with consumer purchases, which are responsible for the huge growth in transactions over the Internet.

Major concerns include how security of commercial transactions over the Internet can be maintained and how the consumer's interests can be protected, including the individual's rights to **privacy**. Added to this are issues associated with protecting a society's values, exemplified by government's role in controlling content on the Internet, particularly in relation to **censorship**.

# CONTROL OF INTERNET CONTENT

One of the first steps in trying to establish a legal framework for any new technology is to classify it to establish how existing legislation may be made to fit the new technology. Although the Internet service provider (ISP) has become the major focus for attempts at legislative controls, there is a wide variation between each country's approach.[1] Singapore, for example, has classified ISPs as broadcasting media, requiring them to be registered. It thereby exercises control by allowing access to only authorised web sites. In the United States, the *Telecommunications Act (1996)* considers the ISP to be a telecommunications carrier. The United States Supreme Court struck down the *Communications Decency Act*, which would have restricted indecent material on the Internet, as unconstitutional and an attack on free speech.

An international working group, the Internet Content Rating Association (ICRA), supported by computer industry heavyweights such as Microsoft, has been formed to establish worldwide standards for content rating.[2]

In Australia, a Senate Select Committee report[3] argued that Internet content should be treated in the same manner as a broadcast medium such as television. One of the outcomes of the report was to make the Federal Government's Telecommunications Industry Ombudsman available to hear complaints from users of the Internet.[4] The more significant outcome, however, was the enactment of the *Broadcasting Services Amendment (On-Line Content) Act, 1999.* This is intended to regulate Internet content hosted both within Australia and offshore by restricting the use of the Internet for transmission of objectionable material including, most importantly, pornography, and by promoting measures to protect children from viewing such material.

The Act requires ISPs and Internet content hosts (ICHs) to comply with guidelines based on pre-existing film and video classifications and encourages the industry to adopt a code of practice or suffer the introduction of mandatory standards by the Australian Broadcasting Authority (ABA),[5] which is responsible for implementing the Act. The ABA is able to initiate investigations into Internet content on its own initiative or as a result of a complaint from the public, and issues notices requiring ISPs or ICHs to take down or deny access to prohibited content.

The Act was introduced in the face of prolonged opposition by industry groups[6] who consider that measures of control are impractical, costly and represent an invasion of privacy of users.

In any event, software is available, such as Net Nanny,[7] which allows parents to block incoming material using key words or phrases and other indicators.

## Censorship on the Internet

### CENSORSHIP FIGHT MOVES TO DETAILS

**The Internet censorship debate has now shifted to the challenges of implementing an incongruous law,** DAN TEBBUTT **reports.**

THE fact Internet censorship is now the law of the land doesn't mean the many voices opposed to the Broadcasting Services Amendment (Online Services) Act 1999 are silenced.

With the emotional rhetoric during the law's hasty passage through the Senate behind them, Internet groups are now focusing on the issues that arise from applying the legislation.

For more conciliatory industry-based groups such as the Internet Industry Association (IIA), this means sitting down to draft a code of conduct designed to minimise the impact on service providers.

IIA executive director Peter Coroneos gave a speech in Washington DC last week suggesting there were considerable virtues in the 'co-regulation' approach.

'The Government provides a legislative framework: and the industry comes in and establishes rules,' Coroneos said. Industry-drafted rules would have the status of 'almost de facto laws'.

In drafting its industry code of conduct, the IIA is working closely with the Australian Broadcasting Authority (ABA) — the body that will administer the law when it comes into effect next year.

If the ISPs appear ready to make a fist of Internet censorship, there are many within the community who remain vehemently opposed.

These groups — recently branded 'maniacs' by IT Minister Senator Richard Alston — held a public seminar in Melbourne last week to discuss the problems users and providers face in applying the law.

Computer law expert Steve White said one of the fundamental elements — the requirement for a restricted access system for R-rated content — was still awaiting definition from the ABA.

He points out that R-style content includes the types of low-level nudity seen on television and in magazines without restrictions.

Another loose end is the status of Web sites that could be construed as games and hence subject to more restrictive classification.

'The critical thing about this legislation is the stance the ABA takes,' White told the seminar.

'If the ABA jumps out on January 1 and starts issuing notices left, right and centre, the industry will feel a lot of pain for not much gain.

'If the ABA is a little more laid-back, it would be fair to say there would not be much impact. It's very difficult to know until someone gets hit.'

Electronic Frontiers Australia board member Jan Whitaker highlighted a recent story in *The Australian* suggesting the ABA may make its list of prohibited sites available to ISPs.

This would expose the folly of content-blocking, because the list would need to go not only to Australia's 600-plus ISPs but also to thousands of companies, universities and non-profit groups that provide Internet access.

The list itself may be subject to Freedom of Information Act requests, Whitaker says.

EFA has regularly been at odds with the IIA over the industry group's more co-operative stance, and Whitaker renewed the attack.

With only some 70 ISPs represented, she says, IIA is 'not a representative body and it is primarily the big end of town'.

Whitaker says the uncertainty and complexity of the law will compound the cost of doing business online.

Even the scope of material covered by the law is in question: all Web traffic is presumably covered by classification rules, but private e-mail is exempt. This gives rise to anomalies over newsgroup traffic, not to mention Web pages fetched through a Web-to-e-mail gateway.

Moreover, broadcast delivery is excluded from the Internet laws, which means pornographic Webcasts could be excluded.

'Some of the silliness is too much to believe,' Whitaker says.

By far the biggest cost fear for ISPs is the network-level filtering that may be necessary to comply with the law.

Connect.com.au technical architect Kevin Littlejohn says a filtering system would cost as much as $2.5 million to set up for an ISP as large as number-three player Connect.

While Alston's aides say the law does not mandate backbone-level filtering, Littlejohn says that is the only way to restrict access to banned material.

'The only way we can block a single page is to put up a scalable, redundant architecture that looks at every packet,' Littlejohn says.

While some sort of filtering is theoretically possible, Littlejohn says, most of the technology is far too immature for network usage.

'The Government is telling ISPs to put this untested equipment between their network and the rest of the world,' he says. 'If that box breaks, the ISP is off the air.'

Littlejohn says the law could advantage US-based companies that sell satellite Net access. The signal would not enter Australia until it reached the subscriber's receiving dish, and the Government would have little recourse against the off-shore vendor.

Institute of Public Affairs media director Michael Warby says the censorship law exposes 'an enormous gulf between what the online community understands to be practical and what the minister has legislated'.

Most parliamentarians have close to zero experience with the Internet, he says.

'Clearly, in the rush to conciliate Senator Harradine and get the bill through the Senate, the Government chose the wrong model,' Warby says. 'The implications of that are still to be understood.'

*www.iia.net.au*
*www.aba.gov.au*
*www.efa.org.au*

**SOURCE:** *Australian*, 2 November 1999, p. 54

## RESEARCH QUESTIONS

1. Has the Act been successful in controlling Internet content?
2. What problems (if any) have been experienced by users and industry groups in meeting the provisions of the Act?
3. Have industry groups managed to change the Government's position on controlling content?
4. To what extent (if any) has the Australian 'model' been adopted elsewhere?

# INTELLECTUAL PROPERTY

The law provides well-established protection for owners of **intellectual property**, which covers many areas of human and corporate endeavour. The Internet provides increased opportunities for eroding that protection in regard to three types of intellectual property: copyright, patents and trademarks.

## Copyright

**Copyright** protects a wide array of material including writings, artwork, music, films, computer programs and extends to broadcast material, quite separate to the copyright in the material which is transmitted.[8] The copyright automatically belongs to the creator, or the owner, from the time of creation of the material.

International treaties such as the Berne Convention provide for protection of Australian copyright owners overseas and vice versa although the rights vary from country to country according to different subject matter. The copyright notice © is not required for protection in Australia.

The copyright owner has the right to use the material in a variety of ways and the rights may be assigned or leased with or without limitations or conditions. Use of copyright material, usually by copying without the permission of the owner, will ordinarily be an infringement of copyright, except in certain circumstances, such as copying of a limited portion of a book by a student (the 'reasonable portion' test).

In Australia, similar copyright protection applies to material placed on the Internet.[9] Screen displays and temporary RAM storage from the Internet are not regarded as the making of copies, although downloading to hard disk and printing are so considered.

Carriers and ISPs do not attract penalties for copyright infringement if they are not responsible for determining the content of the material communicated.

## Patents

A **patent** is a right granted for any device, substance, method or process that is new, inventive and useful. A patent must be applied for at the Patent Office and once granted is legally enforceable and gives the owner exclusive right to commercially exploit the invention for the life of the patent.[10] There is no such thing as a 'world patent'. Separate applications must be made for each country.

Patents covering software or programming related to web sites are the fastest growing sector at the US Patent Office.[11] An example of the legal implications of one such patent is illustrated in the Legal insite on the following page.

# WHO OWNS THE RIGHTS TO CYBERSPACE?

**The first salvo in the e-commerce intellectual property war has been fired over rights to the internet shopping trolley, but where will it end?** GRANT BUTLER **reports.**

Way back in the early history of electronic commerce — 1994, to be precise — an Australian computer programmer called Ernst Van Oeveren came up with what was then a very novel idea: the internet shopping trolley.

The now-ubiquitous tool made it easier for consumers to buy more than one item from a website.

Van Oeveren was working for the National Rural Health Research Institute at the time. Later that year he began working for a web design firm, Ausnet, and extended the metaphor to create one of the world's first online 'shopping trolleys' for the website www.science.com.au.

Around the same time (Van Oeveren says he can't be certain who was first) the United States-based company, Open Market, was developing similar tools. Even though Van Oeveren may have been first, by the end of 1994 the US firm had patented the internet shopping trolley.

Van Oeveren says he regrets not having spent the time and money — $50 000 or more just to patent an idea in Australia and the US — it would have cost to try to claim the invention as his own. 'Our technology pre-dated their application for a patent,' Van Oeveren says, 'but we didn't patent it because we were too busy trying to make money.'

He concedes that Australian developers are relatively lax when it comes to protecting intellectual property rights.

'It's a cultural difference. My experience with Australian innovative companies is that they're smart, savvy technologists but more interested in the technology than protecting themselves in legal frameworks.'

The opportunity that he, and Australia, missed out on was the right to charge royalties to anyone using an internet shopping trolley on a website in a patented jurisdiction. While Open Market hasn't taken up that option, it could be making many millions of dollars by charging fees to anyone using an online trolley — something now so common that critics argue that it, and concepts like it, should not be allowed to be patented.

The internet shopping trolley was just the beginning, and patents related to e-commerce are beginning to flow thick and fast, mainly from pioneering, cashed-up internet firms based in the US.

The internet retail giant Amazon.com has won a US patent for what it calls '1-Click' shopping, a system that records customers' shipping and payment details to save them re-entering the details during subsequent visits.

Amazon has already used its patent to stop rival bookseller Barnes & Noble from implementing a similar system on its website and has extended its patent application to Australia.

According to an intellectual property lawyer from the Melbourne firm Arthur Robinson & Hedderwicks, Michael Pattison, Amazon's claim won't necessarily succeed here.

'Patents in one country aren't automatically good in another.' he says. 'The grant of a US patent doesn't ensure the grant of an Australian patent.'

However, Matt Kraefft, supervising examiner at IP Australia, the government body that grants patents, says Australia's processes are largely aligned with those in the US.

'In general terms, we're going down very much a similar road as the US has done in terms of a liberal interpretation of what can be patented.

'If something can be physically done, and produce a result that is not naturally occurring in nature, then it's patentable.' That includes, he says, e-commerce processes.

Another US company attempting to register patents in Australia is Priceline.com. Priceline pioneered the 'reverse auction' process of inviting consumers to say how much they would be prepared to pay for goods or services, such as a hotel room, then seeing if any vendors are willing to provide at the stated price. The idea sounds suspiciously like an everyday tender process, yet Priceline.com has successfully maintained that its way of doing it on the internet is new and unique. As such, it has been granted a patent by the US authorities.

However, Priceline.com — which is valued at about $US10 billion ($15.19 billion) and was founded by a former patent attorney, Jay Walker — is about to see the strength of its patent tested. In December, the company filed a law suit against Microsoft, arguing that the software giant had infringed its patent by deploying a comparable auction process on its Expedia travel website.

'This will be a good test case because you'll have two parties who finally have the money to get to the bottom on this,' one US patent lawyer, Greg Aharonian, recently told *Wired* magazine.

The core issue is whether it is possible to patent what are essentially business processes, rather than genuine technological innovations. According to Pattison, while it is possible to patent business processes, authorities tend to lack the expertise required to assess whether an e-commerce idea is genuinely 'new' and 'not obvious'.

'A fundamental problem that it [IP Australia] has got — and also the US patent office, I suspect — is that they don't have at their patents office a well-developed knowledge of what is new in this field of e-commerce.'

Pattison cites the example of *Encyclopaedia Britannica* being awarded a patent in 1993 over the then novel technique of using hyperlinks to link pages on CD-ROMs. The US authorities subsequently reversed the decision after realising that such links were a basic building block of the web as invented by the British computer scientist Tim Berners-Lee, that had simply been transferred to a new medium.

It is unusual for a patents commissioner to order the re-examination of a patent, but in another recent case the US patents commissioner has initiated an action which could revoke a controversial patent for a technology that underlies many Y2K computer fixes.

The patent covers 'windowing', which has been in popular use and purportedly allows software to recognise whether a two-digit date represents the 20th or 21st century.

According to *The New York Times*, the inventor, Bruce Dickens, bought the rights to US Patent No. 5,806,063 for $US10 000 in April from his employer, McDonnell Douglas Corporation, which is now owned by Boeing. The patent was granted in 1998 but the company had never made wide use of Dickens' technique.

Another case that is bringing home the patent debate, and with it Australasia's place in the electronic marketplace of the future, involves a new Zealand inventor, Juliette Harrington, and the mighty Yahoo! Inc.

Harrington has patented the notion of being able to buy products from multiple e-commerce websites while remaining within another site — specifically, a 'portal'. The patent is registered under US Patent No 5,895,454 and is for an 'integrated interface for vendor/product oriented internet websites'.

In November, she sued Yahoo! for patent violation, alleging that the directory giant's Yahoo Shopping service is based on the same concept. The case is yet to come to court.

Despite the legal legwork being done to lock down key pieces of the future e-commerce system, there are three factors that could scuttle the plans of Amazon, Priceline and others.

The first is a growing backlash from the technical community that built the internet. Richard Stallman, an industry guru and founder of the Free Software Foundation, which has been instrumental in developing Linux, is asking consumers to boycott Amazon over the 1-Click issue.

Stallman, and others like him, argue that the internet has been able to grow so quickly, and become so economically and socially valuable, because innovations have been made freely available. Any attempt to corner inventions, particularly relatively 'obvious' ones such as one-click shopping, will only reduce the utility of the internet and ultimately damage all e-commerce companies.

'The patent gives Amazon the power over anyone that runs a website ... to control all use of this technique,'

Stallman says on the foundation's site (www.fsf.org). 'Please do not buy anything from Amazon until they promise to stop using this patent to threaten or restrict other websites.'

The second obstacle is jurisdictional. Patents only hold water in the countries in which they are granted and, given that the internet is truly global, companies wanting to use techniques such as one-click shopping have the option of moving their servers to countries that don't honor the patents in question.

While this would be inconvenient, and raise commercial issues, companies such as Barnes & Noble could exercise the option long enough to thwart their rivals' efforts.

The third obstacle, according to Van Oeveren, is technical. He says the internet community has proven adept at building alternative solutions when something, or someone, blocks its path. A key reason he didn't bother to patent the shopping trolley was that he assumed any attempt to impose conditions on its use would only invite the invention of another technique that made his redundant. This may explain why Open Market is yet to enforce its patent.

Van Oeveren says: 'There's great branding ... and kudos in it, but whether they can ever really use it remains to be seen.

'Is it ever going to be that everyone is going to have to pay a royalty to Open Market?'

**SOURCE:** *Australian Financial Review,* 8–9 January 2000, p. 28

## RESEARCH QUESTIONS

1. Has Amazon.com been able to extend its patent for '1-Click' shopping to Australia?
2. What other patents related to Internet commerce have owners tried to protect in the courts?
3. Is there any evidence that patent restrictions are being by-passed by moving operations to other countries where the patents do not apply?

## Trademarks

A registered **trademark** gives the owner exclusive legal rights to use, licence or sell the protected item for the goods and services for which it is registered under the provisions of the *Trademark Act*.[12] A trademark can cover not only words and pictures but also sound and smell. The law provides penalties for infringing a trademark either by using it or by showing something similar to the trademark.

Trademark infringement on the Internet has occurred by the use of **meta tagging**, whereby a word has been incorporated into a site in order to increase the chances of a search engine returning to the site.

# DOMAIN NAMES

Domain names are administered on a national basis around the world. Any name may be registered as a domain name provided that the name has not been previously registered by another company or individual.[13] Registration of a domain name is not backed up by legislation and, like the registration of a business or company name (which does however have a legislative basis), does not automatically give the registrant the right to use that name as a trademark. However, registrants can also register their domain name as a trademark providing it meets the requirements of the *Trademarks Act*.

One aspect of domain names that has necessitated redress to the legal system is domain name squatting whereby individuals have registered famous or significant names with the hope that the owner of the name would be prepared to pay considerable amounts of money to purchase the domain name. While names such as 'wallstreet.com' have been reportedly sold for $1 million or more,[14] court action by well-known companies to protect domain names has been successful where the domain name is in fact a trademark and some success has also been had in protecting well-known names where no trademark existed. Action has succeeded under the legal heading of 'passing off' where the name has been used to induce readers into believing that they are dealing with the real entity. Legal proceedings have also been taken against domain name owners who have registered misspellings of a popular name to catch browsers who mis-type the name they are searching for.

A '.com' can be registered for up to 10 years but '.com.au' domain names can be registered for only two years. It is important to renew the registration as there have been several examples of domain names having been snapped up by competitors or cybersquatters after the web-site owner failed to renew it. The Internet Corporation for Assigned Names and Numbers (ICANN), which oversees the domain name system, has recently established an international system for mediting cybersquatting disputes. The arbitration process provides an alternative to the courts for a company which alleges that a holder of a domain name has no legitimate interest in the name.

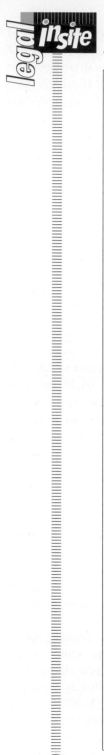

# RULING PROTECTS DOMAIN NAMES
## Legal precedents

BY KIRSTY NEEDHAM

A Federal Court order against a group of Queensland 'cybersquatters' sets a legal precedent for Australian businesses at risk of having trademarks hijacked online, says the CEO of Melbourne IT, Professor Peter Gerrand.

Melbourne IT, Australia's largest registrar of domain names, has obtained an order preventing a Southport couple and an Internet Service Provider from advertising, selling or renting the names Melbourne-IT.com; IT-Melbourne.com and ITMelbourne. com.

Mrs Marilyn Strauss, a conference organiser, and her husband Simon, a retired doctor, must turn the names over to Melbourne IT and pay costs.

The finding comes as the US Government considers a bill that would outlaw 'cybersquatting' and impose fines of up to $300 000 for wilfully registering third-party business trademarks or domain names.

Mrs Strauss said yesterday the Melbourne IT name was registered 'by accident'.

'I had not heard of them,' she said.

Melbourne IT's statement of claim, however, says the domain was registered by Mrs Strauss's company Medical Pain Education the day after five Australian newspapers reported Melbourne IT had won the right to sell the lucrative '.com' domains around the world.

Professor Gerrand sought to register a global name to reflect his company's new, international business, but found it had been taken by the Queenslanders. 'Then when I accessed the name, it was being used to guide you to a site selling domain names,' he said.

Calling itself Australian Domain Names, the site offered to sell or rent more than 50 names associated with companies, cities, sporting or business terms. 'How to own the Sydney Olympics and the rest of Australia as well' was the boast. Among the names were: starcity-casino.com, bigpond-australia. com, ExciteAU.com, eTradeAU.com. and tennis-australia.com.

Mrs Strauss says bigpond-australia does not refer to Telstra's Big Pond Internet Service, but is instead a fishing Website. 'We also have Fish Australia .com. Fishing is a major industry in Australia.'

Mrs Strauss sees a business opportunity in 'developing good addresses' that are easily found on the Web, and wanted to 'get the good ones while they were still available'.

She aimed to rent them out for a yearly fee: 'Some are too valuable for us to sell.'

Professor Gerrand believed the site was trying to pass itself off as Melbourne IT, which would find it in breach of the Trade Practices Act.

'My instruction to Mallesons Stephen Jacques was to win this so that Australian businesses could be confident that names would not be hijacked,' he said.

Mallesons Stephen Jacques partner Mr John Waters said it was the first time that the Australian courts had dealt with cybersquatting, and followed successful action in the UK by retailer Marks & Spencer.

Mr Neil Portland, the managing director of ISP Atnet said his company merely hosted the Website, and regularly conducted domain name registrations for its clients for $40, but did not vet them.

High-profile cybersquatter Mr Brendan Yell, who has registered cdnow.com.au, reports that threatened legal action from an American online CD retailer has not eventuated. Mr Yell does not think the rising involvement of the courts in 'cybersquatting' will kill off the market.

'At the end of the day you have to stay within the letter of the law,' he said.

**SOURCE:** *Sydney Morning Herald*, 13 August 1999, p. 3

## RESEARCH QUESTIONS

1. Has this legal precedent had the desired effect of reducing the incidence of 'cybersquatting'?
2. Has there since been any specific legislation, in Australia or elsewhere, to afford protection to prevent 'cybersquatting'?
3. Have there been any instances of successful legal action against 'cybersquatting' across different jurisdictions?

# JURISDICTION

Every country has established its own network of laws governing most aspects of private and commercial life in response to the country's individual social, political and commercial circumstances. A few legal systems prevail across groups of countries. Australia, together with most of the English-speaking countries, has the 'common law' system inherited from England. However, although this leads to some similarities, any dispute may receive a different interpretation and have a different outcome depending on which state of Australia the events occurred in. Laws established at international forums have been adopted by many national governments, but these represent only a small part of each country's legislative base.

There is a large body of law called Conflict of Laws which is directed toward identifying which jurisdiction's law is to be applied to any dispute; that is, whether it be the state, national, foreign or international law, and which is the most suitable court (or 'forum') in which the dispute is to be heard.

In order for a court to hear a matter with a trans-border dimension, various tests have to be applied to determine the appropriate **jurisdiction**. A key consideration is that one party to the hearing or the subject matter of the hearing must have some connection with its jurisdiction; for example, that a **contract** was signed within the jurisdiction. However, all manner of complications can occur. The other party may be resident overseas and may decide not to appear to defend the proceedings. In that case, even if the court were to make a judgment in the plaintiff's favour, the plaintiff may not be able to enforce the judgment. It is possible to enforce judgements outside Australia only in a limited number of countries (such as the United Kingdom) under reciprocal arrangements.

Alternatively, the aggrieved party may have to take action in the defendant's jurisdiction by commencing new proceedings. The other party may even initiate counter proceedings in a foreign jurisdiction. Further complications arise when evidence required for the hearing is outside the court's jurisdiction and it may not be possible to compel the evidence to be made available, effectively bringing the action to a halt.

These are the sorts of problems that can occur in the more conventional modes of commercial transactions. They are increasingly likely to occur also with transactions conducted over the Internet because much of the trading is conducted outside the existing legislative framework.

# DEFAMATION

The print and broadcasting media are obliged to carefully monitor their outputs to avoid litigation by individuals or companies protecting their interests. It is also necessary for web site owners and bulletin board participants to be careful. Consider, for example, the following situation in the United States. After making allegations about a White House aide on his World Wide Web site, the 'Drudge Report', Matt Drudge was faced with a potentially ruinous **defamation** suit. One article on the defamation suit article commented that 'the Internet has turned anyone with a mouth and a modem into a global publisher'.[15] With reference to jurisdictional matters of defamation, however, it is important to note in this example that Mr Drudge clearly identified himself and both the parties were resident in the same country, the United States. Therefore, United States law could be applied. The situation becomes progressively far more complicated if Mr Drudge:

- resided in another country
- posted the information on a web site located in a third country
- used an ISP in a fourth country
- chose to remain anonymous or used a fictitious name.

All of these would be quite feasible on the Internet and would make it exceedingly difficult, if not impossible, for the offended party to obtain a legal remedy. An illustration of some of these difficulties is provided by a decision in a case involving the Macquarie Bank in the Supreme Court of New South Wales.[16]

It is important to note that email transmissions can also give rise to defamation proceedings. Anything written in an email or that is included in an attachment that is likely to injur the reputation of another person may be defamatory if it is 'published' to a third party. Publication does not need to be intentional but can arise even if you accidentally forward a copy of a defamatory email. As publication will occur in every jurisdiction in which a defamatory email is received, the sender could be the subject of multiple court proceedings!

## Defamation on the Web

# JUDGE REFUSES BANK'S PLEA TO CLOSE 'DEFAMATORY' SITE

## Net and the law

BY ANNE LAMPE, SENIOR JOURNALIST

Macquarie Bank has failed in a bid to shut down an Internet site which, it claims is defaming it and an executive director Mr Andrew Downe. Justice Caroline Simpson yesterday ruled that Australian courts had no jurisdiction to restrain the publication of material over the Net.

In the process, the case has highlighted the limitation of sovereign laws when dealing with the Internet.

Macquarie last Friday sought an interim injunction seeking to shut down the Website, macquarieontrial. com, which includes material relating to the drawn-out litigation between a former employee of a MB subsidiary, Mr Charles Berg, and the bank.

Mr Berg and a colleague, Mr Michael Bell, are seeking about $30 million in damages from MB for alleged unfair termination of an employment contract.

The case has been bogged down in the NSW Industrial Relations Commission, with Macquarie Bank arguing that Australian courts have no jurisdiction to hear disputes over employment contracts entered between the two men and its Hong Kong subsidiary.

Mr Berg now resides in the US and says he and Mr Bell have spent $300 000 on litigation but have not had their grievances aired in court.

On May 24 material in relation to the litigation began to appear on macquarieontrial.com. MB said the material was defamatory and Justice Simpson agreed.

But, she said: 'Any order made by this court would be enforceable only if the defendant were voluntarily to return to NSW. He cannot be compelled to do so for the purpose of enforcement.'

Justice Simpson added that the most significant factors mitigating against the orders being sought was the nature of the Internet itself.

'It is reasonably plain, I think that once published on the Internet, material is transmitted anywhere in the world that has an Internet connection. It may be received by anybody, anywhere, having the appropriate facilities.

'Once published material can be received anywhere, and it does not lie within the competence of the publisher to restrict the reach of the publication.'

She added: 'It is not to be assumed that the law of defamation in other countries is coextensive with that of NSW and indeed, one knows that it is not. It may very well be that, according to the law of the Bahamas, Tadjikistan, or Mongolia, the defendant has an unfettered right to publish the material. To make an order interfering with such a right would exceed the proper limits of the use of the injunction power of this court.'

**SOURCE:** *Sydney Morning Herald,* 3 June 1999, p. 28

**RESEARCH QUESTIONS**

1. Have there been any further cases where a defamation action has failed due to want of jurisdiction?
2. Have any courts in other countries, faced with similar circumstances, reached a different verdict?

# THE CONTRACT

The issue of jurisdiction is particularly important in relation to contracts for goods or services. There is no international law which completely defines obligations under a contract, although it is open to the parties to decide which jurisdiction's laws will apply.

We will use the example of purchasing a CD from a music store to demonstrate the three main elements of a binding contract, which are:

- offer
- acceptance
- consideration.

When you take the CD to the cashier and pay for it, you are making an 'offer' to purchase. The offer is 'accepted' when the cashier takes the money, which represents the 'consideration'. The example of a CD purchase was deliberately chosen. Purchase of CDs via the Internet is a booming business; the CD being a low-weight, high-value item makes it ideal for Internet commerce.

If, when you arrive home, you find that the CD is faulty, you can take the CD back to the store and demand a replacement or obtain a refund of your money. If the store will do neither, you have an action under the general law of contract to obtain recompense or, more conveniently, particularly where small sums are involved, consumer protection legislation. (In New South Wales, the *Fair Trading Act (1974)* will provide the remedy.) You need neither know nor care whose fault it was that the CD was damaged or who made the CD. You are able to obtain recompense from the store because you had a contract with it and the store has legal obligations to provide goods of sufficient quality.

In usual circumstances a store will willingly accommodate you when you return faulty merchandise because your legal remedies would be well known. There would be little point in the store trying to evade its responsibilities as it could not hope to win if you went to court. The store could well reason that you would not bother to go to court for such a small sum. However, because it operates within a local area, it would not want any adverse publicity that could affect consumer confidence and hence sales.

Because a transaction like the one described above was conducted in one place within one state, if you wished to take legal action the local state jurisdiction would provide the remedy. If the transaction was conducted over the Internet and both parties were resident in the one state, in all probability you would also have the same protection as in the example given above. However, you may not be able to ascertain the identity of the party from whom you made the purchase in order to seek recompense for a faulty CD. Overseas Internet advertisers, content service providers and content creators may be completely outside any jurisdiction which could offer redress. In any event, there is the difficulty of obtaining proof of details of the transaction. Web sites can be created and removed in an instant, and the use of hyperlinks confuses the situation still further.

## Fair trading on the Internet

### ON THE WEB, IT'S BUYER BEWARE. BUT WHERE?

BY CARL S. KAPLAN

When the history of e-commerce is written, there will be a long footnote about David J. Loundy.

A persistent Chicago lawyer and music lover, Loundy in the past three months has created an international legal incident over his rebuffed attempt to buy a CD at its listed price from a foreign Web site.

The money at issue in the dispute is small — less than $7 — but the cutting-edge legal issues are complex enough to make an academic swoon with delight.

The international cast of characters is colorful, too. At its zenith, the tempest in a teapot involved a trade enforcement officer from the County Council of Surry, England; the plain-speaking chairman of a small, independent record company based near Newcastle on Tyne, and the chairman's mail-order representative. There's also Loundy, plus a chorus of unpaid American and British legal advisers and law students who have followed the saga with relish on various law-related listserves, not to mention fans and critics of the brouhaha who posted comments on a music newsgroup.

For Loundy the experience has been entertaining and aggravating.

'People ask me why I'm spending so much time on it,' he said in an interview. 'The answer is personal outrage. Also, it will make a great case study for my class.'

Among other things, Loundy, an adjunct professor, teaches classes in Internet law and Internet governance at the John Marshall School of Law in Chicago.

On a more serious note, he says his aborted CD-buying episode highlights one of the problems of Internet commerce. 'If you have a problem with a merchant in another country, you may not have an easy way to fix things,' he said. 'If someone in England, for example, misrepresents the price of a product, you may not realistically have any remedy because they are on the other side of the planet.'

The story began simply enough. Loundy, a lawyer with Davis, Mannix & McGrath in Chicago, is a fan of the British funk rock group Level 42. In January, he learned from an e-mail music discussion list that Boon, a former member of the band, cut a solo album and that the record was available from a British Web site. The site, Rock Relics, was the only seller of the record that Loundy could find.

Clicking on the site, Loundy ordered the CD — where it was advertised for 8.99 pounds, about $14.50 — and received an e-mail acknowledgment of his order. He then received a note from the mail-order representative, Victoria Bowles, stating that the listed price was in error, and that the true price was 12.99 pounds, about $21. Was Loundy still interested?

'I said I still wanted it, but at 8.99,' Loundy recalled. 'My initial thinking was, hey, they offered the CD at a certain price. I accepted the offer and they confirmed my order.' He said under American notions of law, the site's actions would be breach of contract and false advertising.

Later, Bowles wrote Loundy back and asserted that under English law, there was no contract. The Web site's advertisement was not an 'offer' but an 'invitation to treat', an English legalism that means something close to a pre-offer, she explained, adding that she was formerly a courtroom lawyer. Loundy's order was actually the initial offer, she indicated. Having alerted Loundy of the mistake before payment, the company was free to decline the deal. Was Loundy still interested in *Tin Man* at 12.99?

Loundy was unmoved. For one thing, he thought Illinois law should apply to his problem, not English law, since he had ordered the CD from Chicago. He also heard from an English barrister with whom he corresponded that the confirmation e-mail he received after placing his order for 8.99 would likely be viewed as a suitable acceptance under English law, and thus a contract existed on both sides of the ocean.

The back and forth e-mails got hotter. At one point, Loundy suggested the matter be arbitrated online by an independent third party. Rob Ayling, chairman of the Voiceprint Group, which has since taken over the Rock Relics site, wrote back and dared Loundy to sue him in England.

'I said that because he was abusing Ms. Bowles and acting unreasonably,' Ayling said in an interview. 'There was a typo, we never accepted his order and he was given a choice to buy the CD at 12.99 or not.'

Bowles declined to comment.

Loundy responded: 'I was not abusive. I was simply persistent, especially in light of the fact that they told me they had fixed the error, and one month later it still said 8.99.'

Eventually, Loundy was told by one of his legion of e-mail correspondents that he could file a formal complaint with a local County Council, which is authorized to enforce in its vicinity England's Consumer Protection Act of 1987. Loundy duly complained to the Surrey County Council, which is located near Voiceprint.

In early March, Karen Gianfreda, a trading standards officer for Surrey, replied to Loundy that the English consumer protection law, which makes it a crime for a person to give a misleading price indication, could not be applied in his case. Alas, Voiceprint's offense, if any, did not occur in Surrey, but in Illinois, she said. She added, however, that she would have a chat with Voiceprint and explain to them their obligations under the consumer laws.

In an interview, Gianfreda explained why England's Consumer Protection Act did not apply to Loundy. She said the place of the offense is where the price indication is read. Because Loundy read the ad in Chicago, not Surrey, the Surry Trading Practices group had no jurisdiction.

Later, a resident from Surrey — and an e-mail comrade of Loundy's — complained to Gianfreda directly, and thus she was authorized to look into the 8.99-vs.-12.99 matter.

In the interview, she said that after conducting an investigation she decided to take no further action against Voiceprint because, she said: 'I didn't feel it was intentional. They just made a general mistake.' She also said that under English law, Voiceprint was not obliged to sell Loundy the CD for 8.99.

'As of today, I stand waiting to see if I'm going to get *Tin Man* for 8.99,' Loundy said. 'It's just not practical for me to sue someone in England over a few dollars.'

Alistair Kelman, an English barrister who teaches at the London School of Economics, and who recently co-wrote *Electronic Commerce: Law and Practice* (Sweet and Maxwell, 1999), said misunderstandings are bound to happen when consumers go shopping globally, given the diversity of laws and cultural expectations. He quickly added, however, that he believed Loundy was owed the CD at the listed 8.99 price.

What is an American consumer to do if he believes he was ripped off by a foreign Web site? Kelman said that right now, there are really no legal remedies, short of suing abroad, which is not practical for small claims. He said a non-legal solution might be to 'out' a Web site on e-mail lists and try to shame it into changing its practices.

Down the road, Kelman believes international trade groups might sponsor fair-trading guidelines that Web retailers could endorse, thus lending some peace of mind to wary foreign consumers.

For her part, Gianfreda of the Surrey County Council said she would follow-up a complaint from an American with an 'advisory' letter to a Surrey Internet entrepreneur, even if she had no jurisdiction.

Loundy doesn't know it yet, she added, but she's going to send him a free copy of *Tin Man*, courtesy of Voiceprint.

**SOURCE:** *Cyber Law Journal*, 26 March 1999,
www.nytimes.com/library/tech/99/03/cyber/cyberlaw/26law.htm

## EXERCISES

1. Can you find any other examples of trans-border contract disputes involving the Internet?
2. Has any progress been made in establishing any formal channels for dispute resolution for these sorts of problem?

Our simple example does not begin to explore the complexities of contract formation that can occur, for example, where large sums of money are involved and negotiations take place over weeks or months. In such examples the precise time of formation of a binding contract can be crucial. Since early this century, the 'postal rule' applied, the time of contract acceptance was taken to be when the letter containing the acceptance was slipped into a post box (this says a lot about the perceived reliability of the postal service at that time). The legal system has had to cope with a great many other forms of transmission since then. Acceptance of a contract by fax, for example, is taken to occur when the fax arrives on the destination machine. However, no such simple rule can be applied in the case of email transmission. Who is to blame for delay or non-delivery of email, who is liable if a multi-million dollar contract is lost and how can liability be proved? The problem may be due to server failure, network failure, the sender using a wrong email address or the recipient simply not reading his or her email.

To facilitate the orderly conduct of consumer transactions over the Internet, some form of 'electronic contract' is required. In Australia the *Electronic Transactions Act* provides some certainty that electronic transactions will receive the same treatment in law as paper-based dealings. It is based on the *Model Law for Electronic Commerce* prepared by the United Nations Commission on International Trade Law (UNICTRAL).[17] Subject to certain restrictions, the Act provides that where contract law requires writing or a manual signature that this can be done by electronic communication or electronic signature and provides default rules on when and where an electronic message is sent and received.

One of the major issues which will need to be sorted out as part of the electronic contract is electronic funds transfers. This would involve 'electronic signatures', the 'electronic cheque' and digital cash.[18]

The use of credit cards, as 'consideration', for purchases over the Internet does not, of itself, necessarily produce legal issues peculiar to the Internet as the credit card transaction is based on three quite separate contracts: between the issuer and cardholder, the issuer and the merchant, and the cardholder and the merchant. It is more than likely that each one of these contracts was drawn up within one local jurisdiction. Nevertheless, the possibility of **fraud** is greatly increased when the transaction is conducted over the Internet. In an attempt to address the problems of security and also the fact that the credit card is not appropriate for small transactions due to the relatively high cost of processing, a secured electronic transaction (SET) protocol has been developed by the card issuers and is gaining acceptance.[19]

# ADVERTISING

We return to our example of the CD purchase to illustrate the legal aspects of **advertising** and protection for the consumer. Suppose you bought the CD because you saw an advertisement proclaiming The Stones' *Greatest Hits* but you found out that some of the tracks were not great at all or that the Stones' *Greatest Hits* was sung by another group! You have protection and remedies in the various states under legislation that mirrors the *Commonwealth Trade Practices Act (1974)* prohibiting misleading or deceptive conduct in advertising and other areas.

If the store had reproduced the same advertising message on the CD rack, then the consumer protection legislation would give you the same protection under the 'misleading and deceptive' conduct provisions even though the store itself was quite unaware of the misleading nature of the advertisement. Again, the place and identity of the parties are readily ascertainable. Compare this situation with a purchase over the Internet where similar problems could arise as for the case of contract discussed above.

With a view to addressing some of the problems of selling over the Internet, the Federal Government has produced policies and guidelines on consumer protection and building consumer confidence in electronic commerce.[20] The recommendations include the promotion of ethical sales practices.

## SECURITY

The key issues here are the possibility of someone, the 'hacker', gaining access to a communication between two parties which may contain commercial secrets or credit details and deliberately altering the contents of the communication to prejudice the interests of the parties to the communication or using the information for some other illegal use.

Encryption provides the key to providing greater security, and various organisations are considering policies on cryptography. A major problem looming for cryptography as an Internet security measure is the battle by intelligence agencies, particularly in the United States, to ensure that they are able to read any messages sent over the Internet in the interests of national security. Concerns by civil liberties groups and commercial interests are based on the belief that if the intelligence agencies have the facilities to break any given code then sooner or later, and probably sooner, hackers intent on committing a **crime** will be able to do the same.

A handwritten signature provides, in law, valuable evidence as to the authenticity of documents and particularly contracts. The digital signature, by the use of encryption, goes further than the traditional signature by setting up links between the signature and content of the electronic message ensuring that the content has not been altered and requiring a certification authority to regulate the process.

The European Union has in place a legal framework for the recognition of electronic signatures throughout the union.[21] A collaboration of platform, software and technology vendors is developing a specification to facilitate security within the PC operating system.[22] The American Bar Association has also developed a set of guidelines for the use of digital signatures.[23]

Another issue relating to security includes the very real danger of viruses being transmitted by communications over the Internet and the question of where the liability attaches if viruses are responsible for losses to a business. It behoves both the sender and receiver of Internet communications to maintain virus control procedures.

Many early date-dependent computer systems were based on a format with only two digits to represent the year. There were fears that such systems may respond incorrectly to dates after 1999 by interpreting the '00' date as 1900; the potential for disruption to business operations was massive. The consequences of transmission of non-year-2000 compliant data, the so-called 'millennium bug', were seen as potentially serious and a legal minefield. However, 1 January 2000 passed without major incidents.

# PRIVACY

Although security measures can provide some protection to the information transmitted over the Internet, they do not hide the trail created by each transaction. A web server is able to send a program called a 'cookie' over the Internet to be deposited on a user's hard drive without disclosure or consent.

The cookie was introduced as part of Netscape's web technology. When a web browser requests a page from a web server, the web server sends back to the web browser not just the requested page, but also an instruction to the browser to write a cookie (i.e. a record) into the client computer's storage. Once written into the storage, the user can be identified each time he visits the same site thus allowing a profile of the user to be established based on the usage patterns.

Potentially, such an arrangement could have advantages for both merchants and online consumers in the merchant being able to offer a service tailor-made for the user. However, the main objections to the cookie is that it has been introduced to a user's hard drive without disclosure or consent and the information collated could then become accessible to other organisations, including government. Clearly, the objections could be overcome if the user were to be informed if the cookie were to be placed, the uses to which it would be put and given the choice as to whether the user wished to proceed or not. However, the merchant is under no legal obligation to do so.

At present in Australia, the *Commonwealth Privacy Act (1988)* provides privacy safeguards that Federal Government departments must observe in collecting, storing and using personal information. The Act was amended in 1990 to include credit providers but private companies remain unregulated.

In Australia, Victoria has taken the lead in privacy legislation with its draft *Data Protection Bill*[24] based on the Australian National Privacy Principles.[25] Since then the Federal Government, as a result of pressure from various quarters, has announced that it is preparing national legislation. The proposals are for 'light touch' data protection built around a self-regulatory model that allows individual industries to adopt their own privacy codes with legislative provisions applying if an industry code is not adopted.

However, as we have seen earlier, because of the international nature of the Internet any national regulations may not apply to a foreign company. Furthermore, it may not even be possible to determine in which country the company is located so that enforcement of privacy provisions may be impossible.

Although guidelines have been prepared by such bodies as the United Nations, they carry no legal authority. The most influential provision to date is the European Union Council's Personal Data Protection Directive, which was formally adopted in July 1995.[26] This establishes a set of legal principles for privacy protection applicable to both public and private sectors and legislation has since been enacted by all EU member states modelled on the directive.[27]

Although these legal principles apply only in the EU, their effect is far reaching. This is because the directive also prohibits the transfer of data from the EU to countries that do not have adequate data protection laws. Conversely, the import of data from such countries may also trigger the requirement of the importer to abide by the EU directive. This is one of the factors putting pressure on countries such as Australia to improve their privacy protection laws.

## Privacy laws

---

# PRIVACY LEGISLATION KEY TO E-COMMERCE

**If business fails to react to consumer concerns about privacy, government may have to force them to the table.**

BY SUE BUSHELL

A recent survey of the top 200 most accessed Web sites in Australia found more than 90 per cent were failing to adequately inform consumers about the personal information they collected.

An incredible 51 per cent of the 171 Web sites that gathered personal information from the user failed to include a privacy statement on their Web site. Only six per cent had a formal and comprehensive privacy policy, while 43 per cent gave the user some indication of their information practices or privacy policies, but provided minimal information regarding their collection. Just 11 per cent of sites surveyed had an adequate privacy policy.

Alarmingly, some of the worst offenders were sites that typically collected a great deal of personal information from the user, including NineMSN, Telstra, OzEmail, Optus and Qantas.

This is not only short-sighted, it's just plain stupid. As survey author Australian National University law faculty masters candidate Ben Macklin states in his accompanying report: 'The Web site survey gives a clear indication of an Australian Internet market place that is immature and still developing. The scarcity of adequate privacy policies is an important indicator of this.'

There's plenty of solid evidence that consumer concerns about their privacy are impeding the take-up of electronic commerce, especially when it comes to purchasing online. The endless studies showing people remain deeply concerned about privacy must be seen as fair warning to any company that fails to consider privacy issues in its e-commerce, CRM [customer relationship management], data warehousing and marketing efforts.

US organisations have reacted decisively in the face of such consumer concerns, both in recognition of their potential ability to impede the take-up of e-commerce and in fear that if they don't act, the US Government may regulate to force them to act.

Determined to forestall such government intervention, Internet heavyweights responsible for generating about 80 per cent of all Internet traffic, including IBM, Disney and Time Warner, have launched the Online Privacy Alliance, defining a code of practice and developing a privacy symbol to be carried by Web site code observers.

Australian business should look seriously at doing the same. If they don't, the Australian Government may need to consider toughening up the 'light-touch' Privacy Legislation it is due to introduce to the private sector, in the interest of building trust online.

The current proposal is for the Government to base its legislation on the Privacy Commissioner's National Principles for the Fair Handling of Personal Information and the draft Data Protection Bill of Victoria. It would involve the adoption of industry codes approved by the Privacy Commissioner. It would also enforce minimum privacy standards in areas where industry codes are not adopted.

It is not unreasonable for the Government to want to avoid placing an undue burden on business. But the dismal track record of business to date raises fears the 'light-touch' regulation may not be enough. As Macklin says: 'The ... survey reveals that in an environment without legislation, organisations online have not addressed the privacy and security concerns of the consumer.'

If a 'light touch' proves inadequate, the Government may be forced (and well advised) to get heavy.

*Sue Bushell is a Canberra-based political correspondent.*

**SOURCE:** *Information Age*, November 1999, p. 7

## QUESTIONS

1. What progress has been made in Australia in enacting privacy legislation?
2. How have industry codes of practice developed as provided for in the legislation?
3. How effective have the combination of legislation and codes of practice been?

# ETHICS

Anyone engaging in business activities should pay regard to the obligations imposed on them by legislation and industry codes of practice. However, in the absence of legislation or codes, which as we have seen may well be the case in Internet business, what should be the guiding principles in establishing and operating the business? It is here that ethical considerations play a part. They may be thought of as the moral dimension to business. Most professional bodies have established codes of **ethics** to regulate their dealings with their employer, members of the public or clients to ensure that their respective interests are safeguarded.[28]

If you are proposing to conduct business on the Internet, and you are uncertain that what you are proposing is appropriate, you should ask yourselves these questions:[29]

- Are you hiding certain facts because you fear disapproval?
- Are you purposely colouring facts to bias your message?
- If what you were doing was done to you would you feel upset?

- Could anyone object to your action as unfair?
- Will anyone be harmed by your action?
- Do you feel the need to rationalise your behaviour?
- Could a destructive practice or trend evolve?

If the answer to any of the above questions is 'yes', you should reconsider your proposed action. To pursue this topic further, see *Proceedings of the Australian Institute of Computer Ethics*, 14–16 July 1999.[30]

# SUMMARY

There are at present very few legislative controls on the Internet although efforts are being made in various countries and internationally to draw up suitable model laws and guidelines.

Current laws and industry self-regulation have some applicability to Internet transactions within the state or nation. Consumer protection laws provide protection against misleading advertising and faulty goods. However, problems arise in trans-border transactions in determining which country's laws apply and which country's courts have jurisdiction. Problems are exacerbated if the parties to a transaction cannot be determined. This is possible due to the anonymity that the Internet can provide, especially through the use of hyperlinks and the ease of establishing and closing down web sites in a short space of time.

A major hurdle to be overcome is to provide security over Internet communications to prevent fraud. Encryption techniques are being developed to facilitate monetary transfers and ensure that messages are not corrupted accidentally or deliberately by third parties. Hand in hand with the question of security is the question of protecting the privacy of the Internet user who leaves a 'trail' every time he or she uses the Internet that can be followed and recorded.

Lastly, there is the question of who controls the content on the Internet? Countries are adopting different approaches to this issue depending upon their societal and cultural values.

## key terms

| | | |
|---|---|---|
| *advertising* | *ethics* | *meta tagging* |
| *censorship* | *fraud* | *patents* |
| *contract* | *intellectual property* | *privacy* |
| *copyright* | *jurisdiction* | *trademarks* |
| *crime* | *law* | |
| *defamation* | *legislation* | |

## SELLERS MAY BE STROLLING INTO A LEGAL MAZE
### Jurisdiction

BY KATRINA NICHOLAS

Businesses selling or planning to sell over the Internet could soon find themselves in hot water over jurisdictional legal issues, a national law firm has warned.

Allen Allen & Hemsley senior associate Mr Niranjan Arasaratnam, speaking at the eBusiness Symposium in Melbourne yesterday, said the question of jurisdiction was the single most important legal issue confronting the Internet industry.

Jurisdiction problems arise when, for example, a Sydney company sells via the Internet to customers in Perth, or to customers overseas. In these cases there is confusion as to whether customers are covered by legislation in their own jurisdiction, or in the seller's.

The issue arose in a recent US court case where the New York Supreme Court ruled that a Caribbean Internet gambling business had breached New York's ban on cyberbetting. A similar case involves online book retailers Barnesandnoble.com and Amazon.com, accused of breaching German laws by selling copies of Adolf Hitler's book *Mein Kampf* — which is banned in Germany — to Germans via the Internet.

Mr Arasaratnam said these cases demonstrated that any business with an e-commerce operation was potentially exposing itself to the risk of incurring costly and time-consuming legal action.

He said businesses selling overseas or interstate were not only subject to those other jurisdictions' consumer protection laws but also, potentially, to tax laws and licensing fees.

'I think the level of awareness about this amongst e-businesses is low,' Mr Arasaratnam said.

'By selling online, businesses may unwittingly and unknowingly be subject to laws in other States or countries.'

Mr Arasaratnam said adding a disclaimer to an e-commerce site often did not work because sellers had no suitable method to vet where consumers were actually from.

'Determining where a customer is based depending on where the server they are using is based does not work either because, for example, those with AOL would all be deemed to live in Virginia,' he said.

The solution, said Mr Arasaratnam, lay in countries around the globe coming together to negotiate a minimum consumer protection standard. Web sites which met the standard would then be able to display some sort of quality seal or tick of approval.

Europe and the US have already moved to develop such a minimum standard, with the European Commission and Microsoft's Mr Bill Gates indicating support for an Internet charter governing a cyber-jurisdiction.

The Internet charter would govern all aspects of e-commerce, including the protection of privacy, regulation of illegal content, network security and taxes.

However, Mr Chris Shine, partner with Blake Dawson Waldron, said such expensive and expansive measures were not needed.

He said e-businesses should simply make clear all terms and conditions of sale on their Web sites and require customers to click on an 'I acknowledge' button before buying.

In the case involving Barnesandnoble.com and *Mein Kampf*, Mr Shine said the sale would only become illegal once the book was actually shipped into Germany — not at the point of sale.

**SOURCE:** *Sydney Morning Herald*, 2 September 1999, p. 30

## RESEARCH QUESTIONS

1. What progress has been made in developing an international minimum consumer protection standard since this article was published?

2. Does a legal jurisdiction governing Internet transactions, separate from national legal systems, seem a viable proposition?

3. Does clicking on an 'I acknowledge' or 'I accept' button necessarily constitute in law an acceptance by the clicker of an offer made by the web site owner thereby forming a binding contract? Illustrate with examples of recent court cases.

**QUESTIONS**

If you were in the process of establishing a commercial web site in Australia:

(a) What issues would you address in order to safeguard your operation from any legal disputation?

(b) How would you provide users with some confidence that transactions conducted with your site would protect the privacy of the user?

(c) Would you need to investigate the bona fides of linked site(s) if you provided hypertext links to other web sites? Could you protect yourself from legal disputation arising from users who gained access to the linked site through your own? If so, how?

(d) Would your answers be any different if you were establishing your site in:

(i) Europe

(ii) the United States?

If so, how?

## SUGGESTED READING

Adam, N. R. 1999, *Electronic Commerce: Technical, Business and Legal Issues*, Prentice Hall, United States.

Lawson, J. 1999, *The Complete Internet Handbook for Lawyers*, American Bar Association, United States.

Lessig, L. 1999, *Code and Other Laws of Cyberspace*, Basic Books, United States.

O'Shea, P. (ed.) 2000, *E-mail for Business Handbook*, TMTE Group, Sydney.

## END NOTES

1. For current news on national approaches to this and other Internet issues see *Global Internet Liberty Campaign*, www.gilc.org.

2. The Internet Content Rating Association's web address is www.icra.org.

3. For more information see www.aph.gov.au/senate/committee/it_cttee/index.htm.

4. The Telecommunications Industry Ombudsman's web address is www.tio.com.au.

5. The Australian Broadcasting Association's web address is www.aba.gov.au.

6. The industry groups include the Internet Industry Association (www.iia.net.au), Electronic Frontiers Australia (www.efa.org.au) and the Internet Society of Australia (www.isoc-au.org.au).

7. The web address for Net Nanny is www.netnanny.com.

8. For resources on copyright see *The Copyright Page*, www.qantm.com.au/copyright, and the Australian Copyright Council, www.copyright.org.au.

9. For more information see the *Copyright Amendment (Digital Agenda) Act 1999* at www.law.gov.au/publications/copyright_enews.

10. For further information see www.ipaustralia.gov.au.

11. *New York Times* 1999, 'Amazon's one-click suit', in *Sydney Morning Herald*, 25 October, p. 41.

12. For further information see www.ipaustralia.gov.au.

13. For rules and policies on registration see www.internetnamesww.com.au.

14. *New York Times* 1999, 'What's in a name? Big bucks', in *Sydney Morning Herald*, 24 August, p. 28.

15. Kurtz, H. 1997, 'New media, old rules', *Sydney Morning Herald*, Icon, 23 August 1997, p. 14.

16. *Macquarie Bank Limited and Anor v. Berg* [1999] NSWSC 526 (2 June 1999), www.austlii.edu.au/do/disp.pl/au/cases/nsw/supreme_ct/1999/526.html.

17. The United Nations Commission on International Trade Law's web address is www.unictral.org/en-index.htm.

18. See Tyree, A. 1997, *Digital Cash*, Butterworths, Sydney.

19. MasterCard 1999, *Secure Electronic Transaction (SET) Protocol*, May www.mastercard.com/set/.

20. See Treasury Department 1999, *A Policy Framework for Consumer Protection in Electronic Commerce*, October; National Advisory Council on Consumer Affairs 1998, *Consumer Protection in Electronic Commerce — Principles and Key Issues*, April; and Treasury Department and National Office for the Information Economy in the Department of Communications, Information Technology and the Arts 1999, *Shopping on the Internet — Facts for Consumers*, www.treasury.gov.au/publications/consumeraffairs/electroniccommercepublications/.

21. European Commission, 'Commission welcomes new legal framework to guarantee security of electronic signatures', http://europa.eu.int/comm/dg15/en/media/99-915.htm.

22. See Trusted Computing Platform Alliance at www.trustedpc.org.

23. American Bar Association, *Digital Signature Guidelines*, ABA Section of Science and Technology, Information Security Committee, http://abanet.org/scitech/ec/isc/dsg.html.

24. For more information see the Victorian Government's web site at www.vic.gov.au.

25. The Australian Privacy Commissioner's web address is www.privacy.gov.au/publications/index.html.

26. The European Union directive on the protection of individuals with regard to the processing of personal data and the free movement of such data can be found at www2.echo.lu/legal/en/datprot/directiv/directiv.html.

27. For examples see the United Kingdom's *Data Protection Act 1998*, www.hmso.gov.uk/acts/acts1998/19980029.htm.

28. For example, see the Australian Computer Society Code of Ethics web address at www.acs.org.au/national/pospaper/acs131.htm.

29. Based on Parker, C. C. 1996, *Understanding Computers Today and Tomorrow*, Dryden Press, United States, p. SOC 2–22.

30. *Proceedings of the Australian Institute of Computer Ethics Conference*, 14–16 July 1999, www.aice.swin.edu.au/events/AICEC99/.

# CHAPTER

# 11

# Future trends

## LEARNING *Outcomes*

You will have mastered the material in this chapter when you can:

- ◙ understand the concept of the Dot Com economy
- ◙ identify new forms of intermediation
- ◙ define an Internet portal or hub
- ◙ explain the key aspects of online auction technologies
- ◙ describe and explain a virtual private network (VPN)
- ◙ understand XML and its importance to Internet commerce
- ◙ describe the potential impact on Internet commerce of WAP (wireless application protocol)
- ◙ identify the major trends in government and Internet commerce
- ◙ describe how industry structures are changing through new business models.

*'The pervasiveness of information technology, the variety of its benefits to producers and consumers, and the speed of economic change in the digital era have tested the limits of established indices of economic performance.'*

Department of Commerce 1999, *Emerging Digital Economy II*, 22 June, United States Government, www.ecommerce.gov/ede/report.html

The global online economy, through Internet-based commerce, continues to transform industry and commerce; the 'cyber rush' persists. The Internet increasingly influences the way industries work and how companies and customers interact with each other in the twenty-first century. As we have seen in the previous chapters of this book, the Internet is changing business models, but despite the obvious commercial applicability of the Internet, there is no one dominant model emerging as yet.

By now we appreciate that the Internet presents itself to businesses as uncharted territory, forcing firms to seek new strategies that might work in an ever-changing technological and economic environment. Those firms who wish to succeed in Internet commerce have had to confront three unique characteristics: ubiquity, interactivity and speed.[1]

Everywhere on the Internet is accessible to users on what is essentially an unlimited and equal basis — this is ubiquity. The user can go anywhere on the Internet with a minimum of effort and there is no real technological reason for the user to start at a specific spot or web site. Because the Internet is interactive, exciting new forms of interactivity have developed. Software is distributed and tested online, information is exchanged and modified more easily, data is stored online (e.g. using docSpace — www.docspace.com) and virtual organisations can operate more effectively through interacting on a global basis at any hour of the day or night. The speed at which businesses can be established on the Internet places a great deal of emphasis on being first in a particular market category, as has been discussed in chapter 4 under the new P's of marketing. Further, many Internet-based businesses (Dot Com businesses) have been developed as overlays of existing infrastructure, which has reduced start-up costs and time of deployment. The new **Dot Com economy** has arrived.

Because the Internet provides an instant, convenient channel for researching, working, communicating, exchanging and choosing information, Internet commerce is now allowing firms to reconsider which functions they should perform in-house and which are best outsourced. In fact, Forrester Research has coined a new word 'exsourced' and defines an exsourcer as a 'help provider that manages multi-company processes and technologies across the Internet'.[2] In Australia, Com Tech and Internet Security Systems have set up a business to offer virus and hacker protection, router and firewall management, content filtering and analysis for monthly subscriptions. New relationships are being formed to streamline and enhance supply chain processes. Companies such as FedEx and UPS are finding that their roles as logistic intermediaries are expanding, as it is vital that the ordered goods are delivered quickly. American Express, an example of a financial intermediary, now offers an enhanced purchasing card that supports online purchasing by facilitating the process of placing an order, fulfilment, reconciliation, data management and program maintenance. These shifts in process can result in significant cost savings.[3]

The main drivers of business acceptance and uptake of Internet commerce into the next century appear to be:

- continued global expansion, or globalisation
- convergence of media and communications technologies
- increasing awareness and familiarity by consumers and business users of Internet tools
- easier-to-use Internet interfaces (e.g. browsers, directories and search engines)
- new business opportunities in new forms.

There is no doubt that change is the only constant as everything becomes faster and as the rate of change accelerates. Walid Mougayar contends that companies in all industries will face immediate trouble in the twenty-first century if they begin it with less than 25 per cent of their revenue directly dependent on electronic commerce channels.[4] Companies failing to join online business communities could be left behind, missing out on the preferred way of doing business in the next millennium.

David Jonas, Managing Director of Electronic Trading Concepts (ETC), believes that it is possible to pick some general trends for the next two to three years:

- The Internet will continue to grow at an exponential rate in terms of users, sites, bandwidth and volume of trading and information dissemination.
- This will continue to reshape businesses, industries and even national economies across the globe by breaking down barriers, breaking down traditional value chains and reforming them into value networks, facilitating the invention of new businesses, forging new alliances and virtual communities, and ignoring national borders.
- An increasing amount of the time of legislators and government bureaucrats will be dedicated to addressing the complex economic, political and social issues that arise out of the growth of the information society. Much of this will have to be done on a pan-national or global basis.[5]

In this final chapter we will take a look at the emerging new models of digital business, drivers of new trends and unexpected developments, the concerns and influence of government in the internationalisation of economies, and some forward projections for business model trends as Internet commerce continues to grow dramatically into the twenty-first century.

---

## GLOBAL SNAPSHOT

- The number of web users increased by 55 per cent from 1998 to 1999.
- As of May 1999, 171 million people across the globe had access to the Internet; over half of them live in the United States and Canada.
- The number of web hosts rose by 46 per cent.
- The number of new web address registrations rose by 137 per cent.
- **Business-to-business** e-commerce is estimated to rise to $US1.3 trillion by 2003.

*SOURCE:* Department of Commerce 1999, *Emerging Digital Economy II*, 22 June, United States Government, www.ecommerce.gov/ede/report.html

---

# THE DOT COM ECONOMY

The advent of the World Wide Web has provided a classic window of opportunity for new companies to challenge the existing order. Amazon, Yahoo!, eBay and CDNow are pioneers of the Dot Com economy. The extraordinary growth of these young web companies is illustrated by the fact that RealNetworks, Priceline.com and E*Trade have a combined market value of US$31 billion.[6] The table below shows the market values of some other Dot Com pioneers.

| TABLE 11.1 | MARKET VALUES OF FIVE INTERNET COMPANIES |
|---|---|
| **COMPANY** | **MARKET CAPITALISATION AT JUNE 1999 (US$)** |
| 3Com | $9.5 billion |
| Cisco | $176.4 billion |
| E*Trade | $8.1 billion |
| Schwab | $38.5 billion |

**SOURCES:** adapted from TheStreet.com and Flemings Asset Management in T. Power and G. Jerjian 1999, *The Battle of the Portals*, The Ecademy, p. 104, www.ecademy.com

Dot Com companies:
- do business almost entirely on the Internet, that is, they generally have no physical shop-front or outlets
- conduct business by trading information, services or products online.

Throughout the world Dot Com companies are springing up. Many entrepreneurs are now targeting China, which has a huge untapped cybermarket that is tipped to grow rapidly in the twenty-first century. Some developments there include Sina.com, alibaba.com and myrice.com. Australia has seen new listings of Dot Com companies in almost every sector, including such names as Multi-EMedia, Spike, LibertyOne, Swish, Channel E, eCorp, Greengrocer.com and E*Trade.

An economic revolution is occurring in every industry from banking to selling groceries or cars, from planning weddings and birthday parties to managing farms and web servers, from routing container ships to making steel or selling postage stamps. Companies are combining Internet technology and a massive amount of marketing money to compete with companies founded before the Web arrived. Larger older companies may be too slow and too concerned with their histories to compete effectively in the new Dot Com economy. The classic example of the above was seen by the slow reaction of Barnes and Noble to Amazon. The founders of these slick new Dot Com companies believe they can use the 'e' in e-business or the 'm' in mobile e-commerce or the 'w' in wireless e-commerce to create value for customers and wealth for investors before the traditional bigger older companies realise the opportunity.

At a conference in July 1999 in the United States, Schwab president David Pottruck introduced the concept of 'clicks and mortar', the idea that a company actually gains an advantage by being able to serve customers wherever they happen to be — in a store, on the phone, online, or offline in an email program. 'Clicks and mortar' companies therefore value the Internet and must be prepared to pay in order to adopt it as a channel. In turn the sales force or resellers need to be part of the team so that they support the Internet. As well, these companies should have end-to-end integration with the production and fulfilment systems and allow customers to decide how to interact with the company.

Larger and more traditionally structured companies have often found it harder to react quickly to the Internet phenomenon. Some have created their own Dot Com departments and some have formed smaller companies hoping that they can move quickly enough to catch the cyber start-ups. Some have acquired smaller companies that have taken the lead on the Internet; for example, Harris Technology was bought by the Coles Myer Group. Parent companies often find that the effort required to set up an electronic commerce division in-house is potentially too great to justify the investment. Overcoming the built-in barriers in a more conservative organisational structure and thinking and reacting like a venture-backed start-up may take too long. Stockholder pressures, corporate culture and legacy systems are some of the problems bigger companies confront in activating Internet-based initiatives.[7]

John Hagel, a principal at McKinsey and Co. and author of several Internet economy books, says there are four key issues preventing large corporations from competing effectively against Internet-based start-ups. These have been summarised in table 11.2 on the following page.

| TABLE 11.2 | LARGE COMPANIES VERSUS DOT COM COMPANIES — FOUR KEY ISSUES |
|---|---|
| **ISSUES** | **REASONS** |
| lack of aspiration and agility | Some large companies take a defensive mindset. They are not able to envisage how e-commerce could help them grow. |
| lack of experience in dealing with uncertainty | Some large companies react by starting up several broad initiatives so that if one fails, there are other alternatives. |
| funding/finance | Traditional companies have financial restraints such as annual reporting and benchmarking while venture-backed start-ups may be able to lose millions as they build market share as part of their business plan. |
| legacy integration issues | Dot Com companies do not have to deal with legacy applications. As Hagel says, when a large insurance company launches an e-commerce site, for example, its customers expect to have access to all of the new features, as well as access to their current and historical account information. |

Some analysts have predicted that once the slower big companies recognise the effort required to launch Internet-based businesses, they will catch up to the Dot Com companies. Deloitte Consulting has found many of its valuable employees leaving to join the Dot Coms. In the month of January 2000, the company lost 200 of its best people in its 7000 strong United States operations to start-ups.[8] These Dot Com companies may have an early advantage through their nimble, flexible, fast, venture capital-backed approach, whereby they can offer staff the opportunity to make lots of money quickly. However, the next wave of success may belong to those who can deliver a seamless supply chain to businesses and consumers across a global e-commerce network.

## The Dot Com business

### AMAZON VS. EVERYBODY

**Forget Amazon vs. Barnes and Noble, Amazon vs. eBay, even Amazon vs. Wal-Mart. This company has bigger plans. But when will it make money?**

BY KATRINA BROOKER

On the morning of September 28, Amazon.com announced that on the morning of September 29 it planned to make an 'announcement significantly affecting the world of e-commerce'. From Wall Street to Silicon Valley, the effect was immediate.

'I was desperate — calling around all day trying to find out what was going on,' said Mark Rowen, an Internet analyst at Prudential Securities. At the Grand Hyatt in Manhattan, Forrester Research was hosting an e-commerce summit. Toby Lenk of eToys was scheduled to speak. So was Priceline's Jay Walker. Yet all anyone could think about was Amazon. 'Here I am at our conference, and all we can do is talk about what Amazon is going to announce tomorrow,' said Carrie Ardito, a Forrester e-commerce analyst. 'Do you know anything?' Rumor had it that Amazon was opening a real-world store; it was going into business with a big-box retailer; it was launching clothes/travel/office supplies online. 'I heard they were doing something with software,' said Buy.com CEO Greg Hawkins. By the end of the day, on no news other than the announcement of the announcement, the stock market had boosted Amazon's value by $1.5 billion.

At nine the next morning in New York, a crowd of reporters and analysts crammed into the Versailles room of the Sheraton Hotel. The place was buzzing. 'Do you have any idea what this is about?' Rowen pressed a reporter from The Street.com. She didn't, and asked what he knew. 'I heard something about a partnership with Home Depot,' he began, but before he could continue, Amazon CEO Jeff Bezos stepped onto the riser at the front of the room. The din stopped, and five TV cameras trained on him. 'Sixteen months ago Amazon.com was a place where you could find books,' Bezos began, hands folded behind his back as he paced the stage. 'Tomorrow Amazon.com will be a place where you can find anything.' With that, he introduced the latest installment of the Amazon potboiler: the serialized story of one company's ambitious plan to take over the world — the e-commerce world, that is.

Throughout the year, Amazon has been on the move. On average it has announced a major initiative every six weeks. In February it bought 46% of Drugstore.com. In March it launched online auctions — two days after rival eBay announced a secondary stock offering. In May the company took a 35% piece of HomeGrocer.com. In June, 54% of Pets.com. In July, 49% of Gear.com. That same month Amazon opened two new online shops: toys and electronics.

Last month's announcement was Z-shops (an online mall) and All Product Search (a product browser). 'We're always talking about what they're going to do next — they're constantly keeping us guessing,' gushes Forrester's Ardito.

Forget about Amazon as the Wal-Mart of the Web. Bezos is aiming for something even bigger. So big, in fact, that it hasn't been invented yet. 'I get asked a lot, Are you trying to be the Wal-Mart of the Web?' says Bezos. 'The truth is, we're not trying to be the Anything of the Web. We're genetically pioneers. Everybody here wants to do something completely new. I wake up every morning trying to make sure I can confound journalists and pundits who try to encapsulate us in an eight-second sound bite.'

In Bezos' vision, Amazon.com will be the center of the e-commerce universe. Books, pet food, tennis shoes, banjos — whatever e-shoppers want, they can buy it, or locate it, on Amazon.com. Picture Amazon as an octopus, its tentacles reaching out all over the Web. The potential payoff is huge. Investors certainly think so. After Amazon announced Z-shops and All Product Search, its stock rose 23%, to $80 a share. 'This is so big, so important, that you have to be invested in it,' says Morris Mark, a portfolio manager who added to his Amazon stake after the announcement. Pausing, he adds, 'Of course, they've got to make it work.'

That is precisely why the world (the e-commerce world, at least) is addicted to the Amazon saga. Can it pull everything together? Can it fuse all those great ideas into one great business? And can it ever make any money? 'They have a great opportunity, but they could screw it up,' says Henry Blodget, an Internet analyst at Merrill Lynch who made a name for himself last year predicting that Amazon's stock would hit $400. It seemed crazy at the time, but on a split-adjusted basis, he was right on target.

**SOURCE:** *Fortune.com*, 8 November 1999, www.pathfinder.com/fortune/

**RESEARCH QUESTIONS**

1. What are the typical differences between a Dot Com company and a more traditional 'bricks and mortar' multinational company?
2. Name three start-up Dot Com companies with which you are familiar, and describe the approach they use to win business in their chosen market that enables them to compete with larger players.

# BUSINESS INTERMEDIARIES

We considered disintermediation and reintermediation in the last edition of this book. Early Internet commerce theory was that the commercial function of the Internet would be simply to cut out the intermediary — the middle-man — allowing companies such as Dell Computers to put up a web site and sell direct to the teeming masses.[9] Meetchina.com, with a database of Chinese export manufacturers, allows overseas buyers to get specifications and quotes online thereby allowing overseas buyers to bypass middlemen in Hong Kong.[10]

E-commerce capabilities are giving birth to entirely new classes of business intermediaries. Forrester Research groups the new business activities under three headings: **aggregators**, auctions and exchanges. These new activities attack different inefficiencies and provide different opportunities.

**TABLE 11.3** NEW BUSINESS ACTIVITIES

| BUSINESS NAME | AIM | STRATEGY/ADVANTAGE | EXAMPLE |
|---|---|---|---|
| aggregators | to create business communities | supplier content pooled to create a searchable one-stop shopping arena with predefined prices for buyers within a business community | www.supplysearch.com.au www.meetchina.com |
| auctions | to create markets and reduce sellers' losses | sellers and buyers encouraged to participate in multiple, real-time auctions simultaneously — without accruing physical-world search and travel costs | www.gofish.com.au www.stuff.com.au www.priceline.com (an example of a reverse auction) |
| exchanges | to provide vetted players with a trading venue defined by clear rules, industry-wide pricing, and open market information | cost of online industry spot market is a fraction of physical-world cost | electronic-trading network (called an ECN), idea of bandwidth futures trading pit, modelling network traffic, telegeography (www.telegeography.com) and MIDS (www3.mids.org)[11] |

**SOURCE:** adapted from Department of Commerce 1999, *Emerging Digital Economy II*, 22 June, United States Government, www.ecommerce.gov/ede/report.html

# FROM VIRTUAL COMMUNITIES TO PORTALS AND AGGREGATORS

One of the most frequently used buzzwords relating to the Internet has been **portal**. Business-to-business portals appear to have essentially emerged from business-based virtual communities. Within the business sector, portals focused on aggregating information relevant to specific interest groups are referred to as online vertical trade communities. Chemdex.com is an example of an industry-specific portal that allows laboratory personnel to search a vast catalogue of chemical supplies from various providers.

A portal may be defined as a gateway or entry point to the World Wide Web. Portals have been likened to the front page of a newspaper or magazine; an all-in-one web site used to find other sites. Netcenter, LookSmart, Yahoo!, Excite, AltaVista and Freeserve home pages are typical examples of broadly targeted portals. VerticalNet is an example of an aggregation of business portals. Power and Jerjian in their book, *The Battle of the Portals*, predict that pocket portals, an electronic device combining PCs, mobiles, Internet and portal, will act as electronic butlers. A person's personal data shadow (i.e. a personal database of information and transactions) will be accessible via personal computer, laptop, mobile phone or television.[12]

Portals can include email, search engines, news, sport, weather, e-commerce, entertainment, special interest chat groups and links to a myriad of other services. Typical examples include:

- industry-specific portals, such as www.industry.net or www.paperexchange.com
- community-specific portals, such as www.elaunceston.com, www.women.com and www.mymanchester.net.

Following the proliferation of portals across the Web, Jesse Berst claims that the emphasis will switch to **hubs** and **home bases**.[13] The idea of a hub comes from the networking world where it is a central device from which everything radiates. In the Web this means that the hub becomes the focus of activities, not just a gateway to pass through. According to Berst, portals are general interest and may not necessarily have a focus. Hubs are more narrowly organised. To succeed as a hub, a site must surround itself with content, commerce and community appropriate to a specific audience. A home base is a web site to which a user returns in between searching other sites. Personalised start pages being pioneered by the portals (e.g. MyNetcenter) represent early home base ideas. These home bases act as a comfort zone for users and offer such services as email, shopping bots, customised news, calendars and virtual offices.

America Online, Yahoo! and RealEstate.com are transforming from portals to aggregators, bringing millions of customers cheaper Visa cards, lower long-distance rates, and less-costly insurance products. Citibank's strategy is based on the aggregation of one billion customers.

It's possible that cooperative competition will continue indefinitely as the working model for the new economy. Historical versions of this emerging portal-based network economy, such as the early European markets or even the modern shopping mall, were successful because they were able to offer the same valuable proposition that is being offered to Internet customers today — it was cheaper and more time-effective to trade within their walls than outside them.

Business exchanges, particularly in the financial trading world, are being set up. Charles Schwab and Fidelity have collaborated to construct a huge electronic trading network (called an ECN), which operates like a stock market. Soon a global ECN will allow people everywhere to buy and sell financial products 24 hours a day, 7 days a week.[14] John Du Pre Gauntt has advanced the idea that bandwidth (if accepted as a business cost) could be capitalised and traded. He reports there have been several attempts at starting bandwidth trading exchanges, namely Arbinet (www.arbinet.com), Band-X (www.band-x.com) and RateXchange (www.rateXchange.com).[15]

## Vertical trading communities

### VERTICALNET ACQUIRES THREE INDUSTRIAL COMMUNITY SITES

HORSHAM, Pennsylvania — (BUSINESS WIRE) — June 30, 1999 — VerticalNet, Inc. (Nasdaq: VERT), announced today the acquisition of three new communities of content and commerce, bringing the total number of VerticalNet® communities to 43 and extending the company's position as first mover and leader in business-to-business e-commerce on the Web.

'Each of these sites is the leader in its respective industry, and the global industries they focus on are enormous. These market-leading sites provide a very attractive user base, along with significant global e-commerce opportunities. We will leverage each of these assets in members, content and trading activity across a number of VerticalNet sites,' said Mike Hagan, Executive Vice President and VerticalNet co-founder.

The new communities acquired are TechSpex, for the machine tools community; ElectricNet, for electrical power industry professionals; and Oil-Link, a leading Internet community for members of the oil and gas industry. Hagan announced that TechSpex founder Nick Bloom will join VerticalNet as Vice President, and ElectricNet founder Bob Libbey will join VerticalNet as Industry Manager.

TechSpex serves builders, users and suppliers of machine tools and related peripherals. The site includes a comprehensive database of machine-tool model specifications with a proprietary technology that allows for parametric searching on the database to obtain an analysis of which models best meet users' needs. Members can obtain purchasing quotes online through a partnership between TechSpex and the American Machine Tool Distributors' Association. TechSpex will be the first online community in VerticalNet's Manufacturing and Metals Group.

'TechSpex technology will allow VerticalNet members to drill much deeper into the manufacturing side of their business, another instance of our leadership role in bringing VerticalNet community members the most useful and convenient buying platforms,' Hagan noted.

ElectricNet, a leading destination for electrical power industry professionals, offers the dominant online buyer's guide for the power transmission and distribution industry and includes classified career sections, company and product spotlights and an industry events calendar among other services. The ElectricNet website will be part of VerticalNet's Environmental Group.

'VerticalNet will offer ElectricNet members the enhanced content of the entire VerticalNet community, with expanded e-commerce synergies across the community and particularly with Power Online, another of our leading vertical sites,' Hagan added.

Oil-Link, a popular portal for executives and engineers in the global oil and gas community, received a 'Selected Site' ranking by the Dow Jones Business Directory. The site includes industry news and information, a number of online services, plus a growing clearing-house for industry transactions. Oil-Link will be integrated into VerticalNet's existing Oil and Gas Online community, making Oil and Gas Online that industry's leading portal.

### About VerticalNet

VerticalNet, Inc. (www.verticalnet.com), is the Internet's premier developer of business-to-business communities of content and commerce.

The company currently operates 43 vertical communities grouped into ten sectors: ADVANCED TECHNOLOGIES: Aerospace Online, Computer OEM Online, Medical Design Online, Test and Measurement.com, Plant Automation. com, Embedded Technology.com; COMMUNICATIONS: Wireless Design Online, Photonics Online, Fiber Optics Online, RF Globalnet.com, Premises Networks.com, Digital Broadcasting. com; ENVIRONMENTAL: Water Online, Pollution Online, Public Works Online, Solid Waste Online, Power Online, Pulp and Paper Online, Safety Online, ElectricNet.com; FOOD AND PACKAGING: Food Online, Food Ingredients Online, Beverage Online, Bakery Online, Meat and Poultry Online, Dairy Network.com, Packaging Network.com; FOODSERVICE/HOSPITALITY: Foodservice Central.com; HEALTHCARE: Hospital Network.com, Nurses.com and E-Dental.com; MANUFACTURING AND METALS: TechSpex; PROCESS: Chemical Online, Pharmaceutical Online, Hydrocarbon Online, Semiconductor Online, Paint and coatings.com, Adhesives and Sealants.com, Oil and Gas Online; SCIENCE: Bioresearch Online, Drug Discovery Online, Laboratory Network.com; SERVICE: PropertyAndCasualty.com.

This announcement contains forward-looking statements that involve risks and uncertainties, including those relating to the company's ability to grow its user and advertiser bases, its advertising and commerce revenues, and to continue to generate profits and positive cash flow from operations. Actual results may differ materially from the results predicted, and reported results should not be considered as an indication of future performance. The potential risks and uncertainties include, among others, the company's limited operating history, the increasingly competitive and constantly changing environment for advertising sales and for VerticalNet, the early stage of the Web as an advertising and commerce medium, and the company's dependence on advertising revenues and on third parties for technology, content and distribution. More information about potential factors that could affect the company's business and financial results is included in the company's Annual Report on Form 10-K for the year ended December 31, 1998 and the Company's Prospectus dated Feburary 10, 1999. 'Management's Discussion and Analysis of Financial Condition and Results of Operations', 'Factors Affecting Our Business Condition', 'Competition', and 'Proprietary Rights' are on file with the Securities and Exchange Commission (http://www.sec.gov) ...

VerticalNet is the registered trademark of VerticalNet, Inc. All other names are trademarks and/or registered trademarks of their respective owners.

**SOURCE:** VerticalNet, 30 June 1999, press release, www.verticalnet.com/press_release_arch_front.html

1.  Find four examples of vertical trade communities and list their range of services. Compare the list — how many are offering Internet commerce transactions like online ordering and e-payment?
2.  How do you believe broad-based portals like Yahoo! and Netscape will keep their 'stickiness'? (Stickiness, in relation to Internet commerce, is a term applied to customer loyalty — the reason why customers return to a web site.)

# ONLINE AUCTIONS

As outlined in chapter 2, **online auctions** are already changing the face of electronic commerce. In many cases they are add-on businesses for online retailers, another form of buyer interaction. Sites offering online auctions have redefined business for collectors, resellers, consumers and shipping companies. They can create international markets linking like-minded individuals on different continents in communities of interest. People can auction their collections of magazines, such as the *Saturday Evening Post*, online and find a buyer from Japan.

The giant of the global online auctions, eBay attracted 84 million hits on web pages by consumers in the first quarter of 1999. It was second only to Yahoo! in terms of the number of minutes that visitors spent at the site (called stickiness). Using a business model where sellers pay for the site's costs, eBay has been consistently profitable despite the fact that it does not have to handle the goods itself. Anyone auctioning goods must pay eBay a fee, as well as a percentage of the sale

Priceline.com is a 'name your own price' online auction model, referred to as the Reverse Auction model in chapter 2. It allows would-be buyers to name the highest price for airline tickets, then checks whether major airlines will sell a seat at that price.

The success of consumer-oriented auctions may be emulated or even surpassed by business-to-business auctions. In this model, companies sell surplus inventory or commodities like electric power or medical equipment generally either to invited dealers or pre-screened partners.

Online auctioneers are expanding their inventory to include a wider range of goods to keep buyers coming back. Real-world livestock auctioneers Cattle Offerings Worldwide (COW) has been online since 1995. Upscale auction houses, often in association with Internet partners, are going online. The second-largest auction house in the world, the 250-year-old Sotheby's Holdings, has signed up 1500 art dealers for its auction site, which was launched in July 1999.

To date, online auctions have faced surprisingly little pressure for regulation, even from consumer advocacy groups, as all parties are reluctant to stifle the boom.[16] This new industry must address many controversial elements before it can become a permanent fixture, including fraud, taxes and the sale of regulated goods ranging from wine to weaponry.

# AUCTIONS MAKE BID FOR NET DOMINANCE

BRAD HOWARTH
■ E-commerce

ONE-to-one auctions will become the most pervasive form of online commerce, according to a senior research scientist with IBM.

Stuart Feldman, of IBM's JT Watson Research Laboratories, said the method of fixed-price consumer purchasing worked because it was too difficult for consumers to shop around for a bargain.

However, this issue disappeared on the Internet, where it was comparatively easy for buyers to run price comparisons.

Mr Feldman said his views were based on the success of online personal auctions sites, e-Bay and OnSale.

But he added that the concept would quickly extend to a business-to-business model for companies that had supply or demand issues they wished to address quickly via the spot market.

'We're already seeing some sites trying to sell industrial goods such as metals and fabrics where the quantities are very large and the values high,' he said.

By hosting auctions with third parties on the Internet, buyers and sellers could remain anonymous, thus protecting their activities from the rest of the market.

Mr Feldman said several stock exchanges had already shut down their pits due to the popularity of mechanised commodities trading, while the Internet extended the potential customer base for sellers and increased the supply opportunities for buyers.

The building blocks for auction sites were already developed. IBM was working with several customers eager to take advantage of auction technology.

These sites involved incorporating auction technology as part of the business chain within the regular procurement processes.

Mr Feldman predicted many companies would move to a purchasing model which would incorporate spot-buying through auctions in conjunction with longer term fixed-price purchasing — the latter in place to protect companies from price spikes on the spot market.

'We see this sort of thing growing very rapidly in standard large business environments,' Mr Feldman said.

'Over the next year or two we're going to see many very interesting applications.'

The consumer auction technology would also continue to grow and evolve to the point where suppliers would compete for consumers' business.

'I have every faith that 10 years from now I will have a communicator gadget that I walk around with and one of the possibilities would be to enter a list of groceries and have companies bid to sell them to me,' Mr Feldman said.

IBM was also working on intelligent agent technology that would help to negotiate the best price on behalf of buyers.

**SOURCE:** *Australian*, 1 June 1999, p. 47

## QUESTIONS

1. How are online auctions changing the rules of online commerce?
2. Are there drawbacks to online auctioning compared to the more traditional form of auction?
3. What is a Dutch auction on the Internet?

# VIRTUAL PRIVATE NETWORKS

A **virtual private network (VPN)** utilises a public network, such as the Internet, to transmit private data. VPNs are an emerging form of extranet that may become a viable replacement for traditional wide area networks (WANs). It is vital that the data is kept secure, confidential and maintains its integrity when it is being transmitted over the Internet. Creating an extranet over existing Internet infrastructure brings international companies closer to the idea of operating as a virtual enterprise. A VPN could also be thought of as a collection of technologies such as host authentication using Secure Shell (SSH) protocol or protocol tunnelling using encryption (and sometimes compression) to create secure connections or 'tunnels' over regular Internet lines.

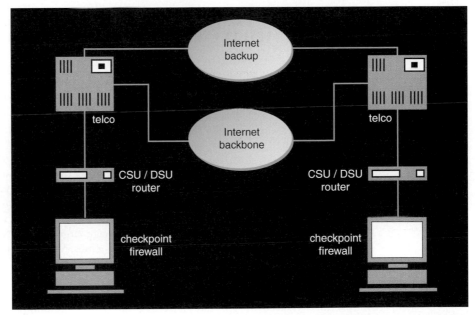

**FIGURE 11.1:** Flow chart of a virtual private network.
**SOURCE:** FishNet Security 1999, www.kcfishnet.com/vpn.html

The cost advantages of a virtual private network are generally acknowledged as:
- cheap and easy access rather than using the more expensive traditional remote access solutions (e.g. leased lines).
- reduction in infrastructure cost and complexity by utilising a company's existing investment in the Internet

- eliminates access and maintenance costs to support 1800 numbers or banks of modems for direct dialling and long-distance call charges.

For companies with multiple locations, telecommuters, mobile workers or the need to exchange information with trading partners, a VPN offers a viable alternative to such traditional remote access solutions as X.25, leased lines, frame relay, 1800 numbers and long-distance modem dial-in.

The VPN brings the best features of the wide-open Internet to the secure and reliable world of private services such as leased lines or a frame relay service. Although the concept of a VPN has been largely associated with establishing encrypted tunnels across the Internet for the use of 'road warriors' or telecommuters, the majority of IP-VPNs (Internet protocol-based virtual private networks) will be hosted on private networks.

It appears that the VPN market will expand rapidly in 2000 and beyond. VPNs have matured from the early stages of investigation of feasibility and commercial viability into a corporate reality. Driven mostly by security and cost factors, VPN deployments should double in the next 18 months.[17]

## business insite | From public to private networks and back again

### LIGHT AT THE END OF THE TUNNEL — NEW TOOLS HOLD OUT HOPE FOR CUTTING VPN COSTS

SALVATORE SALAMONE

Everybody's talking about virtual private networks (VPNs) lately. And it's no wonder why. By all reputable accounts, the market is wired to explode over the next two years. But before providers get too excited about offering these services, they better make sure they have the tools in place to handle the quality of service (QoS) and performance requirements inherent in the service level agreements (SLAs) that will drive the VPN market's growth.

Help may be on the way through products offered by a variety of vendors that are trying to address VPN management issues. Right now it's not clear how effective all these offerings will be. For carriers, however, finding products that let them easily deploy and manage VPNs is essential,

because the worldwide market for VPN services is expected to reach $8.85 billion by 2001, says Michael Howard, principal analyst and founder of market research firm Infonetics Inc. (San Jose, Calif.).

'Until now, Internet VPNs have been limited by the lack of integrated intelligent tools required to deploy and manage large-scale VPN services,' says Eric Zines, VPN analyst with the consultancy TeleChoice Inc. (Boston). Typically, providers deploying site-to-site VPNs, which link corporate branches together, have had to create distinct VPN tunnels between each corporate site. Each tunnel has had to be created one at a time, with the provider manually entering critical information such as the Internet protocol (IP) addresses and tunneling protocols associated with each connection within the site's network. It has been a time-consuming process because each site may require a number of distinct tunnels with varying service requirements. Creating a 30-node VPN could take 60 hours.

Such labor-intensive work to initially establish a managed VPN and the additional work needed to add new sites have prevented many service providers from offering VPNs. But a slew of new products introduced this month by equipment companies, including Xedia Corp. (Littleton, Mass.), Internet Devices Inc. (Sunnyvale, Calif.) and Spring Tide Networks Inc. (Boxborough, Mass.), are trying to address this problem by letting service providers deploy and manage VPNs via policies that designate such things as network topology and security levels for different types of connections.

By enabling centralized policy-based end-to-end provisioning of site-to-site VPNs, these products promise 'quicker, simpler VPN deployments, which will ultimately lead to higher revenue returns for VPN providers,' says Zines.

Many of the new products have both policy-based management and QoS capabilities. Concentric Network Corp. (Cupertino, Calif.), which is using Xedia's Access Point QVPN, offers a managed VPN service that lets an information technology (IT) manager control QoS by giving the manager the ability to ensure that certain VPN traffic gets a higher priority than other traffic. To feasibly offer managed VPN services, providers need tools that bundle tunneling, encryption, bandwidth management and policy-based management. In the past, these features were offered in different devices. But Xedia and other vendors are consolidating all these features into one box.

'This makes it easier for a carrier to reduce costs,' says John Lawler, VPN product line manager at Concentric. But providers also face rising operational costs that will come from distributing VPN software and providing technical support to remote users.

'We're going to be in the software distribution business for the next few years,' says John Summers, senior product manager of VPN services at GTE Internetworking (Cambridge, Mass.).

**SOURCE:** CMP Media, Inc. 1999, *TechWeb*, May, issue 410, www.techweb.com

## QUESTIONS

1. What do you think the difference is between the value-added network service providers, such as GEIS and AT&T, who emerged in the early 1990s, and new VPN service providers?
2. Why are VPNs of interest to large corporations in particular?

# ENTERPRISE INFORMATION PORTALS

**Corporate intranets**, now being called **enterprise information portals (EIPs)**, are being used to manage the knowledge within the organisation. (See the case study on Sydney Water in chapter 1, pages 15–17.) Internet users are familiar with a web browser interface (even an operating system such as Windows 98 has modelled its appearance on such an interface). As a result, corporate intranets have applied the same model to the distribution of information to their employees. Corporate intranets are also sometimes called a business intelligence portal (BIP). The challenge of the EIP is to manage the knowledge within the organisation. An EIP site may include a search engine covering the entire intranet, a categorisation of information on the site, news sources, links to internal sites and popular external web sites, and the ability to personalise the page. The EIP may help to provide a framework for data, turning information into knowledge for employees to use.

The main features of an EIP are as follows:

- an easy-to-understand 'map' of the data (**metadata**). One such tool is Mindmap, an easy-to-use piece of software that maps the business organisation's web site.
- the ability to publish all types of information — data, word processing files, spreadsheets, audio, video, images, streaming video, HTML, email, reports, etc. Many companies find it useful to train their staff online using streaming video. The School of Computing Sciences at the University of Technology is a registered Cisco Academy and several staff members are trained as Cisco Certified Network Administrators using online Cisco material.
- management of user profiles. Information technology (IT) should be able to administer individual and group profiles alike, and individuals should be able to fine-tune their own profiles within the boundaries established by IT. The Cisco material, for example, is set up so that instructors see certain materials including teaching tips, while students have their own profile that, obviously, does not show the tips.
- the ability to support triggers or alerts (exception reporting), which is a key component of an EIP
- both push and pull implementations. An EIP should 'pull' information to publish to the appropriate receiver, based on the profiles, and also 'push' information on a regular basis.[18]

In figure 11.2 you can see that a portal must provide access to data warehouses, desktop documents, sales force automation, customer relationship management and enterprise resource planning systems.

Users should be able to subscribe, design, create, collaborate on, publish and distribute information efficiently and effectively on the business's EIP. EIPs should:

- increase productivity
- be easy to use
- allow users to focus on the content, context and relevance of corporate information
- lead to improved decision making.

The GartnerGroup believes that 80 per cent of early adopters of technology will have put together an intranet portal by the year 2000. Some intranet portals have even accepted revenue-producing advertising to help defray the cost.

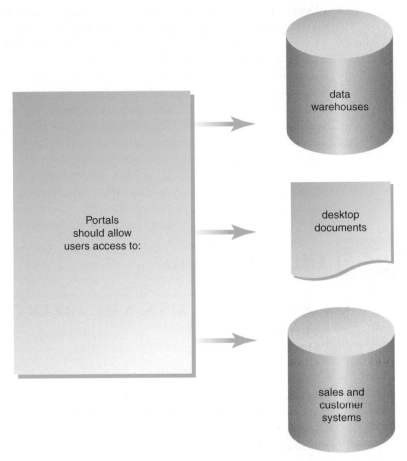

*FIGURE 11.2:* Portals within an organisation

# XML AND STRUCTURED METADATA SYSTEMS

*Because rich media (and much of the computer industry) has so much money, they are able to corral the debate on the future on the Web around bandwidth, bandwidth, bandwidth. A much more important debate is being ignored. It has to do with information structure, structure, structure.*[19]

XML stands for extensible markup language. It is a meta language — a language for defining other languages. It is used to define text markup so that the text can be used and interpreted by different applications, including those that present information to people. It resembles HTML (hypertext markup language) which is the markup language used to describe how text should be formatted for the Web. However, the usefulness in XML lies in the fact that new tags such as 'ProductNumber', 'ProductName', 'Year' and 'Position' may be defined. XML applications are useful to businesses as they allow non-technical personnel to update web pages easily — it becomes as simple as filling in a form.

XML is a universal representation that can be used to prepare text not only for the Internet and other electronic applications. Other applications include:

- electronic publishing to various media, including paper, the Web, CD-ROM, hand-held devices, audio, even Braille
- electronic data interchange
- defining a single, common data format that could be used for interchange among different applications, such as Microsoft's PowerPoint, Word and Excel
- exchanging consumer financial information among financial institutions. OFX, the new financial data exchange standard, is being translated into XML.
- creating standard patient descriptions for data sharing in the healthcare industry.

Thus, the same XML data could be presented to the consumer on the Web, processed by the consumer's bank, and transferred to a third party for an electronic funds transfer. The GartnerGroup expects XML to exceed the use of HTML for publishing applications by the middle of the year 2000.[20]

## XML and e-commerce

### ENTERPRISE APPS: XML TAKES ON E-COMMERCE
BY JAMES E. GASKIN

When Extensible Markup Language was approved by the World Wide Web Consortium in February 1998, the standards gurus hoped XML would offer a more efficient way to publish Web pages. But developers quickly realized that the power of defining their own tags separate from the file contents meant data could be defined and easily exchanged. This ability, tied tightly to Web publishing initially, spread to more data interchange situations and now has XML taking on e-commerce.

Companies trading together must share common data definitions, such as whether address means a physical address or a network address. XML syntax uses matched start and end tags, such as 'and' to define information within a file. This syntax has three advantages: it's easy for humans to read, easy for machines to process and has the look and feel of HTML.

'XML makes quick and dirty implementations compared to EDI,' says Benoit Lheureux, research director for GartnerGroup's application integration and middleware strategies division.

EDI is the e-commerce standard used by some large companies and their trading partners, but is considered too complex and overkill for medium and small companies.

Unlike XML, EDI is not text-based and is hard for people to read. 'XML makes it easy for vendors to agree on [formats] for purchase orders and the like,' Lheureux says. Developers and tools vendors are quicky exploring XML, and products using XML are readily available for Web publishing applications. Many data integration and exchange products powered by XML have been announced, but most won't ship until this summer.

**SOURCE:** *InternetWeek*, 5 April 1999, www.internetweek.com/trends/trends040599.htm

### QUESTIONS
1. Why is XML and metatagging so important to Internet commerce?
2. Will XML have an impact on **knowledge management** within a corporation?

# WIRELESS APPLICATION PROTOCOL

Wireless application protocol (WAP) is an industry open standard to facilitate the easy access to information by handset users. Wireless carriers can exploit Internet Commerce opportunities as they can send targeted information such as banking details, stock trading and travel information to end users.[21]

Advances in wireless telecommunications infrastructure have led to improvements in basic services, which in turn are being seen as commodities. Now applications are being added to the basic services. For example, the Swedish Postal Bank (Postbanken) and Teli's Mobil Smart service allows consumers to make Giro payments from their mobile telephones. In Singapore, Citibank clients can use their mobile telephones to access account balances, pay bills and transfer funds.[22]

Everyday tasks, including making telephone calls, doing banking, trading shares, organising business and personal affairs, and sending email, will be done more efficiently because of the power and convenience of wireless applications combined with the decreasing cost of wireless usage. The most popular applications for WAP have been weather reports, stock quotes, traffic reports and news reports. Additional business functions include access to company telephone directories and the ability to check the telecommunications carrier account via the Internet. The devices that deliver these services will vary from mobile telephones to hand-held devices. Information technology users will no longer have to be confined to their offices, working at their desktops — the age of the mobile worker, equipped with a variety of hand-held, wireless devices offering mobile applications is here.

Emerging and developing nations can bypass the wired telephony model and move directly to a wireless infrastructure for basic telephone service. This will create tremendous demand for business applications — and help make wireless technology a ubiquitous global communications medium.[23]

## Mobile commerce

### NOKIA TARGETS CALL-IN COMMERCE

Nokia is launching a service that will enable consumers to place secure Net orders using a mobile phone.

Nokia, the Finnish telecom equipment maker, said on Monday that it would launch the pilot program later this year with payment card group Visa International and Finnish-Swedish banking group MeritaNordbanken, a European leader in electronic banking. For the pilot, the phones will be equipped with a plug-in card that will provide Visa payment services to MeritaNordbanken customers.

The project will develop systems for secure mobile wireless payment over the Internet and at points of sale using Wireless Application Protocol (WAP) technology.

Consumers will be able to use their mobile phones to pay over the Internet via mobile telephony networks, as well as at merchant points of sale using Bluetooth technology for short-range

communication between electronic devices.

'What we are really announcing is that soon consumers will be able to jump the queue at retailers to pay — or access the Internet anywhere to order and pay for goods and services,' a Visa executive said in a prepared statement.

Using the secure e-commerce system, customers will also be able to download applications to an EMV (Europay-MasterCard-Visa)-compliant bank card.

**IBM goes with Spyglass**
IBM on Monday picked a Web browser to use on its digital set-top platform, but it is not a product of Netscape or Microsoft. Big Blue will use Spyglass' Device Mosaic browser and Internet technologies to create electronic programming guides, video-on-demand services accessible from the set-top box.

IBM Microelectronics will license the technology to set-top box manufacturers targeting the digital video broadcasting market.

**SOURCE:** *Wired News Report*, 24 May 1999, www.wired.com/news/technology

### EXERCISE

Read and discuss the article above. What do you believe are the possibilities for 'mobile commerce' using wireless technology? Will 'wireless' replace 'wired' over time?

# THE FUTURE OF E-MARKETING

A world governed by networks is rewriting the rules on how to build companies, market products (**e-marketing**) and create value. So-called **network effects** are the basis for the new approach to marketing business involving different markets, different business models, and entirely different business strategies.

A classic example is Hotmail, now part of Microsoft, which opened its doors in July 1996. Today Hotmail has become a case study for its fast-forward approach to attracting customers and creating value. Hotmail had 12 million subscribers within 18 months of launching. In 1999, with 50 million registered users, Hotmail is the largest web-based email service on the Internet.

The Hotmail example is well known, and the electronic marketing phenomenon it created has become known as **viral marketing**. Hotmail users, simply by sending emails, were helping the company spread the news about the advantages of free email. They were 'infecting' new users and the infection rate increased, rather than decreased over time.

The principle behind viral marketing is that in the new Internet economy, companies don't sell to their customers. Current customers sell to future customers. In exchange for a free service, customers agree to recommend the service. Hotmail has proven particularly attractive to young people travelling around the world. They meet at Internet Cafes to read and send their email. In the marketing world it is a given that the message is more powerful if spread by people who know other people. Recipients of Hotmail messages are almost always friends, travelling companions, relatives or business acquaintances of the sender. Each email carries an implied endorsement by someone whom the recipient knows.

Ransdell[24] quotes the following examples of network effects and viral marketing. NetZero, for example, offers a lifetime of free Internet access in exchange for allowing a one-by-four-inch window to be displayed that broadcasts targeted ads. NetMind, a service that automatically notifies subscribers of changes to their favorite Web pages, has attracted seven million customers in three years. Homestead, another start-up, lets users create private web sites for free. When users send their password that allows family and friends to access the site, it comes with a link encouraging them to set up their own page.

---

## FOUR LAWS OF VIRAL MARKETING

**1. That's what friends are for**

Network-effects companies have to be great at signing up new customers. But truly great network-effects companies also know how to keep the customers they have. The way to do that is to create products that are so easy to understand and so compelling to use that people enlist their friends.

**2. The freer it is, the faster it spreads**

Sooner or later, business comes down to money. But with network-effects companies, later is better. If a service tries blatantly to charge its subscriber base in every way imaginable, new users will be reluctant to spread the word. In these early days, many of these services are free, and light on revenue generation.

**3. Cafes beat train stations**

The big difference between a cafe and a train station is that people seek out reasons to spend time in the former — and try to pass through the latter as quickly as possible. One of the best indicators of an Internet site's value is customer loyalty: How long do people stay? How often do they return?

**4. Size does matter**

In a world of network effects, the bigger you are, the harder it is for you to be dislodged. By the time a virus spreads to the point of being an epidemic, its growth curve relative to a new entrant is daunting.

*SOURCE:* E. Ransdell 1999, 'Network effects', *Fast Company*, issue 27, p. 208

---

It would seem that the ultimate value of network effects comes down to the lifetime value of a customer.[25] An investment is required to acquire a customer; a further investment is needed to service the customer. Then a certain amount of revenue is derived from that customer. The revenue that is generated through 'monetising' customers, whether it is from subscription fees, e-commerce or advertising, should exceed the cost of acquiring and servicing those customers. Networks operate under the principles of increasing returns. Old-economy companies do not work in the same way.

From the perspective of creating shareholder value, a handful of companies — Microsoft, AOL, Amazon.com, eBay, Yahoo! — are clear-cut cases of increasing returns.

# insite  Viral marketing is spreading

**business**

## SALES FORCE

### A free Internet service provider? A free PC? There must be a catch, and there is, reports IAN CUTHBERTSON.

IN the US and the UK, 'free' has become the operative word for e-mail clients, Internet service providers — and in one quite famous case, for complete PCs. So how did this come about? More importantly, how does it work?

In the case of the free PC, the deal is a testament to both the power of advertising and the ever-decreasing cost (and simultaneously increasing power) of computer technology. Free PC (www.free-pc.com) expects to ship the first 10 000 computers — Compaq Presario 333MHz multimedia systems with 15-inch monitors, CD-ROM and floppy-disk drives — in the second quarter of 1999. Eventually, idealab!, the US Internet giant behind Free PC, hopes to deliver a free PC to each of the estimated 1.5 million hopefuls who have applied for one.

And the catch? Advertising, night and day. And not just when you're online with the free ISP that comes with the free computer — but on the hard disk itself. In order to qualify for a free PC, potential recipients must agree to the monitoring of their Internet habits. They must also supply a vast amount of personal information, which is used, of course, to specifically target the animated banners that will feature at all times, no matter what program you are using, along the bottom and right-hand side of your screen.

Or, make that the company's screen, as it must always remain. Though this could make concentration on, say, a mammoth spreadsheet task distracting, to say the least, the offer does make computer technology and processes available to students and the cash-strapped who might otherwise miss out. Meanwhile, reports on the Internet claim that users are deserting pay-as-you-go ISPs in droves to sign up with companies providing free Net access. In the US, NetZero, a free ISP, claims to have signed about 500 000 users. In the UK, Freeserve describes itself as 'the UK's first fully featured free Internet service'. But though Freeserve may have been the first, it certainly won't be the last.

British Telecom, for example, has announced a free ISP called BT Click-Free — and even Richard Branson has jumped on the bandwagon, announcing recently that Virgin Net will offer free access to its existing 150 000 customers from April 1, 1999, and to the general public from May 1, 1999.

Closer to home, Australia's first and only free ISP, Internet 4 Free (www.in4free.com.au) is up and running, though currently only in the Brisbane area (other major centres are expected to have access to the service by Christmas).

Although it sounds like a contradiction, Internet 4 Free has a one-off charge of $199, nominally to cover the purchase of its *FreeCast* software, which will place a movable advertising banner on your screen, no matter which browser you use.

**290**  Internet Commerce: Digital Models for Business

Thereafter, Internet access is free, for good. A demo of *FreeCast* is downloadable from the site, so you can see how unobtrusive it is. Potential users may have to wait for connection for up to a maximum of 20 days, but, according to marketing manager Kerry Robinson, this is to maintain a modem access ratio of 7:1 — a figure he claims is higher than that provided by many leading — and charging — ISPs.

Internet 4 Free is headed by CEO David Delaney, of David Delaney Advertising. But according to Robinson, in this case 'a computer nerd has come to the marketers, rather than big business with all their dreamy ideas, hauling in the nerds to put some legs on what they've got'.

The system is the brainchild of technical designer James Collins, who sounds most unlike a computer nerd, but admits to a little nervousness about being gazumped by the competition.

Convinced that the system is groundbreaking and technologically significant, Collins says, 'The actual production of this system started in 1997, but in fact it is my life's work. I believe that it's going to cause waves that will echo everywhere — which is why I'm a little reluctant to divulge too much about the technology.'

Robinson mentions that there have been howls of 'You'll never do it' and 'It'll never work' from some sections of the industry, but the team clings resolutely to Collins's vision. He would not be drawn on future developments, but added tantalisingly, 'There are going to be more and bigger stories down the track — perhaps within a few weeks — so keep an eye on us.'

So, is the road to freedom lined with advertising banners? Quite probably. But chances are, there will always be those willing to pay for a private run on the information superhighway.

**SOURCE:** *Australian*, 27 March 1999

## EXERCISES

1. What are the common marketing principles each of these ISPs ascribe to?
2. How long can they maintain a competitive edge?
3. How do they illustrate the theory of viral marketing?
4. Investigate each of the following web sites and report on the similarities and differences between them:
   (a) www.homestead.com
   (b) www.netzero.com
   (c) www.netmind.com.

# E-LOYALTY PROGRAMS TO ACCELERATE INTERNET COMMERCE

One aspect of customer relationship management (see figure 11.3 on the following page) are **e-loyalty programs**, similar to the idea of frequent flyer points in the real world, which are emerging as an accelerated form of marketing for Internet-based commerce in the cyber world. Companies like Beenz.com, MyPoints.com, ipoints, Netcentives, Inc. and Cybergold, Inc. have launched marketing programs for online retailers where consumers receive 'chits', or points, that can be redeemed for products and services. Customers who visit participating web sites, make online purchases, provide personal information to be used in targeted e-mail promotions, refer friends or participate in trial offers are rewarded with points. Cybergold's program allows consumers to transfer cash rewards to their credit cards. Points are acquired as customers visit participating web sites, make online purchases, provide personal information to be used in targeted email promotions, refer friends or participate in trial offers.

Internet businesses may benefit in a variety of ways from e-loyalty programs, including:

- increased traffic to their web sites by attracting new customers
- increased customer loyalty
- the opportunity to track customers across multiple visits more easily. It is important to be careful that you do not alienate customers by invading their privacy. This can cause a customer backlash as happened with DoubleClick early in 2000.[26]
- the opportunity to engage, upsell and cross-sell to highly targeted consumers through email. Again, this must be handled with care.

**FIGURE 11.3:** Customer relationship management.
**SOURCE:** R. Kalakota and M. Robinson 1999, *e-Business: Roadmap for Success*, Addison-Wesley Longman, p. 119

Compiling detailed customer information databases appears to be the long-term strategy for Internet loyalty companies. Not only can these Internet marketing companies sell the information they gather on customers (with some restrictions), they can also drive profits by creating 'consortiums' of related web sites, all of which offer incentive points, making it more likely that customers will stick to those related sites. However, privacy advocates oppose the creation and on-selling databases of personal web behaviour. In January 2000, a Californian resident sued DoubleClick, alleging the company used sophisticated technology to identify web surfers, track their web usage and obtain confidential information without their consent.[27]

To be successful, e-loyalty programs must provide real value to the marketer, the online retailer (e-tailer) and the consumer by offering a package of services that can be scaled to business requirements. Above all, it is clear that the privacy of the consumers must be valued and protected for the consumer to trust the scheme in the first instance.

When incentive programs simply involve discounting or other giveaways, businesses can become locked into price wars. But when incentive programs deepen and broaden the marketing relationship with information, both companies and consumers stand to benefit from the long-term relationships created.[28] (See also chapter 7 for more information on customer relationship management).

# THE ROLE OF GOVERNMENTS IN INTERNET COMMERCE

The role of governments in Internet commerce is being widely debated across the globe. Because of the global nature of e-commerce, there are efforts being made to formulate an international policy.[29] A number of key committees, comprising major government representatives, are considering such issues as the legal framework, taxation, intellectual property protection and the removal of barriers to competition. These committees are from organisations including the OECD, the United Nations, the Global Information Infrastructure, the World Wide Web Consortium, and many more.

The Working Party for the Information Economy (WPIE) is the working group within the OECD that drives economic analysis and associated issues on business-to-business e-commerce. It is responsible for:

- reviewing and evaluating economic and social implications of e-commerce
- submitting to the OECD committees and council an analysis of the factors that encourage the uptake of e-commerce
- analysing the policy frameworks for the information economy.

Key studies conducted by the OECD and the US Department of Commerce in 1998/99 suggest that:

- the macro-economic impact of business-to-consumer e-commerce will be positive but is unlikely to be significant for some time
- the impact of business-to-business e-commerce is much more significant
- the contribution of the 'information economy' to US economic performance rests largely with the IT sector rather than the more recent phenomenon of e-commerce.

Internet commerce in government is predominantly concerned with the delivery of services online. Steve Curran, Director of ETC Electronic Trading Concepts in Australia, believes that these trends include:[30]

- increasing amounts of information available online
- development of 'entry points' and other means to improve the ease with which this information can be located
- increasing availability of online transactions and increasing confidence in being able to conduct these transactions securely
- minimising the need for the public and business to repeatedly enter data when conducting interactions and transactions with government

- integrating government's online services with conventional services to improve the overall efficiency and convenience of service delivery.

The added value these 'entry points' provide includes:

- providing pathways to information that do not rely on the user having a knowledge of the government or departmental structure, i.e. without having to know who provides the information
- providing search engines which can locate required information by searching for key words in the documents and other information resources stored (or hosted) on the site
- enhancing this search capability to include information held on other sites and increasing the relevance of search results through the use of consistent 'descriptions' of information by government agencies
- links to related information sites.

The Business Entry Point, managed by the Commonwealth Government and developed collaboratively by all levels of government in Australia, provides a world-leading example of these value-adding elements.

## The Business Entry Point — an Australian Government initiative

The Business Entry Point makes it easier for Australian businesses to deal with the Government. Currently through the entry point, businesses can:

- access current information on a wide range of government assistance programs and services, and on topics such as taxation, record-keeping, superannuation, occupational health and safety, customs, intellectual property protection and workplace relations

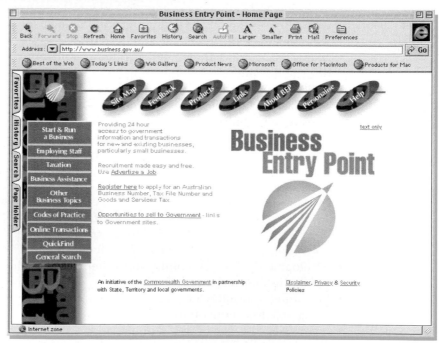

**FIGURE 11.4:** Home page for the Australian Government's Business Entry Point

- gain a better understanding of their obligations, for example, as an employer and for taxation
- tailor their query to suit their business and area of operation
- privately and securely undertake a number of initial business registrations which are tailored to the businesses needs.

Information about licences, codes of practice and a broader range of transactions will be added in the near future.

The entry point provides access to resources from approximately 50 Commonwealth Government agencies, 100 State and Territory Government agencies and 125 industry associations.

# United States and e-commerce

The United States Government released the report *Emerging Digital Economy II* in June 1999. This report recognised that e-commerce and the IT industries that make e-commerce possible are growing and changing at breathtaking speed, fundamentally altering the way Americans produce, consume, communicate and play.[31]

The Government is aware of information technology's growing importance to the United States' economy, the convergence of technology and telecommunications, and the impact of technology on ordinary citizens. As the information technology and telecommunications industries grow increasingly important to the US economy, e-commerce could become a legislative battleground. High technology companies normally adopt a laissez-faire stance, while governments tend to want to protect consumers through legislation.[32]

## Let the market decide

### SENATE SUBCOMMITTEE HEARS ARGUMENT FOR 'HANDS OFF' E-COMMERCE

BY MARY HILLEBRAND

At a hearing on Internet standards yesterday, a handful of e-commerce watchers told the U.S. Senate Science, Technology and Space Subcommittee to let the market decide how and where global electronic commerce matures.

The witnesses largely echoed the sentiments of countless other Internet executives and researchers who have been telling anyone who will listen on Capitol Hill, in both chambers, to leave this nascent business alone for a few years and see what develops.

Some on yesterday's panel, however, argued that a slightly more complex mix of government assistance and market forces will yield the most progress toward interoperability.

'Any effort toward global interoperability in electronic commerce must walk the fine line between market-driven solutions and government initiatives,' argued Andrew Whinston, director of the University of Texas Center for Research in Electronic Commerce.

### Standards a must

Whether the government or the industry handles the details, all agreed that some type of technical standards are needed to make sure the Internet does not become a splintered set of commercial enclaves using different, mutually exclusive technologies.

'Timely and appropriate standards are critical to the long-term commercial success of the Internet, as they allow products and services from different vendors — and different regions — to work together, facilitate robust competition, and reduce uncertainty in the global marketplace,' U.S. Department of Commerce General Counsel Andrew Pincus said.

Setting those standards, however, gets complicated as global e-commerce and the competitive nature of the private sector are factored in, the panelists said. 'If several years ago a standard-setting body or a government agency had sat down and tried to define e-commerce standards or structures, no person, no matter how enlightened, could have hoped to envision the future and develop protocols to serve all the needs that have emerged,' Wal-Mart Stores, Inc. Senior Vice President of New Business Development Glenn Habern said.

Habern added, 'We believe that this period of dynamic growth is just beginning, and some conditions will hold true in the future, namely that no standard-setting body could hope to replicate the innovations that will be introduced according to the demands of commerce itself.'

The Commerce Department agrees, Pincus said, noting that governments of all types — in all regions of the world — should resist the temptation to define and regulate Internet technology. In a way, he argued, standards are already being developed.

'More often than not, the standards we take for granted today are in fact products and services that are broadly used and implemented on a global and national basis. These so-called 'de facto' standards are driving the growth and use of applications of the Internet, and are moving faster than both traditional and non-traditional standards-setting organizations can keep pace with,' Pincus said.

On top of the natural development of e-commerce technology based on business needs, some businesses are voluntarily working together to ensure interoperability, according to CommerceNet President Randy Whiting.

CommerceNet, for example, is a non-profit member-driven group focused upon improving the value of businesses through innovation in electronic commerce. 'We provide a variety of programs that support member research, invention, experimentation and collaboration,' Whiting said. 'Our major area of focus is on interoperability and its impact on technology, applications, public policy and business models.'

### Whither the government?

There is still a role that the government can play in this process, the witnesses argued, as a facilitator of cooperation. For example, Pincus said, the National Institute of Standards and Technology has already begun working with companies to improve interoperability and define technical standards for broadband wireless access technology.

In fact, some testified that the government's oversight, even if passive, might be necessary to protect weaker businesses. 'Leaving standardization entirely up to market players will not guarantee that such an effort will not be anti-competitive,' Whinston argued. 'For example, a standard-setting session among competitors may be a disguised conference for collusion.'

> The government can also lead by example, as Whiting put it, by being a 'first mover' in the implementation of interoperable e-commerce technologies. Under the direction of the Departments of Commerce and Defense, many federal government agencies have been moving toward paperless commerce and reducing barriers to electronic commerce between the government and the private sector.
>
> By making the early moves, Whiting said, the government can 'more strongly and effectively influence the direction and adoption of interoperable e-commerce'.
>
> **Global example-setting**
>
> Pincus noted that the government should also 'strive to reduce the abuse of standards by governments to create technical barriers to global electronic commerce.

**SOURCE:** *E-Commerce Times*, 29 October 1999, www.ecommercetimes.com/news/articles/991029-2.shtml

**QUESTIONS**

1. Should governments take an interventionist approach to global Internet commerce?
2. How can governments lead by example in e-commerce?

# INTERNET COMMERCE WORK FORCE TRENDS

Jobs are both created and destroyed by technology, trade and organisational change. The overall effects of electronic commerce on employment are:

- the creation of direct new jobs (e.g. in 1995 there were few web masters, in fact many people had never heard the term)
- the creation of indirect jobs created by increased demand and productivity (e.g. delivery/fulfilment specialists)
- job losses (due to workers of retailers or other intermediaries being replaced by electronic commerce).

Gains and losses may differ by industry, by geographic area and by skill group. To assess the impact of electronic commerce, it is essential to understand which industries it is generating, which industries will experience new growth and demand because of electronic commerce, which types of job will be destroyed and which created, and what the overall needs are in terms of skills.[33]

A number of industries are affected by electronic commerce:

- The distribution/fulfilment sector is directly affected. Physical goods (e.g. groceries) still need to be delivered whereas movies and music can be delivered electronically.
- Industries related to ICTs (information, communication and technology — the infrastructure that enables electronic commerce) are affected (e.g. as the Internet grew so did the need for routers such as Cisco).
- Content-related industries (information-related goods and services, entertainment, software and digital products) are affected (e.g. TrendMicro

sells its virus protection software PC-Cillin over the Internet at www.trendmicro.com).

- Transactions-related industries (i.e. those affected by the size and type of economic transaction such as the financial sector, the postal sector, advertising, travel and transport) are affected.[34] The United States Postal Service (www.usps.com) sells stamps over the Internet.

Businesses have been affected by the growth in electronic commerce. They have to become flexible organisations and increase their operational efficiencies. Both small businesses and multinationals are having to compete in a global environment. The increased competition, global access and organisational change are impacting labour markets by influencing employment demand, wages and skill requirements.[35]

Electronic commerce is certainly driving the demand for IT professionals but it also requires IT expertise to be coupled with strong business application skills, thereby generating demand for a flexible, multiskilled work force. The United States Government Department of Commerce predicts that by 2006, almost half of the US work force will be employed by industries that are either major producers or intensive users of information technology products and services. IT workers continue to earn more than non-IT workers. Innovation has:

- caused a surge in demand for highly paid IT personnel such as computing scientists, electrical engineers, telecommunications experts
- created new IT jobs such as web masters and online marketing experts
- changed skill levels for non-IT jobs; for example, motor mechanics now use computers to test engines, etc.
- raised minimum skill requirements for many occupations.

As Internet adoption moves to a 'transaction' model, there is a growing need for increased integration of Internet front-end applications with enterprise operations, applications and back-end databases. The lack of staff to support ongoing Internet/intranet maintenance and development, coupled with integration problems and cost and time overruns, drives demand for outside services providers to help plan and implement solutions. Some companies are moving their information technology sectors to India where there is a large pool of IT workers and pay rates are lower. Countries such as Australia are losing many of their skilled IT workers to the United States and Europe where they can earn more money. Activities in demand include security design and firewall implementation, web page design and creation, and Internet/intranet application development.[36]

With the spread of electronic commerce, and the consequent re-engineering of business processes and changes in competitive paradigms, software will increasingly be used to create business value. Electronic commerce will thus sustain a high demand for IT personnel. This is expected to exacerbate what has been called a critical shortage of IT workers.

The same innovations in computing and telecommunications technologies that are rapidly creating jobs in some industries are causing jobs to be lost in other industries. This is referred to as a 'churning' effect in the US Government's *Digital Economy II* report. New occupations are being created while others are being redefined and workers must undertake continuing education and worker retraining. Workers of the twenty-first century must be 'multi-skilled' and commit to lifelong learning and retraining in order to remain flexible in rapidly changing labour markets.

The demand for skilled labour in the IT industry is being driven by the growth of IT itself as well as attrition among the work force. According to IDC, 20 per cent of IT jobs had to be filled in the United States alone in 1999. The lack of a skilled IT work force is a worldwide problem. By 2002, in Western Europe alone, there will be 1.4 million fewer skilled workers than IT jobs.[37]

Organisational life is also becoming much more fluid and dynamic with almost no 'standard' work day or working pattern. The Internet and intranets make possible 'anytime/anyplace' work. This flexibility is already enabling millions of individuals to work part-time or on a self-employed basis. (Refer to the idea of the 'business of one' as discussed in chapter 1.)

# INDUSTRY STRUCTURAL CHANGE

What we are seeing is a break with the traditional way of organising economies along industrial lines. This new economic model has portals emerging as a central plank and new intermediaries/infomediaries being established. Anthony deLeon of Andersen Consulting believes that as power shifts from industry to consumer, companies will move from industrial groupings to clusters of companies servicing particular types of customer desires, or intentions. It is a transition phase as the economy moves from its industrial framework to an electronic network. When the transition phase is over, the alliances will be more defined.

Successful companies in the new economic model will be the ones that know the most about their customers and follow customer relationship principles. They are able to bring together goods and services tailored to the individual customer, and delivered at a single time- and cost-effective point — the 'my' portal.

There is an increasing trend to the unbundling of organisational functions and in many cases the outsourcing and/or exsourcing of these. The Managed Funds Industry in Australia and internationally is such a case where investment application and redemption processes are outsourced. Often one provider will handle the functions of competing organisations. Such a move would not be possible without electronic commerce.

The electricity industry is another example. E-commerce is an important part of breaking the nexus between distribution and supply, which is at the heart of much restructuring in the electricity industry.

One of the key drivers to consolidation in the finance industry is the necessity of integrated e-commerce systems and the cost of developing them and integrating them with legacy systems. This is reinforced by increasing perceptions that customers are demanding bundled or 'wrapped' financial services, and the reality that start-up organisations are seeking to provide these. Banks in Australia have seized the opportunity to keep their customers coming back by offering other services as illustrated in 11.4 on the following page.

| TABLE 11.4 | BANKS ADD VALUE FOR CUSTOMERS |
|---|---|
| **BANK** | **OTHER OFFERINGS** |
| St George Bank, www.stgeorge.com.au | Shoplink online mall (www.shoplink.com.au) and eCash |
| National Australia Bank (NAB), www.nab.com.au | partnered with FreeOnline.com.au to give clients free access |
| Australian and New Zealand Bank (ANZ) www.anz.com.au | partnered with Free.net.au to give clients free access and joined with E*Trade to add share trading (www.etrade.com.au) |

*SOURCE:* adapted from D. Braue 2000, 'Bank portals could be the next Yahoo!', IT News, *Sydney Morning Herald*, 7 March, p. 3c

E-commerce can move markets towards much better information, and it is widely expected that wider market reach, a greater number of buyers and sellers in a market and improved information is leading to an irreversible shift in the balance of power between producer and consumer. It is possible that cooperative competition will continue indefinitely as the working model for the new economy. Cooperative competition ('coopertition' is the buzzword that has been coined) will continue indefinitely as the working model for the new economy. Pfaffenberger speaks of a value constellation where businesses look upon suppliers and customers as allies and consolidate the relationship with them.[38]

# THE NEXT GENERATION INTERNET

In 1996 a project known as **Internet2** was born in Chicago, involving more than 154 American universities together with representatives from a few high-tech and telecommunications companies. The project is establishing gigabit-per-second points of presence nationwide on a very-high-speed backbone network (vBNS). It will give people more control over how their information is used and, as it will be more secure, it will be of great interest to Internet commerce companies. Once the wide bandwidth represented by Internet2 moves from academia into the corporate world, a set of new, powerful web applications will appear.

In February 1999, Internet2 went live on the Abilene fibre optic network developed by the University Corporation for Advanced Development, Indiana University and corporate partners Cisco Systems, Nortel Networks and Qwest Communications International. The three companies have invested an estimated $US500 million in this superior Internet. With speeds up to 2.4 gigabits per second, Abilene is potentially 85 000 times faster than a standard 28-Kbps connection. The research effort is concentrated on higher bandwidth with the aim of making a large pipe available to everyone, including end users in their homes. And that is going to enable a new set of services and applications for home and business use.[39]

# SUMMARY

Internet commerce still has a long way to go. Building the infrastructure to do business on the Web will ultimately give way to a more mature, methodical approach to exploiting this new sales, marketing and customer-service channel while continuing to nurture and develop existing ones. The successful companies will create web-based efficiencies customers will embrace, although power will be transferred to those customers in the process.[40]

Technological innovation and the global expansion of commerce are the forces combining to contribute to the further growth of Internet commerce, particularly among the developing nations.

It is clear that the most important change that Internet commerce will bring will be the way businesses and people interact with one another and the way products and services will be offered. Aggregators, e-auctions and online exchanges will become the new electronic marketplaces of the future, running on broadband or on wireless or mobile appliances.

Differentiated and customised products will offer more choices than mass-produced goods, for which firms with sufficient economies of scale will have the cost advantage.

In this book we have considered digital models for both consumer and business-to business Internet commerce, we have explored the issues that in some ways are perceived to be obstacles to the further development of web commerce — issues such as security, taxation, and legal and ethical considerations, and we have speculated on future trends and the overall changing global marketplace.

Internet commerce will provide countless opportunities and challenges to our economies and societies. Traditional institutions, such as banks, universities, established business intermediaries, the media and publishing houses are now finding it necessary to redefine their roles in the new global commercial environment.

## key terms

| | | |
|---|---|---|
| aggregators | e-marketing | metadata |
| application service provider (ASP) | enterprise information portal (EIP) | network effects |
| | | online auction |
| business-to-business | home base | portal |
| corporate intranet | hub | viral marketing |
| Dot Com economy | Internet2 | virtual private network (VPN) |
| e-loyalty program | knowledge management | |

## WEB SERVICES DISPLACE SOFTWARE

... Increased use of the Internet will cause competitive pressure to change in the markets for many kinds of packaged software. In our November briefing, we discussed a new type of business model — Web services. As Internet technology continues to mature in 1999, Web-based services will become an increasingly significant component of the business plans of software developers, electronic commerce vendors, and other Internet companies.

Presently the new business model takes three different shapes. First, software vendors have determined that many products they once delivered as packaged applications can be more economically sold, distributed, and maintained as networked services managed remotely. Second, numerous companies are giving away Web-based services so that they can fuel product sales on their sites. And a third group is also giving away similar services, but in the hopes of attracting traffic for advertising or other subsidiary revenues.

Included in the first category are companies that use the network to run applications for maintaining their customers' payroll, benefits, and human resource records, as well as companies like Portal Software, which distributes a billing application to a client's network and manages it over the Web. Such software used to be delivered on shrink-wrapped CD-ROMS or floppy disks that had to be installed on every computer that required access to them; now the programs are stored on a remote server managed by the service provider, and employees of the customer company can access the data using their Web browsers. Upgrades, installation, and other technical hassles are offloaded onto the service provider.

Fees for such services are generally based on a subscription model — a significant change for application developers, which formerly relied on large, lump-sum payments that were subject to delay or cancellation by clients. Subscription-style payments can also help buyers, who can pay for as much or as little of the service as they need incrementally.

A second use of Web services is illustrated by Cisco Systems, which this year will generate about half its revenues from online sales. By enhancing online transactions with Web-based product-configuration services and technical consultations — some of which are free — Cisco directly encourages customers to return to its site to purchase additional goods.

Internet supersites like Amazon.com illustrate the third type of Web-services business model. The online bookseller's recent purchases of PlanetAll and Junglee allow it to offer free electronic address books and comparison shopping, respectively. Although the shopping service may sometimes refer users to competing sites, Amazon.com hopes that both services will entice consumers to make it their 'home' retailing site for books and other merchandise. In theory, this additional traffic will then translate indirectly into more sales.

As corporations continue to increase their reliance on the Internet, the Web-services business models will become more widespread. By the end of 1999, we're sure to see companies from many different industries making Internet-distributed services an essential part of their plans for growth ...

**SOURCE:** *Red Herring Magazine* 1998, from 'Ten Trends for the Post-PC World', December, www.redherring.com/mag/issue61/trends.html

## QUESTIONS

1. How do the business models for aggregators/portals and web services differ? How are they the same?
2. Name three companies you are aware of that are now offering web-based services for software access and usage.
3. Do you think that web-based distribution services will accelerate the uptake of e-commerce by small- and medium-sized enterprises?
4. What other industries might make use of Internet-distributed services, other than the software industry?
5. Do you believe this statement may be true? '**Application service providers (ASPs)** (web-based service providers) may soon replace ISPs.'

**QUESTIONS**

1. What do you believe are the main inhibitors of Australian companies taking up Internet commerce at this point?
2. What new media, apart from television and mobile telephony, do you think may deliver Internet-based commercial transactions and business information in the future?
3. Are there some aspects of business which do not lend themselves to online delivery? Explain.
4. Will some countries' economies be disadvantaged because of the Internet? Explain.
5. Will 'e-business' just be 'business' in the near future? Explain.
6. Make five predictions for future trends in Internet commerce in the next decade.
7. If usage costs dramatically increase, will Internet users use the Internet?
8. Will the global marketplace diminish?
9. What are the other possibilities for next generation Internets?

## SUGGESTED READING

Aldrich, D. F. 1999, *Mastering the Digital Marketplace: Practical Strategies for Competitiveness in the New Economy,* John Wiley and Sons, Inc., New York.

Hagel, J. and Singer, M. 1999, *Net Worth*, Harvard Business School Press, United States.

Herzenberg, S., Alic, J. A. and Wial H. 1998, *New Rules for a New Economy: Employment and Opportunity in Post-Industrial America*, Cornell University Press, United States.

Kalakota, R. and Robinson, M. 1999, *E-Business: Roadmap for Success*, Addison-Wesley Longman, United States.

Kelly, K. 1998, *New Rules for the New Economy: 10 Radical Strategies for a Connected World*, Viking Press, United States.

Mougayar, W. 1997, *Opening Digital Markets: Battle Plans and Business Strategies for Internet Commerce*, McGraw-Hill, United States.

Seybold, P. B and Marshak, R. 1998, *Customers.Com: How to Create a Profitable Business Strategy for the Internet and Beyond*, Times Books, United States.

Shapiro, C. and Varian, H. R. 1998, *Information Rules: A Strategic Guide to the Network Economy*, Harvard Business School Press, United States.

Tapscott, D., Lowy, A. and Ticoll, D. 1998, *Blueprint to the Digital Economy: Wealth Creation in the Era of E-Business*, McGraw-Hill, United States.

Tapscott, D. 1997, *Growing Up Digital: The Rise of the Net Generation*, McGraw-Hill, United States.

Ware, J., Gebauer, J., Hartman, A. and Roldan, M. 1998, *The Search for Digital Excellence*, McGraw-Hill, United States.

## END NOTES

1. Kenney, M. and Curry, J. 1999, *E-Commerce: Implications for Firm Strategy and Industry Configuration*, July, E-conomy Project working paper, Berkeley Roundtable on the International Economy (BRIE), http://brie.berkeley.edu/~briewww/pubs/wp/ewp2.html.

2. *E-Commerce Today* 2000, 'Security "exsourcing" emerges in Australia', issue 79, 24 February, www.ecommercetoday.com.au.

3. Department of Commerce 1999, *Emerging Digital Economy II*, 22 June, United States Government, www.ecommerce.gov/ede/report.html.

4. Mougayar, W. 1998, 'Buy land while land is cheap' and Wilder, C. 1998, 'Peer into the Net's future', *InformationWeek*, 4 May, www.informationweek.com.

5. Jonas, D. 1999, *Future Trends in E-Commerce*, ETC Electronic Trading Concepts presentation.

6. Ransdell, E. 1999, 'Network effects', *Fast Company*, issue 27, p. 208.

7. Duvall, M. 1999, 'To spin off or not to spin off', *Inter@ctive Week*, 18 October, www.zdnet.com.

8. Jackson, D. 2000, 'Dashing for dot.coms', *Australian*, 7 March 2000, p. 38, www.australianIT.com.au.

9. Davidson, J. 1999, 'Evolving e-economy shifts the balance of power', *Australian Financial Review*, 12 March.

10. McCarthy, T. 2000, 'China dot now — Joseph Tong: Meetchina.com', *Asia Time*, 28 February 2000, p. 18.

11. Du Pre Gauntt, J. 1999 'The network is the market: financing Internet bandwidth', *On the Internet*, January/February, pp. 22–9.

12. Power, T. and Jerjian, G. 1999, *The Battle of the Portals*, The Ecademy, England, www.theecademy.com, pp. 82–4.

13. Berst, J. 1998, 'What's next after portals?', *ZDNet AnchorDesk*, 1 July, www.zdnet.com/anchordesk/story/story_2263.html.

14. Ellis, J. 1999, 'Change partners', *Fast Company*, issue 28, p. 351.

15. Du Pre Gauntt, J., op. cit.

16. Clark, T. 1999, 'Sites redefine buying online', *CNET News.com*, 24 February, www.cnet.com.

17. Huang, M. 1999, *First VPN Virtual Private Network*, October, www.FirstVPN.com.

18. Atre, S. 1999, 'Enterprise information portals, the right way', 18 May, *PlanetIT*, www.planetit.com.

19. McGovern, G. 1999, 'The Web and the TV', *New Thinking*, NUA web site, 24 May, www.nua.ie/newthinking/archives/newthinking323/index.html.

20. *Executive Edge*, 1999, 'Strategic planning assumption', May, GartnerGroup, www.ee-online.com.

21. Smith, B. 1999, 'Wireless Wakes up to E-Commerce', *Wireless Week*, 1 February, wweb@cahners.com.

22. Birch, D. 1999, 'Mobile financial services: the Internet is not the only new digital channel', *Electronic Markets, Business Briefing: Electronic Commerce: An Analysis of Electronic Commerce and Perspectives on the Future*, World Markets Research Centre, England, p. 97.

23. *Red Herring Magazine* 1998, 'Ten trends for the post-PC world', December, www.redherring.com/mag/issue61/trends.html.

24. Ransdell, op. cit.

25. ibid.

26. Bridge news 2000, 'Web ad policy a "mistake"', *Australian*, 7 March, p. 3.

27. ibid.

28. Stear, E. 1999, 'Stampede: are Internet trading stamps the key to customer retention?', *Executive Edge*, GartnerGroup, October–November issue, www.ee-online.com/oct/oct_tech.htm.

29. Alliance for Global Business 1999, *Trade-Related Aspects of Electronic Commerce*, World Trade Organisation, April, www.wto.org.

30. Curran, S. 1999, 'Regional Summit Tool Kit — Practical Leadership Strategies', Online Australia Conference, April, www.onlineaustralia.net.au.

31. Department of Commerce, op. cit.

32. *Red Herring Magazine*, op. cit.

33. Organisation for Economic Cooperation and Development 1999, *The Economic and Social Impacts of Electronic Commerce: Preliminary Findings and Research Agenda*, February.

34. ibid.

35. Department of Commerce, op. cit.

36. Organisation for Economic Cooperation and Development, op. cit.

37. International Data Centre 1999, 'The workforce of the information age is changing even faster than the information technology' press release, 22 February, www.idc.com/Press/default.htm.

38. Pfaffenberger, B. 1998, *Building a Strategic Extranet*, IDG Books, United States, p. 6.

39. Wilcox, J. 1999, 'Expanding the information highway', *TechWeb*, 6 July.

40. Kindel, S. 1999, 'Reassessing e-Commerce', *Executive Edge*, GartnerGroup, February–March, www.ee-online.

# Web sites listed by chapter

# APPENDIX 1

www.ssw.com.au
*SSW Database and Internet Consultants, Sydney*

www.davidjones.com.au
*David Jones*

www.cyberconsult.com.au
*Cyber.Consult*

www.setco.org
*Secure Electronic Transaction*

www.openbuy.org
*Open Buying on the Internet (OBI) Consortium*

www.consult.com.au
*www.consult*

www.sydneywater.com.au
*Sydney Water*

www.fairfax.com.au
*John Fairfax Holdings*

www.aptstrategies.com.au
*APT Strategies*

http://ozsearch.com.au
*OzSearch Internet Guide*

www.cisco.com
*Cisco Systems*

www.icann.org
*Internet Corporation for Assigned Names and Numbers*

www.noie.gov.au
*National Office for the Information Economy*

www.iana.org
*Internet Assigned Numbers Authority*

www.aunic.net
*Aunic Registry*

www.apnic.net
*Asia Pacific Network Information Centre*

www.internic.net
*Internet Network Information Centre*

http://arin.net
*American Registry of Internet Numbers*

www.ina.com.au
*Internet Names Australia*

www.auda.org.au
*.au Domain Administration*

www.netregistry.com.au
*NetRegistry*

www.hills.com.au
*Hills Industries*

## CHAPTER 2   Business models for Internet commerce

www.anzwers.com.au
*ANZWERS search engine*

www.rpdata.net.au
*RP Equipment*

www.successful.com
*Successful.com*

www.ninemsn.com.au
*ninemsn*

www.yellowpages.com.au
*Yellow Pages*

www.socs.uts.edu.au/cpe/
*Continuing Professional Education (CPE), University of Technology, Sydney*

www.woolworths.com.au
*Woolworths*

www.sofcom.com.au
*Sofcom*

www.gw2k.com.au
*Gateway 2000 Australia*

www.coop-bookshop.com.au
*Co-op Bookshop*

www.wineplanet.com
*The Wine Planet*

www.hilton.com/hotels/ADLHITW/index.html
*Adelaide Hilton Hotel*

www.sold.com.au
*Sold.com.au*

www.priceline.com
*Priceline.com*

www.ebay.com
*eBay*

www.cba.uga.edu/~rwatson/iim
*Site on Integrated Internet Marketing*

www.zdnet.com/enterprise/e-business/solutions/stories/0,5918,2315043,00.html
*Story on Internet commerce*

## CHAPTER 3   Technology basics

www.blackwell-science.com/products/journals/isj.htm
**MISQ** *and* **Information Systems Journal**

www.autobytel.com
*Autobytel*

www.asx.com.au
*Australian Stock Exchange*

www-cec.buseco.monash.edu.au
*Centre for Electronic Commerce at Monash University*

http://home.netscape.com
*Net Search*

www.disney.go.com
*Disney*

www.netscape.com/netcenter/index.html
*Netscape*

www.microsoft.com
*Microsoft*

www.public.iastate.edu/~PremCourses/dutchauc.html
*Competition in the Dutch Flower Markets*

www.isworld.org/isworld/ecourse
*Site for e-commerce resources*

www.time.com
*Time's Pathfinder web site*

www.davnet.com
*Davnet*

www.optusnet.com.au
*Optusnet*

www.tradegate.org.au
*Tradegate ECA*

www.gateway.com/accessories/
*Gateway Accessory Store*

www.wap.org
*Wireless Application Protocol*

www.mp3.com
*MP3*

www.cisco.com/universal/data/doc/cintrnet/ito/55168.htm
*Cisco Systems*

www.ninemsn.com.au
*NineMSN*

www.lycos.com
*Lycos*

www.excite.com
*Excite*

www.violet.com
*Gift service*

www.ibook.com
*iBook — online publisher*

www.infocus.com
*InFocus — online publisher*

www.groupweb.com.email/es_soft.htm
*Groupweb Directories*

www.w3.org/hypertext/www/History/1989/proposal.html
*WWW Consortium*

www.mastercard.com/press/970718a.html
*MasterCard*

Internet Commerce: Digital Models for Business

www.jcc.com/sql_stnd.html
*SQL Standards Home Page*

www.goliath.wpine.com.au/cu-seeme.html
*Information on the development of CU-SEEME*

www.oasis-open.org
*Organisation for the Advancement of Structured Information Standards*

www.wingspan.com
*WingSpanBank*

www.napster.com
*Napster for MP3*

## CHAPTER 4 World Wide Web commerce

www.dell.com.ap/au/index.htm
*Dell Computer*

www.davidjones.com.au
*David Jones*

www.ht.com.au
*Harris Technology*

www.abc.net.au
*ABC Online*

www.greengrocer.com.au
*Greengrocer.com.au*

www.librgirl.com.au
*Sancella (Libra products)*

www.cyberhorse.com.au
*Everything to do with Horses*

www.shark.com
*Greg Norman site*

www.oncourt.com
*Patrick Rafter tennis site*

www.netcraft.co.hk.survey
*Netcraft web server survey*

www.iko.com.au
*Interactive Knowledge Online*

www.cart32.com
*Cart 32 Shopping cart*

www.interworld.com
*Interworld*

www.WingspanBank.com
*WingspanBank*

www.qantas.com.au
*Qantas*

www.theecademy.com
*The Ecademy*

www.ecommercetoday.com.au
*E-Commerce Today*

www.unece.org/trade/untdid/texts/d422_d.htm
*Electronic Data Interchange for Administration, Commerce and Transport*

www.edi.wales.org/cstudie4.htm#Catnic
*Catnic Group*

www.epf.net/Prev.Mtngs/Jan97.Mtng/Presentations/Odell/sld002.htm
*Electronic Payments Forum*

http://digicash.com
*eCash Technologies Inc.*

www.cybercash.com
*CyberCash Inc.*

www.cs.newcastle.edu.au/Research/pabolins/mseg.html
*University of Newcastle*

www.adb.org
*Asian Development Bank*

www.internet.net
*Internet Shopping Network*

www.yahoo.com/Business_and Economy/Electronic_Commerce/
www.yahoo.com/Entertainment/Automobiles/General_Motors
*Yahoo!*

www.southwire.com/wgta/mempages/cemc/cemcover.htm
*Southwire Company*

www.interaccess.com:80/users/numusic
*InterAccess ISP*

www.lubricants.dupont.com:80/
*Krytox Performance Lubricants*

www.microsoft.com/indonesia/EVENTS/SLIDES/TrackC-3_files/
frame.htm#slide0108.htm
*Microsoft*

www.mastercard.com/set/
*MasterCard*

www.zdnet.com/zdnn/content/inwo/0323/296952.htm
*ZDNet*

www.idg.net/new_docids/transaction/electronic/internet/vendors/secure/even/
popularizing/implementedmew_docid_9-48998.html
*IDG Online Network*

www1.bnm.gov.my
*Bank Negara, Malaysia*

www.bot.or.th/bank/public/findata/Mbpolicy/MonetaryPolicy.htm
*Bank of Thailand*

www.asic.gov.au
*Australian Securities and Investments Commission*

www.apca.com.au/Paymentsystems.htm#Financial
*Australian Payments Clearing Association*

www.anu.edu.au/people/Roger.Clarke/ElectronicCommerce/EPMIssues
*Roger Clarke's Electronic Commerce Pages, Australian National University*

www.ivans.com/about/index.cfm
*IVANS, Inc.*

www.neology.com/portfolio/fstc.cfm
*Neology Information Design*

http://mir.com.my/lb/econ_plan/contents/press_release/110899merge.htm
*Malaysian Internet Resources*

CHAPTER 6 **Security issues, networks and electronic commerce**

www.genome.wi.mit.edu/WWW/faqs/wwwsf1.html
*World Wide Web Consortium*

www.auscert.org.au
*Australian Computer Emergency Response Team*

www.cert.org
*Computer Emergency Response Team*

www.ec.gov.sg/policy.html
*EC Business Policy Helpdesk, Singapore*

CHAPTER 7 **The Internet customer**

www.nua.ie/surveys
*NUA Internet Surveys*

www.inter-Merchant.com
*Inter-Merchant*

www.doubleclick.com.au
*DoubleClick*

www.digitalme.com
*Novell, digitalme*

www.novell.com/lead_stories/1999/oct05/index.html
*Novell*

www.ansett.com.au
*Ansett*

www.barnesandnoble.com
*Barnes and Noble*

www.aol.com
*American Online*

www.CDNow.com
*CDNow*

www.nrma.com.au
*NRMA*

www.amazon.com
*Amazon*

www.smh.com.au
**Sydney Morning Herald**

www.emarketer.com
**eMarketer**

www.sunherald.com.au
**Sun Herald**

http://advisor.internet.ibm.com/inet.nsf
*Commerce Assistant program on IBM site*

www-personal.umich.edu/~sgupta/hermes/
*Hermes Survey Consumer Survey of World Wide Web Users*

www.ecommercetoday.com.au
**E-Commerce Today**

www.washingtonpost.com
**Washington Post**

| CHAPTER 8 | **Organisational communication** |
|---|---|

www.commerce.net
*CommerceNet*

www.octel.com
*Octel Messaging*

www.news.com.au
*The* **Australian**

www.messenger.com
*Octel Messaging*

www1.sinet.uq.edu.au/sinet6/home/default.asp
*University of Queensland Student Information Net*

www.cisco.com
*Cisco Systems*

www.woolworths.com.au/vendorguide/index.stm
*Woolworths*

www.ford.com.au
*Ford Australia*

www.employment.com.au
*Commonwealth Government Employment site*

| CHAPTER 9 | **Taxation of Internet commerce** |
|---|---|

www.teletask.com.au
*Teletask*

www.datamation.com
*Datamation*

www.sigraf.co.yu/sigraf/oblasti/sgi/www/intmain.html
*SiGraf WEB*

www.pctoday.com
**PC Today**

www.ecommercetoday.com.au
**E-Commerce Today**

www.sunherald.com.au
**Sun Herald**

www.ispo.ce.be/ecommerce
*European Union's 1997 Communication*

www.oecd.org/dsti/sti/it/ec/index.htm
*Organisation for Economic Cooperation and Development*

www.revenue.irglov.ie
*Irish government paper on eCommerce and the Irish Tax system*

www.offshore.com.ai
*Vince Cate site*

www.smh.com.au
**Sydney Morning Herald**

www.news.com.au
*The* **Australian**

www.ato.gov.au
*Australian Tax Office*

www.afr.com.au
**Australian Financial Review**

www.iitf.nist.gov/eleccomm/ecomm.html
*Information Infrastructure Task Force*

www.nhdd.com/nta/ntaintro.htm
*United States National Tax Association Tax Project*

http://e-com.ic.gc.ca
*Canadian Electronic Commerce Strategy*

www.connect.gc.ca.
*Connecting Canadians*

www.taxia.com.au
*Taxation Institute of Australia*

www.cpaonline.com.au
*Australian Society of Certified Practising Accountants*

| CHAPTER 10 | **Legal and ethical issues** |
| --- | --- |

www.nytimes.com
**New York Times**

www.gilc.org
*Global Internet Liberty Campaign*

www.icra.org
*Internet Content Rating Association*

www.tio.com.au
*Telecommunications Industry Ombudsman*

www.aba.gov.au
*Australian Broadcasting Association*

www.iia.net.au
*Internet Industry Association*

www.efa.org.au
*Electronic Frontiers Australia*

www.isoc-au.org.au
*Internet Society of Australia*

www.netnanny.com
*Net Nanny*

www.qantm.com.au/copyright
*The Copyright Page*

www.copyright.org.au
*Australian Copyright Council*

www.law.gov.au/publications/copyright_enews
*Copyright Amendment (Digital Agenda) Act 1999*

www.ipaustralia.gov.au
*IP Australia*

www.internetnamesww.com.au
*Internet Names Worldwide Domain Registration*

www.austlii.edu.au/do/disp.pl/au/cases/nsw/supreme_ct/1999/526.html
**Macquarie Bank Limited and Anor v. Berg** *[1999] NSWSC 526 (2 June 1999)*

www.unictral.org/en-index.htm
*United Nations Commission on International Trade Law*

www.mastercard.com/set/
*MasterCard, Secure Electronic Transaction (SET) Protocol*

www.treasury.gov.au/publications/consumeraffairs/electroniccommercepublications/
aapolicyframeworkforconsumerprotectioninelectroniccommerce/index.asp
*Treasury Department 1999,* **A Policy Framework for Consumer Protection in Electronic Commerce,** *October*

www.treasury.gov.au/publications/consumeraffairs/electroniccommercepublications/
consumerprotectioninelectroniccommerce%2Dprinciplesandkeyissues/contents.asp
*National Advisory Council on Consumer Affairs 1998,* **Consumer Protection in Electronic Commerce — Principles and Key Issues,** *April*

www.treasury.gov.au/publications/consumeraffairs/electroniccommercepublications/
shoppingontheinternet%2Dfactsforconsumers/index.asp
*Treasury Department and National Office for the Information Economy in the Department of Communications, Information Technology and the Arts 1999,* **Shopping on the Internet — Facts for Consumers**

http://europa.eu.int/
*European Commission*

www.trustedpc.org
*Trusted Computing Platform Alliance*

http://abanet.org/scitech/ec/isc/dsg.html
*American Bar Association,* **Digital Signature Guidelines,** *ABA Section of Science and Technology, Information Security Committee*

www.vic.gov.au
*Victorian Government*

www.privacy.gov.au/publications/index.html
*Australian Privacy Commissioner*

www2.echo.lu/legal/en/datprot/directiv/directiv.html.
*European Union directive on the protection of individuals with regard to the processing of personal data and the free movement of such data*

www.hmso.gov.uk/acts/acts1998/19980029.htm
*United Kingdom's* **Data Protection Act 1998**

www.acs.org.au/national/pospaper/acs131.htm
*Australian Computer Society Code of Ethics*

www.aice.swin.edu.au/events/AICEC99/
**Proceedings of the Australian Institute of Computer Ethics Conference,** *14–16 July 1999*

## CHAPTER 11  Future trends

www.ecommerce.gov/ede/report.html
*Emerging Digital Economies II*

www.docspace.com
*docSpace*

www.consult.com
*www.consult*

www.ecademy.com
*The Ecademy*

www.pathfinder.com/fortune
*Fortune.com*

www.supplysearch.com.au
*SupplySearch*

www.meetchina.com
*MeetChina.com*

www.gofish.com.au
*goFish*

www.stuff.com.au
*Stuff Online Auction*

www.priceline.com
*Priceline.com*

www.telegeography.com
*TeleGeography, Inc.*

www3.mids.org
*MIDS*

www.paperexchange.com
*Paperexchange.com*

www.elaunceston.com
*Launceston's Community Portal*

www.women.com
*Women.com*

www.mymanchester.net
*MyManchester*

www.arbinet.com
*Arbinet*

www.band-x.com
*Band-X*

www.rateXchange.com
*RateXchange*

www.verticalnet.com
*VerticalNet*

www.ebay.com
*eBay*

www.kcfishnet.com
*FishNet Securities*

www.techweb.com
**TechWeb**

www.planetit.com
**PlanetIT**

www.internetweek.com
**InternetWeek**

www.wired.com/news/
**Wired News**

www.homestead.com
*Homestead*

www.netzero.com
*Netzero ISP*

www.netmind.com.
*Net Mind*

www.ecommercetimes.com
**E-Commerce Times**

www.trendmicro.com
*Trend Micro, Inc.*

www.usps.com
*United States Postal Service*

www.stgeorge.com.au
*St George Bank*

www.nab.com.au
*National Australia Bank (NAB)*

www.anz.com.au
*Australian and New Zealand Bank (ANZ)*

www.etrade.com.au
*E\*Trade*

www.business.gov.au
*Commonwealth Government Business site*

www.wto.org
*World Trade Organisation*

www.nue.ie
*Nua*

www.ee-online.com
**Executive Edge**

www.ecommercetoday.com.au
**E-Commerce Today**

www.redherring.com
**Red Herring** *Communications*

www.zdnet.com
*ZDNet*

www.oecd.org
*Organisation for Economic Cooperation and Development*

# APPENDIX 2

**Web
sites
listed
by
industry**

## Banking/Finance

www.anz.com.au
*ANZ Bank*

www.amp.com.au
*AMP Society*

www.afr.com.au
**Australian Financial Review**

www.asx.com.au
*Australian Stock Exchange*

www.axa.com.au
*AXA Australia*

www.colonialfirststate.com.au
*Colonial First State Investments*

www.citicorp.com.au
*Citicorp Bank*

www.commbank.com.au
*Commonwealth Bank*

www.eyonline.com.au
*Ernst and Young Online*

www.macquarie.com.au
*Macquarie Bank*

www.mastercard.com
*MasterCard*

www.national.com.au
*National Australia Bank*

www.pricewaterhousecoopers.com
*Price Waterhouse Coopers*

www.stgeorge.com.au
*St George Bank*

www.tradewizard.com.au
*Trade Wizard Pty Ltd*

www.westpac.com.au
*Westpac Bank*

## Computer industry

www.adobe.com
*Adobe Systems Inc.*

www.allaire.com
*Allaire Grap*

www.apple.com
*Apple Computers*

www.aiia.com.au
*Australian Information Industry Association*

www.brother.com
*Brother Corporation*

www.compaq.com.au
*Compaq*

www.dell.com.au
*Dell Computer*

www.estrategies.com.au
*eStrategies — e-commerce consulting*

www.firmware.com.au
*Firmware*

www.hotwired.com/synapse
*Synapse: technology, culture and society*

www.ibm.com
*IBM Corporation*

www.interworld.com
*InterWorld*

www.macromedia.com
*Macromedia*

www.microsoft.com
*Microsoft Corporation*

www.netscape.com
*Netscape*

www.oracle.com
*Oracle*

www.ozemail.com.au
*Ozemail*

www.sap.com
*SAP*

www.sausage.com.au
*Sausage Software*

www.sun.com
*Sun Systems*

www.ssw.com.au
*Superior Software*

www.tpis.com.au
*TP Information Systems*

www.unisys.com
*Unisys*

www.wired.com
**Wired News**

www.yahoo.com
*Yahoo!*

## Indigenous organisations

www.atsic.gov.au
*Aboriginal and Torres Strait Islander Commission (ATSIC)*

www.aiatsis.gov.au/index.htm
*Australian Institute of Aboriginal and Torres Strait Islander Studies*

www.alga.com.ai/indig.htm
*Australian Local Government Association — Indigenous Issues*

www.austlii.edu.au/car/
*Council for Aboriginal Reconciliation*

www.indiginet.com.au
*Jumbonna — UTS, Centre for Australian Indigenous Studies*

www.koori.usyd.edu.au
*Koori Centre, University of Sydney*

www.auckland.ac.nz/lbr/maori.htm
*Maori Electronic Resources*

www.nntt.gov.au
*National Native Title Tribunal*

www.webmedia.com.au/tandaya
*Tandanya — Australian Aboriginal Cultural Institute*

## Insurance

www.ampgeneral.com.au
*AMP General*

www.aii.com.au
*Australian Insurance Institute*

www.axa.com.au
*AXA Australia*

www.colonial.com.au
*Colonial Group*

www.fai.com.au
*FAI Insurance*

www.hannangroup.com.au
*Hannan Group Global Insurance Solutions*

www.ica.com.au
*Insurance Council of Australia*

www.iinz.org.nz
*Insurance Institute of New Zealand*

www.lawcover.com.au
*Lawcover — Professional Indemnity Insurance*

www.legalandgeneral.com.au
*Legal and General Australia*

www.qbe.com.au
*QBE Insurance Group*

## Law

www.auslii.edu.au
*Australian Legal Information Institute*

www.copyright.org.au
*Australian Copyright Council Home Page*

www.the-bar.com.au
*Barristers' Reference Page*

www.butterworths.com.au
*Butterworths: Legal Publishers*

www.cch.com.au
*CCH Australia*

www.fitzroy-legal.org.au
*Fitzroy Legal Service Online*

www.fl.asn.au
*Foundation Law*

www.lawcouncil.asn.au
*Law Council of Australia*

www.lawnet.com.au
*Ozemail LawNet*

www.aph.gov.au
*Parliament of Australia*

www.phillipsfox.com.au
*Phillips Fox Lawyers*

www.law.house.gov/
*US House of Representatives*

## Mining and manufacturing

www.amcor.com.au
*AMCOR*

www.bhp.com.au
*BHP*

www.boeing.com
*Boeing*

www.csr.com.au
*CSR*

www.ford.com.au
*Ford Australia*

www.gec.com
*General Electric*

www.hills.com.au
*Hills Industries*

www.johnsonjohnson.com
*Johnson & Johnson*

www.kelloggs.co.uk
*Kelloggs, UK*

www.mim.com.au
*MIM Holdings*

www.mot.com
*Motorola*

www.riotinto.com
***Rio Tinto***

www.samsung.com
***Samsung Electronics***

www.toyota.com.au
***Toyota***

www.wmc.com.au
***WMC Ltd***

## Popular culture

www.australian.aust.com
***The* Australian Online**

www.abc.net.au
***Australian Broadcasting Corporation***

www.cdnow.com
***CDNow***

www.eonline.com
***eOnline***

www.sofcom.com.au/TV/
**Australian TV Guide**

www.dominis.com/Zines
***E-Zines Database***

www.foxtel.com.au
***Foxtel***

www.mtv.com
***MTV***

www.mca.com.au
***Museum of Contemporary Art, New York***

www.nme.com
***New Musical Express***

www.theonion.com
**The Onion**

www.pccmag.com/toc.html
**PopCulture-Corn *Magazine***

www.rollingstone.com
**Rolling Stone *Magazine***

www.sanity.com.au
***Sanity***

www.sony.com
***Sony***

www.wired.com
**Wired News**

## Retail

www.amazon.com
*Amazon*

www.the-body-shop.com
*The Body Shop*

www.dstore.com.au
*DStore*

www.esprit.com
*Esprit*

www.gleebooks.com.au
*Gleebooks*

www.greengrocer.com.au
*Greengrocer Online*

www.interflora.com.au
*Interflora, Australian Unit*

www.myerdirect.com.au
*Myer Direct On-line*

www.ozvideo.com.au
*OzVideo — Online Video Supermarket*

www.plusone.com.au
*Plus One Marketing: Australian Business Bookshop (can pay with e-cash)*

www.radiorentals.com.au
*Radio Rentals*

www.realestate.com.au
*Real Estate.com*

www.travel.com
*Travel.com*

www.toyspot.com
*Toyspot*

www.virtual-showroom.co.uk
*Virtual Showroom — Vehicles*

www.woolworths.com.au
*Woolworths*

## Sport

www.arl.org.au
*Australian Rugby League*

www.ausport.gov.au
*Australian Sports Commission*

www.australian.aust.com/sport.htm
*The Australian Online: Sport*

www.bathurst100.com.au
*Bathurst 100*

www.aus.cricket.org
*CricInfo — The Home of Cricket on the Internet*

www.golf.com.au
*Australian golf site*

www.horsenet.com.au/raceclub.htm
*HorseNet Australian Racing Directory*

www.ninemsn.com.au/homepage.asp
*Wide World of Sports*

www.ozsports.com.au
*Links to Australian Sports Sites*

www.pgatour.com
*PGA Tour site*

www.scrum.com
*Rugby Union*

www.exploratorium.edu.sports/index.html
*Sport!Science*

www.S2h.tas.gov.au
*Sydney-to-Hobart Yacht Race*

www.olympic.org/games/sydney
*Sydney 2000 — Games of the XXVII Olympiad*

www.corelwtatour.com
*Women's Tennis Circuit*

## Tourism/hotels

www.australia.com
*Australian Tourist Commission*

www.biztravel.com
*Biztravel.com: the Internet company for business travellers*

www.bookit.com.au
*Bookit Online*

www.thetrip.com
*Business Travel Information/Services*

www.tourism.gov.au/welcome.html
*Department of Tourism*

www.fodors.com
*Fodors Travel Online*

www.frommers.com
*Frommer's Encyclopedia of Travel*

www.itn.com
*Internet Travel Network*

www.lonelyplanet.com.au
**Lonely Planet** *Travel Guide*

www.expedia.msn.com
*Microsoft Expedia*

www.peppers.com.au
*Peppers Hotel Group Australia*

www.rydges.com.au
*Rydges Hotels and Resorts*

www.statravel.com.au
*STA Travel*

## Universities — Australia

www.acu.edu.au
*Australian Catholic University*

www.adfa.oz.au
*Australian Defence Force Academy*

www.anu.edu.au
*Australian National University*

www.bond.edu.au
*Bond University*

www.cqu.edu.au
*Central Queensland University*

www.csu.edu.au
*Charles Sturt University*

www.curtin.edu.au
*Curtin University of Technology*

www.deakin.edu.au
*Deakin University*

www.cowan.edu.au
*Edith Cowan University*

www.flinders.edu.au
*Flinders University*

www.gu.edu.au
*Griffith University*

www.jcu.edu.au
*James Cook University*

www.latrobe.edu.au
*Latrobe University*

www.mq.edu.au
*Macquarie University*

www.monash.edu.au
*Monash University*

www.murdoch.edu.au
*Murdoch University*

www.ntu.edu.au
*Northern Territory University*

www.qut.edu.au
*Queensland University of Technology*

www.rmit.edu.au
*Royal Melbourne Institute of Technology*

www.scu.edu.au
*Southern Cross University*

www.swin.edu.au
*Swinburne University of Technology*

www.adelaide.edu.au
*University of Adelaide*

www.ballarat.edu.au
*University of Ballarat*

www.canberra.edu.au
*University of Canberra*

www.unimelb.edu.au
*University of Melbourne*

www.une.edu.au
*University of New England*

www.newcastle.edu.au
*University of Newcastle*

www.nd.edu.au
*University of Notre Dame*

www.unsw.edu.au
*University of New South Wales*

www.uq.edu.au
*University of Queensland*

www.usyd.edu.au
*University of Sydney*

www.unisa.edu.au
*University of South Australia*

www.usq.edu.au
*University of Southern Queensland*

www.utas.edu.au
*University of Tasmania*

www.uts.edu.eu
*University of Technology, Sydney*

www.uwa.edu.au
*University of Western Australia*

www.hawkesbury.uws.edu.au
*University of Western Sydney, Hawkesbury*

www.macarthur.uws.edu.au
*University of Western Sydney, Macarthur*

www.nepean.uws.edu.au
*University of Western Sydney, Nepean*

www.uow.edu.au
*University of Wollongong*

www.vut.edu.au
*Victoria Institute of Technology*

## Universities — New Zealand

www.aut.ac.nz
*Auckland Institute of Technology*

www.canterbury.ac.nz
*Canterbury University*

www.lincoln.ac.nz
*Lincoln University*

www.massey.ac.nz
*Massey University*

www.otago.ac.nz
*Otago University*

www.auckland.ac.nz
*Auckland University*

www.waikato.ac.nz
*Waikato University*

www.vuw.ac.nz
*Victoria University of Wellington*

## Universities — Other

www.bath.ac.uk
*University of Bath*

www.cam.ac.uk
*University of Cambridge*

www.harvard.edu
*Harvard University*

www.hku.hk
*University of Hong Kong*

www.nus.edu.sg
*National University of Singapore*

www.ox.ac.uk
*University of Oxford*

www.stanford.edu
*Stanford University*

www.taylors.edu.my
*Taylors College, Malaysia*

www.temple.edu
*Temple University*

# GLOSSARY

A useful web site for definitions is www.whatis.com.

**advertising:** the act or practice of bringing anything, such as a business activity, to the attention of the public

**Advertising model:** a business model based on offering advertising space on web pages to obtain revenue (*see also* banner advertisements)

**Affiliation model:** a business model that encourages web-site owners to sign up under what is known as an associate or affiliate program. For example, Amazon invites web-site owners to sign up to sell the bookseller's inventory. Once approved the affiliate is sent an email with instructions on how to set up links and banner ads. These affiliates do not directly sell but merely direct web surfers to the online store, which takes and fills the order. The merchant then pays the affiliate a small set fee for playing the rainmaker.

**agents:** electronic shopping software tools that assist users to search the Internet for product items. Users interact with a shopping agent by submitting agent requests. The agent then searches relevant online shops for items matching the search criteria. One example is the web site at www.mysimon.com.

**aggregators:** web sites that create a business community by pooling supplier content to create a searchable one-stop shopping mall with pre-defined prices for buyers within a business community. In business-to-consumer e-commerce, people (aggregators) band together to buy similar articles (such as Palm Pilots) in an attempt to drive down the price for each article as they are buying more than one.

**application service provider (ASP):** software providers who rent out rather than sell their software or part of their software to consumers

**AS 4269:** the Australian Standard for complaint resolution, which establishes the minimal conditions for resolving disputes

**attachments:** files, such as word-processed or spreadsheet files, that are sent along with an email.

Most email packages support several common standards for sending attachments across the Internet, such as UUencoding and MIME. Receivers of an attachment are then able to either save the attachment to their disk or launch the appropriate program to read the file (*see also* multipurpose Internet mail extensions)

**Auction model:** a business model that uses real-time or live auction bidding on the Internet

**AusCERT (Australian Computer Emergency Response Team):** a single, trusted point of contact in Australia for the Internet community to deal with computer security incidents and their prevention (www.auscert.org).

**authentication:** a means of countering the threat of masquerade. Online data and information transmission in electronic form require that the message sent reaches the intended recipient and only that recipient.

**availability:** a requirement so that the communications infrastructure and the network systems in place can receive and send information and data and enable electronic transactions in business

**banner advertisements:** passive advertisements that are encountered by simply visiting a web page. They usually appear across the top or bottom of web pages.

**bookmarking:** a means of creating a list, stored in a browser, of the title and URL of favourite pages or sites on the web. It assists users to quickly return to the web page in a future session. It is sometimes called a 'hotlist'.

**browser:** a software application used on the web that allows the user to navigate and view various Internet resources, move to other documents via hypertext, view images, listen to audio files, etc.

**business-to-business:** refers to companies doing business with other companies on public networks like the Internet and its derivations, extranets and intranets. Organisations benefit from having a common standard for information sharing and exchange. The outcome will mean shifting the business model from a supply chain to a supply web.

**censorship:** the suppression of material in media, such as books, films, etc., that is deemed to be objectionable on moral, political, military or other grounds

**CERT (Computer Emergency Response Team):** an overarching trusted point of contact for the Internet community to deal with computer security incidents and their prevention

**'click-through' advertising:** advertising on a web page that takes an Internet user to the site of the advertiser. By clicking on the advertisement, the user is routed to the advertiser's URL.

**'clicks and bricks' model:** (*see* 'clicks and mortar' approach)

**'clicks and mortar' approach:** refers to a business that has an online presence from which it sells its goods and also a physical presence from which it sells its goods. The idea is that a company actually gains an advantage by being able to serve customers wherever they happen to be — in a store, on the phone, online, offline or in an email program.

**common gateway interface (CGI):** specifies a standard mechanism for a web server to communicate with a script or program running on the same server in order to pass data between them

**comparison shopping:** being able to compare the prices of the same products in different outlets. In Internet commerce this can be achieved by using intelligent agents, which do the searching and return to the user a report showing product availability, price and a link to the relevant online stores.

**complaint resolution:** the process by which businesses receive and process customer complaints (*see also* AS 4269)

**compliance:** ensuring that the population complies with a country's laws, such as those on taxation

**conference:** using the Internet so that a group of people in different locations can hold interactive meetings. Cheap software, such as Net-Meeting, enables people to see one another on screen and even collaborate using interactive electronic whiteboard software.

**confidentiality:** concerned with the notion that there is protection from intrusion, that no one can access the contents of data or information

being sent and that no one can identify who is sending or receiving a message

**contract:** an agreement between two or more parties creating obligations that are enforceable or otherwise recognisable at law

**cookies:** files that a web server stores on a user's computer when a web site is visited. A cookie gathers information about the user.

**copyright:** the exclusive right, created by law, to make copies of, or otherwise control, a literary, musical, dramatic or artistic work for a certain number of years. Copyright is included in the all-embracing term 'intellectual property', which extends to industrial property providing protection to patents, inventions, trademarks and industrial designs.

**corporate intranet:** a business intelligence portal (BIP) or enterprise information portal (EIP). An EIP site may include a search engine covering the entire intranet, a taxonomy showing clearly what's available on the site, news sources, links to internal sites and popular external web sites and the ability to personalise the page. The EIP may help to provide a structure for data, turning information into knowledge for employees to use.

**CPM (cost per thousand presentations model) advertising:** the method of counting the number of clicks per thousand on any given advertisement. It is used to help establish advertising rates.

**crime:** an act, a failure to act or other conduct which is prejudicial to the community, rendering the person responsible liable to a fine or other punishment

**Cryptolope:** IBM's trademark for its *crypto*graphic enve*lope* technology. Cryptolope objects are used for secure, protected delivery of digital content and can be compared to secure servers. Both use encryption to prevent eavesdroppers from stealing or interfering with content. Both use digital signatures to offer the end user a guarantee that the content is genuine.

**customer:** any recipient of information or products. For example, a customer can be a purchaser of a CD, the reader of a report or any other recipient of a product.

**customer relations:** occur when a supplier interacts with and seeks to enhance the relationship with a customer

**customer security:** the integrity of the consumer's data transmission; for example, somebody stealing a customer's credit card details from the Internet. Customer security concerns differ from those of business proprietors.

**Cyber Brochure model:** the placing of information sheets, brochures and information items on a web site

**CyberCash:** a company (www.cybercash.com) that offers payment services for credit card, micro-payment and Internet cheque transactions. CyberCash services credit cards securely over the Internet by linking storefronts with credit-card processors providing authorisations in real-time at the time of purchase. They also offer the CyberCoin® Service, which provides special tools to deliver information to the user, which can either be the content for which the user is paying or an electronic receipt that pro-vides access for the user to get to the content elsewhere. This system is particularly useful for 'pay-per-view' areas, selling small programs and utilities online, selling one-day passes to sites that otherwise require monthly subscriptions or 'pay-per-play' games.

**data integrity:** refers to protection of data at all levels, from the operator (the human element) to the systems being used (browsers, networks, servers and communications infrastructure)

**defamation:** the publication of a false or derogatory statement about another person without lawful justification

**DigiCash:** a company that marketed Ecash, the Internet implementation of David Chaum's anonymous electronic cash system. This Ecash system uses electronic tokens to exchange goods and services in an online environment. Banks are used to verify the value of the token.

**disintermediation:** the connecting of producers and consumers directly, cutting out the intermedi-aries such as wholesalers, distributors and retailers

**domain name:** the part of the URL following the two forward slashes that identifies an Internet host site

**Dot Com economy:** refers to an economy where Dot Com companies are those companies specifi-cally formed to do business almost entirely on the Internet, i.e. they generally have no physical shopfront or outlets, and they conduct business by trading information, services or products online

**e-cash:** digital cash

**e-loyalty programs:** an accelerated form of marketing for Internet-based commerce. Companies like Beenz.com, MyPoints.com, ipoints, Netcentives, Inc. and Cybergold, Inc. have launched marketing programs for online retailers where consumers receive 'chits', or points, that can be redeemed for products and services.

**e-marketing:** (*see* viral marketing)

**EDIFACT (Electronic Data Interchange for Administration, Commerce and Transport):** a standard for EDI transactions

**electronic data interchange (EDI):** computer-to-computer exchange of business information, such as orders and invoices, between customers and vendors

**electronic funds transfer (EFT):** the exchange of money electronically, such as the electronic transfer of funds from one bank account to an account in another bank

**electronic funds transfer at point of sale (EFTPOS):** allows for the transfer of value electronically at the checkout in a shop or supermarket

**electronic payment system (EPS):** an information system designed to record, transfer, store and process data about goods and services purchased

**electronic purchasing:** the use of any electronic tech-nology to transact or buy goods, services or information

**email:** an application which allows messages to be transmitted via data communications to elec-tronic mailboxes. The text or multimedia mes-sages are transmitted asynchronously.

**encryption:** the process of enabling information/ data/knowledge to be coded in such a way that it cannot be read without a decoding system or key

**enterprise information portal (EIP):** (*see* corporate intranet)

**ethernet:** a communications standard commonly used in local area networks for transmitting data among computers on a network

**ethics:** a system of moral principles by which human actions or proposals may be judged good or bad or right or wrong

**extensible markup language (XML):** a meta language — a language for defining other languages. It is used to define text markup so the text can be used and interpreted by different applications, including those that present information to people. XML allows developers to develop custom tags such as product-number, product-name, etc. Will allow for rich searches and allow transaction processing tasks to be imple-mented by browser and web server. XML, derived from SGML, retains SGML's power while reducing its complexity. Unlike HTML, XML allows the developer to create new tags which describe the data, and optionally create a set of rules called Document Type Definitions (DTDs). Any standard XML parser can read, decode, and validate this text-based, self-describing document, extracting the data elements in a platform-independent way so that applications can access the data objects through yet another standard called Document Object Model (DOM).

**extranet:** a collaborative network that uses Internet technology to link businesses with their suppliers, customers or other businesses that share common goals

**extra-organisational communication:** communication that occurs between members of an organisation and some external person

**fat client system:** fully configured desktop computers with local storage, operating systems and peripherals. In these systems, data is most commonly centralised. However, applications are located on the desktop.

**file transfer protocol (FTP):** a communication protocol that is used to transmit files over the Internet

**firewalls:** refers to both the software and hardware that stands between the Internet and a corporate network for security access control

**flat-fee advertising:** occurs when a single set rate is billed for advertising (e.g. selling an advertisement at $100, regardless of how many times it is viewed)

**fraud:** obtaining material advantage by unfair or wrongful means. It involves the making of a false representation knowingly, without belief in its truth or recklessness.

**frequently asked questions (FAQs):** documents stored on a web page which list the most commonly asked questions and answers about topics, services or products

**fringe benefits tax:** a tax on a non-salary component of a person's income. Some taxpayers seek to minimise their taxation burden by using flexible salary packages, sometimes known as 'salary sacrifice'. In such a case, a person might have his or her children's school fees paid directly to a school or his or her parking fees paid directly to the parking station. This money therefore does not appear as salary and lowers the taxpayer's tax burden.

**GENTRAN:** software allowing ordering and transmission of transactions to occur electronically. GENTRAN may be downloaded via the Internet and then installed on a remote computer.

**Goods and Services Tax (GST):** a tax on goods and services at a fixed rate; for example, adding 10–15 per cent to every meal served at a restaurant to raise revenue for the government

**Gopher:** a menu-type program that helps users locate and retrieve files on the Internet

**gross domestic product (GDP):** refers to the total value of all the goods and services produced domestically by a nation during a year

**groupware:** an application that allows many people to interact together. This software is often used to run virtual meetings.

**hacker:** someone who accesses a computer system without permission

**Hermes Survey:** refers to the ongoing consumer surveys of web users carried out by Georgia Tech in conjunction with University of Michigan. Each survey contains such useful information on consumer behaviour on the Web.

**home base:** a site to which a user comes back in between searching other sites

**home page:** a web page that is the starting point for accessing information at a site or in a particular area. It can also be the Web page that is chosen to display each time the browser software is started.

**'hot desking':** a system whereby employees work from home, and on the days they need to come into the office, they sit wherever they can find a desk

**hotlink:** a word, picture or feature highlighted within a document that triggers the link to another document which may be located on another computer in some other location in the world

**hub:** a central position from which everything radiates — it becomes the focus of activities, not just a gateway to pass through

**hypertext:** software technology that allows for fast and flexible access to information. Users browse and retrieve information by following hotlinks rather than following a linear structure.

**hypertext markup language (HTML):** a page description language used to compose and format most of the content found on the Web. It defines hypertext links between documents. It is a subset of standardised general markup language (*see* standardised general markup language).

**hypertext transfer protocol (HTTP):** a multimedia transport protocol used in communications between browser clients and web host computers

**income tax:** an aggregate tax, whereby the liability is arrived at by considering the aggregate result after adding up all items of assessable income and subtracting all allowable deductions. Income tax imposes a personal liability on the person who derives the income. Thus, personal identity is extremely important. In cases of a taxpayer defaulting on payment of income tax, the identity, whereabouts and financial position of the taxpayer are all relevant.

**Integrated Internet Marketing model (I²M):** a model that tries to coordinate Internet facilities to market products and services, mould customers' attitudes, and establish and maintain the corporate image

**intellectual property:** an all-embracing term covering copyright, patents and trademarks. The term describes those rights that protect the product of a person's or corporation's work by hand or brain against unauthorised use or exploitation by others.

**interactive mail access protocol (IMAP):** allows for better control over the way messages are delivered. When a user connects to a mail host, the user is able to see a one-line summary of each message. This allows the user to selectively download the messages that the user wishes to receive. Selective deletion of email is also possible.

**Internet:** a network of computer networks. It allows public access to information on a huge number of subjects and allows users to send messages and obtain products and services. It works because there are agreed rules or protocols about how information is exchanged.

**Internet2:** a project to establish gigabit-per-second points of presence nationwide. Internet2 went live in late February 1999.

**Internet Commerce Customer Service Life Cycle:** a model that separates the service relationship with a customer into four distinct yet overlapping phases: requirements, acquisition, ownership and retirement

**Internet protocol:** a set of traffic rules, procedures and standards designed to allow transmission of data and information

**Internet protocol television (IP/TV):** a protocol that allows the delivery of full motion video to desktop PCs via existing Internet protocol data networks, instead of requiring dedicated video cable, monitors and viewing rooms (*see* http://www.precept.com)

**Internet shopping mall:** a collection of virtual businesses, each of which may pay some fee to the mall proprietor, who then markets the entire mall. The Internet shopping mall simply develops an economy of scale in marketing and other services.

**intranet:** a locally-operated hypertext environment generally using TCP/IP architecture and services which is delivered to browser software on networked PCs and desktop workstations. It is just like the Internet, but can usually be accessed only from within an organisation. It is privately developed and operated within a business or organisation.

**intra-organisational communication:** communication that occurs within an organisation

**IT audit (information technology audit):** the systematic checking of all IT components in a business system

**Java:** a programming language used as a software development tool for the Internet

**Java applets:** programs written in the programming language, Java. The applets are downloaded to client machines. These applets then execute on a user's machine.

**Java Beans:** a portable, platform-independent component model written in the Java programming language. Java Beans' components are reusable software components that can be manipulated visually in a builder tool.

**jurisdiction:** the power of a court or judge to hear an action, petition or other proceeding, and the district or limits within which the judgement or orders of a court can be enforced

**just-in-time:** systematic management process for the delivery of component parts just in time for their use in a production process

**just-in-time information:** information that is timely and relevant. It is produced when it is needed, with little lead time.

**knowledge management:** the name of a concept in which an enterprise consciously and comprehensively gathers, organises, shares and analyses its knowledge to further its aims

**law:** the body of rules which a State or community recognises as binding on its members or subjects

**legacy systems:** refers to existing company databases (often ones that have been developed in third-generation languages such as COBOL) or back-end systems, such as EDI (electronic data interchange). Developing e-commerce systems often requires integration with legacy systems, which often hold critical corporate data.

**legislation:** the body of laws enacted by the legislature

**listservs:** programs that provide automatic processing of many functions involved with mailing lists or discussion groups. Emailing specific messages to it will automatically subscribe (or unsubscribe) a person to the mailing list. These programs also answer requests for indexes, FAQs, archives of previous discussions and other files.

**local area network (LAN):** a networked group of computers, usually within an organisation, contained in a small geographic area such as a building

**metadata:** refers to the corporate information that is modelled and ultimately stored in the corporate database

**meta tagging:** refers to the technique whereby a word or words are incorporated into a site to increase the chances of a search engine returning the site. This tag, <META> part of the HEAD of an HTML document, provides information that describes the document in various ways. It contains valuable information for search robots to use in adding pages to their search indexes. It can also be used to search locally for similar files or files that need reviewing or updating. Information in each <META> tag is expressed as a NAME= and value= pair. The NAME can be used to distinguish one type of <META> statement from another.

**middleware:** software that operates between an application, such as a database or email program, and the transport layer that performs the services and hides the details of that layer. For example, in a database situation, a client program might send a request message, the database middleware program passes the request to the database middleware on the server machine. This then puts the request in whatever format is needed to get the desired data. These programs are useful for linking database servers to traditional legacy database programs (e.g. written in COBOL).

**money:** unit of value used in exchange

**money laundering:** the placing of money, gained by illegal means, such as from selling illicit drugs, into general circulation so that its origin cannot be traced. In Internet commerce, there is concern that it might be possible to launder money from criminal activities by shifting it electronically between different accounts and countries.

**multipurpose Internet mail extensions (MIME):** a TCP/IP standard used on the Internet to allow electronic mail headers and mail bodies to contain information other than plain text. It enables mail transfer in complex organisations.

**Netscape:** a computer software company that markets Internet and World Wide Web software, such as Netscape Navigator and Netscape Communicator

**network effects:** refers to a world governed by networks. It is rewriting the rules for how to build companies, market products and create value.

**non-repudiation:** a requirement that the sender and recipient of messages can validate their role in the transmission of data

**online auction:** real-time or live auction bidding on the Internet

**Online Yellow Pages model:** a web business model using menu systems to point to other sources and information

**ontology:** in information technology, the working model of entities and interactions in some particular domain of knowledge or practices, such as electronic commerce or 'the activity of planning'

**Open Buying on the Internet (OBI):** a standard and an open, flexible design for business-to-business internet commerce. It is intended for high-volume, low-dollar transactions that account for 80 per cent of most organisations' purchasing activities (www.openbuy.org).

**packaging:** one of the old five P's of marketing. In cybermarketing it is essential to make the product attractive to buyers by giving incentives, such as discounts, if the product is bought online.

**paradigm:** the third new P of marketing. It is a pattern example or a model way of doing things.

**paradox:** the first new P of marketing. It is a statement or proposition which, on the face of it, seems self-contradictory, absurd and at variance with common sense, but which upon investigation may prove to be well founded or essentially true.

**passion:** the fifth new P of marketing. Cyber marketers must be passionate about their Internet commerce site. The Internet is an exciting communication channel and the web-site business needs to persuade the consumer to visit the web site.

**patents:** refers to government grants to inventors granting them the sole right to make use and sell such inventions for a limited time

**people:** one of the old five P's of marketing. The cyberbusiness must not forget that people, including the people who run the business and the people who interact with the business, are vital.

**Performance and Assessment Results (PAR4):** software that maintains a record of key performance indicators and is used by managers in conducting performance appraisals of employees

**perspective:** the second new P of marketing. It is vital to view the products from the consumer's perspective. The cyberbusiness must determine those consumer requirements the product or service satisfies and how it satisfies those requirements differently and better than its competitors.

**persuasion:** the fourth new P of marketing. All businesses try to persuade people to buy their product or service. As Internet commerce is a new medium, companies are attempting different ways to persuade people to their site and get them to buy. To master persuasion, it is essential to concentrate on credibility, content and involvement of the listener.

**place:** one of the old P's of marketing. This is no longer such a vital consideration as the cyberbusiness can be on a service in a garage or in a home study. The business must realise that the market is now potentially a lot larger than if it was setting up a real store.

**point-to-point protocol (PPP):** a protocol that provides a method for transmitting packets over serial point-to-point links. It is a standard for telephone modem communication between a user's personal computer and an Internet service provider (ISP).

**Portal model:** a business model where a web site is designed to offer a variety of Internet services from a single convenient location (*see also* portals)

**portals:** web sites designed to offer a variety of Internet services from a single convenient location. The goal of the portal is to be designated as your browser's startup page. Most portals offer certain free services such as a search engine; local, national and worldwide news, sports and weather; references such as yellow pages and maps; shopping malls; email and chat rooms.

**Poster/Billboard model:** a simple Internet commerce business model that allows businesses to use email headers and footers, signature blocks or greeting cards to advertise their business

**post office protocol (POP):** a TCP/IP protocol used in electronic mail that allows users working on intelligent devices such as personal computers to do a lot of work on local devices. POP may also refer to 'point of presence', which is a site with a collection of telecommunications equipment, usually digital-leased lines and multi-protocol routers.

**price:** one of the old P's of marketing: the product must be affordable to the target market. One of the great advantages of the Web is that products can be sold more cheaply because the large infrastructure of a physical shopfront is not necessary.

**privacy:** the right to not have one's private life intruded upon or unjustifiably brought into the public arena. The issue of privacy is imperfectly recognised in many legal systems.

**product:** one of the old P's of marketing. It is vital that the company that wishes to go into online commerce has a product that consumers will require. If a company has had a successful business selling via catalogues, it is likely that such products will also sell well over the Internet, particularly if they are finance, travel or automobiles. A complete range of products should be available as consumers are frustrated if they believe they can buy a product in store but not online.

**promotion:** one of the old P's of marketing. It is still vital to promote the cyberbusiness to ensure online customers will buy from the site. Such promotion might be on traditional forms of advertising, such as advertisements in print, radio or television media.

**protocol:** a set of traffic rules, procedures and standards designed to allow transmissions of data and information

**proxy:** a small program that is able to read messages on both sides of a firewall

**Reverse Auction model:** a business model where bidders set their price for items such as airline tickets or hotel rooms and sellers decide whether to supply the items. This was originally set up by Priceline.com (www.priceline.com).

**sales tax:** an example of transaction tax, whereby liability results from an imposed tax on particular types of transactions. For example, a consumer buying a car is subject to a sales tax on that car and the advantage for the government is that the car dealer collects the tax.

**search engine:** a program that gathers and sorts through information on the Web

**Secure Electronic Transaction (SET):** encrypted data transmission, which allows financial transactions to occur. SET is used by banks to engage in financial transactions with customers via the Internet.

**security:** protection of information systems and operating systems from illegal or unauthorised interference

**serial line Internet protocol (SLIP):** a standard that enables TCP/IP packets of information to be sent between different types of computers

**server:** a special purpose device within a LAN that performs a specific function. For example, the file server will provide access to the shared files for all LAN users. The file server is usually a computer that has no other function in the network.

**server security:** refers to keeping network servers safe from attack. The servers normally store various software packages which enable mail, FTP, news groups, network operating systems, the Web, CGI scripts and Telnet. Security checks must be done on networks servers and regular tests made on its operation and on the security of each of the component software packages it operates. This involves not only implementation of a security policy and security audit, it requires the use of additional features to ensure screening and repetitive testing.

**simple mail transfer protocol (SMTP):** a TCP/IP protocol used on the Internet to deliver messages between electronic mail hosts and to specify message structure

**smart card:** a credit-sized card containing a computer chip which is capable of receiving, processing, storing and transmitting monetary information

**standardised general markup language (SGML):** a protocol which defines documents in a plain text using tags which are embedded in the text to specify the definition

**stored value card (SVC):** a card which stores information about value which can be used in exchange for goods and services

**structured query language (SQL):** a standard fourth-generation language for relational database systems

**Subscription model:** an Internet commerce business model that has been borrowed from publishing. Just as a consumer might subscribe to a monthly or weekly magazine, so too a consumer is able to subscribe to an online version of such a magazine or any product with updated versions offered on an on-going basis.

**supply chain:** description of the structure and/or process used in bringing together components in a production process. It is simply the staged process of sourcing, producing and distributing goods and services.

**target advertisement:** an advertisement that users can click on and be automatically directed to the web page belonging to the advertiser. For example, by clicking on an advertisement of IBM ecommerce on the Web Wombat site, the Internet user would be redirected automatically to their web site.

**tax avoidance:** refers to schemes to lower the taxation burden, such as moving money offshore. In Internet commerce, the key issue will be the extent to which the Internet will allow business activities to be undetectable or anonymous, so that the taxing and auditing requirements of the existence and identity of persons or transactions cannot be determined. The migration of businesses to the Internet may be partially driven by the tax avoidance and evasion opportunities it presents.

**tax evasion:** refers to activities, generally illegal, aimed at ensuring that tax is not paid. A high level of non-detection could lead to tax evasion in a highly-competitive global business environment where businesses may be forced to adopt non-compliance facilities to compete with other businesses, thus exacerbating non-compliance (*see* tax avoidance).

**tax neutrality:** a concept which rejects the imposition of new or additional taxes on electronic transactions. Neutrality requires that the tax system treat similar income equally, regardless of whether it is earned through electronic or existing means.

**telecommuting:** refers to an employment situation where employees are able to work from home rather than at the usual workplace. The use of information technology and improved tele-communications make this a feasible option for employees. It is sometimes called teleworking.

**teleworking:** (*see* telecommuting)

**templates:** style sheets containing such information as font, style, spacing, formatting information and possibly text that might always be used such as headings and titles. Such templates may be useful in defining the layout of a commercial web page.

**thin client system:** a user interface where most of the computing is done on a powerful back-end server

**3.5.7 model:** an Internet commerce business model that lays the foundation for commercial success by focusing on using the Internet as a business communication tool. It advocates three steps to a better focus, a five-dimensional strategy and a seven-point tactical guide for doing business on the Internet.

**total quality management (TQM):** a management system designed initially to assist the post-war reconstruction of industry in Japan. It is based on continuously improving the quality of all component parts and processes in a manufacturing system or service industry. Total quality management is an organisation-wide approach to total customer satisfaction and continuous improvement.

**TRADACOMS:** a protocol or standard for EDI transactions

**trademarks:** refers to signs used, or intended to be used, to distinguish goods or services provided in the course of trade by a person from goods or services provided by any other person. These signs could be letters, words, names, signatures, numbers, devices, brands and even a smell or scent.

**transmission control protocol/internet protocol (TCP/IP):** a set of commands and communication protocols used by the Internet to connect dissimilar systems and control the flow of information. This protocol allows users of the Internet to find information, use email, interact with other businesses, find personal details of people who have developed their own home pages, exchange business information and data or download software from the Internet.

**uniform resource locator (URL):** the defining terminology that identifies other web sites and specific web pages. A URL is a means of specifying a resource by incorporating the protocol, machine address, path and filename.

**value-added network (VAN):** an online service which provides proprietary software to communicate with firms registered with the service

**very-high-speed backbone network service (vBNS):** a spine or backbone which allows very-high-speed interaction for the next generation Internet

**viral marketing:** based on the premise that in the new Internet economy, companies don't sell to their customers; current customers sell to future customers. In exchange for a free service, customers agree to recommend the service.

**virtual private network (VPN):** utilises a public network, such as the Internet, to transmit private data. VPNs are an emerging form of extranet implementation that may become a viable replacement for traditional wide area networks (WANs).

**virtual atmospherics:** part of the Integrated Internet Marketing model, where the web site should allow the customer to experiencee an organisation's atmosphere without actually being there

**virtual reality modelling language (VRML):** a language that allows graphical representations and models generated by computers to be broken into smaller components and transmitted across the Internet

**Virtual Storefront model:** a full information service designed to include the marketing of a business' services, products, online purchasing and customer support on the Internet

**virtual wallet software:** an electronic storage of 'virtual cash' or financial credit. A user places an amount of money or credit in his or her virtual wallet, and deducts specified amounts in financial transactions.

**virus:** a program written with malicious intent that is loaded into the computer system of an unsuspecting victim. It normally tries to destroy or interfere with the running of other programs or applications on the host computer and aims to spread through multiple computer systems.

**web surfers:** users who jump from site to site on the Web. Such users may be likened to people who use their television remote controller to 'channel surf'.

**wide area information server (WAIS):** a system that helps users to search remote databases on a network

**wide area network (WAN):** a network that spans a large geographical area (e.g. across a state, a country or the globe). Nodes on the network communicate using communication channels such as telephone lines or satellites.

**wireless application protocol (WAP):** an industry open standard to facilitate the easy access to information by handset users. It was engineered with the low bandwidth of current mobile technology which have small monochrome screens. WAP is a specification for a set of communication protocols to standardise the way that wireless devices, such as cellular telephones and radio transceivers, can be used for Internet access, including email, the Web, newsgroups and Internet Relay Chat (IRC). While Internet access has been possible in the past, different manufacturers have used different technologies. In the future, devices and service systems that use WAP will be able to interoperate. The WAP layers are: wireless application environment (WAE), wireless session layer (WSL), wireless transport layer security (WTLS) and wireless transport layer (WTP). The WAP was conceived by four companies: Ericsson, Motorola, Nokia, and Unwired Planet (which is now Phone.com). IEEE 802.11 is emerging as the standard for wireless LANs. Bluetooth technology will enable many different devices to share information seamlessly.

**wizards:** specialised applications that reduce the complexity of using an application. For example, Sofcom has wizards that enable novices to design commercial web pages.

**World Wide Web (the Web, WWW):** a graphical hypertext environment that operates within the Internet. It contains a collection of distributed documents, referred to as 'pages', located on computers all over the world.

**worm:** a malicious program designed to corrupt an information system or operating system. The worm propagates and exists independently. It does not have to attach to another program or part of the operating system to propagate, unlike a virus.

**X.12 protocol:** a standard designated by the American National Standards Institute as the standard for EDI

**X.25 protocol:** an international standard for connecting devices to a packet-switching network

**X.400 protocol:** a family of open systems interconnection (OSI) protocols used to deliver messages between electronic mail hosts and to specify message structure

**X.500 protocol:** a standard which describes how to create a directory containing all the electronic mail users' names and their addresses

**X.509 protocol:** used for public key digital certificates. It is used by secure socket layer (SSL) protocol as part of a two-phase handshake protocol for server and client authentication.

# INDEX